Confrontations with

CONFRONTATIONS WITH TYRANNY

Six Baltic Plays
with introductory essays

Edited by
ALFREDS STRAUMANIS
Southern Illinois University

WAVELAND PRESS, INC.
Prospect Heights, Illinois

OR 11/82

For information about this book, write:
Waveland Press, Inc.
P.O. Box 400
Prospect Heights, Illinois   60070

The materials in this volume have been prepared, in part, under the grant OEG-0-74-9158, Drama and Theatre of Baltic American Youth. The U.S. Office of Education has waived all rights under copyrights in materials supported, in part, under the above identified grant, in accordance with Section 12a of the USOE Copyright guidelines, but subject to the free copyright license reserved to the Government under that section.

Printed in the United States of America.

To ANDRIS
and all others of the second generation
Balts in America.

PREFACE

This volume in many ways is a first among similar anthologies. It is for the first time that plays originally written in the three Baltic languages—Estonian, Latvian, and Lithuanian—appear together in English translation under the same cover. It is for the first time these plays are selected according to their themes in an attempt to explain a common destiny of people who either physically, philosophically, or in spirit have exiled themselves from their original environment. It is also for the first time that a collection of drama addresses itself not only to the student of comparative drama but especially to the many "ethnic millions" that are part of the American multicultural society, hoping to facilitate a positive exchange of cultural values among them.

Although a collection of Baltic plays in English translation has been a dream of some individuals in the Baltic communities for many years, only due to a grant from the Ethnic Heritage Studies program under Title IX of the Elementary and Secondary Education Act this dream has reached its fulfillment. The collecting of materials, translating of plays, and the research of many years finally seemed to have significance, and an impetus was generated resulting in the present collection with additional translations that could fill many more volumes. These additional translations are critically reviewed by the members of the Baltic Theatre project in the Theatre Department of Southern Illinois University at Carbondale for inclusion in future collections. At the same time guides for teachers are being prepared together with bibliographies of source materials. In view of the above, therefore, the present volume should be considered only a part of the materials destined to be developed and used for the Baltic ethnic heritage and multicultural studies.

In order to appreciate drama to the fullest extent, however, one must observe it enacted on a stage where the characters become alive and the actions develop the story more forcefully than words can ever tell. Three of the six plays in this volume have been produced in English language by professional and university theatre ensembles, as well as by community theatre groups. Data concerning some of these productions is appended

7

to the production photographs included in this volume.

Most of the translators and essayists whose works are included in this volume are initial members of the Baltic Theatre project. Information about them can be found under *Contributors* on the last pages of this book. Information about the authors of the original plays is included in the introductory essays.

Acknowledgments concerning copyrights and authorizations, as well as credits for photography are mentioned at the point of use. We would like as well to acknowledge with gratitude the moral and additional financial support extended to the Baltic Theatre project by many individuals of Baltic descent, their organizations, and scholarly institutions. Our thanks go to the Southern Illinois University Foundation for establishing a Baltic Theatre Fund; to Dr. Michael R. Dingerson, Director of the Office of Research and Projects at SIU, and his staff; to Dr. Ilse Lehiste and Dr. Valters Nollendorfs, past and present presidents of the Association for Advancement of Baltic Studies; to the research assistants, and, especially, to the many volunteer translators of plays intended for inclusion in future volumes for their enthusiasm and devotion. Their list is too long and their contributions too varied for a detailed description.

A.S.

CONTENTS

INTRODUCTION

The words of Emma Lazarus have a promising sound for the "huddled masses yearning to breathe free" throughout the world; and the Statue of Liberty, within the pedestal of which these words are graven, is the beacon of hope. During the last 200 years, thousands after thousands have listened to their sound; and still other thousands one day may hope to see the beacon light shining for them at the gateway to the land of the free.

The word "freedom", however, can mean different things to different people in different places at different times. The basic freedoms guaranteed by The Constitution of the United States are more liberal than those in the many lands from which the immigrants had come. However liberal these freedoms may be, there is to them—especially in the minds of the first and often still of the second generation immigrants—a condition attached: complete negation of one's past. The rationale for this condition is sound: why immigrate to a land without having the intention of becoming its citizen? Therefore, sound seems also the "melting pot" principle, still advocated by its staunch defenders. Many immigrants have accepted it as the only way of life, their new life, and many will do it in the future.

It is good to look into the future, it is good to accept change, for without change, progress cannot be made. Progress, though, is an obvious part of our culture—we are a nation on the move: we have built railroads in order to open the wilderness, we have changed the wilderness into fertile fields, we have found riches hidden in the earth, we have accumulated wealth and control it from our comfortable offices in the cities we have built. However, as soon as our railroads stop bringing profit, as soon as our fields become barren, as soon as we have exhausted the riches found in the ground, we leave them all. We move on, as there still is new abundance somewhere else in this great land of ours, and, if the city from which we controlled our wealth happens to be too far, we leave it, too, and it becomes a concrete and asphalt jungle in which those who are less fortunate than we can roam.

We are a nation on the move. We are without roots—they were rejected by the melting pot. We are like cut flowers in a container filled with water which will sustain us only as long as we are willing to fulfill our function of pleasing the eye of the beholder. And the mycelial hyphae that could lead us back to our group, tribal or national archetype, remain only in our memory.

Or do they? There have been great migrations before. As a result new nations have been formed, new cultures established. Some of them still survive. But those new nations were the results of one single migration. Waves after waves of new immigrants arrive on our shores, immigrants of the same stock as those who had arrived here many years before. And these new immigrants remind us of our lost roots, our former home lands, our ancestry. They remind us that we have negated part of ourselves, a scintilla like part, without which, however, a human being, an individual cannot really be complete.

The recent attempt to study the heritage of the many ethnic units that compose our nation might help in finding a common denominator for our multicultural society through which a unity can be reached and the parts will be truly integrated into the whole. The concept of universality implies that in any particular there is something common to all. And because this study concerns itself with the immigrants of Baltic descent, we should hasten to add that they are as particular and at the same time as universal as any other ethnic group, be they the descendants of the original inhabitants of this continent or of the many other ethnic forefathers who have settled here for one reason or another. The only difference might be the ratio between the particulars and universals.

The Baltic ethnic groups in the United States of America—descendants from the Estonian, Latvian, and Lithuanian immigrants—are nothing more than conglomerates of individuals with the same traditions, which are kept alive in this country to the fourth generation. The original language quite often is abandoned with the third generation, but the traditions remain. They include the mythology that has been communicated orally from generation to generation through legends, folksongs, and proverbs that were written down only starting with the national awakening in the 19th century. At that time they were patterned after earlier models of Western European nations, therefore they are not always completely reliable, especially as far as the mythology is concerned. The above mentioned sources, though, give us ample information about the life styles, the philosophies of the individuals belonging to the same nationalities, as well as the ethics and aesthetics developed during a period of more than four thousand years of living on the Eastern shores of the Baltic Sea.

Throughout the ages drama has reflected the human condition facilitating the identification of man regardless of his origin. Drama has recorded the problems and conflicts man has with his fellow man and his environment. One can argue that drama, while depicting man of different eras in varied geographic, economic, social, or political environments, is the most objective source for study of man. To show man as he is, in other words, to create verisimilitude is an important facet of drama, because it is meant for immediate consumption by the dramatist's contemporaries in the form of a performance. Drama may be considered objectivity in action where the characters, situations, and conflicts, as well as the germinal ideas, are palatable to the consumer and in agreement with the philosophy of his time. And, even though drama has not always kept "the mirror up to nature," but has been used as a weapon toward other ends, it still remains a true reflection of the human condition.

For this reason we have chosen the drama of the Baltic immigrants in order to show the particular, as well as the universal qualities of these three ethnic groups.

There are many aspects of the Baltic immigrants worth considering: their history, economics, demography, culture, among others. But because our primary goal is the study of the Balts as ethnic groups in this country, we propose to start by asking, why the Estonians, Latvians, and Lithuanians left their respective countries and came to the United States of America? In order to make our study relevant to the reader of today, we chose to study the most recent dramatic works of these nationalities. Before making this decision we considered the plays that were written and produced during the first major immigration period around the turn of the century. Our findings were that, although entirely different political and economic conditions prevailed during the first period as compared to the second, which started after World War II, the same basic reason forced the Balts to leave their home lands during both periods: fear of tyranny.

Thus the title of the first collection of Baltic plays: *Confrontations with Tyranny.*

There are many kinds of tyranny, as there are many ways of reacting against it. Throughout their histories the Balts must have experienced them all, because the relatively young Baltic literatures are filled with themes as varied as the masks hiding the true faces of tyranny. Varied are also the reactions against it as depicted in the Baltic novels, short stories, poetry, and modern fairy tales. These reactions range from one extreme to the other. In a fairly recent novel, *Graves Without Crosses* by

Arved Viirlaid, translated from the Estonian by Ilse Lehiste, the tyranny is raging, and the natural reaction to it is fighting without a compromise, as if death would be the only answer to all ills. In an allegorical fairy tale, *Pussy's Water Mill* by Kārlis Skalbe, translated from the Latvian by W.K. Matthews, where Pussy, after being tyrannized by many and at the end saved by a good king, who asks him what punishment he wishes for the malefactors, answers: "I bear no grudge. When, as a beggar, I went out into the world there were sufferings enough. Why add to them? Rather let joy increase," we are shown the other extreme.

All the plays in this collection deal with tyranny as a universal evil. They depict the particular only as far as the reaction against tyranny by specific characters in given situations would occur. There are three plays written by Baltic dramatists under soviet rule and three written by dramatists in exile. The introductory essays to each play, besides informing about the playwright, are suggesting certain interpretations in order to facilitate the understanding of the characters and their actions in a given play. These essays, although striving towards impartiality, do not profess having the only interpretation, as we trust the reader's ability of finding the deeper meaning on his own.

Our ultimate hope is that the material presented in this collection will at least partially explain the reasons why so many Balts chose to seek freedom instead of tyranny.

Carbondale, 1976   Alfreds Straumanis

PHOTOGRAPHS

CONFRONTATIONS WITH TYRANNY

FIVE POSTS IN A MARKET PLACE, Act One. Director: Sidney Walters; Scenography: Herbert Senn and Helen Pond; Costumes: Sonia Lowenstein; Lighting: Richard Nelson. The REPERTORY COMPANY AT THE GATE THEATRE, New York City, March 1961. Photo: Charles Caron.

FIVE POSTS IN A MARKET PLACE, Act
Three.
The REPERTORY COMPANY AT THE GATE
THEATRE, New York City, March 1961. Photo:
Charles Caron.

FIVE POSTS IN A MARKET PLACE, Act Three.
Director: Alfreds Straumanis; Scenography: Peteris Rožlapa; Costumes: Mary Rose; Lighting: James Utterback. SOUTHERN PLAYERS, Southern Illinois University at Carbondale, May 1975. Photo: Andris Straumanis.

FIVES POSTS IN A MARKET PLACE.
Unit set by Pēteris Rožlapa. SOUTHERN PLAY-
ERS, Southern Illinois University at Carbondale,
May 1975. Photo: Andris Straumanis.

MAD CHRISTOPHER, MAD, poster.
Designer: Raymond T. Kurdt; Photo: John
Anderson.

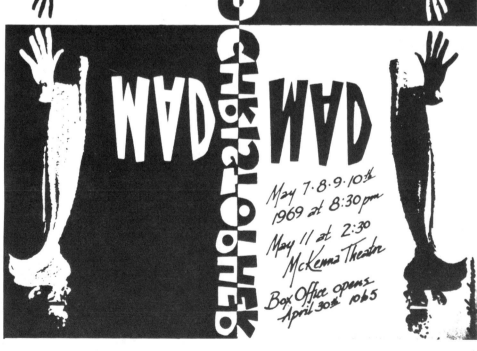

MAD CHRISTOPHER, MAD, Act One. Director: Alfreds Straumanis; Scenography, lights and costumes: Raymond T. Kurdt. NEW PALTZ PLAYERS, State University of New York, New Paltz, May 1969. Photo: John Anderson.

CINDERELLAGAME. Cinderella: Linda Mays, Prince: Devin Scott.
Director: James E. Dwyer; Scenography: Michael Goldberg; Costumes: Yako; Lighting: Joseph Krames. LA MAMA E.T.C., New York City, April 1971. Photo: Roger Martin.

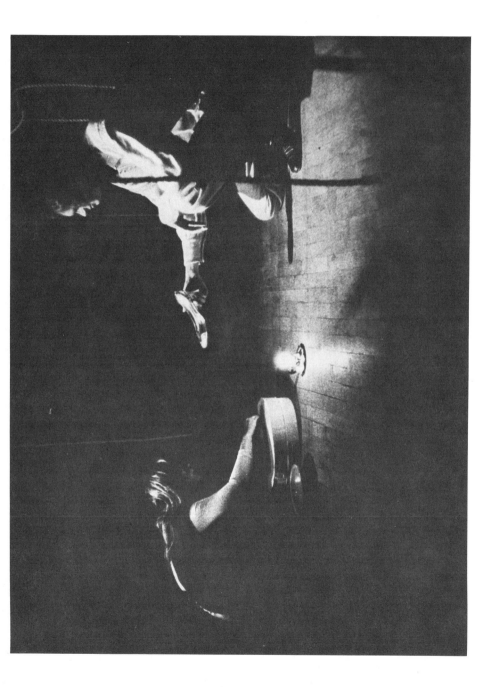

CINDERELLAGAME. Prince: Devin Scott.
LA MAMA E.T.C., New York City, April 1971.
Photo: Roger Martin.

FIVE POSTS IN A
MARKET PLACE

by
Algirdas Landsbergis

Translated from the Lithuanian by the
author

Introduction to
Five Posts in a Market Place

Drama has never been the dominant genre in Lithuanian literature. An epic poem, *Metai* (The Seasons) by Kristijonas Donelaitis (1714-1780) stands at the threshold of the written literary tradition; lyrical poetry and narrative prose have led the way in its development, at least to the point in time marked by the end of the Second World War. There have been some powerful historical plays written by Vincas Krėvė-Mickevičius (1882-1954) and by Balys Sruoga (1896-1947), but both authors achieved distinction in other genres as well, Krėvė in prose and Sruoga in poetry.

During the postwar years, Lithuanian drama made considerable progress, both in the numbers of new playwrights and in the quality of their accomplishments. Nevertheless, some of the most important pioneering talents turned to the theater only after they had proved themselves in verse and most particularly in prose.

Among the Lithuanian writers in exile, Algirdas Landsbergis is such a talent. Born in 1924, Landsbergis reached his full maturity just at the time when Lithuania as a country was undergoing one of the most agonizing crucibles in its entire history, the return of the Soviet power in 1944. The onslaught of the red army, accompanied by the tidal wave of political genocide and terror, forced Landsbergis to flee to the West, along with thousands of his compatriots, among whom were many intellectuals, writers and scholars. It was there, in a postwar Displaced Persons camp in Germany, that Landsbergis begain writing in earnest. His first publications appeared in an iconoclastic "little magazine" called *Žvilgsniai* (Glances) which had gathered young Lithuanian literati interested in new directions, open to contacts with the Western literary and philosophical developments, and inclined to reject the romantic patriotism which was expected of the Lithuanian artists in exile.

After a number of short stories and one major novel, *Kelionė* (The Journey, 1954), Landsbergis turned to drama. His first published play was *Vėjas gluosniuose* (Wind in the Willows, 1958), a mystery play about the miraculous appearance of Saint Kazimir, the Patron Saint of Lithuania, to the Polish-Lithuanian army on the eve of a victorious battle against the Russians in the sixteenth century. It is a lyrical and philosophical play, not without a touch of humor. Its main proposition is that the imperfect earth, upon which erring humans must meet their uncertain destiny, is yet able to provide the distant heaven with insights into suffering, love and the yearning for perfection. The next play, *Five Posts in a Market Place*, written in 1958, after several previous performances in Lithuanian and English, is our present topic. It was followed by *Meilės mokykla* (The School for Love, 1965), a comic and lyrical, avantguardist *tour de force* about a small-time Lithuanian speculator and dream merchant named Leviathan who comes to America and builds a fantastically successful business empire upon the premise that America, indeed, the world, needs a Dale Carnegie-type course in the art of love. After several smaller plays, Landsbergis published, in 1973, a second edition of *Wind in the Willows*, together with a companion play, *Willows in the Wind,* a comic travesty of the first piece which nevertheless reveals some new insights that could not be reached in the original serious treatment of the theme.

Five Posts deals with one of the most traumatic and complex experiences of the Lithuanian nation, the bloody and protracted guerilla warfare against the Soviet power which lasted some seven or eight years, from about 1945. Like many other countries in Central and Eastern Europe, Lithuania was caught between Russia and Germany, the two ideological grindstones, imperialistic in purpose and fanatical in conviction. The Soviet occupation of 1940 came first, bringing along a way of life which included as a matter of course the constant tyranny over the mind, arbitrary arrests and mass deportations. When the Germans attacked in 1941, there were a few breathless days of freedom during which many Lithuanians took up arms to drive the Russians out. The German occupation, however, turned out to be just as terrible, and the people were left with only one hope—that somehow the Germans would be defeated before the Russians came back. This could have resulted in a situation allowing for the restoration of Lithuanian independence. It did not happen. The Russians returned, victorious and powerful and bent on destroying all their enemies, real and potential. For a tyrant, a people whom he oppresses is by definition an enemy. Expecting the worst, the Lithuanians seriously began to doubt the possibility of their survival as a people, and many decided that if one must perish, it is better to go down fighting. The guerilla movement grew out of this desperate feeling. It lasted for seven or eight years and brought the country untold suffering, drowning its towns and villages in blood. For the first few years the guerillas operated with marked success. The Soviet government in the smaller towns and in the countryside became demoralized, the Soviet-style "elections" were disrupted, and the collectivization of agriculture slowed down considerably. This gave the guerillas hope that they could hold on somehow until the Western democracies would come to their aid. Gradually and painfully, the guerillas understood that no real help from outside will ever come, and in the meantime the Soviets kept pouring in more and more troops, until they finally crushed all armed resistance in the protracted, bloody agony. After this, it took a long time for the devastated country to recover from its nightmare, to learn how to "bend with the wind" and how to develop subtle means of resistance or, if this were not possible, to find ways of surviving within the demands of the regime.

Landsbergis' play *Five Posts* reflects to some degree most of the aspects of this guerilla war. The grim and total determination of the guerillas to keep fighting to the bitter end, past all hope, can be seen in Antanas' unyielding resolve to carry out his last orders even after the destruction of the underground headquarters from which they came. The young woman Aldona, who works as a secretary to the district Prosecutor and is at the same time a secret guerilla agent, exemplifies the search for new alternatives when she attempts to lure Antanas away from his terrible task, so that he would survive to be with her and to chart some possible future course for their lives. Gražina, who grew from a pig-tailed highschool girl to the full stature of womanhood while serving the guerillas as a messenger has learned so much about death and about survival that she could become an effective representative of the generation which might lead the country out ot its tragic blind alley of uncompromising resistance. There were many young people like Gražina who actually undertook and to some extent accomplished this task, but Gražina herself belongs among those who could not force themselves to adjust to the regime, because she had been the witness of the full horror of its deeds. Her parents, on the other hand, might be the truest survivors of all, because they have no plans to resist, openly or covertly, nor do they think of joining the new order. They merely cultivate the soil, planting potatoes, grain and vegetables, knowing that all regimes, tyrannical or not, will have a need of people who make things grow. Then again, some of the youngest children, inspired by the spirit of the armed fighters, were ready to carry on the proud flame of national resistance into the uncertain dawn of the future which may quite possibly be bloody again. Such a boy in the play brings flowers to the five posts in the market square, where the bodies of the dead heroes are left to rot as an example to the population.

The realities of the guerilla war, however, were much too complex to be reflected fully in the three-act play. This entire tragic period of

Lithuanian history requires a work of epic dimensions—it could provide more than enough material for a classic novel of the kind that were written in the nineteenth century, something like Tolstoy's *War and Peace*. Moreover, these events need the distance of time to focus their tangled patterns into a comprehensive, meaningful whole. Landsbergis, however, writes from another distance—that of exile, where our vision is blurred by insufficient knowledge of what really went on from day to day and by the pain of dispossession which may cause us to draw larger than life the figures of those who remained at home to face the battle that was ours to fight as well. Landsbergis therefore uses history only as a backdrop against which he builds an artistic structure of his own, expressing universal human feelings, issues and ideas which remain relevant to our search for meaning in life whatever the setting. He simplifies the plot line to the point where it becomes almost a symbolic frame, a device to bring out complexities of a different order, namely those that pertain to our inner life, where the real battles are fought between emotions and reason, duty and love, faith and despair. Antanas, the leader of a very small guerilla detachment, perhaps the last one in the whole land, receives orders to kill the hated public Prosecutor who has relentlessly pursued the freedom fighters through seven long years of "search and destroy" operations and of inhuman torture in the interrogation cells. The plan is to lure the Prosecutor into the open by means of a staged wedding between Antanas and Aldona, the Prosecutor's secretary who has been secretly working for the guerillas. High Communist dignitaries will be present, and they will be killed together with the Prosecutor when the right moment comes. The author of this plan is Aldona herself, and she has another idea in mind—to convince Antanas to go through the wedding in earnest so they could both later withdraw into the fabric of the country's life without any more killing. Antanas, however, resists Aldona's pleas to change his mind, in part because of his determination to follow his duty and in part also because he no longer wishes to marry Aldona, having gradually fallen in love with Gražina during his guerilla years. Failing to convince Antanas, Aldona arranges for him to meet the Prosecutor alone, face to face, because she has a good reason to expect that Antanas will not be able to bring himself to shoot him. The reason is that the Prosecutor had a long time ago written a book, *The Statuary of the Future*, which contained ideas and visions that had inspired Antanas, who was a sculptor before the war, to believe in the creative principle of life. When the two men meet, Antanas finds out that this same hated Prosecutor is indeed the author of the book, and he cannot force himself to shoot. The Prosecutor, however, understands from this gesture of reverence to his former self how far he has gone along the path of complete moral self-destruction. This convinces him that his time has come to die. During the wedding ceremony, he provokes Antanas and his assistant Jonas to kill him, whereupon both guerillas are also destroyed by the security troops.

This simple outline of the plot sustains a complex system of stages devices and symbols which transfer all the issues to another dimension. One of the most important devices is the figure of the Commentator. He appears on stage as someone from a distant future, where mankind has learned to subordinate its passions to reason and can therefore hardly comprehend the time in which Antanas fought and died. The Commentator resembles a liberal intellectual of the professorial type, and he presents the play to us almost as if it were a classroom lecture. His relation to the other characters can be described as a series of contrasts. He is safe in the dimension of the future, while the players are deeply committed to the present, where they stand on the brink of destruction. They are creative and passionate, while the Commentator is, at most, academic and inquisitive. He is privileged to enter the play itself even as he comments upon it and to withdraw at will from its agony of suffering, but the players have nowhere to escape and are themselves the bearers of the cross. In this way, the Commentator, standing between the audience and the play, able to speak directly to both, becomes a kind of personalized inner voice across time and distance, a voice describing the essential human experience in the play.

The Commentator relates to the play on at least four different planes, each of which may have several facets of its own. First of all, he stands before the audience to describe his task: "I am here to introduce you to a strange story.... I enter here to tell of these men on whom a sky of extreme demands and total decisions fell one day." The audience is thus asked to perceive itself as the Commentator's contemporary, but since we know that our age has not at all conquered its passions by reason, the Commentator's rational stance acquires a bitter ironic meaning. Then he proceeds to the action itself, but in a special dimension, where he is not a participant in the plot but converses with the players, as it were, inside their own minds, testing the validity of their purpose and reflecting their own inner doubts. This occurs several times in the play at critical moments, when the movement of action is suspended in order to bring out the complexities of its implications. In this manner he questions the guerillas at the beginning about the meaning of their plan while at the same time he establishes before the audience the symbolic function of certain objects: a knife and some crude wooden carvings by Antanas. The knife, a sculptors's tool, has been transformed into a symbol of his weapons, and we perceive that, while Antanas' determination to fight in order to preserve the principles of freedom and creativity grew over the years, his own ability as an artist declined while he was using his "knife" for the purposes of killing. At another time, just before the wedding ceremony, the Commentator speaks from this special plane to Jonas about the man's modest dreams of a little house and some flowers in the future and tempts him with the regime's offer of amnesty, to deflect him from his decision to kill and die together with Antanas. A dramatic confrontation on this same level occurs when the Commentator, in the guise of a photographer, freezes the action on the split second of camera flash in order to try and convince the Prosecutor that he ought not to provoke Antanas to kill him. At issue here is the Prosecutor's insistence that he will not discard his "rationalistic" philosophy, which does not permit the moral dimension, even if he now sees that it may have been absurd: "Concede that all my life work—the perfect voyages charted by my reason—were only a senseless maze leading nowhere?!" In reference to his own face which, like the portrait of Dorian Gray, now shows all the stages of his moral deterioration, the Prosecutor expresses his final decision to die—a decision in which, as in that of Antanas, we hear at least as clearly the voice of pride as that of principle: "If both faces are sodden and blue-veined with absurdity, I'll serve neither! I'll go alone!"

The third plane on which the Commentator appears is that of a regular member of the cast, a contemporary and a participant in the historical moment. There he takes up secondary roles, similar to those of an observer, while he again questions the players' thoughts and attempts to deflect them from their purpose. The difference is that he can only pretend to know no more than the players do; in fact, he remains an omniscient narrator of the entire drama and therefore, paradoxically, must fail to understand the deepest motives of the people he speaks with, because their convictions arise in part from their ignorance of the historical perspective. A clear example of the Commentator's dilemma is the scene where he, in the guise of a beggar, tries to convince a little boy not to put flowers next to the posts in the market square:

COMMENTATOR: My child, you aren't one of those who place flowers on the posts, are you?

BOY: Me?! No! And what if I did? It's not for you to understand.

COMMENTATOR: Why shouldn't I understand, Child? I know life. Don't be too bold—you'll soon be cold. Who has might, has right.

. . . .

BOY: Did you ever put flowers on a place that's very dear to you when it was not allowed?

COMMENTATOR: No. To be honest, I never did. Who knows, maybe I missed something.

BOY: I'm sure you did.

The boy emerges here as the greater sage, one who knows the wisdom of the heart. This in turn, contradicts the apparent meaninglessness of Antanas' blind determination to fight to the end, because his own conviction, and the boy's, is what the entire struggle is about—the ultimate human values.

Finally, the Commentator enters the stage as a poet, a reader of verse strongly reminiscent of Lithuanian folk songs, gentle and lyrical and resigned to the centuries-old fate of the nation to keep dying forever in battles it did not seek but must fight in order to preserve its physical existence as well as its humanity. These songs serve as prefaces to various stages of the action, thus lending the events themselves a moving lyrical quality.

As noted before, the Commentator's entrances into the play on one plane or another also help establish the symbolic function of various objects. Most of the other characters continue to elaborate these symbols and in the process depict themselves as something more universal than mere participants in a tragic episode of long ago, in a forgotten country. One may in fact perceive a circular sequence of symbolic objects, beginning and ending with the five posts of the play's title. These posts are a silent presence before the action begins. It was the Prosecutor's idea to put them up in the market square and to tie to them the bodies of dead guerillas, so that, in his own words, the town could be edified by "this majestic spectacle: ants, methodically destroying the bodies of those who dared to raise their hands against history." One could visualize these dead men, standing at the posts, as if they were statues, the creations of time gone mad. This allows for the connection of the posts with the Prosecutor's book: *The Statuary of the Future,* where he had envisioned a coming time of men and women of marble-like perfection, free from emotional complexities and moral prejudice. The juxtaposition between these statues of the mind and the rotting corpses describes quite clearly both the frightful irony of the distance between unreal dreams and repulsive reality and the catastrophic destruction of the Prosecutor's mind. A further link in the chain are the little wooden figurines which Antanas was carving in his guerilla hideout, pitiful echoes of his once powerful artistic vision. We are shown an example of what he tried to create before all the madness descended upon the land. In Antanas' former studio there are clay sculptures of figures captured in their dynamic surge of movement, a statuary embodying men's feelings and not their dead utopian logic. Antanas did not have the time to cast them in bronze, and now they are all decaying, returning to the dust from which they came, just like the dead freedom fighters at the posts. The Prosecutor's book enters again as a symbol during his encounter with Antanas; it outlines his profile as a decaying corpse in his own right, a far cry from the marble perfection of his dreams. At the same time, both the Prosecutor and Antanas emerge as two people who have one esential thing in common: through the author's use of subject-symbols they reveal themselves as thinkers in images and not in logical abstractions. They are, as the play makes clear at several points, in their essence artists and not "men of intrigue and action." Consequently, in this time of tyranny, described by the representatives of the new order as a new ice age, they are both doomed to perish, and it does not matter that one of them attempts to fight the advancing glaciers, and the other—to join them, to become "an icicle in the flow."

Landsbergis' play reveals one crucial aspect of any encounter with tyranny: such encounters are never simple, and men do not achieve heroic stature through a single-minded devotion to their ideals, for that would be too easy and would too much resemble what Matthew Arnold has described as ignorant armies clashing in the night. No struggle is worthwhile, none has a universal and everlasting quality if the deepest values of those who stand up for freedom do not undergo their own crucible in the clash of arms. Therefore, the terrible events in Lithuania some years ago are illuminated by Landsbergis in such a way that they acquire relevance, become a contribution, to the principles and ideals of the American revolution as well, because it, too, did not achieve its present greatness without painful defeats and without the multiple agonies which result from the questioning of one's own conscience.

Rimvydas Šilbajoris

FIVE POSTS IN A
MARKET PLACE

CHARACTERS

COMMENTATOR
ANTANAS: 35, leader of a guerilla detachment, formerly, a sculptor
LEONAS: 26, a guerilla, former high school student
JONAS: 30, a guerilla, formerly a carpenter
GRAZINA: 19, high school senior, liaison worker for the underground
PROSECUTOR: 60, professor of Law, public prosecutor for the occupation government
ALDONA: 30, secretary in the Prosecutor's office, agent for the underground
BOY: 9
FATHER: Father of Grazina, old
MOTHER: Mother of Grazina, old
DEPUTY: High official of the occupation government
CHAIRMAN: Official of the occupation government, middle-aged

Place: A forest and a town in a small country.
Time: Our century.

ACT I

(*The curtain is open. One sees an empty stage of an abandoned theatre. The COMMENTATOR steps out from the audience. He is well-groomed, middle-aged, a comfortable man whom you have often met: prim but not insensitive, intelligent, pleasantly bookish.*)

COMMENTATOR: Good evening, ladies and gentlemen. I am here to introduce to you a strange story. (*The stage becomes gradually lighter. ANTANAS, JONAS, LEONAS enter slowly. They are dressed as typical guerillas of our century. The set becomes completely visible. It pictures the interior of an underground pillbox, made of timber and planks. A narrow staircase leading to the surface. Bunk beds. Boxes. A battery transmitter. A typewriter. Weapons.*) It is our century. Recognize the rot and rust? You see an underground guerilla pillbox in the middle of impenetrable forests. It is the year that saw the end of the armed resistance in a small country against a mighty totalitarian conqueror. I enter here to tell of these men on whom a sky of extreme demands and total decision fell one day. I will describe an unusual wedding during that year; a wedding and a dark plan to kill a man. (*The COMMENTATOR approaches JONAS from behind.*) What do *you* think of the plan, Jonas?

JONAS (*rapidly and excitedly*): It's good! I may be a plain guerilla, but I can appreciate a clever plan. (*Points to ANTANAS.*) The leader and I come to the district town for a wedding. The leader is the groom. I'm his best man. We're from the capital city. The top officials of the enemy come to the wedding party at the Town Hall. The Prosecutor comes—the Prosecutor who has stayed away from every public event until now. (*Points to LEONAS.*) Leonas and two men from our head-quarters take places in the house across the street. We shoot! We kill! Leonas covers our retreat, we all escape in a truck. (*Grabs a knife and stabs repeatedly a wooden block on the table, enacting the climax of the assassination.*) The prosecutor—whom we've failed to kill for seven years—He's dead.—And I hope it's a bullet from my gun that gets him.

COMMENTATOR: But you know nothing about him.

JONAS: He mocked those he condemned. It cheered him when families were torn apart. No one knows his real name? All right—no one knows the devil's real name either! The devil also has a past!

(*The COMMENTATOR pulls out the knife from the block, walks over to LEONAS, and slips the knife into his hand together with the question.*)

COMMENTATOR: And you, Leonas, how do you feel about the plan?

(*LEONAS drops the knife which the COMMENTATOR picks up.*)

LEONAS: I hope our headquarters drops it. There is no guarantee that the Prosecutor will come to the wedding party. The town is teeming with soldiers. The plan is really a death trap covered with a bridal veil!

COMMENTATOR: So much afraid of death?

LEONAS: No, I am not afraid of death. To go away, to fight alone—that I fear! (*Points to ANTANAS.*) I've always felt safe in his company. I cannot leave him, and yet I cannot tell him that!
(*The COMMENTATOR walks over to ANTANAS and slips the knife to him.*)

COMMENTATOR: And *you*, as leader of the group?

ANTANAS (*grasping the knife hard*): I will go ahead with the plan. It's headquarters orders. But I have doubts.
(*ANTANAS picks up a half-finished wood-carving and starts retouching it.*)

COMMENTATOR: What doubts?

ANTANAS: The author of the plan—Aldona—I know her very well. Our wedding plans were made seven years ago. The war separated us. We hadn't met since, except for a couple of notes: a luxury with our overworked messengers.

COMMENTATOR: But she does work for the underground, like you?

ANTANAS: She's been one of our most valuable members—the way she managed to get a job in the Prosecutor's office. Even now I cannot forget recall the handwriting of her mind—soft lines on an aspen leaf. I try to picture her drafting the plan and I cannot.

COMMENTATOR: Why don't you tell your men everything you know?

ANTANAS: It would only breed new doubts in them. Tomorrow they must be steel: spotless and efficient. Doubt is rust.

COMMENTATOR: Which only leaders can afford, right? Doubts about the plan, doubts about your hands that used to sculpt such perfect features.
(*ANTANAS turns his eyes from the COMMENTATOR to the carving in his hands. He once more runs his fingers over the features of the carving. His face shows pain and disappointment. With a definitive gesture he puts the carving away.*)
(*The COMMENTATOR turns to the audience, takes a copybook from one of the boxes.*)

COMMENTATOR: It's time to touch the yellowed pages of their songs; time to begin.
(*The COMMENTATOR starts reading the song from the copybook. Music of the concertina. The lighting changes to depict the atmosphere of an underground pillbox. ANTANAS, JONAS and LEONAS take their places in it.*)

COMMENTATOR: Nightingale, dear nightingale,
              Hasten homeward through the seas.
              Songs have never been so sad,

There were never times like these.

Once you see your native land,
You will wonder where all went . . .
And the branch where once you sang,
And the tree—all is lament . . .

(*During the second verse, LEONAS' shrill tubercular cough is heard.
Singing, the COMMENTATOR crosses the stage and disappears.*)

JONAS: I hope the poor girl didn't get lost like a couple of years ago.

ANTANAS: Grazina knows this forest better than the foxes and the beavers.

JONAS: That time when she caught a cold—what a wonderful nurse you were, Sir. You didn't get a wink of sleep watching her, and she couldn't close her eyes looking back at you.—Anyway, it was good to hear a woman sneeze around here. No male messengers for me!

ANTANAS (*to LEONAS*): I'm afraid you cannot wait any longer.

LEONAS (*with sudden determination*): If she doesn't come, I'll stay here!

ANTANAS: Jonas, take a quick look outside. Listen for suspicious sounds, any.

JONAS (*mockingly*): Oh, let me stay . . .

(*JONAS goes out slowly, taking a long look at LEONAS.*)

LEONAS: You didn't want him to hear us. Are you ashamed of me?

ANTANAS: I'm too proud of you. Why should he see you in a moment of weakness?—You will go now. The two men from the headquarters must have arrived at the mill already. You cannot keep them waiting.

LEONAS: If you only would understand!

ANTANAS: You were the youngest in our group; you and Grazina. What was purgatory to others must have been hell to you; and what was hell to them, for you there's no name. I didn't forget it for a single moment.

LEONAS: Will you let Jonas go in my place, and take me with you?

ANTANAS: That would upset the entire plan.

LEONAS: You have your own doubts about the plan, don't you?

ANTANAS: Headquarters has analyzed it to the last bullet. (*Warmly.*) All will end well, Leonas. We'll succeed tomorrow. Look beyond tomorrow. Look into the future.

LEONAS: The future? If, by some miracle, I should be washed up on that shore, what would lie ahead for me? I would gasp there, with my lungs in shreds, like a stranded fish. And I would still turn my head toward the past.

ANTANAS: We must put the past aside! It holds us back, and we must go on!

LEONAS: All of it? That afternoon when you and I met in the park, by accident, before the war?

ANTANAS: Even that afternoon!

LEONAS: The sun was copper. The flowers were chrysanthemums. The book in your hands was "The Statuary of the Future"; it fit your hands better than the gun.

ANTANAS: The words of that book; the beauty of that afternoon; *all* our loyalties—everything lead us here! But we are soldiers who don't stop in the middle of the road to gaze at their pasts. Here only the present counts—and the future.

LEONAS: That meeting with you—it set me on a long train of thought. I began to read, to search. A spark was born, which you helped ignite— merely to be buried now in this tomb of a pillbox.

ANTANAS: We will preserve it. One day we'll carry it out into the sunlight, like a jewel in our palms. This is the tie that binds us, Leonas. And that's why you've always meant more to me than the others.

LEONAS: Yes, yes, I'm grateful, but...

ANTANAS: Discard gratitude, speak—we haven't much time left.

LEONAS: No, I can't. D'you think I have no pride? To admit...

(*JONAS enters.*)

JONAS (*to ANTANAS*): Not a sound, Sir. Just the usual pitchblack rustling, like the devil's behind.

ANTANAS: (*to LEONAS*): It's time you got ready.

LEONAS: Time to get rid of me!

JONAS (*to LEONAS*): Let your feet do the talking now.

LEONAS: And you, why do you rush—to be hung on the posts in the market place?

ANTANAS: Leonas, please!

JONAS: Please? That won't stop the tantrum.

ANTANAS: (*to JONAS*): I didn't ask you for advice!

JONAS: I couldn't help it.

ANTANAS: Jonas! Must I ask you to recite the book on discipline?

JONAS: Yes, Sir, what about discipline? I was sure that you'd put Leonas against the wall for such carryings on, and what do I hear—"please!"

ANTANAS (*to JONAS*): We have a big job ahead, and I will not permit loose tongues. (*More softly.*) Leonas is overtired.

LEONAS: No excuses, please! I resent it!

JONAS: There were others, tired and sick.

ANTANAS: Was I less patient with them?

JONAS: Like a father, perhaps, but not a pampering mother.

ANTANAS: Now I see—I have brushed two hornets nests.—Jonas, look straight into my eyes and say it; say everything.

JONAS: I can speak bluntly, Sir, whether I look at my navel or at a hole in the wall. There was a time when there were forty of us. I hate to complain, but then you didn't ask me to look straight into your eyes. Then Jonas was the last one. Jonas, you'll gather firewood! Jonas, do the wash! Jonas, you've failed to memorize the instructions again!— Then you didn't take much notice of Jonas. But this same Jonas had a dog's luck—even in dying, he is the last.

ANTANAS: Jonas, they are no more. Do you envy the dead?

JONAS: I envy nobody. I'm plain mad! Here we crouch, covered by the same earth, and these young gentlemen, these students still manage to get away with the cream.

LEONAS (to ANTANAS): Why waste your time explaining to him? He'll never understand!

JONAS: But, of course, how could I understand! Black hands—dark brain! (To ANTANAS) You're not a local man, Sir. You were never in this district before the war. Myself, I grew up here. When still a youngster, with the snot dried under my nose, I used to watch Leonas clatter by to Mass in his parent's black carriage. He was as white as a priest's palm. One day—I can see it as clearly as now—his mother presented us dirty kids with candy. She didn't hand them to us—no— her thin fingers just threw a handful into our midst.

LEONAS (to JONAS): Don't touch my mother! Let her rest in peace and don't root around her with your blind snout! From the first day here I was a "man of wealth," an outsider.

ANTANAS: Nonsense, Leonas!

LEONAS: Does it matter that I shall never see this broken down estate again?

JONAS (to LEONAS): I bet you would grab that poor little estate, with your nostrils trembling, if times could only change!

ANTANAS: If these seven years haven't made you two brothers, nothing ever will! (To JONAS.) How can you leave for tomorrow's task, if this is what you think of him?—Here's an amnesty leaflet. Those who give up now don't get killed.

JONAS: By God, if you go on talking like that, I'll do it! So it's only you who can stick it out until the end. We're for lighter chores, no? I'll show both of you that I can hold out as long as you, or even longer! (*Moment of silence.*)

ANTANAS: Forgive me, Jonas. I shouldn't have mentioned amnesty. No, I have no right to reproach you on these things. No matter how black the enemy, the past—the silent film of misery over the children's eyes—has followed us even under the earth.

JONAS: How well you speak. Reminds me of your lecture courses in the forests. Speeches, statues, recitations! And for us, even cursing is forbidden. Did you expect us—drenched to the skin, our stomachs glued to the backs—to break into the national anthem at a handclap? When a good curse would've been like a glass of brandy, or an hour of sleep. Instead, they try to make alter boys of us. The hell with everything!

ANTANAS: Hold your tongue, Jonas!

JONAS (*provokingly*): I say—the hell with all this rotten mess!

ANTANAS (*his composure disappearing*): We're in the front line! I order you to stop!

JONAS: I puke on your goddamn front-line, on your goddamn decrees, on your goddamn everything!

(*Knocking outside. All three grab their guns. The knocking continues, and they recognize the code sound. LEONAS rushes up to open the cover. GRAZINA comes down the staircase, followed by LEONAS.*)

ANTANAS: Grazina!—Grazina... Do you have everything?

(*GRAZINA's face is expressionless. She rips up the lining of her jacket, takes out a wad of papers, gives them to ANTANAS.*)

ANTANAS: Passports, draft certificates, employment certificates, official traveling certificates... Good job. They look quite authentic. Who did you see at headquarters?

GRAZINA (*breaking down*): There's nobody more to see! There's no more headquarters!

(*She breaks into tears.*)

ANTANAS: What are you saying?

GRAZINA (*through tears*): I had hardly left headquarters with the papers—I got into town—and then I heard: Their pillbox was discovered. I saw trucks, jammed with troops, racing toward the forest. Headquarters was surrounded.—They blew themselves up. Two survived. They had left in the morning for some special job.

ANTANAS: Nobody to change the order now. (*To LEONAS.*) Your two men are at the mill. I order you to go meet them!

(*LEONAS gives ANTANAS a long look and suddenly dashes out.*)

JONAS: I'll go look around.

(*JONAS slowly goes after LEONAS.*)

GRAZINA: What's happened to Leonas?

ANTANAS: Last night I had a dream. I dreamt I was in my old workshop, with my sculptures. A storm was howling outside. Suddenly the roof blew off. Rain gushed down. Lightning struck, again and again, like a whip. I tried to cover my statues, to protect them but it was useless.

49

They were splitting, crumbling, melting. Their stone eyes were those of my own men, reproachful.

GRAZINA: Tell me, is there some special plan?

ANTANAS: Grazina, I'm surprised you ask!

GRAZINA: What will you do, where will you go?

ANTANAS: We'll go on fighting. But we shall leave here; we can't come back again.

GRAZINA: And I?

ANTANAS: Your work is over. You have one more important journey—home. I have one more care—that you get home safely. Then, destroy everything that has the imprint of your journeys through the forests and start another life.

GRAZINA: I don't want to return safely! I don't want a new life!

ANTANAS: It's an order. Don't forget—until you reach home, you are still under my command.... Grazina, this means very much to me. I should have sent you home when you were twelve.

GRAZINA: I'm nineteen!

ANTANAS: I remember the day you found us. Such a little daredevil, quick-eyed, your braids astray. Still have the brown dress you wore that day?

GRAZINA: My little sister is wearing it now.

   (*She wearily sits down and takes off her wet shoes and knee-high stockings.*)

GRAZINA: Antanas—please—always remember me as I am—nineteen years old.

ANTANAS: How could I ever forget you? You came to us when our fight had just begun. Over parched grass; in autumn rains; by frozen paths; your little feet—each year more sure, each year stronger—kept seeking the way to our hiding place. You have seen us in our victories and brightest hopes. You grew taller, while we lost battles and lives. You kept growing more beautiful, while our wounds clotted and refused to close. I'll always remember you at nineteen, because thanks to us you might never reached thirteen.

GRAZINA: When I was thirteen—and fourteen—after each journey you used to help me dry my feet. I always looked forward to it while crossing the swamps. For several years now I have missed your hands. Why don't they help me anymore?

ANTANAS: Don't you understand? Grazina, Grazina. I also used to sit and wait for you by the fire. Like an impoverished sculptor's my hands would try to recreate your feet from air and memories. But when your fifteenth autumn came, I could not deceive myself any more: the little girl would never come back again—a young woman was knocking at the cover of our cave. I had to step back.

GRAZINA (*challengingly*): Why? Doesn't a woman feel more and deeper than a girl?

ANTANAS: No more of that!

(*A moment of silence.*)

GRAZINA: All right—no more, but under one condition. This evening is the last; no more food, no more fire, no more hands will wait here for me in the future. Help me to dry my feet as you did when I was fourteen.

(*ANTANAS turns away.*)

GRAZINA: Nobody ever anymore. Only foxes and badgers will find the way to your cave.

(*ANTANAS sits down next to her. He takes her foot and gently strokes it.*)

ANTANAS: You won't have colds anymore.

GRAZINA: My feet are girlishly naive. Now they believe that your hands will never part from them.

ANTANAS: Your promise, Grazina—your promise.

GRAZINA: I'll change the subject. It's been so long since you have given me one of your wood carvings. I have them lined up on a special shelf. My mother teases me—she says I'm still playing with toys. She thinks some dreamy-eyed beardless youngster from my school makes them for me.

ANTANAS: They have been turning out—primitive. My hands seem to have lost—at least, for now—their special strength, and gentleness, and patience that gives life.

GRAZINA: It isn't true! Antanas, you have been so good, so gentle, so very patient with me. With no time on your hands, with all the cares on your shoulders, you've still managed to teach me.

ANTANAS: I only tried to salvage for myself what I learned once. As the years went, I had less and less to offer to you. The forests, the steel, the blood have crowded my mind with their dark formulas. Look at our typewriter. We can write almost nothing with it anymore; it lacks the letters "m" and "o". The same has happened to me, to all of us.

GRAZINA: I'd be happy all my life with the seven letters of your name. Without "m" and "o".

ANTANAS: Tomorrow our forest experience will be quite useless to you. No more running, hiding, looking for cover. You'll have to live and to resist in a completely different way. The regents are next month, aren't they? What are your grades now? Not too good?

GRAZINA: Medium.

ANTANAS: You must have good grades. Promise you'll try to get into a university.

GRAZINA: Dull, dull lies.

ANTANAS: Their lies will not affect you. Your reason, your feelings, your senses—your entire body will reject them. Your little feet—whenever they recall the dampness of the swamps. I tried to give you a background in history, art, literature. Hold on to it. Promise me to learn.

GRAZINA: But I don't want to learn! I want to go on living as before. My home is here—at your side. Here I have peace; I'm away from the loudspeakers, the glaring posters, the faces of stone.

ANTANAS: Grazina, I don't like to hear you talk like this.

GRAZINA: I don't need scolding. I get enough of that at home. You're not my father!

ANTANAS: I need only a few more years.

GRAZINA: Forgive me. I didn't mean to be rude. What are you to me? Tell me what are we to each other. Then I could carry the word with me, embrace it when I wake. Tell me the word!

(*A moment of silence.*)

ANTANAS: I'm thirty-five! Your whole life lies ahead of you. It has so many promises for you—for you alone. Times may change. Summer nights still await you, unheard songs and unseen faces. In your future, young men are waiting, a little timidly and very hopefully, to start a conversation with you. Girls never stop dreaming, even in slavery; they'll dream forever of such things.

GRAZINA: And women? You said I was a young woman.

ANTANAS: A woman and a girl at the same time. Yours is the most dangerous age: when—some years from now—you'll look back at some of your feelings today, you'll laugh.

GRAZINA: It isn't true! Our word, Antanas, our word!

(*ANTANAS rises.*)

ANTANAS (*very severely*): We in the forests are meant for death! The living should keep away from us. The farther, the better.

(*Silence. GRAZINA begins putting on her stockings, shoes and jacket.*)

GRAZINA: Antanas, will this madness ever end?

ANTANAS: It will. Otherwise, all we've been doing would be meaningless.

GRAZINA: Then—when it's over—promise that you'll come to me.

ANTANAS: I promise. When the last battle is over, I will come to you.

GRAZINA: Will you walk with me—as far as the clearing, at least?

ANTANAS: I cannot. I'd like to very much, but I cannot. Grazina, I have nothing to give you for our parting—will you take one of my few secrets? You know the apartment house by the hospital, in the district town. There's a shed in its backyard. I left my statues in it. The janitor, if he's still alive, knows. Ask him to keep them a little longer; don't tell anybody else. Visit them sometimes.

GRAZINA: Thank you, Antanas. There couldn't be a lovelier gift.

ANTANAS: Good-bye, Grazina.

(*He kisses her forehead.*)

GRAZINA: May God keep you, Antanas.

(*She suddenly kisses him on the mouth. He is taken aback, but then he cannot restrain himself and responds. A long tender kiss.*)

GRAZINA: You will come—I know. We'll be together, we'll have time, endless forests of sunlit time. I will never look at another man. I will never marry—until you come.

(*She turns around and leaves by the staircase.*)

ANTANAS: Grazina, be careful. Follow the clearing.

(*The sound of the closing entrance cover.*)

ANTANAS: Grazina...

(*For a moment, ANTANAS stands motionless. Then he takes an iron bar and begins to demolish the radio set. JONAS comes down the staircase.*)

JONAS: Beg your pardon, Sir, but what's the sense smashing that piece of junk? It's shot, anyway.

ANTANAS (*angrily*): If the enemy discovers our cave, let them think— those guerillas had a good receiver and transmitter they exchanged messages with abroad, they didn't want to leave it to us.

JONAS: Very clever, Sir. (*Hesitation.*) Sir, I've committed a breach of discipline....

ANTANAS: I'll postpone the punishment—there's no time left. (*More warmly.*) And, please, don't call me—Sir—any more. Leonas must be now way into the forest.

JONAS: I'm standing outside and I think—we have become like children. All we need is a trifle, and there's a lump in the throat. It's night outside, the trees are whispering, the dew is on, and—Grazina's voice in the darkness. A woman's voice in the night—it almost makes me lose my breath. God, how I craved for a concertina standing outside there, alone. At least to finger it a couple of times, even without a melody.

ANTANAS: You saw her—going away?

JONAS: There were tears on her cheeks. Warm tears in the moonlight.

ANTANAS (*in a military tone*): It's time to start moving. Have you cleaned your rifle?

JONAS: Yes, Sir.

ANTANAS: We'll bury the rifles at the edge of the forest. We'll use pistols.

(*ANTANAS takes from one of the boxes an empty meat-can and a battered flashlight, and places them in the middle of the floor.*)

ANTANAS: It's good we saved the empty meat-can and the flashlight. If they do get into our cave, let them think that we received aid from abroad.

(*While ANTANAS is speaking, JONAS looks around affectionately, walks to the bunk-beds and gently touches them.*)

JONAS (*without listening to ANTANAS*): Just think, it's been seven years since that Prosecutor started raging. And we have lived here seven whole years. They destroyed those who didn't have shelters—then they smoked out the shelters—and now their bloodhounds are already sniffling for us, their men are crawling to surround us: through swamps, through marshes and under the earth. God knows, perhaps we are the only ones left in the whole country.

ANTANAS: How many children have grown up during these years: What will they be like? What will become of them? What do they think about us?

JONAS (*still not listening to ANTANAS*): Antanas, do you remember the blacksmith, and the brown-haired teacher? How those two used to sing: no bounds and no end.

ANTANAS: No end... until two stray bullets.

JONAS: And the captain's two-fingered hand, and how he used to roll the cigarettes. Every night when I climb into bed, I touch the dried out patches of his blood.

ANTANAS: Slowly, so slowly they separated themselves from us; joint after joint, hemorrhage after hemorrhage. Even now they aren't completely gone.

JONAS: Let's not leave these beds here. I'll break them to pieces.

ANTANAS: No, let them stay. I buried a copybook with our songs under one of them. Many years might pass before anybody discovers it. And then the people will carefully lift our bunk-beds into the sunlight, find our songs—and remember us.

JONAS: Seven years...

ANTANAS: And five posts... Let's go!

(*They leave. Lights fade out.*)

(*Lights go on—the office of the PROSECUTOR. Two chairs. A file cabinet. ALDONA is sitting, the steno pad on her knees. The PROSECUTOR is looking out the window.*)

PROSECUTOR: Five posts in the market place. (*He pauses.*)

ALDONA: Mr. Prosecutor, is there more dictation?

PROSECUTOR: Yes, start a new page. (*In a dictating tone.*) The market place once upon a time. Barter in the sun and horse dung in the snow. Copper coins wet with perspiration, and motionless women in carriages, like freshly excavated statues. A small, green country, dreamy and stubborn, still sinking in the marshes of dark centuries.

ALDONA: Excuse me, but what is this?

PROSECUTOR: The opening lines of my memoirs. I wanted you to take down at least the first two chapters—before you run away, forever.

ALDONA: I shall read them with the greatest interest.

PROSECUTOR: No government will permit their publication. But—let us go on.

(*As he speaks, the five posts emerge slowly in the background.*)

PROSECUTOR: Seven years ago, I stood in the market place and watched a cart full of guerilla corpses clatter by. My eyes wandered from the corpses to a huge ant-hill in the middle of the market place. In that instant my idea was born. The next day a post was erected by the ant-hill. Soon two more posts rose on either side. Throughout the heat of the resistance, naked corpses adorned the posts. The one by the ant-hill was usually reserved for the highest in rank. In that way, a nondescript market place was transformed into a dramatic example and a majestic warning to the population.

(*ALDONA lowers her head.*)

ALDONA: Mr. Prosecutor, please.

PROSECUTOR: Yes?... Aldona, how pale you are.

ALDONA: I would like to be excused. You said yesterday I could leave earlier.

PROSECUTOR: Of course. I intentionally forgot your wedding eve—to keep you longer. A last fitting of your gown?

ALDONA: Last minute visits.

PROSECUTOR: I'm expecting a fateful visit myself.

ALDONA (*very tensely*): What do you mean?

PROSECUTOR: The Chairman of the town and the Deputy from the capital city—one of the great old figures of the New Order.

ALDONA (*relaxing*): Oh, they... They will attend the wedding, won't they?

PROSECUTOR: They hinted so. The Deputy will make a formal call on me early tomorrow. It will be perhaps my last chance to take a stand, any stand, to have a say before a high level audience. The town was important because of the guerilla war. From now on only petty officials with dull briefcases will come here on rare assignments.

ALDONA: I'm sure there are more interesting things in store for you.

PROSECUTOR: I shall never forgive your future husband. He cuts the dialogue which I hoped would continue much longer. For at least one more year. I won't live more than that.

ALDONA: You can't be serious. Your health is excellent. A year has passed already without any attempt on your life. The headquarters of the bandits has been destroyed, the entire guerilla movement crushed.

PROSECUTOR: A couple managed to escape.

ALDONA: You *will* come to our wedding party—it was a promise.

PROSECUTOR: When I had to hide myself at home; when the guerillas reigned over the forests and villages, even then I wouldn't have missed your wedding. Why should I miss it now?

ALDONA: You are generous with your compliments today.

PROSECUTOR: It's high time, Aldona. Everything is coming to an end, and I must be totally frank. I'm going to miss you very much. Without you, this town will be only a retired man's anecdote, a song hummed by a balding clerk. With the end of the guerilla war, the last diversion will be gone. Only emptiness will remain. And—the shadows.

ALDONA: What shadows?

PROSECUTOR: You promise not to laugh, don't you?—A crowd of shadows from the last seven years. Silent, persistent and inhumanly patient, they circle me, and they stare.

ALDONA: Those you have prosecuted?

PROSECUTOR: In the villages they call me devil, and parents threaten their misbehaving children with my coming. When they hear my name, they hide at once. It's good to be able to hide. Do you know why judges wore long black robes in the olden days? So they could crouch within them and hide from their shadowy visitors. We, the judges of the new order, stand naked in our street clothes.—Aren't you the least bit afraid of me?

ALDONA: No. When I was a little girl, I used to be afraid of bloated eyes, hook-shaped noses and canine teeth. Later I realized that terror lives within. Today I know that people who carry terror in their breasts are the most helpless and the most to be pitied. They do not deserve fear—they *are* fear themselves.

PROSECUTOR: I appreciate your frankness, Aldona. (*Suddenly, in a PROSECUTOR's tone.*) Would you define my activity here as a crime?

ALDONA (*evasively*): You did your duty...

PROSECUTOR: Those people stood in history's path. Sentimental students, moss-covered farmers, superstitious goodwives.... To think that they once had their government, their laws, their prisons.... Oh, they paid dearly for my six months in their prison.

ALDONA (*with a touch of sarcasm*): Will that be a chapter in your

56

memoirs?

PROSECUTOR: Aldona, when my complaints begin to bore you, please warn me.

ALDONA (*sincerely*): You are the least boring person in our town.

PROSECUTOR: Would you believe that I haven't confessed this much to anybody in my life?

ALDONA (*half-jokingly*): That's almost a confession of love.

PROSECUTOR: The word is terribly inaccurate. Let us rather say that I—District Prosecutor, sixty years old—like to be near you, to hear your voice, to read the story of my life in your beautifully listening eyes. I am very selfish—I need you. (*ALDONA rises and turns away.*) Forgive me, please. Farewells were never my strong point.

ALDONA: All those you prosecuted would agree with that.

PROSECUTOR: A well-aimed shaft. All. Everybody. Nothing but shadows. Not a single exception. Do you think I might be capable of an exception, a single exception?

ALDONA: These matters are far beyond my competence or knowledge.

PROSECUTOR: Yet your eyes say—"I hope so." I'm grateful for your hope; I might even repay it.

(*ALDONA remains silent.*)

PROSECUTOR: You still haven't forgiven me. Will it help if I tell you the secret of my wedding gift? It is my most valuable possession. There may be only one copy of it in the entire world.

ALDONA: A book?

PROSECUTOR: Yes, written by a man whom you wouldn't recognize now, under a different name. Five people may have read it, including four censors—although it was meant for millions.

ALDONA: I forgive you—I think.

PROSECUTOR: To prove that you forgive me fully—may I bring this gift to you tomorrow morning?

ALDONA: No! (*A long pause.*) Why not...

PROSECUTOR: Eleven?

ALDONA: Eleven—I'll be waiting. But now I must go.

(*Darkness. COMMENTATOR appears. He fishes out the copybook from his pocket and finds the page.*)

COMMENTATOR: How weak is man, how frail and small,
    The greatest kingdoms once will fall
    Like ant-hills, and shall pass away
    On Judgement Day, on Judgement Day.

(*The lights change to an evening hue. It is the market place. COMMENTATOR exchanges his tweed jacket for a shabby one. Then he puts on dark glasses and sits down on the floor with his concertina,*) *impersonating a blind beggar.*)

COMMENTATOR (*seriously*): We have arrived at the center of the maelstrom. This is the market place. The guerilla ranks have now thinned out so much, that the posts have been empty for several months.

(*BOY enters the empty stage and cautiously looks around. He is hiding something close to his chest under his shirt. COMMENTATOR puts the concertina down and lifts his finger, listening.*)

COMMENTATOR: Nine year old feet and freshly picked flowers. Do I guess right?

BOY: You're just dreaming old man. There are no flowers.

COMMENTATOR: My child, you aren't one of those who place flowers on the posts, are you?

BOY: Me? No! And what if I did? It's not for you to understand.

COMMENTATOR: Why shouldn't I understand, child? I know life. Don't be too bold—you'll soon be cold. Who has might, has right.

BOY: Aw, what can you know—you're much too old.

COMMENTATOR: And therefore very wise.

BOY: Did you ever put flowers on a place that's very dear to you, when it was not allowed?

COMMENTATOR: No. To be honest, I never did. Who knows, maybe I missed something.

BOY: I'm sure you did.

COMMENTATOR: Could be, could be.—Good of you to keep company of an old man. Just sit here and imagine—what a thrill it will be to grow up: to wear long pants, to shave, to kiss a girl, to get drunk. And then, to become somebody.

BOY: Like what?

COMMENTATOR: The people—they are all somebody. Even a beggar like me is somebody.

BOY: I'll be just a boy. Why should I be somebody? Nobody likes the policeman. The grocer is always grumbling. Even my father is unhappy.

COMMENTATOR: You should be the government—that's the best somebody. You know, the men who slide by in black cars, stuffed with good food, in imported underwear.

BOY: People spit on the sidewalk when these cars go away.

COMMENTATOR: Psst, quiet! I hear two pairs of feet.

(*The BOY glances around. JONAS and ANTANAS enter from the other side of the stage.*)

JONAS: I must look ridiculous. I feel ridiculous in this suit.

ANTANAS: Your dark one, for tomorrow, will fit you better. The watchmaker—where you'll sleep over—has had it made to your measurements.

JONAS: The poor man will go broke. The price of a good suit today! If I could only give him something.

ANTANAS: I'll try to get some money.

JONAS: But how?

ANTANAS: I hid some banknotes in this town seven years ago. But that's my worry. You know the town. Where is Aldona's street?

JONAS: I'm all confused. All the street names've been changed. It should be in that direction. (*He notices the posts.*) Look—the posts!

(*JONAS crosses himself with a sudden motion.*)

ANTANAS: Empty...

JONAS: Only rags were left of the men from headquarters—not enough to hang here, is there, Prosecutor?

ANTANAS: The Prosecutor! A dark blot; to be hit, slashed, torn to pieces. For all the waiting, the teeth-gnashing, the bleeding of seven years. The Prosecutor—nothing else matters now!

JONAS: What are you waiting here for? Trouble? The longer I look at these things, the more I shiver.

ANTANAS: Take a good long look: You'll do better work.

JONAS (*noticing the BOY*): Someone else is looking at them—with different eyes. Seven more years, and he'll strut in the enemy's uniform. He may be the one who'll catch us, if we're still alive.

ANTANAS: He can direct us to Aldona's street.

JONAS: Be careful. Better ask him in the enemy's language.

(*ANTANAS goes to the BOY and whispers to him.*)

BOY (*shaking his head*): No! No! I don't know that language: I don't speak it.

(*ANTANAS and JONAS smile at each other.*)

ANTANAS: Tell me, son, how do we get to the Street of the Glorious Future?

BOY: That way, across the market place, right past the prison.

ANTANAS: Thank you, son. Thank you very much. (*He squats next to the BOY.*) Tell me, do you usually play here?

BOY: I'm not playing!

ANTANAS: Why not? When I was your age, what games we had. Cops and robbers, cowboys and Indians. I'm sure you know them.

BOY: Sometimes we play war.

(*ANTANAS strokes the BOY's head and notices the flowers. He gently pulls them out and shows them to JONAS.*)

ANTANAS: Lilacs. (*To the BOY, very seriously.*) Isn't it time for you to go home?

(*The BOY snatches the flowers from ANTANAS.*)

BOY: No.

(*ANTANAS holds him tight.*)

BOY: Let me go, mister! Let me go!

COMMENTATOR: What's happening? Help!

JONAS: Shut up, you old rag-pile! Do you want trouble pouring in on us?!

(*ANTANAS releases the BOY.*)

ANTANAS: Everything's all right, old man. Nobody is harming the boy.

(*ANTANAS kisses the BOY's forehead.*)

JONAS (*to BOY*): May God protect you.

ANTANAS: Jonas, go straight to the watchmaker's and get a good night's sleep.

JONAS: That's your best order yet. I'll sleep like mad.—And you?

ANTANAS: I'll get that money for the watchmaker. Don't worry—it's nothing dangerous. See you tomorrow.

(*ANTANAS and JONAS leave. A moment of silence.*)

BOY: It's quiet now, isn't it?

COMMENTATOR: Like a tomb. Only at the other end of the town, a woman's bare feet and the weight of water pails. The first lamplights splash in the puddles like newborn chicken.

(*The BOY gets up.*)

COMMENTATOR: Don't go yet! I'll show you a trick. I'll tell you a fairy tale about the tin soldier. You never heard it before.

BOY: No, thank you, you are very good, but I must go.

COMMENTATOR: You'd love the fairy tale about the tin soldier!

BOY: Tomorrow, old man.

COMMENTATOR: Is there anything I can do for you?

BOY (*taking a step up-stage*): If you hear heavy boots, warn me.

COMMENTATOR: I will, son.—Your voice is trembling. Are you afraid?

(*The BOY takes another step up-stage.*)

BOY: A little, just a little.

COMMENTATOR: What will be left of your soft body,
    Lilac-young, flower-like body;
    Only the bones by ants picked clean
    And little worms where eyes have been.

(*During the COMMENTATOR's song, the BOY cautiously takes out the bunch of flowers from under his shirt and smooths them. Then, with a sudden determination, he turns and dashes up-stage. The lights fade out.*)

(*The shed emerges from darkness. A faint glimmer of moonlight from a small window high above. ANTANAS enters the shed stealthily, takes one more glance outside, then cautiously closes the door. A*) *moment of hesitation. Then, slowly, he walks toward the statues. He searches around and pulls out an old suitcase from behind them. He kneels down, opens it, and takes out an oil cloth wrapping, which he unfolds to check several banknotes in it. The moonlight illumines the suitcase more brightly. ANTANAS puts the money aside and takes out a crumpled dirty smock, a sculptor's hammer, a chisel. He surveys each of them with wonderment and caution, as if they were extremely fragile. His eyes wander from the tools to the statues which are flooded by moonlight.)*

ANTANAS: What inquisitive moonlight. No more the gentle, the lullaby-ing syllables of the forest moon. Well, my respects, city moon. I've grown unused to your razor of curiosity, to your profile of a prying art critic. There is a question on your lips—what does a sculptor feel revisiting the world of his creation after seven years? Will you help me to re-enter the world, city moon?

(ANTANAS gets up and slowly uncovers the statues. As he speaks, his curious hands move over their features.)

ANTANAS: My "Sleeping Soldier"—hardly recognizable—returning to the nothingness from where he came. He must have wondered why, knowing that clay wasn't made to last for seven years, I didn't return in time to recast him in more lasting materials. Poor "Soldier"... The "Athlete"—still in flight, seeking and straining as when I left him. Ah, my "Young Girl with a Dying Deer," still closest to my heart. Are you hinting that it shows too much violence for a pastoral theme? It is the imprint of the age, you ageless faraway observer, an imprint which I never wanted to delete. "Reject time's ills, but embrace time's wounds." This my heart dictated seven years ago, and it still whispers the same message now.—One thing I grant my Olympian critic, I must expand, use new materials. The Athlete, a new better version, should be done in bronze. Bronze—rich, noble bronze. If only the war would have started a couple of months later! I was all ready to enlarge my workshop, to build a brick kiln for baking the mold. Two months—and I could have started working in bronze. Oh, how I craved for it! And the Girl, my Girl with the Dying Deer! I'll do you in wood, a completely new arrangement. The grain of wood, how it will emphasize the composition. I came to know wood better than any other material; trees are my brothers now. I'll work in bronze and in wood, do you hear? All the new things I'll fashion now, a whole world of forms waiting!

(As he speaks, the moonlight begins to wane.)

ANTANAS: My plans—what do you think of my plans?

(The moonlight is now pale as before the conversation. ANTANAS

stands silent for a while. He looks up to the window.)

ANTANAS: A city cloud... Farewell, city moon.

(*A fragment of ALDONA's room emerges from the darkness on one side of the stage. A white curtained window. A bed. A candle on the table. ALDONA, her head covered with a shawl, waiting by the window.*)

(*On the other side of the stage, lit very dimly, is the room of GRAZINA's parents. GRAZINA stands by the window upstage. FATHER and MOTHER sit on benches on both sides. The COMMENTATOR stands at the side of the stage.*)

(*Suddenly ALDONA freezes with expectation. She can hardly believe that she is hearing steps. She dashes to the door and flings it open. ANTANAS is outside. For a moment neither of them moves. Then he steps in, and she embraces him.*)

ALDONA: Antanas—Antanas.

ANTANAS: Yes, Aldona.—Yes.

ALDONA: Oh, my dear, you must be exhausted.

ANTANAS: Nothing as bad.

ALDONA: Come, sit down, right now.

(*ANTANAS sits down on the bed, and ALDONA next to him. She takes his hands and regards him silently. Then he jumps to his feet suddenly, goes to the window, glances out for an instant, and gives a couple of slight taps at the wall.*)

ANTANAS: Is it safe here?

ALDONA: We can talk to our hearts' content. My neighbor is a widow with four little ones. She's stopped listening to the outside world. (*ANTANAS sits down again.*) I didn't do much talking myself during my enforced widowhood.

ANTANAS: You'll notice my words have also become few and ungainly.

ALDONA: Then we'll gaze at each other silently for the next ten years. (*A pause.*) You were late. Nothing went wrong, did it?

ANTANAS: No, everything went as planned.

ALDONA: Did you stop over somewhere?

ANTANAS (*a moment of hesitation*): No.—Just at the forest edge, to change our pillbox clothes.

ALDONA (*caressing his hand and touching his sleeve*): This jacket seems a little short. And look at your shirt, a patch!

ANTANAS: It was the best they had, the good people. Jonas is having even more trouble with his clothes. He's getting his dark suit from the watchmaker, where he's sleeping over.

ALDONA: Wait till I show you your wedding suit!

(*ALDONA dashes out. ANTANAS sags, the exhaustion beginning to*

overwhelm him. ALDONA comes back holding up a dark suit and a snow-white shirt. ANTANAS makes an effort to sit straight again.)
ANTANAS: This must have cost you a fortune.
ALDONA: Remember, I didn't have anybody to dress up for. Saving was easy.
(She puts down the suit and the shirt on the chair and again sits beside him.)
ALDONA: I was afraid you'd never come. I ran out on the street several times. I even stopped a strange man once. *(ANTANAS closes his eyes momentarily.)* Oh, God, you must be starved, and I'm sitting here and talking away. I kept rewarming your favorite pancakes. I'll have them in a minute.
(She quickly embraces him and runs out. He yawns, stretches, touches the bed, marvelling at the blanket and the sheet. He cannot resist the temptation to lie down. Instantly, he falls asleep.)
ALDONA *(backstage)*: Would you like me to prepare a bath for you?—Dear Antanas, how pale you've become.—You will have cranberry jam, won't you?—You still like tea, of course. Oh, Antanas, my hands tremble from joy. I have so much, so much to tell you!
(She comes in and stops, surprised. She strokes his hair, then lifts his head, arranges the pillow, takes off his jacket and shoes. Meanwhile, the stage is growing darker. She sits down in the chair beside him and draws the shawl over her shoulder. The other side of the stage becomes light.)
(The room of GRAZINA's parents emerges from the darkness: GRAZINA, FATHER, MOTHER, COMMENTATOR in their previous positions.)
FATHER: She's going to tell me where she spent last night! She is—even if I have to drag her through the streets by her hair!
MOTHER: Her shoes wet, her hair astray, at the cock's crow—what a shame!
GRAZINA: The forest dew was on my feet, my hair, my eyes.
FATHER: She's turned into a real savage; you wouldn't find another like her in the whole district.
MOTHER: The eyes, the tongues of our neighbors! God forbid: she'll never be married!
FATHER: If a single dog barks about it in the village, I won't forgive her.
MOTHER: The times have changed, father. The young are baited against the old: our words have no worth any more.
COMMENTATOR *(to GRAZINA)*: You were in the forest. You said good-bye, but you couldn't go home. Hidden behind a tree, you waited for them to leave the pillbox. You followed them with your eyes, but you

knew you couldn't approach them.

GRAZINA: They stepped carefully on the tall grass, like young, green reapers. He walked behind his friend, placing his feet into the footprints before him. With such care, so softly and yet so strongly—like everything he used to do.

COMMENTATOR: The grass that bears the footprints of those who'll die soon, is graveyard grass.

GRAZINA: No, he is alive!

FATHER: What did she say?

MOTHER: I understood her better when she was still under my heart.

FATHER: What does she care if the bread basket is empty, the milk pail dry and even bacon doesn't buy a pane of glass?

MOTHER: Her fingers have always been empty—now they don't miss the wool sliding through them, they do not hurt.

FATHER: Yet one must live, even with a foreign millstone around his neck.

MOTHER: Where are the bones of those who hurled themselves against the might?

(*A wave of women's wailing rises and falls from the direction of the town. GRAZINA freezes. FATHER, MOTHER and the COMMENTATOR listen attentively.*)

GRAZINA: Did you hear it? (*To the COMMENTATOR.*) What has happened?

COMMENTATOR: Someone is being taken to prison.

GRAZINA: Antanas!

(*ANTANAS suddenly sits up in bed.*)

ANTANAS: What was it?

ALDONA: Nothing, nothing. There are always some women crying.

(*ANTANAS goes back to sleep.*)

COMMENTATOR: No. It's a nine year old boy. They've seized him in the market place.

CURTAIN

ACT II

(*The stage grows lighter, slowly.*)
(*ALDONA's room. A window. White curtains respond to a slight breeze. A white basin, a large pitcher with water and a towel on a bureau. A doll in folk costume on the table. Chairs. ANTANAS is asleep on the bed. He is dressed, except for his jacket and shoes. ALDONA sits on a chair and watches him. The COMMENTATOR stands beside her and sings.*)

COMMENTATOR: Whitely dawns the day,
   Darkness steals away,
   My beloved alone
   Sleeps beyond the dawn.

   Yet for all my hoping
   His eyes will not open,
   For he sleeps so still
   Deep beneath the hill.

ALDONA: Softer, please. No more dark songs for me. The dawn is as white as a bridal veil, and I see him again after seven years.

COMMENTATOR: Admit, you are afraid of his awakening.

ALDONA: I wait and I tremble.

(*Light fades out on ALDONA and the COMMENTATOR. At the same time, GRAZINA is picked up by the light on the right side of ANTANAS' bed.*)

GRAZINA: Where are you now? Where are the flowers that will blossom on the morning of our wedding?

ANTANAS: Were I to see you again, I would break the seven seals of steel and duty that have closed my lips. An army of words of love is impatient to break their long wait.

GRAZINA: There is a birch tree on the way to church—all moonlight and green tears—born the same day as I. Proud and sad, it will look at me walking in white at your side.

ANTANAS: A linden tree grows by the church stairs—my young heartbeat still embraces the rind of its memory. Now it will see me beside you and cry out.

GRAZINA: The aisle to the altar, so terribly long.

ANTANAS: As I slide the ring on your finger, I hesitate: will I be able to take such peace, such happiness—can a bullet-scarred and burnt out tree ever bloom again?

GRAZINA: Your lips have already forgotten the taste of lead and fire;

your lips next to mine.

(*Light fades out on GRAZINA, ALDONA and the COMMENTATOR emerge again, waiting by ANTANAS' bed.*)

ALDONA: He's waking! And the more he wakes, the more he is my bridegroom. Straight and young, as seven years ago; singleminded, like lightning.

COMMENTATOR: Let me warn you—seven years is a long time.

ALDONA: He couldn't have changed!

(*Exit the COMMENTATOR. Faint steps outside the door. Man's whistling of a carefree song. ANTANAS opens his eyes and jumps up from the bed.*)

ANTANAS: Who's there?

ALDONA (*smiling*): It's only the postman.

ANTANAS: A fantastic profession.—What time is it?

ALDONA: Ten thirty.

ANTANAS: What? Why didn't you wake me up?

ALDONA: Good morning Antanas.

ANTANAS (*more gently*): Good morning.

(*A moment of silence.*)

ALDONA: I'm waiting.

ANTANAS: For what?

ALDONA: Last night you were too tired for a good night kiss. This morning you are too confused—and no good morning kiss.

ANTANAS: I'm sorry.

(*He kisses her on the cheek.*)

ALDONA: You are forgiven. (*She gently kisses him.*) In fact, I forgive you everything in advance. Everything save one.

ANTANAS: And what crime could that be?

ALDONA: That you should stop loving me. Some women must have crossed your path during those seven years—prettier, younger than I. There was even talk.

ANTANAS: What talk?

ALDONA: Oh, empty, empty talk. I didn't pay attention. I've forgotten already.

(*ANTANAS abruptly steps to the wash-basin and takes off his shirt.*)

ALDONA: You tossed and turned throughout the night while I kept watch.—You know, during my years of waiting I said I'd watch you sleep, one hour for each lost year. And so I did.—You tossed. Sometimes you smiled. Tell me about your dreams.—the dreams of our wedding eve.

ANTANAS: Unreal, even for dreams.

(*He hurriedly begins washing his face.*)

ALDONA: Will you say that I'm too greedy—I even want your dreams? So, I'll confess—I want to have them, your smallest thoughts, everything. Will you say that I used to be more reserved? Yes, but hunger is a terrible thing.

(*ANTANAS finishes washing his face. ALDONA hands him the towel.*)

ALDONA: There's a grey hair—several—a whole little forest. You'll have to tell me how you got each of them. To describe every snowfall. (*ANTANAS is still looking at the towel without using it.*) Dreaming again?

ANTANAS: It's too soft, to shamelessly clean.

(*A full-throated bell outside the window. ANTANAS freezes tensely.*)

ALDONA: Just a school bell. We're neighbors to a schoolyard.

(*ANTANAS begins drying his face. A noise of children's voices rushing outdoors.*)

ALDONA: The sounds of peace—you have forgotten them. You'll have to go to school now to learn them again.

(*ANTANAS holds the towel to his face and listens. His eyes meet a statuette on the shelf. He puts down the towel, carefully picks up the statuette and surveys it.*)

ANTANAS: To think that once I made this with my door wide-ajar to the sun, with my heart open to laughter, to children's voices. (*He slowly sits down on the chair, the statuette still in his hand. The children start a song outside.*) It was seven hundred years ago, on a different planet. And I am stumbling here—a blind man's bluff—on unfamiliar sounds. I trip over objects from my past—a backwoodsman among the bric-a-brac of forgotten drawing rooms.

(*ALDONA takes his white shirt from the chair and begins putting it on him. He resists half-heartedly, but she is adamant.*)

ALDONA: I'll be your teacher. I can lead you back—to the sounds, the things of peace. We'll re-enter it together. (*She kneels down beside him. A moment of silence. Her look slides down to his shoes. She speaks with light gaiety.*) We'll start with your shoes. They need a much better job of shining. Remember, officially you come from the capital city.

ANTANAS: I worked on them for hours. But they've been too long in the forest dampness. The forest... (*He looks at his shoes, at her, then at the open window through which the children's song is flowing inside. Then he suddenly pulls his hand away from hers, jumps to his feet and shuts the window. The song ceases.*) No more of peace now! There is no peace! These sounds are counterfeit and they know it! D'you think that any power—God included—could ever erase that hissing when the foam of last words mingles with blood in a friend's mouth; or the cracking of the universe of a skull under a heavy boot? These sounds shall reverberate through all time and make peace impossible!

(*ALDONA seizes his arm.*)

ALDONA: But Antanas...

(*ANTANAS frees himself.*)

ANTANAS: Let's get on with our work! Anything about Leonas? Have they reached the city yet?

ALDONA: No, not yet... For a moment I had a feeling that you were avoiding my touch.

ANTANAS: I didn't. Believe me, I didn't want to offend you.

(*A moment of silence.*)

ALDONA: What will you eat? We can talk while we eat.

ANTANAS: Thanks, but I'm not hungry.

ALDONA: But you must eat. You won't be able to avoid drinking at our wedding party. And it's time you started getting used to me setting the meal times.

ANTANAS: My body has changed. Aldona. My mouth, my palate, my vocal chords. Remember that when you hold me up to the young soft-spoken man of seven years ago. Remember and be understanding.

ALDONA: With all my heart. I'll search patiently for the features of your face and your mind that seem absent now, and find them again. I'll find that your face is more than a scream frozen by will power—as it looks to me now.

ANTANAS: There were no mirrors in the forests, but I remember looking at a strange face reflected in a puddle.—You've changed, too, Aldona. The plan to kill the Prosecutor—the plan that you inspired was a great surprise to me. It's high time you tell me more about it! And about the Prosecutor. What kind of man is he?

ALDONA: You mean—was.

ANTANAS: Be serious!

ALDONA: I am! His face is just a ruin of what it had been—that's why nobody recognizes him. Everything's in the past for him. He lives in sad memories—how once he used to be a thinker, a creator. I have a feeling that he's looking for death, as some people struggle for survival.

ANTANAS: We'll give him all our assistance!

ALDONA: Please, Antanas! I hear an echo of gun clatter in your voice. Hear me out. While in hiding from you, he has burned and crumpled up inside his armor like a dry thorn bush. In his hallucinations, his victims come to steal his peace.

ANTANAS: This I can understand—to each his own ghosts. For all of us who take part in our times: the devil's side or the angels'! No skies of peaceful stars, just constellations of ghosts.—But we're at war, Aldona! Forget the Sunday philosophy circles of our young days. He has committed ugly crimes and he must die.

ALDONA: But life has already destroyed him. To open the coffin and kill the corpse? Not you—I can't imagine you as a tool! Leave him to God!

ANTANAS: We are two soldiers now and nothing else! We have an order that we both swore to obey, and that nobody can change any more. We're one against a thousand. Without an iron discipline we will be blown away like chaff. I demanded this discipline from others, I must demand it from you and—from myself.

ALDONA: Please don't go on. These terrible seven years—they've managed to turn part of you to stone; what was once warm skin, blood, thought, feeling—now grey stone, as grey as the enemy.

ANTANAS: I don't understand you any more. Are you still with us? Answer me! Why did you propose this idea to kill the Prosecutor, and now you do your best to talk me out of it?

ALDONA: Don't be afraid, Antanas. I haven't done anything to harm the cause. They are still enemies for me. I'll do everything I'm told. But I have my personal war as well. And in that war I am the sole commander.

ANTANAS: There's only one war in this country, and you can read it's mark on every face.

ALDONA: There is my own war to save you.—How I waited for you through all these years. I was afraid you'd become hardened; only, I hadn't guessed how much. This plan was my last chance to get you out of the forest. I hoped that seeing life beyond the pillboxes would save you from turning completely to stone. On that hope I built everything!

ANTANAS: If you had only asked me whether I wanted to be saved and to survive your way. You had no right to slip your dream among the military plans.

ALDONA: My dream has its feet on the ground. It's you and the rest of the guerillas that live in the clouds. You know, as I do, that armed resistance lives by hope. But there is no more hope.

ANTANAS: To panic is a feminine privilege!

ALDONA: Have you been listening to the foreign radios? Nothing! Nothing!

ANTANAS: The silence must be only temporary. They'll have to understand. Aren't we fighting for the freedom of the whole world?

ALDONA: And the world? It has forgotten you. What do we all seek? That you and our love survive in it. In what way? Yours? No!

ANTANAS: And what is your way?

ALDONA: Has it never occurred to you? Didn't it strike you that there haven't been any mass deportations for three years? Has it escaped you that they've stopped using open terror? Were you blind not to see that they are keeping their word of amnesty for guerillas?

ANTANAS: And the way, the way?

ALDONA: Armed resistance only provokes the enemy. We must try to stay alive, to sneak into official posts, to sustain our culture, to keep our children ours, and—slowly—to improve things.—Quite a few people think that way.

ANTANAS: They sleep in soft beds. If they'd have lived on naked grass and damp earth, as I have, they would think otherwise!

ALDONA: There are things more difficult than open combat. If you could only feel the coarse cloth of my seven years!...

ANTANAS (*disregarding her*): And what about the youth, our youth?! Haven't we given them a gift of an example? Last night we stopped a little boy and he, proud as a cock, refused to speak to us in the enemy's language! Looking at him I had no doubt that we were right.

ALDONA: You are especially dangerous to the young people—to the children who still place flowers by the five posts in the market place.

ANTANAS (*softly*): He had lilacs...

ALDONA: Antanas, as time goes on, there will be fewer and fewer of these flowers. Some day the posts will rot and break and flowers will return to the hands of brides and to the peaceful graves where they don't waken dangerous memories.

ANTANAS: How smooth, how painless! And we, guerillas, what is our lot in this "peaceful" world of yours?

ALDONA: For you, Antanas, it's life. For all of you it's one more sacrifice—to leave the scene, to change your lives, to go into oblivion. Sometime, in the future, you will obtain justice.

ANTANAS: You spoke of me and stone. You should listen to the word "future"—that noble prostituted word—as it comes from your mouth like a piece of some lewd inhuman metal. Try to look into that future, at its people. Can you not see them in the warmth of their beds, entangled in the dirty sheets of lies; touch their endless sweat of fear? Will you dare to say that these people would be able to rise if dawn should break? Your heart bleeds for the children; brace yourself for the children of the future. They will be born from the seed of many fathers: the general's, the censor's, the executioner's. The contours of their brains will resemble the buckle of the policeman's belt. What will these children do if morning ever rises?

ALDONA: You have so little confidence in freedom! It doesn't die that fast. Antanas, your pride is blinding you! I'll prove that I am right: the Prosecutor will be here at eleven!

ANTANAS: What?

ALDONA: He's bringing me his wedding gift.

ANTANAS: But, why?

ALDONA: Because I know you can't kill him. Will you face him alone?

ANTANAS: You shall see!—Eleven, you said? Take some food over to Jonas' place. Be back with him here in half an hour. Not earlier.

ALDONA: I'll do that.—I love you, Antanas. As I touch your hand again...

ANTANAS: There is no time! Hurry now!

ALDONA: God be with you.

(*ALDONA goes out.*)

(*ANTANAS checks his gun. He crosses the room a couple of times, then sits down. The lights go out.*)

(*PROSECUTOR's office. A vase with flowers on the table. DEPUTY, CHAIRMAN and PROSECUTOR enter.*)

DEPUTY: You are exemplary hosts, gentlemen. No sooner than I have arrived, and you present me with a freshly captured guerilla, still warm.

CHAIRMAN: Mister Deputy, the doctor says he will stay unconscious no longer than fifteen minutes. We can resume the questioning then.

DEPUTY: Enough time to make a decision. Would you sum up what we know, Mr. Chairman.

CHAIRMAN: His name is Leonas. Caught with a gun. Looks frail. Wouldn't talk.

DEPUTY: How many guerillas did escape from the headquarters pillbox before yesterday?

CHAIRMAN: Two men.

DEPUTY: That would leave only one at large.

PROSECUTOR: And, perhaps, a couple of survivors from another pillbox.

CHAIRMAN: Aren't these figures wonderful? Like the last drops from a faucet.

DEPUTY: He must be made to talk.

PROSECUTOR: I don't think he will.

DEPUTY: How do you know?

CHAIRMAN: Yes, how? All the time you wasted waiting for him to open his eyes? Why?

PROSECUTOR: To read in them. To compare with what I read in others. To chart his spirit.

CHAIRMAN: Metaphysical games!

PROSECUTOR: You aren't a man to waste time with such games my dear colleague.

CHAIRMAN: It's his mouth we have to open, not his eyes!

DEPUTY: I used to indulge in these games once, Mr. Prosecutor. What did you read in his eyes?

PROSECUTOR: Above all—strength. Unusual strength beneath that deceptively fragile blue.

CHAIRMAN: Assuming that you are right—which you aren't—our new methods of questioning will take care of it.

PROSECUTOR: He will remain silent. And if the methods are applied, he won't survive.

DEPUTY: I must confess, I had imagined you differently.

PROSECUTOR: How, Mister Deputy?

DEPUTY: More—like the sword of justice. Do you understand me? The most advanced form of simplicity, steel poised to fall swiftly on the enemies.

PROSECUTOR: Well I had also imagined myself differently, although I had in mind more precious metals.

DEPUTY: Mr. Prosecutor, the important activities here are coming to an end. We will be assuming a more paternal attitude, strict and yet protective. We shall even forgive sometimes, although without spoiling the people.

PROSECUTOR: In other words, the sword of justice will remain poised and polished, but mainly as a reminder.

CHAIRMAN: I say, our steelly veteran is really softening. Never seen flowers on his desk before.

PROSECUTOR (*pointing to the vase with flowers*): This is an official exhibit, and the chairman knows it. A boy was arrested last night for placing flowers by the five posts. Before you is the main exhibit of evidence.

DEPUTY (*touching the flowers with his finger tips*): Lilacs whithered by history's lightning. The last of their kind.

PROSECUTOR: I suggested to the security police that they drop this flower case. It seems to be an isolated event.

DEPUTY: How unlike you again.—But we are digressing along a flower path. We must make a decision.

PROSECUTOR: On the contrary, Mister Deputy, we have just arrived at the right path. There are crossroads in the lives of men and of systems of government. At one of these crossroads there must be a flower bush or a lilac tree. There must be life. Those who once drafted the blueprint of the New Order, didn't they think of one crossroad in the far distance where flowers wouldn't be out of place?

DEPUTY: What an immense question, put in the terms of small-time gardening.

PROSECUTOR: It's time we start using words that have root in living things. This is a turning point. Active resistance lies before us like a broken branch. Let us make this young man, this Leonas, a case to mark history's turn. He won't give away any information. If tortured, he won't survive...

DEPUTY: So, then...

PROSECUTOR: Then let him live.

CHAIRMAN: And all this because of a pair of eyes!

DEPUTY: Gentlemen, in this new phase, we must change some attitudes. We must mingle more with the plain people, make our educating presence felt in their simple rituals—that's why I am attending the wedding. We also must remove some symbols that evoke unnecessary resentment. We will retain some punitive symbols to keep a healthy dose of fear. But—mark this well—we shall never spare our avowed enemies!

CHAIRMAN: And anyway, nobody will know about this Leonas. We'll say he died from battle wounds.

DEPUTY: Our Chairman has a unique gift of making complex things clear. Yes, we cannot lose. At best, we get the information, at worst— we dispose of a potential risk.

PROSECUTOR: Mister Deputy, this is my case more than anybody else's! The decision is mine by obvious right! You know my contribution of the past seven years, the era of corrosion and devouring, the era to which I gave the great symbols of the five posts and the ants. For long months I saw the whole world as an ant heap. But that era is finished. Now I demand a tangible act to seal its end. A deed to show that the New Order rejects the notion of perennial sacrifice. The deed is the life of this young man Leonas.

DEPUTY: Mr. Prosecutor, you've put your finger on the core of our disagreement. It is the ants. The ants, gentlemen, are organized, industrious, obedient things. What we need now is more of their spirit, not less. They move in perfect harmony, they move from dawn and far into the night, and as they move they think only of what is useful. The New Order highly respects them and intends to go on learning from them.

CHAIRMAN: Bravo!

PROSECUTOR: I worked for a rule of reason, Mister Deputy. I am not inspired by patterns of moving ants. I demand a vote to which I am entitled!

DEPUTY: Too many personal pronouns—you betray yourself, Mr. Prosecutor. (*To the CHAIRMAN.*) My dear Mr. Chairman, would you check to see if our captive has come to his senses.
(*CHAIRMAN goes out.*)

DEPUTY: Long ago, my friend, I was somewhat like you. I remember enough to understand you, too little to be disturbed in my lucid peace. I reached a plateau where the personal pronoun doesn't count any more. And if you ever pass that crossroad, you will also understand that measured sacrifice will be necessary as long as there are men to be ruled. To stop it would mean to invite chaos and our own end.

PROSECUTOR: It must be a fascinating land, where you live beyond the crossroads. Is this the farthest frontier of the New Order?

DEPUTY: For the few who know what it means to rule.

PROSECUTOR: It is so far that you can hardly hear what I am saying. Don't you think you might profit once from what is unfamiliar to you?

DEPUTY: Quite the contrary—your case is only too familiar. Admit it, you have bad nights. You may see faces of those you prosecuted, or hear voices. I once did! But I managed to master my fears. Now these are frozen voices on other planets.

PROSECUTOR: You know extremely much, Mister Deputy.

DEPUTY: I know even more. Didn't you write once that gigantic glaciers of the New Order are on the way, glaciers that will change the surface of the earth. And then you wrote that a man of reason does not try to stop the glacier and risk being crushed. He rather adapts himself to the glacier, in the form of a crystalline icycle, and travels with it.

PROSECUTOR: I may have written it. At this moment, in this room, it sounds very strange.

DEPUTY: Authors often forget what they have written. We never do. We are keeping the chart of your spirit. Yes, Mr. Prosecutor, we take a risk when we accept intellectuals into high positions. Like you, often they are not men of action. Sooner or later their shoulders give way to the weight of reality. They become unable to look into history's terrible eyes and to fulfill her demands.

PROSECUTOR: You didn't come here for the wedding alone.

DEPUTY: This town is ripe for readjustment; your fame has spread too widely around here. And although we respect intellect, we have now to choose a plainer person, better suited to the new phase.

PROSECUTOR: The Chairman seems to answer your needs perfectly.

DEPUTY: You'll serve in a less exalted position: no more the fiery sword over the rebels, but a kitchen knife over thieves and embezzlers. But you will serve and be useful. When we meet at the wedding I expect to see you cleansed of all uncertainties. There I will also wear my public mask. And there we shall present a solid front, a picture of unity, an example for the populace.

(*CHAIRMAN comes in.*)

CHAIRMAN: He has regained consciousness.

DEPUTY: We shall resume the questioning. I just told Mr. Prosecutor that you are taking over all the main functions in town. In any new political cases to be tried, he will be under your direct supervision.— Let us go now. (*To PROSECUTOR, who remains standing still.*) Will you join us in the questioning?

PROSECUTOR: No. My part in the questioning is over.

DEPUTY: Very well. I'll see you at the wedding.

CHAIRMAN: Don't take it hard, my friend. We'll get along.

(*CHAIRMAN and DEPUTY leave the room. In the doorway they pass the COMMENTATOR, who enters with a load of files in his hands. The PROSECUTOR steps to the table and clutches the flowers in the vase. The COMMENTATOR's voice and bearing are those of a middle-aged clerk.*)

COMMENTATOR: These are the files you had asked for, Sir. Your cases of the last seven years.

(*As the PROSECUTOR does not answer, the COMMENTATOR puts the files down on the table. Then he notices a smudge of blood on the PROSECUTOR's finger.*)

COMMENTATOR: Sir, you've cut your finger!

PROSECUTOR (*looking at the smudge*): No, my good man, no! It isn't a cut. I held a young man's chin in my hand, waiting for his eyes to open. There was a trickle of blood from his mouth.

COMMENTATOR (*visibly disturbed*): Excuse me, Sir, but I am not supposed to know what goes on in the cellar. As far as I'm concerned there is no cellar.

PROSECUTOR: Even if someone is about to die there?

COMMENTATOR: I know nothing, Sir, nothing.

PROSECUTOR: Ants, ants, ants. Do you like ants?

COMMENTATOR: If you say so, Sir.—Shall I dust off the files?

PROSECUTOR: No! Dust to dust. The chin I held will be dust. The life of the eyes. The life of a flower. Tell me, why are no human acts like flowers?

COMMENTATOR: I don't know, Sir. I don't grow flowers.

PROSECUTOR: Splendid, my good man, splendid. Think hard now before you answer. Can intellectuals be men of action?

COMMENTATOR: I would be presumptuous to think of such things, Sir. The people in the government take care of that.

PROSECUTOR: They do, they do. One faces them. The last chance. And suddenly they are invincible. Why? Because they are puffs of grey smoke, or white tombs. Oh, to battle a giant or a windmill. But a puff of smoke doesn't bleed. Tombs are beyond defeat.

COMMENTATOR: You are certainly right, Sir.

PROSECUTOR: And you're a perfect conversation partner. (*He opens the drawer and takes out a book.*) My book—a flower of long ago. I am to deliver it now. Then, no more dealings with flowers. (*He thrusts the flowers from the vase into the COMMENTATOR's hands.*) Now throw these out! And stop staring at me! Go home! Get ready for the wedding feast! We'll celebrate the new era! Go!!!

(*Darkness. The light on the COMMENTATOR who straightens out and crosses to the other side of the stage, where ANTANAS is sitting.*)

COMMENTATOR: You've had time to brood inside over what Aldona said. Don't you suspect now deep inside that she might be right? The lion's time is past—now the fox takes the field.

ANTANAS: Who are you?

COMMENTATOR: Someone who wants to clarify your story.

ANTANAS: To play peeping Tom when I confront that man? As if the dust of hesitation that settles now on my waiting hand were not enough.

COMMENTATOR: Help me to understand. I have some questions before the knock on the door. There are things to disentangle.

ANTANAS: I have no time for disentangling. I must act—for my country's sake.

COMMENTATOR: Tell me, when the pain of defeat makes you choke is it because you suffer for your country, or for yourself as well?

ANTANAS: I tried to think of my country's life alone.

COMMENTATOR: Tell me—before we hear the knock—in your little forest world you proclaimed the state of tomorrow, a state without serfs and without tyrants. Did you sincerely believe in such a state?

ANTANAS: Not always, I admit. But in our deepest moments—yes! When in retreat we had to leave a wounded friend behind us and heard him explode himself with a grenade—we did believe. When we saw prisoners herded into cattle cars for deportation and gnashed our teeth and couldn't help—we did believe. When a girl of twelve, disdaining danger for her life, brought us a message from headquarters and told us that she'd be back again—then we believed. During such moments we couldn't have fought for anything less.

COMMENTATOR: But suppose Aldona is right? If all this civilization is nothing but a sunken city, isn't your fight then only a vain and hopeless gesture? (*A knock at the door.*) If she is right—then you were born to be an artist and not a man of conspiracy, of action. (*Another knock.*) Then—what a fatal burden is this duty you imposed on your own shoulders.

(*The COMMENTATOR steps back into the shadow.*)

ANTANAS: Come in.

(*The PROSECUTOR enters. He is dressed in somber black and holds a book in his hand. Seeing ANTANAS, he hesitates for a moment. A shadow of fear.*)

PROSECUTOR: Good day. Is Miss Aldona in?

ANTANAS: She had an unexpected errand.

PROSECUTOR: Well, I will...

(*He prepares to leave.*)

ANTANAS: But do come in, Sir—she may be back any moment.

PROSECUTOR: Well, for a few minutes. I'm the District Prosecutor.

ANTANAS: Won't you sit down?

(*The PROSECUTOR sits down.*)

PROSECUTOR: You are the groom, aren't you?

ANTANAS: Yes.

(*The PROSECUTOR catches ANTANAS's intense look.*)

ANTANAS: Will you have a glass of sherry?

PROSECUTOR: No, thank you.—A sports instructor, I'm told. (*Suddenly, in a Prosecutor's tone.*) Did you serve in the army of the new order?

ANTANAS: I did. (*He puts his hand in his gun pocket.*) I've been decorated for marksmanship.

PROSECUTOR: Anyway, that was long ago. I always thought that your present profession was easier—softer.

ANTANAS: Why? I cannot complain.

PROSECUTOR: Your hands are as hard as a woodchopper's or a blacksmith's.

ANTANAS: We handle some hard implements.—It's touching to think how, in your profession, you did find time to shake simple people's hands.

PROSECUTOR: But I didn't. I probed their hardness with my eyes, in the courtroom. These people have a common gesture to plead their innocence—they open their mouth mutely and turn their palms outward. As if the stony plainness of their hands was proof they were innocent, like statues.

ANTANAS: But they were men, and therefore guilty. You had a genius for finding guilt where lesser talents would have failed. Still I confide to you a sentimental frailty—I wish these simple people had been found innocent, and others guilty.

PROSECUTOR: Ah, familiar echoes. Have you also heard voices at night or seen shadows?

ANTANAS: Voices? Shadows?

PROSECUTOR: I say this is hopeless sentimentality, young man. As part of a travelling glacier you should not have such feelings.

ANTANAS: What voices? What shadows?

PROSECUTOR: A healthy-minded sportsman interested in such dark matters.

ANTANAS: You underestimate today's sportsmen.

PROSECUTOR: Do I? How many relations, would you say are possible between a man and a woman: brother and sister, father and daughter, husband and wife? And you are quite justified if you wonder—what sort of man is this old goat? Why does he visit her alone, on her wedding morning?

(ANTANAS takes out his hand from his pocket. His curiosity is awakened.)

PROSECUTOR: A secret father, perhaps? Or an old lecher, who lurks to seduce young brides-to-be? What else, what more could there be between a man and a woman?

ANTANAS: There are so many things that bind a man to a woman. There are the pledges of distant years, the obligations of the past. (*Directly to the PROSECUTOR.*) Or—when a man is pressed to unburden his heart, there she stands, promising peace, understanding—salvation.

PROSECUTOR: A remarkable vocabulary. (*He stands up.*) Will you do me a favor and give this to Aldona. I can entrust my gift to you— you're not the ordinary sportsman that I had expected.

(The PROSECUTOR gives ANTANAS the book. ANTANAS takes it without looking at the title.)

ANTANAS (*emphatically*): You are not going yet, Sir!

PROSECUTOR: (*ignoring him*): Small, isn't it? But very rare—perhaps, the only copy in the entire world. And, in one man's life, it is the best thing he has ever done, or will do.

ANTANAS (*reads the title of the book*): "The Statuary of the Future!"

(He is unable to concel the shock of recognition.)

PROSECUTOR: You know this book?

ANTANAS: Yes...

(The PROSECUTOR sits down wearily on the chair, his back to ANTANAS.)

PROSECUTOR: I think I'll take that glass of sherry.

(ANTANAS walks to the cabinet in the back of the PROSECUTOR and slowly pulls out his gun.)

ANTANAS: But—how did you come to own it?

PROSECUTOR: Through the author, directly through the author.

ANTANAS: The author—why did he call it "Statuary of the Future?"

PROSECUTOR: Because it was a book about a perfect world to be created from the stuff of humanity, as an artist makes it from marble.

ANTANAS: "Can men, try, convict, execute each other?"

PROSECUTOR: Yes, that was the question with which the book began... The author sought support for his ideas; then he believed he had found it—in the philosophy of the New Order.

ANTANAS: What a strange alliance!

PROSECUTOR: His alliance with them was inevitable. In the rest of the world, all was autumn and dusk, small hour thoughts and middling deeds. In the empire of the New Order, a majestic flame was burning with the only worthy purpose—to change the world. And so this man dreamt that with his genius he would shape history, would make the managers of the New Order dance like marionettes...

ANTANAS: But was turned into a marionette himself!

PROSECUTOR: The government of the New Order wasn't interested in his theories; it even found harm in them. And perfect care was taken that he doesn't have time to write, to spin his thoughts—only to act, to dance at their bidding.

ANTANAS: Compassion—in your lips?

PROSECUTOR: They sent him back here instead, as a judiciary official. Oh, they knew how this transfer would affect him. Revenge against his former country—contempt for his own impotence—discovery of fear, and hate of that fear and of himself...

ANTANAS: And now? And today?

PROSECUTOR: They'll simply disregard him now. They know that never again will he give birth to ideas and raise them to manhood. He's just an old and barren woman upon an empty winter field.... But now, enough of this fairy tale about useless relics. It is his own fault—he had to stick to the philosophy of law. He was a promising thinker, but not a man of rule, of conspiracy, of action.

(At the impact of the last sentence, ANTANAS clenches the gun with both hands and, then, with a sudden decision, pockets it. He pours a glass of sherry and gives it to the PROSECUTOR.)

PROSECUTOR: Thank you. *(He empties his glass.)* How could you have know this book?

ANTANAS: Just... by accident. A friend of mine had a copy. He admired it deeply. He said... it was extremely rare—censors, you know.

(PROSECUTOR rises and looks searchingly at ANTANAS.)

PROSECUTOR: Your eyes are most interesting. You haven't told me everything about yourself. There is more in your eyes than the Sports

Institute and the wedding.

ANTANAS: You're wrong.

PROSECUTOR: I happen to be an expert on eyes. I've spent long years studying them. Before the war I used to teach in a university in this country. I used to love the auditorium full of young eyes, their attentiveness, hunger, devotion. How revealing were the eyes of the people I prosecuted. In them—between terror and resignation—an entire life would flash by in a few seconds. But yours—they resemble a pair of eyes I saw today—strength beneath that deceptively fragile blue; strength and a burnt-in mark of tragedy.

(*The PROSECUTOR shakes ANTANAS' hand and goes to the door. ANTANAS does not move, as if petrified.*)

PROSECUTOR: I will see you at the wedding party.

(*The PROSECUTOR leaves.*)

(*After a few seconds ANTANAS, with a sudden motion, pulls out his gun and dashes to the door. But the door remains closed; ANTANAS raises his fists, bangs at the door and, with his head bowed, remains in the same position for a few seconds. Then he wearily steps to the chair and collapses in it, his head in his hands.*)

(*ALDONA and JONAS enter.*)

JONAS: Where is he? What happened?

(*ALDONA stands in a silent triumph.*)

ANTANAS: Nothing!

JONAS: Why? Why?

ALDONA (*with a gentle smile*): Why?

ANTANAS: I couldn't...

JONAS: How—couldn't you?

ANTANAS (*pulling himself together, with difficulty*): I realized—that if I killed him now—Leonas and the other two would be in danger.

JONAS: But how?...

ANTANAS: Enough questions! I order—no more questions! I give orders here! I've decided to kill him at the wedding party! It will be better. The signal remains the same—have you got our train tickets? Understand? "Have you got our train tickets?" The Prosecutor will die at the wedding! (*He turns to ALDONA.*) Do you hear? He will die at the wedding!!

(*Darkness.*)

ACT III

(*The COMMENTATOR appears at the edge of the stage with a camera and a tripod. Music.*)

COMMENTATOR: O my wreath of rues, thy scent
          No more green with innocence.
          O my braid, gold silken ones,
          No more glistening in the sun.

          O my hair beneath the veil
          No parting in the gale...

The marriage has been sealed. They gave their false names. They signed with heavy hands. Outside her hair parted in the breeze. Thus to the Town Hall they came for their wedding feast....

(*The COMMENTATOR buries his head under the dark cloth of the camera and begins to adjust it. The stage lights up in a flash. Loud dance music erupts. It is the Town Hall. Benches lined up against the wall. Colored paper ribbons hang from the ceiling. A concertina on one of the benches.*)

(*ANTANAS and ALDONA are posing for a wedding photograph. The flash of light startles somewhat. JONAS and the PROSECUTOR walk over to them. The COMMENTATOR pushes the camera out. ANTANAS whispers into JONAS' ear. JONAS exits.*)

PROSECUTOR (*to ANTANAS*): Now I'm convinced that you served in the army.

ANTANAS: Why?

PROSECUTOR: You started with genuine shock at the photographer's flash. Such are the reflexes of war veterans. The memories of the front still seem to be very much alive in you.

ANTANAS: Did you doubt me when I told you I had been in the army?

PROSECUTOR: I did—automatically. Such are the reflexes of public prosecutors. I suspect everybody, including you and, consequently, I check every statement.

ANTANAS (*half-jokingly*): What is your verdict in my case?

PROSECUTOR: I reserve the verdict until the last moment.

(*ALDONA joins them.*)

PROSECUTOR: Aldona, your husband is the most serious sports instructor I've ever met.

ALDONA: Did you think that I would choose an ordinary sports instructor?

PROSECUTOR: But he could be a little happier now.

ANTANAS (*with a pretended gaity*): Don't forget, this is my first marriage.

ALDONA (*to the PROSECUTOR*): Why are the Chairman and the Deputy so late?

PROSECUTOR: They are busy with something.

ANTANAS: With what? It's a holiday, isn't it?

PROSECUTOR: Listen, young man, one shouldn't worry about officials on such a day. What if they don't come at all? Your eyes and your thoughts should be for your bride alone.

(*ALDONA kisses ANTANAS' cheek.*)

ALDONA: Do you hear, young man?

(*The COMMENTATOR enters and respectfully greets the PROSECUTOR.*)

COMMENTATOR: Excuse me, Sir. The Chairman and the Deputy want you "downstairs." Very urgent.

PROSECUTOR: You must be mistaken. I am not taking part in the questioning.

COMMENTATOR (*confidentially*): Oh no, Sir. The two that were just brought in there are beyond any questioning, unless one believes in heaven.

PROSECUTOR: Two more?

(*The PROSECUTOR goes out*)

ANTANAS (*to the COMMENTATOR*): What's "downstairs?"

COMMENTATOR: A cellar—thick walls, privacy. The town prison is jampacked, the interrogation room always crowded. Perhaps a new, a very special case. But I've said too much already.

(*The COMMENTATOR leaves. ANTANAS glances questioningly at ALDONA.*)

ALDONA: No, it can't be our men. We would know.

ANTANAS: And Jonas? Where did he disappear to? He was supposed to check if Leonas and others had arrived.

ALDONA: He'll come. Antanas, please, try to look a little happier, otherwise they'll suspect.

ANTANAS: I think the Prosecutor suspects already. I don't like his questions, his allusions.

ALDONA: How blindly, aimlessly you hunt each other. And only twelve years ago your ideas were the same. Admit—admit, Antanas—he's just a victim!

ANTANAS: A victim? Who isn't then? This chairman and this deputy for whom we're waiting? And all the bemedaled generals and pompous stalwarts, down to the smallest torturer whose worn-out heel crushes a cigarette on a floor caked with blood? Guilt has never been pure, but it goes on screaming for retribution.

ALDONA: He's guilty, yes! He is a leper—do you hear—a leper! But, Antanas, there comes a time when one has to kiss one's leper. Otherwise, there'll never be an end. You are about to do it, no matter how much you protest—you weren't able to kill him!

ANTANAS: Leprosy! It has infected everything (*He seizes her hands.*) What is there left of that girl I once discussed so many things with—a gentle girl, thoughtful and modest? Everything is infected—time itself has become leprosy!

ALDONA: She never discussed anything. She only listened—so attentively, always so silently. And now you're shocked when the "gentle" girl speaks her own mind.—Antanas, you are hurting me! (*Music suddenly stops backstage. ANTANAS releases her hands. A moment of tense waiting. Then applause is heard.*)

ALDONA (*relieved*): It's only the Deputy. Come—we must greet him.

(*ANTANAS and ALDONA leave.*)

(*JONAS enters from the other side and looks for ANTANAS.*)

JONAS: Antanas.

DEPUTY (*offstage*): Dear friends, it is with the greatest pleasure that I convey to you the strongest congratulations of the new order. (*JONAS notices the concertina on the bench. At the same instant, the voice of the DEPUTY in the background stops. JONAS turns his eyes away from the concertina and attempts to proceed to ANTANAS, but the temptation is too great. He again looks at the concertina, steps closer to it and gently strokes it. Then, with a quick movement, he puts it on and starts playing softly.*)

(*The COMMENTATOR enters and sits down on one of the neighboring benches. He looks at JONAS and smiles encouragingly. JONAS replies with a somewhat guilty smile.*)

JONAS: I love the concertina. Violins are for grasshoppers, clarinets for polkas, but the concertina touches the depth of my heart. As soon as I hear it, I can't help dreaming.

COMMENTATOR: I understand you very well. Go on playing, and I shall try to guess your dreams. God—you are dreaming—if all this warring and fighting could end some day. I don't ask for much. A little house with some lilac trees around. I, sitting on a bench in front.

JONAS: Yes, yes. Inside, a woman's voice speaks of good things: bread and milk, sun and rain. When she laughs—like doves, like forest streams—I close my eyes and I feel like someone is brushing my face with a bunch of lilacs.

COMMENTATOR: And in the bath, voices of children are splashing as

83

the loving force of the mother's hands slides along their soft skin.

JONAS: Then I lean back, the clean shirt makes my skin shiver, and I pick up the concertina.

COMMENTATOR: Have you seen this new offer of amnesty? (*He takes from his pocket a leaflet and gives it to JONAS. JONAS reads it.*) It's quite generous. If you'd give up now, you'd get away with some three years of prison. And after that—didn't they once say your hands were made of gold? A couple of years more and you'd prosper a little. Then, if you're still smart, you'd slip into a manager's chair in some little factory. And the lilacs should go on blossoming, and the women overflowing the houses and streets as ever forever. Ten years, less maybe, and all your dreams will have bodies. (*JONAS finishes reading the leaflet and clutches it in his hand.*) You realize that otherwise, you may not live to see this coming night, I want to help you.

(*JONAS stands up and turns away from the COMMENTATOR. A moment of internal struggle. Then he cringes, turns back to the COMMENTATOR and returns the leaflet to him.*)

JONAS: Thank you and no, Sir. Let them stick this amnesty, you know where. Without freedom, my woman would forget how to laugh, I'd be afraid of my own children; and my lilacs—they would smell like old fish.

COMMENTATOR: Freedom, you say. What freedom? Individual, environmental, metaphysical?

JONAS: Why so many words? I only want to breathe, that's all. Just smell the air here.

COMMENTATOR: But my dear young man—freedom! The greatest brains of your era are still arguing about what it is; if it exists at all.

(*JONAS takes the concertina again. He starts playing softly, looking straight before him.*)

JONAS: I wish somebody would round up these "greatest" brains and bring them here and stick their noses in our blood-soaked earth.

(*JONAS continues to stare ahead and play. The COMMENTATOR waits for a second, then lowers his head and leaves. At that moment, the voice of the DEPUTY is heard again.*)

DEPUTY (*offstage*): Long live the new order which this nation has married for an eternal union!

(*Applause. Music. Enter ANTANAS. JONAS hurriedly puts away the concertina and jumps to his feet.*)

ANTANAS: Where have you been?

JONAS: I—got held up for a minute.

ANTANAS: Did you meet them?

JONAS: No. People are whispering that half an hour ago, three trucks of security police roared out of town—machine guns and all.

ANTANAS: There can only be one target for them—our three friends. No more guerillas in the district. Something is going on in the cellar here. Anything suspicious about it?

JONAS: Two uniformed guards by the cellar door.

ANTANAS: We may never see our men again. You realize that without them, our chances of escaping are one in a hundred?

JONAS: Why didn't you blast his brains out this morning?

ANTANAS: Is your gun in order?

JONAS: It is.—You could have killed him without a mouse squealing about it. I feel sick. I don't trust anybody any more!

ANTANAS: You can always trust me! We're friends, aren't we—faithful friends.

JONAS: I don't know anything any more. I don't even trust myself. And what about Aldona? Tell me, do you trust her completely?

ANTANAS: We—can trust her.

JONAS: When she came to me today, she kept questioning me about you and Grazina. What the devil did she need to know about that for?

ANTANAS: About Grazina? Why didn't you tell me earlier?

(*ALDONA enters.*)

ALDONA: They've caught our men!

ANTANAS: Where? When?

ALDONA: One—this morning. The others—half an hour ago. The soldiers brought them to town. They're here, right below us.

ANTANAS: Alive?

ALDONA: I don't know.

JONAS: If any one of them speaks...

ANTANAS: Leonas... Sick and tired.

ALDONA: I haven't noticed anything suspicious yet. But we can't risk waiting. We can still leave—for our honeymoon trip. It would seem logical enough: we're young, impatient.

JONAS: It does make sense. With all these security men around—we may not have time to reach our guns. (*To ANTANAS.*) Couldn't we try to knock them off another time, in a few months?

ANTANAS (*slowly*): You may be right. (*To ALDONA.*) Yes, Aldona, I concede—one phase of the guerilla war is over! Right now it wouldn't help our country if we killed them all and died with them. (*He silences her attempt with his hand.*) We'll still fulfill the order. Those under the earth will understand why our guns will be silent today. Instead, Jonas and I will try to break across the border. If we could only reach the other side and bare our wounds before the peace and plenty of those people—God!—they would wake up, and understand

and help us.

ALDONA: And I?... And I?

ANTANAS: Taking a woman along would be suicide for all three of us. (*To JONAS.*) Jonas, go mingle among the guests, stay close to the exit, watch, listen. We'll join you in a minute.

JONAS: Antanas—I was a fool to mistrust you. I think—I understand you now.

(*JONAS turns around hurriedly and leaves.*)

ANTANAS: Aldona, when you denounced our fight, when you told me our country would survive—in your way—you were thinking of us two, of us alone. You knew about Grazina and you were afraid that she would take me away from you.

ALDONA: Yes. My ideas were nourished by love and sorrow—but does it make them wrong?

ANTANAS: It is not for me to be the accuser. This is the last time we'll talk alone. I wish I hadn't forgotten how to use words. I do respect you deeply. I must tell you the truth....

ALDONA: What truth? The girl you met? So the gossip was true. But I understand you—you were lonely. She's only a passing episode, isn't she?

ANTANAS: The truth about our love. I knew it the very moment I saw you last night. But, then, this love never was real. You described it well—a would-be artist flattered by a pretty, mild-mannered girl who admired his "profound" talk. "Soft lines on an aspen leaf"—that was the picture of your mind, of your always yielding language, of the soft outlines of our relation—that I took with me to the forests. Now the leaf has grown alien, the love has withered in seven autumns!

ALDONA: These are only words—rash, feverish, spoken in danger! Reassure me, Antanas, please! Just now, when you spoke of our past, of the aspen leaf, there was a warmth, a gentleness in your voice. It comes deep in you where your love for me still lives.

ANTANAS: There's no more time nor space for soothing words, for more deception. Aldona, I love her. It may have been the loneliness, the forests, the strange new life—it doesn't matter. Forgive me—I do love her.

ALDONA: No! No! (*Overcome by sudden weakness.*) I feel so weak! Why wasn't all this struggle and seeking one short brilliant blaze, and then—a plunge into darkness? All I wanted was to get you out of the forests and to survive together. As long as I hoped to save you, to have you, I didn't tremble once. Now I'm afraid! I'm afraid!

(*Enter JONAS, PROSECUTOR, CHAIRMAN and DEPUTY.*)

JONAS: Attention, newlyweds. The guests of honor.

86

PROSECUTOR (*to ANTANAS*): May I introduce: the groom—our Deputy—the Chairman.

DEPUTY: Very pleased to meet you. And the bride, still blossoming like a rose.

CHAIRMAN: Best wishes to you both, best wishes.

PROSECUTOR: You never dreamt, of course, that your wedding would coincide with a historic event. Mark today's date: whenever you celebrate your wedding anniversary, you'll also commemorate the end of the guerilla resistance in our district.

ANTANAS: Why? What happened?

PROSECUTOR: Our soldiers caught the last bandits who escaped from the demolished cave before yesterday.

CHAIRMAN: We knew that two of them had escaped. But the third was young Leonas: his parents used to live ten miles from the town until they were resettled—permanently—as a dangerous element.

DEPUTY: But why would they head straight for town?

PROSECUTOR: Perhaps they had a definite task.

CHAIRMAN: What task?

PROSECUTOR: To spoil the wedding, for example.

(*General laughter.*)

DEPUTY (*to PROSECUTOR*): I'm glad to see you heeded my advice, Mr. Prosecutor. Your public mask sits perfectly. Your wit is back, the brooding, the uncertainty are over.

PROSECUTOR: It is because my mind is made up, Mr. Deputy.

(*Backstage, from the street, a song is heard. The music in the hall subsides.*)

CHAIRMAN: Ah! There march our boys!

DEPUTY: Don't they sing beautifully? Proudly, somehow.

PROSECUTOR: Haven't they defeated three enemies?

CHAIRMAN: Point of order, Mr. Prosecutor, point of order. Your jibe is quite unwarranted. Wasn't it thanks to them, these brave boys, that we had only three bandits left. They are proud, because this is a victory after seven years.

JONAS (*automatically*): Seven years...

CHAIRMAN: Madame Aldona, you don't mind if I invite our fighting men here for a toast of beer. I'm buying three cases. They've deserved it.

DEPUTY: An excellent idea.

ALDONA: We... shall be honored.

(*The COMMENTATOR appears.*)

CHAIRMAN (*to the COMMENTATOR*): Listen, old man—stop the soldiers and invite them inside in my name.

(*The COMMENTATOR exits.*)

ANTANAS: Mister Deputy, distinguished guests. You've made my very happy by coming here today. I'll also be very privileged to have a glass of beer with your gallant soldiers. (*The rumble of many boots— the SOLDIERS enter the hall backstage.*) But, as head of the family, I'm obliged to tell you that my wife is impatient. She insists that we leave.

PROSECUTOR (*surprised*): Now? So soon?

CHAIRMAN: Ah, the honeymoon. We understand, yes, we do. We too have been yoong. Where to, Madame Aldona?

ALDONA: To... the seashore.

CHAIRMAN: Youth and the ocean. This is—somehow—optimistic, new-order-like. We cannot permit this historic coincidence to pass unnoticed. Our press must use this story. How many noble themes here: the struggle between old and new; the death of criminal resisters and a new order wedding. We must make a group picture for the press! Photographer! Photographer! (*The COMMENTATOR pushes his tripod camera.*) The newlyweds in the middle. I *do* love meaningful photographs. Me next to the groom. Mr. Prosecutor next to the bride. Closer, don't be bashful.

(*They pose. The COMMENTATOR directs them standing by his camera. He raises his hand. The stage is filled with very bright light. At the same moment, the music in the background ceases. The group remains frozen in its position except for the PROSECUTOR. He steps forward to meet the COMMENTATOR, who walks toward him.*)

COMMENTATOR (*confidentially, to PROSECUTOR*): You were expecting more from them—you hoped they had come here to kill you.

PROSECUTOR (*also confidentially*): I did. All the suspicious details. And his eyes!

COMMENTATOR: Weren't you complaining—just yesterday—that the judges of the new order no longer have their black robes to hide in. (*He takes the black cloth from the tripod camera and offers it to the PROSECUTOR.*) Isn't it wonderful—all you have to do is to take this robe, to put it on and slowly live away. It will not be your life, but you will die your own death.

(*PROSECUTOR takes the black cloth and wraps himself up in it. He looks around, stares at the CHAIRMAN and the DEPUTY, and with a sudden contemptuous gestures takes the cloth off and tosses it at the COMMENTATOR.*)

PROSECUTOR: Take back your rag, tempter! I will not bow! If I were to cringe, and shrink, and hide—I would admit that my shadows are real, that the ancient moral superstitions are true. Concede that all my life's work—the perfect voyages charted by my reason—were only a senseless maze leading nowhere? I refuse, as I refuse to put the tombstone of this faceless town on my chest! If both faces of the world are sodden and blue-veined with absurdity, I'll serve neither! I'll go alone!

COMMENTATOR: Let these men go. Let Antanas live. You both must live!

PROSECUTOR: To live? To fade away in this grey town where one more shadow—blood trickling down his chin—will be waiting at my door. To become as the Chairman—or the Deputy, there are no other choices. A puff of smoke or a white tomb. No! I want to be liberated from it all. And I've got one more card, one more trick. They may be tough, these guerillas, but they are still very sensitive about one thing...

COMMENTATOR: Please, don't

(*The COMMENTATOR tries to prevent the PROSECUTOR from rejoining the group, but the PROSECUTOR frees himself and hurries back to his place. The COMMENTATOR returns to his camera. The PROSECUTOR joins the rest of the group. The COMMENTATOR raises his hand, as before the beginning of the conversation with the PROSECUTOR. At that moment, the light returns to normal. The music resumes. All rise from their chairs.*)

COMMENTATOR: Thank you.

(*ANTANAS stretches out his hand to the DEPUTY.*)

ANTANAS: Sir, it was a great pleasure...

PROSECUTOR: One moment, young man. The Honorable Deputy has rightly called today's events historic. Now, I don't think it would be fair to rob the newlyweds of this occasion to witness the last, the most important decision of this memorable day.

ALDONA (*with suspicion*): What decision?

PROSECUTOR: We have three bandits. And in the market place we have the posts and the ant-hill—the great educational theatre for the people of this small stubborn country. As the creator of this theatre, I propose that a spectacle be staged.

ANTANAS: What?! Are they still alive!

PROSECUTOR: They won't disturb your wedding.

ANTANAS: Did they—say anything?

CHAIRMAN: Nothing, nothing at all. Two of them died right away, except this Leonas.

ANTANAS: Leonas?!

PROSECUTOR: He lived for several hours, but they weren't able to get one word out of him. Even the most advanced methods didn't help.

CHAIRMAN: Is this the place to discuss such details? As for the corpses, the best thing would be to bury them at the edge of the forest, at night. We have won the battle; the next task to make the population forget it as soon as possible.

ALDONA: Please, I may be interfering in affairs far above me, but I beg you, I beg you—change your mind. I want the memories of my wedding clean and bare of posts and corpses in the market place.

PROSECUTOR: Aldona, I'm ready to grant you anything but this. It is my last attempt at selfishness, at peace.

ANTANAS: You won't have peace! (*ANTANAS pulls out the book from his breast pocket and thrusts it into the PROSECUTOR's hand.*) You know the words of this book by heart. Make peace with them or forget peace forever!

(*PROSECUTOR tears the book in two and throws it away.*)

PROSECUTOR: The man who wrote these words just died!

CHAIRMAN: Gentlemen, I will have none of that confusion! My word prevails, and I resolve that the exhibition of the corpses in the market place would now serve no purpose. I'm sure that the Deputy will agree with me.

PROSECUTOR (*deliberately, in a florid orator's style*): Your decision, Mr. Chairman, is too rash. I am compelled to say that it has definite traits of defeatism. Why? The Chairman does not correctly estimate the vitality of the resisting elements. One phase of the struggle is ending, and he says—now let us loosen the reins, let us sit back in our chairs. Friends, we cannot ever afford to forget that the fight never ends. These people are dead, but microbes from their bodies, from their ideas, are already rising in this balmy afternoon to infect others. They are rising now, while softness and mildness are proposed in this very room. The fight goes on forever. Whoever holds out without compromises, without softening—will triumph in the end!

DEPUTY: Brave! The Sword of Justice! Of course, the Prosecutor is right.

CHAIRMAN (*confused and frightened*): You misunderstood me. I agree. The bodies must be exhibited in the market place!

ALDONA (*to the PROSECUTOR*): Please, I beg you... An exception, a single exception—you promised!

PROSECUTOR: Aldona, some day you'll understand why I couldn't change anything. Perhaps, you'll even forgive me. But it must be so. (*PROSECUTOR turns to ANTANAS and stares at him challengingly.*)

ANTANAS: Jonas, don't wait for us.

PROSECUTOR: Your wedding day will always be connected with the majestic picture of justice: ants, methodically destroying the bodies of those who dared to raise their hands against history—until only their rags are left and shoes: doomed shapes distorted by the mud of forests.

ANTANAS: Jonas, I want our train tickets! HAVE YOU GOT YOUR TRAIN TICKETS?

JONAS: Antanas—my friend—yes, I've got your train tickets!

(*A knowing smile appears on the PROSECUTOR's face. ANTANAS' hand is at his inside pocket.*)

JONAS: Yes!

(*JONAS also reaches in his pocket. They pull out their guns. ALDONA's scream. At that very moment the light goes out. Complete silence. The song of the Nightingale is heard. The stage becomes light again. The room of GRAZINA's parents. GRAZINA stands by the window. FATHER and MOTHER sit on the benches.*)

GRAZINA (*frightened*): Did you hear?

MOTHER: What?

GRAZINA: Gunfire—from the town.

FATHER: It's children, rattling sticks along the fence.

MOTHER: Such sounds deserve a deaf ear. The fox always hurries away from the hunters.

FATHER: For us it's different sounds. The rustling of the wheat, the creaking of a closing gate.

MOTHER: The laughter of the linen, the language of the fire.

GRAZINA: For me—ice bursting on the river of my hope, a jubilant meeting of the floods.

FATHER: The backs of our forefathers have bowed and bent and turned to stone. But they have borne it all and outlived the chains and the hands that forged the chains.

MOTHER: Quietly, to suffer, patiently to endure, and thus to live, to outlive, to live away.

FATHER: It's already three summers since they've stopped deporting people.

MOTHER: This fall we will have more potatoes than during all these seven years.

FATHER: Only to clench the teeth—to forget, to endure and to live.

GRAZINA: Never to forget, never to forget.

MOTHER: From our patch of land we'll be able to take a sack of potatoes to the town.

FATHER: Who knows—maybe to sell it in the market place as in the old days. To purchase nails, and glass and wheelgrease.

GRAZINA: There are posts in the market place and spots of blood!

FATHER: The posts will rot, the rain will wash away the blood, and the stones will forget. (*Knocking at the door.*) Who's there?

COMMENTATOR (*offstage*): A poor passerby with news.

(*FATHER gets up to let the COMMENTATOR in. The COM-MENTATOR comes in. He holds a large bunch of lilacs in his hand.*)

COMMENTATOR: Good evening to all.

FATHER: Good evening. Sit down, old man. You look tired.

MOTHER: What beautiful lilacs. I've never seen such around here.

COMMENTATOR: I picked them in a garden that is not of this earth—that blossomed in the dreams of one man. He is dead and the garden lies empty.

GRAZINA: You speak about death. What else do you know?!

COMMENTATOR: I was trapped in the middle of hell. There was a wedding in the Town Hall. Suddenly, out of the clearest sky, the groom and his friend pull out their guns and blast the Prosecutor. What bedlam followed. The two never got to fire another shot—their heads smashed by rifle butts, trampled to death by boots. Of the officials, only the Prosecuter died. Now they're tying these two and three others to the posts in the market place. The groom, as leader, goes into the ant-hill.

(*GRAZINA faints and the COMMENTATOR prevents her from falling with the hands free of flowers.*]

FATHER: Grazina, daughter!

MOTHER: Dearest child!

(*GRAZINA slowly comes to, as she inhales the scent of the flowers near her face. She straightens up.*)

GRAZINA: You said they were married? That is not true—he is my betrothed! Did she fight at his side?

COMMENTATOR: No, she surrendered and confessed everything. Most probably she will have to live.

GRAZINA (*to her parents*): You worried if I would ever be married. Be glad now, because I'm leaving for my wedding. (*She takes the flowers from the COMMENTATOR.*) My flowers, you are from the land of dreams; you'll fit my hands at the altar.

FATHER: I forbid you.

(*MOTHER grabs her by the hand.*)

MOTHER: It's death! Death ends everything.

GRAZINA: Nothing ever ends!

(*She frees herself from the MOTHER and runs out.*)

FATHER: Go after her!

MOTHER: Stop her! She is running to her death!

COMMENTATOR: Too late. She's on her way to the altar.

(*FATHER and MOTHER go after her.*)

COMMENTATOR (*to the audience*): Time to leave. What can I tell you more? Words are humble and heavy in my mouth. Listen instead to the steps of a little boy who, in every century, walks to his place of sacrifice clutching a bunch of flowers to his heart. Listen to the ashes of those who were burned; to the solitude of those buried in snow. Listen to the winter-wombs of manless brides and to the quiet of men in death's bridal bed. Listen and don't forget, never forget....
(*The COMMENTATOR, his head bowed, walks slowly across the stage and off.*)
(*The music of the wedding song is heard softly. GRAZINA, in a bride's pose and in a bride's step, holding flowers to her bosom, walks on slowly, passing the COMMENTATOR on his way off. Neither sees the other.*)
GRAZINA: My beloved awaits me. His happiness will be so heavy that he will not rise to meet me. Our bed will be cobblestones and our cover will be the sky. His left hand will find my head and the right will embrace me. The bullet-pierced body of my beloved resembles a honeycomb. His words of love, treasured unsaid for me, are meat and milk in his mouth. The blood from his lips is wine spilt on our wedding cloth. (*GRAZINA kneels. The five posts appear in the background.*) How beautiful is my beloved, like a deer frozen in an eternal leap. (*ANTANAS' statues become visible behind the posts.*)

CURTAIN

THE AWAKENING

A play in three sequences:

Footsteps
La Cumparsita
The Awakening

by
Antanas Škėma

Translated from Lithuanian by
Kristina Škėma-Snyder

Introduction to
The Awakening

Antanas Škėma was born in Lodz, Poland, November 29, 1911, and died in an automobile accident in Pennsylvania, September 11, 1961.

Škėma returned with his parents to Lithuania in 1921. He studied medicine, then law, in the University of Kaunas. In 1935, he began to study drama. From 1936 to 1940 he was an actor with the Lithuanian State Theater in Kaunas, then moved to Vilnius in 1940 to become an actor and director in the Vilnius State Theater, where he remained until 1944.

In Germany he continued his work as an actor in several Lithuanian theaters in the displaced persons camps until 1949, when he came to the United States and became an elevator operator. While in the United States he was elected to membership in the PEN International Writers' Club.

Škėma's published works are *Nuodėguliai ir kibirkštys* (*Charred Stumps and Sparks*), 1947, a collection of short stories, including a one-act play, *Viena Vakara* (*One Evening*); *Šventoji Inga* (*Saint Inga*), 1952, short stories; *Čelesta* (*Celeste*), 1960, a series of sketches written in the "stream of consciousness" manner; *Balta droubulė* (*The White Shroud*), 1958, a novel; and the plays *Pabudimas* (*The Awakening*), 1956, *Žvakidė* (*The Candlestick*), 1957, and *Kalėdu vaizdelis* (*The Christmas Play*), printed in *Metmenys*, (*Pattern Sketches*), a Lithuanian cultural magazine of the younger generation, in 1961. Several stories, an unfinished novel, and plays remain in manuscript.

The death of Antanas Škėma in a highway accident in 1961 brings to mind the fatal crash which took the life of Albert Camus. Such an absurd way to die was cruelly, ironically appropriate for these men who understood absurdity so well.

By his death Antanas Škėma also vindicated his belief that the universe is governed by absurd and pitiless laws which require that vengeance be exacted upon those who disturb its dead, inhuman order by exercising their gift of imagination. In his works, the main protagonists usually perish at the highest point of their creative consciousness, when they become rebels against the inherent meaninglessness of the universe. It

From *Perfection of Exile: Fourteen Contemporary Lithuanian Writers*, by Rimvydas Šilbajoris.
Copyright 1970 by the University of Oklahoma Press.

does not matter that they challenge the world not as a conqueror would but in the effort of love, asking only that reality should assent to transfiguration by the spirit of poetry living in the heart of man. If there is God, as we hope there is, and if He is good, as we must believe, the creative effort of man should bring him the reward of fulfillment. What happens instead is that man is obliterated forever in the bottomless void. Škėma's work, therefore, leaves the impression of a tense and worried attempt to puzzle out this impossible state of things. It resembles a tortuous and prolonged dialogue with an incomprehensible, silent God whose presence reveals itself only in the suffering and destruction of man.

The people we meet in Škėma's works for the most part carry within themselves pieces of their broken hearts; they search for their Father in whom they must believe—some because they are mere children, too young to countenance the possibility of nonbelief and others because they had been so cruelly punished for the creative and questioning spark they possess that they have become nothing but fearful, obsequious slaves of the nameless power which struck them. Such a slave is Antanas Garšva in the novel *Balta drobulė* (*The White Shroud*), when he prays feeling the vault of madness—the equivalent of death for the poet—closing inexorably over his head:

Lord, You see how unhappy I am.
I know I come too late, but save me.
I promise
I will tear up my notes, my poems,
I will not think the way You do not wish.
I will pray,
I will enter a monastery.
Lord, help me at least in my death.
I believe You forgive at the last moment
For all of one's life.
Lord, Lord, into your hands...
Oh, no, I'm just a miserable human being, Lord.
Looooord!

The people in Škėma's works, live in our time, when the pillars of the world have become so shaky that one or two atomic bombs will knock them down altogether. In such a world, games with God are no longer possible—unless played by madmen—and the last prayer of Garšva is a scream of terror coming from a heart that is humble and faithful yet filled with total despair. We can listen to this scream again in Škėma's play *Pabudimas* (*The Awakening*). There is a woman being led to execution by the Soviet secret police; we do not see her on stage, but only hear her voice:

98

I won't go, I don't want to any more. Let go of my hand—there's a nice fellow—just for a moment. All right, I'll rest for a minute, all right, all right. Don't, you're hurting me, I won't go I said, I won't go. All right, don't drag me, I don't want to, I don't. Please don't drag me, I don't want to, I don't want to, all right. I don't want to, I don't, I don't, all right... (*The words turn into a scream, the steps conquer, they drag the woman on. The scream vanishes behind the door.*)

The Communist god here is quite different from that in *The White Shroud*, but in both instances the essence of the prayer is the same—helpless terror. Both powers are equally immovable. Adam committed the original sin and was punished, but he, at least, tasted of the fruit of paradise and could know good and evil. Today this fruit is already rotten—we don't know even this much any more—and yet the punishment goes on.

Such is the first impression upon reading Škėma. A rebellion, we are told, is an effort to assert one's human dignity. The mighty creative fire of the Renaissance was lit when the long-suffering medieval slave of God stood up and proclaimed his desire to be human. In *The Awakening*, Kazys, a Lithuanian rebel against the Soviet rule put to terrible and revolting torture, also cries that he wants to be human, but in the middle of his cry, "his face becomes all wrinkles, tears spurt from his eyes, animal groans issue from his throat."

If we listen well, we can hear this horrible scream in every critical experience undergone by Škėma's protagonists, as if this were the ultimate wisdom, the last word of the philosophers, the final "amen" after the prayer of an innocent child.

Paradoxically, at times Škėma seems capable of hearing a note of triumph in his human cry of despair. This would seem to go against all logic, but Škėma knew, as did Dostoevsky's Underground Man before him, that logic is the province of limited minds—minds that dwell safely inside the walls of what they call reality and therefore cannot begin to understand the quality of a creative act. The finger writes two and two makes four. Who does not believe in happiness is a pessimist. Who tortures and kills is a soulless monster. Who betrays his own people to the enemy is a despicable traitor. In Škėma's work, however, two and two may well add up to infinity. His ideas are not abstracted from human experience and cut to manageable size on the writer's desk. They remain as organic parts of a living man, and therefore their nature and validity is subject not as much to logic as to the infinite variety of unpredictable human responses to life in which passion, fear, desire, and inspiration may well play the dominant part.

In *The Awakening*, for instance, the Soviet secret police investigator,

Pijus, attempts to force Kazys, his former friend, successful rival, and now an underground hero, to betray resistance secrets by torturing Elena, the woman they both love but Kazys has married, before Kazys' eyes. Pijus continues to love both his captives and also secretly hates them both with the fury of the defeated. Now he wants to win his victory by means of the power given him by an ideology which, as he thinks, stands for the immutable laws of history. Pijus has accepted this ideology not for its intrinsic values but for the hypnotic force of its perfect logical design, from which he hopes to derive his own personal perfection and invincibility. "The sun," says Pijus, "makes the fragile flower grow; the sun also burns out deserts. Water has the same quality, and so does fire, so does earth itself. In our system man shall acquire his greatest possession: absolute objectivity." As it turns out, however, it is precisely this objectivity that Pijus lacks in the performance of what he thinks is his duty but what actually amounts to a desperate and tortured effort to resolve his own endlessly complex dilemma which he himself cannot begin to comprehend. And so he loses again. Having set up the inhuman torture of Kazys and Elena, he cannot bear their suffering and shoots Kazys, without having learned his secrets, on a sudden impulse of pity. Pity has destroyed the invincible force to which Pijus had committed himself. Loving both Kazys and Elena, he has tortured them both, and while torturing them he has understood that he possesses no right to do so in the name of his truth because he does love them in human terms. His truth forsakes him, and he himself falls into the hands of the Communist police. In his last hour he prays again, striving to believe in a different God, repeating the Lord's Prayer after the priest Antanas, another of his victims. Thus the protagonists all perish, but what remains is stronger than the darkness enveloping them. It is man's love for freedom, in the name of which Kazys and Elena die and remain victorious, and man's love for man, which constitutes the tragedy and the glory of Pijus. In this way, the noble qualities of man remain triumphant, and in their agony Škėma's heroes receive a priceless gift—the same tragic dimension in which resounds the terrible voice of Christ: "My God, my God, why hast thou forsaken me!"

For this reason, the experience of tragedy in Škėma's works can never be described in human terms alone. His protagonists possess the paradoxical ability to function as symbolic representations of the many-faceted relationship between man and God, without themselves becoming larger than life. They do not fit the definition of a tragic hero as someone whose qualities elevate him far about his fellow men, and yet their lives, their passions and sufferings, are comprehensible only in relation to an all-encompassing moral and metaphysical idea. In *The*

Awakening, as in other works, we meet a number of individuals who seem to be struggling with nothing more than their personal problems, but the outcome of the struggle always implies something about the nature of good, of evil, and of eternity. The priest Antanas, for instance, waits in fear and trembling for his inevitable death, but over and above his anguish there is the much greater agony of constant thought about his sister who committed suicide because Antanas would not allow her to leave the monastery even though she could no longer live the life of the nun without perverting her own humanity. The terrible question that this priest must face in his hour of death is this: Is it really true that absolute faith demands an absolute commitment? By insisting that his sister must remain in the monastery, has Antanas perhaps committed a blasphemy by transforming the suffering God into a granite idol, born of man's perverse imagination, no different in essence from the "absolute objectivity" which Pijus professed to believe? His moral principles, turned monstrous without the human quality of mercy, come to haunt him in the revolting nightmare of a toothless, idiotically grinning Madonna. Both Pijus and Antanas are forsaken by their respective gods, the priest because he did not know pity and the secret police interrogator because he did. It is quite appropriate, therefore, that they should both kneel down to pray at the end of the play, searching together for still another God.

A curious facet of Škėma's art is his handling of characters. While acting out their lives on the purely human plane, they seem to be aware somehow that what they do has no reality except in terms of the symbolic. They take a strangely impersonal attitude toward their very personal conflicts and very genuine death, as if they know that all the world is indeed a stage and that they are only acting out their parts in some metaphysical mystery. Kazys and Pijus, for instance, locked in desperate combat, show no personal hatred toward each other but rather the solidarity of two actors performing a terrible ritual. Similarly Elena, after unspeakable tortures and after the death of Kazys, can speak to Pijus with an unearthly calm, explaining to him the issues of their struggle and the reasons for her ultimate victory.

Škėma's heroes, symbolic of ideas and forces greater than themselves, blend in the reader's mind into a single hero—an embodiment of the spirit of poetry in man. The image of the poet always emerges from the tension between love and death. Death and love appear in many guises, evoke a multitude of emotions, ideas, actions, create and destroy many answers to the riddles of the universe. Škėma demonstrates this with special dramatic clarity in his plays, in which his man-poet, burdened with a multitude of complex and contradictory private emotions, is confronted with an enormous and tragic reality requiring radical action and fatal decisions. In *The Awakening*, the extreme situation of the torture room in the Soviet prison forces the actors to destroy one another and themselves, almost as if in some nightmarish dance, with Kazys, Pijus, and Elena going round and round, holding hands with love and death.

In another play, *Žvakidė* (*The Candlestick*), similar complex and tortured poetic personalities try to work out their destinies and fulfill their private desires while the reality of the given moment is crashing down over their heads like a giant wave about to engulf them all. The scene is Lithuania in 1941, in the last few days of the first Soviet occupation, just before the German attack. The last Lithuanian victims of Communism are going to their deaths, often betrayed by their own people. One such traitor is Kostas, a bitter and complex figure. As a child he yearned for music and love but was rejected by his family, and his love turned to hatred or, rather, put on the mask of hatred without ceasing to be love, however perverted. Similarly, his music rises up like a fierce dark stream entering and distorting the Bach toccatas he plays on the organ of an abandoned church. The church is empty because Kostas has betrayed its parson, his father's brother, to death.

Kostas has a brother, Antanas, who, like Abel in the Bible, represents the figure of light. Noble and humble, radiant with love, he nevertheless remains guilty of the fact that their parents loved him and not Kostas. As the German advance turns the sky blood red, Kostas, tortured by the growing awareness that he became what he is out of jealousy, decides to cut through his tangled inner conflicts by taking a resolute step toward damnation. He kills his brother with a huge candlestick before the altar in the church. The Cain and Abel theme thus introduced removes the conflict from the context of a specific time and place and makes it a recurring theme from the very beginnings of human history, translated again by Škėma into the framework of love and death. Kostas brings death to Antanas (and himself) in revenge for the love he was refused in childhood. Antanas, through his love and trust, achieves his fulfillment, which is death.

In these two plays there is a determined effort by Škėma to discern the principles of good and evil through the tangled web of contradictions, ironies, and fears in the shadow of catastrophe. In his next piece, called *Kalėdų vaizdelis* (*A Christmas Play*), Škėma seems at first to give up this effort altogether. We can no longer point our finger to the supposed villains and heroes. All are only sufferers, and through their sins they search for self-fulfillment, half-blinded with alcohol, fear, and pain. The whore, Magdalena, for instance, has always wanted to be a dancer and to strew flowers under the feet of priests in processions. Now she sleeps with many men, but "even so, every time I was in bed with a man, I imagined that I was dancing, dancing very beautifully and elegantly." Panašus (his name translates as "he who resembles," i.e. Christ, although he is, perhaps, a madman and an imposter) kisses her gently on her maidenly lips as one would kiss an innocent. Two other people, Skaidra and Danguolė his wife, seem to be in an irrevocable conflict, but from their mutual heartrending explanations the reader understands that the issue is not hatred or guilt but simply suffering; they have been so created that they cannot help hurting each other. Panašus invites them both to join his feast of joy, to taste water turned into wine.

The way Panašus-Christ gathers everyone in to the shelter of his love creates a feeling that A Christmas Play, far from being a story of crime and punishment, is an apotheosis of universal forgiveness or, possibly, of universal agony in the name of One who has given meaning to all human suffering through his own Calvary. This feeling is present in the dialogues, in the quarrels; everything is permeated with the expectation of some great love which would embrace everyone sorrows, sins, revolting vulgarity, and all. What we see is the face of humanity covered with dirt, sores, and pus—a face waiting to be kissed by the Redeemer. Quite logically, therefore, the action is set on Christmas Eve. This is the time of expectation. Ironically, also, the place is a mental hospital, described in such a way as to suggest that the whole world might really be nothing but a madhouse, waiting insanely for something that never did happen and never could.

The character of Skaidra in A Christmas Play absorbs, supersedes, and transfigures the characters of Pijus and Kostas in the two previous plays. As if he feels himself to be the actor called upon to portray the greatest human sin, Skaidra raises his hand not against other people but directly against Panašus-Christ. And Panašus tells him quite clearly that this is his task. "Do your work, Skaidra," he says, almost as if this were the eleventh commandment of God. Because of this, the role of Skaidra-Judas acquires a special kind of nobility. His task is terrifying, but because it must be done, we are almost thankful to Skaidra for having taken upon himself this sin. We all murder God in many ways in our hearts, but it is Skaidra who literally performs the deed, thus taking up the burden of all our sins. In this way he paradoxically begins to resemble Christ, because His cross, too, is made of all our sins. If we were now to assume that Judas represents the principle of death, and Christ the principle of love, we can see how, in a final paradox, their roles in the fate of mankind blend into one.

We have previously said that Škėma's heroes seem to challenge the world in an effort of love. The world responds to this effort by completely obliterating the challenger in the end, but the first step toward destruction is to make man realize that he is not wanted on earth. The whole world is ruled by logical inevitabilities which, in their dead clarity, are entirely incomprehensible to the living imagination. The blind laws of the universe do not admit the possibility of its poetic transfiguration, and for this reason the universe remains unreal for Škėma's man-poet. He is doomed to be a stranger, an exile.

Such understanding of the fact of exile separates Škėma rather sharply from some other Lithuanian writers for whom exile is merely physical—the loss of the homeland, its meadows, brooks, native villages, and of people dear to them. In Škėma's works exile is a general human condition, insofar as "human" specifically means imagination, creativity, and a yearning for immortality in an organic fusion with the very source of being. A man is an exile because his spark of divinity alienates him from the earth, his mother. The only way back to the native soil is over the threshold of death.

This deep-seated conflict between the imperative need to belong to the world (or, rather, with the world to ultimate reality; Škėma has stated that "both worlds are unreal, the actual and the one created by me. In a real world they would blend into one") and the unavoidable necessity of remaining a stranger is reflected in all facets of Škėma's fiction, first of all, perhaps, in his style. We find tender, warm descriptions that seem to weave together man's own consciousness and the throbbing vitality of nature into a rich and colorful tapestry of being. In contrast, we also find bitterly ironical statements, juxtapositions of highest exultation and lowest animal needs, as if Škėma, burdened by the foreknowledge of his heroes' doom, wanted to expose the cruel mockery of their situation in a kind of tortured revenge for the indignity inherent in man's bondage to nature's laws. A typical example is the picture of a man with diarrhea, sitting in the outhouse and contemplating the blueness of the sky through a heart-shaped hole in the door. Torn by such contrasts, the narrative often resembles a confused mosaic of accidental sights and inner visions, of masks and living faces, of past and present, and of distant places continuing the landscape directly before one's eyes. It does seem to represent a recognizable picture even on the surface, but its real meaning lies in the symbolic relationship of one piece of mosaic to another.

Škėma's longest work, the novel *The White Shroud*, is concerned with the same issues that exist in his other works. The main hero, Antanas Garšva, is again a poet, trying to create, to feel life as profoundly as he can. The deeper his feeling is, the greater the suffering. While still in high school, Garšva learned the precepts of Schopenhauer: "optimism is a bitter mockery of human sorrow; life is evil because life is struggle; the more perfect an organism, the more perfect is its suffering." The novel is full of life, but it begins with Garšva attempting suicide and ends with him becoming insane.

The defeat of the poet is due to the fact that he always sacrifices too much to poetry. Religion and poetry have at least this much in common—that they demand from the elect their full devotion, a renunciation not only of the world but also of themselves. Generally speaking, love may be said to increase the measure of perfection in man, to deepen his capacity for feeling, to bring him nearer the poetic consciousness. But to a poet love is a hindrance, for it provides a shelter, a home, protection from reality, whereas a poet should always remain vulnerable to reality, since poetry is pain. Garšva meets Elena and falls in love and then deliberately renounces his love, cuts the thread of human ties and remains alone. This refusal then destroys his heart. Reality is the organic and irresistible urge to love and be loved. Refused, this urge turns into still another fury driving Garšva into madness. Nevertheless, the very process by which a poet is defeated in this life brings a rich treasure of new thoughts, new experiences, new understanding. And this is the meaning of the creative life. In his defeat, Garšva remains victorious for our sake, just as Kazys and Elena are victorious in *The Awakening.*

After all the human agony revealed by Škėma, the lasting effect of his work is one of a mysterious elevation of the soul, as though it were a priceless, though painful, gift. We might return to the ideas of Schopenhauer, which Garšva pondered so carefully: the more perfect an organism, the more perfect the suffering. Perfect suffering is pain beyond enduring, made from the same rare jewels that went into the making of the kingdom of heaven. This may well be the essence of Škėma's perception of the world. When spiritualized, this suffering is the goal toward which man strives in Škėma's works. This is why death is needed, for it is the ecstasy which raises man to his highest degree of perfection.

Rimvydas Šilbajoris

THE AWAKENING

CHARACTERS:

PIJUS
KAZYS
ELENA
PRANAS
FATHER ANTANAS
A WOMAN IN THE CORRIDOR

FOOTSTEPS

(*A cell in the N.K.V.D. building in Vilnius. A small barred window. A metal bed chained up against the wall. A stool. In one corner a bucket with a wooden lid. FATHER ANTANAS is pacing evenly from the door to the wall with the window—four steps forward and back again. After a few moments the echo of steps in the corridor unite with his. At first they are far away and muffled, then they grow louder. FATHER ANTANAS stops, smooths his hair and buttons his cassock. Then, as though remembering, he crosses himself. The steps stop near his cell. The door is unlocked, opened, and a voice is heard from the corridor:* In there! *KAZYS enters. The door is closed and locked. The sound of metal shoes is heard receding slowly. KAZYS stands silently by the door. When the footsteps are no longer heard*):
F. ANTANAS: Blessed be the name of Jesus Christ.
KAZYS (*silent for a moment*): Oh, forgive me, it's you here. They brought me in from the light. The light bulbs are strong in the corridor... And it's rather dark in here. (*Gives him his hand.*) Hello.

107

F. ANTANAS (*offering his hand*): For ever and ever. Amen.

KAZYS: So be it. (*They shake hands.*) My name is Kazys.

F. ANTANAS: I am Father Antanas.

KAZYS: A pleasure. (*He smiles.*) Forgive me again. It's really no great pleasure. This is my first time in jail.

F. ANTANAS: Mine also.

KAZYS: How long?

F. ANTANAS: Four days.

KAZYS: Have they interrogated you yet?

F. ANTANAS: No, not yet.

KAZYS: Well, we've made a start at least. (*Looks around.*) So this is it. (*Points to the window.*) Which wall is that?

F. ANTANAS: As far as I can tell, it's a garage. I often hear cars and see smoke.

KAZYS: Thanks. And this is the only piece of furniture? (*Tries to lift the stool.*)

F. ANTANAS (*smiles*): I tried too. Unfortunately it's nailed to the floor.

KAZYS: So that prisoners can't fight. (*A pause during which both observe one another.*) But, you're shaven?

F. ANTANAS: Every morning they take me to the washroom. There a N.K.V.D. man hands me a razor and soap. The washroom is divided into sections. I shave and he watches. (*Points to the bed.*) That's the bedroom. It will have to do for both of us.

KAZYS: It seems the number of guests has increased. How many hours allowed for sleeping?

F. ANTANAS: From ten at night till six in the morning.

KAZYS: Science has proven that eight hours of sleep are sufficient for an adult. That is, if you sleep peacefully. Do you sleep peacefully, Father?

F.ANTANAS: Not peacefully. I dream.

KAZYS: So. (*Noticing the bucket.*) And that's the bathroom?

F. ANTANAS: In the mornings you're allowed to use the ones next to the washroom.

KAZYS: I like that. What about the food?

F. ANTANAS: A slice of bread in the morning with a cupful of warm water, for lunch—a cup of soup, in the evening—cold water and a slice of bread.

KAZYS: In other words (*pointing to the bucket*) this is very necessary and the toilet is not. What did you do during those four days here, Father? Oh, forgive me, perhaps I shouldn't ask, but...

F. ANTANAS (*interrupting him*): It's all right. I prayed.

KAZYS: Prayer helps?

F. ANTANAS: Very much...

KAZYS: Do you repeat the same prayers or do you search for new ones?

F. ANTANAS: That's a strange question.

KAZYS: Don't answer, then.

F. ANTANAS: I repeated my favorite prayers.

KAZYS: In other words, if I followed your method, I'd have to turn over the same thoughts in my mind and I'd feel more peaceful.

F. ANTANAS: You don't pray?

KAZYS: No. It doesn't help. (*Pause.*) Is it always quiet here?

F. ANTANAS: During the day—always. Except when they're bringing food. At night it's uneasy.

KAZYS: Oh?

F. ANTANAS: At night there are cars outside the window and last night a man was shot.

KAZYS: How do you know?

F. ANTANAS: I heard footsteps in the corridor. Many footsteps. There was also a sound as though they were dragging a heavy sack on the floor. Perhaps they're dragging the condemned man, I thought. I looked through the keyhole. The blue pants of the N.K.V.D. men passed and in the middle, for a split second, there was a pair of brown pants—immobile and wrinkled. And they talked. Then doors closed and finally I could hear four muffled shots. When they returned, the brown pants weren't there.

KAZYS (*bending over the keyhole*): Yes, you could only see the pants from here. (*Stands up.*) You're right, now I remember. We're at the end of the corridor and it ends with doors. And... beyond them they shoot. Perhaps they won't have to drag us on the floor, Father. We only have to walk a few steps. And what did he say?

F. ANTANAS: I understood only a few words—he was murmuring. One was "tomorrow", and the others— "I don't want to."

KAZYS: Not very profound words before dying. Naturally, you couldn't fall asleep that night, Father?

F. ANTANAS: I recited my favorite prayers and fell asleep. I had the most vivid dream of my life... (*becomes silent*). May I tell it to you? Don't be so amazed, these are unusual circumstances.

KAZYS: Please go on, Father.

F. ANTANAS: I was kneeling in an empty church. There were many candles burning. The Blessed Virgin, in our great altar—she has a most beautiful face—the Blessed Virgin suddenly smiled and I felt good... Then I stood up, and the flames separated from the candles and hung near the cupola. As though the flames were wings of fire... (*He stops.*) Perhaps you'll laugh, young man?

KAZYS: No, I don't laugh at dreams.

F. ANTANAS: When the Blessed Virgin smiled again I saw that she had no teeth. It was more frightening than listening to the last words of the condemned man.

KAZYS (*softly*): Pardon me, but after the dream did you recite your favorite prayers?

F. ANTANAS (*looks at KAZYS for a long time. Silently mouthing the word.*) No. I crossed myself just before you were brought in.

KAZYS (*taps on the wall*): Don't our neighbors answer?

F. ANTANAS: No. I tried the first two days. This wall is very thick. I imagine there are people in the next cell.

KAZYS: You're right. When they were taking me through the corridor I noticed there was a wide space between the doors. Too bad. I can remember the Morse Code rather well. (*Searches through his pockets and takes out three mangled cigarettes, some matches, and a piece of a matchbook cover.*) I'm in luck. I got only one punch in the jaw and I hid the cigarettes. But Pranas is still there. Do you smoke, Father? (*FATHER ANTANAS nods his head.*) Good. We'll share one—and save the others for life's more important moments. (*Hands F. ANTANAS the cigarette and lights it carefully. F. ANTANAS inhales greedily. KAZYS puts the cigarettes, matches, and cover back into the lining of his coat.*) What did they grab you for?

F. ANTANAS: I'm the parish priest of Salmenas. Three weeks ago I gave a sermon they didn't like. (*Takes a couple of puffs.*) I compared them to red devils.

KAZYS: The devils contributed a lot to man. For example, they invented tobacco. My dear father, would you leave me a few puffs?

F. ANTANAS (*smiles rather embarassedly*): Excuse me. I got dizzy and... forgive me. (*Hands over the cigarette.*)

KAZYS: It's all right. What can you do? Smoking is egotistical.

F. ANTANAS: As far as I can understand, two of you were caught. You mentioned Pranas...

KAZYS: Yes. They told Pranas to stay... in the room. Do you remember the waiting room?

F. ANTANAS: I remember.

KAZYS: They didn't hit you?

F. ANTANAS: No. One spat in my face. I said: "May God forgive you." He spat again.

KAZYS: Was he small and dark, with a broken nose? (*F. ANTANAS nods his head.*) It's cold in here, Father.

F. ANTANAS: At night it's even colder. (*KAZYS looks around.*) The radiators are near the ceiling. Unfortunately they're warm only in the morning. What time is it?

KAZYS (*looks at his left wrist. Smiles.*): It's a habit. I forgot they took my watch. It's about nine o'clock in the evening.

F. ANTANAS: I, too, forgot that they remove everything. Forgive me. In an hour they unlock the bed and we'll go to sleep.

KAZYS: It will be warmer together. When did they drag... that man?

F. ANTANAS: Let's see... about this time... a half an hour before they unlock the beds.

KAZYS: Ah, that is so-called psychological pressure. So that everyone could hear. (*Long pause.*) Talk about something, Father. I've run out of subjects.

F. ANTANAS (*as though awakened from a sleep*): Talk? Talk about what?

KAZYS: Perhaps you'd like to ask me something?

F. ANTANAS: Ask you something? (*Thinks for awhile.*) Is it still snowing outside?

KAZYS (*lively*): It's falling. Still falling. All of Vilnius is covered with snow. Great balls of snow rest on the saints' statues in front of the Cathedral. They look like snowmen. But the air is pleasant, Father. It's about two degrees. Children are sliding on the icy sidewalks and throwing snowballs. I saw them from the car when they were bringing me here. One of them got a snowball right in the face and he cried. It was a pleasant face.

F. ANTANAS: Do you have a family?

KAZYS: I have a wife. She's young, and our friends say—rather pretty.

F. ANTANAS: You must make a good looking couple.

KAZYS: Oh, you know how to compliment. The women must have liked you, Father. Please don't misunderstand me... (*F. ANTANAS smiles.*) Good. You have white hair. Was it once curly and shiny?

F. ANTANAS (*smiling*): I must admit the devout old ladies couldn't take their eyes off.

KAZYS: Didn't I say so? (*Both laugh. While laughing they look at each others eyes and the laughter dies when both notice the sadness.*) Why are you standing, Father? Please sit down.

F. ANTANAS: Thank you, but I don't want to.

KAZYS: You don't want to... then what would you want?

F. ANTANAS (*quietly*): That they would finally take me out. (*Looks at KAZYS*) There, to that room.

KAZYS: There will be time. First they'll interrogate us.

F. ANTANAS: It won't take long for me. Perhaps they'll do without it.

KAZYS: How do you know?

F. ANTANAS: I know. They were supposed to liquidate me in the woods.

111

Li-qui-date. That's their word.

KAZYS: Their logic is cold. It tolerates murder.

F. ANTANAS: Who thought up this logic?

KAZYS: Wise people... continue, Father.

F. ANTANAS: After I gave the sermon, three weeks passed. They warned me and I asked the bishop to transfer me to another parish. To a corner of Lithuania in the Kretinga district. I've lived in Šalmėnas for twenty years. Many of my parishioners followed me to the station. Women cried aloud and even some of the men had tears in their eyes. People pushed a package of food into my hands. Perhaps they loved me. There were no N.K.V.D. agents at the station, but as soon as the train started to move, two of them appeared. We didn't reach Vilnius. We got out at Paneriai and got into a car. Then they led me into the room you know. The small, dark man with the broken nose was sitting there. He asked "Why the devil did you bring him here? He was supposed to be liquidated." The agent answered "We didn't have specific instructions." "But I called on the phone," the little man said. It was obvious that he called two minutes after they left to arrest me. Then the little one ordered them to put me in here. "For the time being," according to him. When it was time to leave, he spat on me. They were two minutes early and it has cost me four whole days. That is why I listen to footsteps all the time and when I hear them, I think I've heard them before. I hear them all the time, and they're in the corridor, coming closer, and closer, and closer, and I don't know any longer which are real and which are the ones I hear. Listen. Don't you hear them?

KAZYS: No.

F. ANTANAS: But I hear them.

KAZYS (*quietly*): At first you said, "It's quiet here during the day." And you said nothing about these footsteps. You said, "I pray and prayer helps me." And now you tell me that you hear footsteps all the time. Just footsteps. Did I misunderstand you, Father?

F. ANTANAS (*shouts*): Quiet!

KAZYS: Oh, forgive me. (*Pause.*)

F. ANTANAS (*quietly*): Please forgive me. When was the last time you prayed?

KAZYS: When did I pray?... I was fifteen.

F. ANTANAS: Why did you stop?

KAZYS: Prayers weren't useful any more.

F. ANTANAS: You decided not to believe in God?

KAZYS: I didn't try solving that problem.

F. ANTANAS: And up to fifteen?

KAZYS: I had to learn Latin and prayers and, according to my father's strange imagination, telegraphy. And telegraphy wasn't even needed in jail. After a while when I could avoid praying, I stopped. I resemble my mother. She didn't even know what a toothache was. While dying, she smiled with a full mouth. When the priest left her she said, "My child, you know that I allowed the priest to come so that Father wouldn't worry." I respect my mother very much. (*KAZYS starts whistling a cheerful tune.*) That's her tune. She often played it on the piano. You know what she said to me, Father, when she kissed me for the last time? "Try not to be afraid, son. Fear causes a lot of unhappiness." And I try to overcome fear, Father. (*He walks towards the window, jumps up, grabs the bars, raises himself by the hands and stays that way a few moments. Then he jumps down lightly.*) You're right. There are garages in front of us. They're dark now. And what a starry night! It stopped snowing, Father. I've never seen such bright stars. Maybe it's because this bulb is so weak.

F. ANTANAS: May I ask what your profession is?

KAZYS: I wanted to become a great writer, but I'm a mediocre journalist. Shall we smoke one more cigarette together, Father?

F. ANTANAS: Perhaps we should save it for life's more important moment?

KAZYS: There will be only one important moment in our lives.

F. ANTANAS: There beyond the door?

KAZYS: No, those few steps.

F. ANTANAS: And you're sure you won't be afraid?

KAZYS: I'll try not to be. (*Takes out the cigarette and hands it to F. ANTANAS.*) You smoke first. (*F. ANTANAS stretches out his hand, but suddenly it drops.*)

F. ANTANAS: Hear it?

KAZYS: What?

F. ANTANAS: Footsteps coming. Hear them?

KAZYS (*quickly moves towards the door, listens*): No. It's silent. You only thought you heard them, Father.

F. ANTANAS: Tss... Quiet. (*Listens.*) Now they've reached the third or fourth cell from ours and they've stopped. (*Quickly.*) Listen. Can you hear now that it's quiet?

KAZYS: It's always quiet here.

F. ANTANAS: They're walking again. They're coming close to our cell, Are you deaf?

KAZYS: My hearing is rather sensitive, but...

F. ANTANAS: They've stopped again. I think they're near our neighbor's cell. (*Both strain to hear.*) They're moving, moving.

113

(*KAZYS lies down with his ears to the ground.*)

KAZYS: It's quiet. Devilishly quiet.

F. ANTANAS (*whispering*): They're here. They're standing in front of the door.

(*The door's window is opened and someone's eyes look in and then close the window. KAZYS gets up and walks towards F. ANTANAS.*)

KAZYS: Do you have a handerchief?

F. ANTANAS (*mouthing the word*): Yes.

KAZYS: Where is it?

F. ANTANAS: Here.

(*Takes a handkerchief out of his pocket. KAZYS takes it and wipes the sweat off F. ANTANAS' forehead. F. ANTANAS puts it back into his pocket.*)

KAZYS: Did the window ever open before?

F. ANTANAS: No. This was the first time.

KAZYS: Now you can sit down. (*Takes F. ANTANAS to the stool and sits him down.*) So. There are no more footsteps. They've disappeared.

F. ANTANAS (*laughs*): You say they've disappeared? You say there's no more? They echo and I ask myself, "Did I have the right?" Why did I send my sister to the pond? I'm like them. The same kind of sinner. The same kind of judge. I heard the way a man screamed next door when he was being killed. I am guilty that he was shot. I am guilty that they torture and send them to Siberia. I am guilty that they liqui-date.

KAZYS: Calm yourself, Father.

F. ANTANAS: A cigarette. (*KAZYS hands him a cigarette and lights it.*) Would you listen to my last confession?

KAZYS: Me?

F. ANTANAS: You.

KAZYS: But, I ...

F. ANTANAS: I know. I don't ask for absolution from you. I don't ask for anything and I don't demand anything. I have to say a few words to you. I can't die with only myself. All my life I've been taught: you have to confess your sins, you have to give your most secret thoughts and wants to someone and at the same time they require me to gather into myself their many sins and judge and punish and forgive. I've been two people all my life—two. The accused and the judge. It's good that you came. It's good that you demand nothing. I don't have to be a judge. You don't ask me to judge. And having judged, you don't ask me to forgive you. How good... (*He notices that he smoked the whole cigarette.*) Like a child I smoked the whole cigarette and left you none.

KAZYS: This time you needed it more.

F. ANTANAS: Love thy neighbor as thyself. May I shake your hand?

KAZYS: Let's not become sentimental. That will destroy us. There's no place for sentimentality in jail.

F. ANTANAS: Your hand. (*KAZYS gives his hand. F. ANTANAS holds it in his for a few moments.*) Your fingers are cold. When I first shook your hand it was warm.

KAZYS: I'm not cold.

F. ANTANAS: I rarely felt a handshake. Often my parishioners kissed my hand and it was as though it were dead. They kissed His feet over the holy water the same way. I wasn't a human being to them. I was a living statue.

KAZYS: Did you doubt God?

F. ANTANAS: I believed and still believe in Him. Only I want to reach Him with a pure conscience. (*Silent for a minute.*) You don't understand me. This thought came to me here, in jail. The thought that I was a small God, at least to them, my parishioners, those that attended church. I didn't have the right to waver, to kneel, to sin, not before them. The halo of the virtuous priest shone around me all the time. I don't have the right to be human the same as they, wavering, kneeling, sinning. Oh my God, how I cried, like a small child in my garden house...

KAZYS: Why did you cry in the garden, Father?

F. ANTANAS (*quietly*): Because she left the garden. Her name was Regina. My sister. We grew up in an orphanage, and then—she entered a convent and I left for the priesthood. One night, thirty years ago, she came to me. She had great faith in me, I was her brother, she believed in me. She said, "I can't any more, Antanas. I'm suffocating. I can't pray any more. I see the sun, moon, stars, I hear laughter, I can't, I don't want to turn into wax." She was a wonderful girl, her eyes glowed like stars. I sent her back that night and then cried and bit my hand not to cry. (*Stretches out his hand.*) There's the scar. You can see how white it is.

KAZYS: Where did your sister go?

F. ANTANAS (*impassively*): She committed suicide. That same night. She jumped into the pond. They didn't find her for quite a while. I saw her corpse. (*Walks towards the wall and leans his forehead against it, stands for a minute, then turns around.*) You say there are no more steps? You say they disappeared? They echo all the time. Her steps. The same steps to the door, beyond which one is shot. Perhaps she didn't think anything while walking to the dirty water? Maybe she just repeated "I don't want" and "tomorrow" like those brown

115

slacks. And then they found her like that. With no eyes. Sometimes I begin to believe that jail is my payment for the pond.

KAZYS: If you left the cell, what would happen then?

F. ANTANAS: I won't leave the cell. That would be a miracle.

KAZYS: And what if this miracle did occur?

F. ANTANAS: It would be a miracle.

KAZYS: Would you go back?

F. ANTANAS: I don't know. I would probably enter a monastery.

KAZYS: And now? (*F. ANTANAS looks questioningly.*) Will you succeed in dying, Father?

F. ANTANAS: Here any solution loses meaning.

KAZYS: You say it loses meaning, Father? And what of the few seconds beyond that door? You walk and hear them breathing. And you know—their guns are aimed at the back of your head. And suddenly you lose your balance because all through life the earth swayed under your feet. You break out in a cold sweat and your knees shake. You probably fall on your knees and beg for mercy although you know there is no mercy. You asked for mercy many times during your life and no one had any for you. And now, howling from fear, stinking, torn by cramps, you writhe on the ground until finally they shoot you. Not from pity. Quite the opposite. They shoot because they have orders.

F. ANTANAS: And what do you offer?

KAZYS: To go to your death very simply. You faint... and then it's your business, Father.

F. ANTANAS: That's what I think. I faint and... revive in God.

KAZYS: Calmly, without fear?

F. ANTANAS: I'm afraid. I'm very much afraid.

(*Now footsteps are heard, in the corridor. At first dull, then more clear. The footsteps stop in front of the cell. Then F. ANTANAS walks toward KAZYS and embraces him. The doors are unlocked and PRANAS is pushed inside. His face is beaten. He speaks Lithuanian well, but has a slavic accent.*)

KAZYS: Pranas!

PRANAS: Yes, here I am.

KAZYS: Did they interrogate you?

PRANAS: You can see they did.

F. ANTANAS: I didn't drink all the water for supper. Here's half a cup. Why don't you wet your face?

PRANAS: I'd much rather drink it.

F. ANTANAS: Please do.

(*Hands him a tin cup.*)

PRANAS (*drinks looking at KAZYS*): What is he in for?

KAZYS: The Father gave a sermon. Now he's waiting to be shot. They've brought him here by mistake. Someone called too late and left him to live for a while. (*To F. ANTANAS*) His name is Pranas. We were both arrested in my apartment.

PRANAS: We're lucky. We won't be shot now. They want to know where we hid the weapons.

KAZYS: So, they've guessed that we collected weapons. I thought they would.

PRANAS: Yes, only they don't know where.

KAZYS (*to F. ANTANAS*): They beat up Pranas for nothing. A small group of people met in my apartment and we discussed the possibilities of freedom. We anticipated war, so we collected weapons. Pranas doesn't know the location of the warehouse. Only the most trusted know. Our underground is organized rather well.

PRANAS: You don't even know why they beat you.

KAZYS: Poor boy. (*Runs his hand through PRANAS' hair.*) Self-respect is a bad business, isn't it? (*PRANAS is silent.*) They interrogated you in the other room?

PRANAS: No. They took me to the second floor. To a clean and attractive room. Stalin's picture was hanging on the wall and a well-dressed type sat behind the table. He spoke Lithuanian and smoked "Moscow" cigarettes. (*To F. ANTANAS.*) Too bad you don't have any more water.

F. ANTANAS: I'm sorry.

PRANAS (*to KAZYS*): Now you and your underground can be satisfied. I've been baptized.

KAZYS: You've waited for baptism, boy. Perhaps you'll be able to say: our underground soon. If you hold out until the end.

PRANAS: You'll probably count my corpse as a true member.

KAZYS: Possibly.

PRANAS: You won't have enough people if you are so mistrusting.

KAZYS: We will have true people.

PRANAS: You will be caught one by one, slaughtered, and that will end it. God, it's a curse. To suffer and know you're mistrusted. I wanted to prove myself constantly, I kept asking you for an assignment, a tough and important one. I wanted to be informed like the "most trusted" and you were the only one who consistently opposed me. Now you can see what happened. The most mistrusted one was baptized first.

KAZYS: Am I wrong, or do you stink from whiskey?

PRANAS: At first they gave me something to drink. The whiskey was

Russian. The bottle read: 57 percent. It was good. Then... Here's where he put out his cigarette.

. (*Points to his cheek.*)

KAZYS: They've made a tactical error. They should have arrested me when I was taking the weapons to the warehouse. If they knew that we were collecting weapons...

(*Stops talking.*)

PRANAS: You think they moved too soon?

KAZYS: I think so.

PRANAS: They plan to find out here.

KAZYS: From you?

PRANAS: No. I haven't been informed.

KAZYS: Can you imagine, I haven't either.

PRANAS: Do you think you'll hold out?

KAZYS: I think so. And you?

PRANAS: It's a little harder for me. I'm losing my balance. They didn't hit me for the meetings in your house. They asked for the location of the warehouse. That's all they'll ask for. They said, "We will discuss this question again." You don't understand me?

KAZYS: You will have to suffer for the idea. It becomes less concrete and it's hard for you to bite your tongue.

PRANAS: I cried. I didn't want to scream and I didn't, but suddenly I felt the tears. The tears rolled down my cheeks and they laughed.

KAZYS (*walks over to PRANAS, turns his head towards him and looks him in the eye*): If I told you the location would it really be easier for you?

PRANAS (*slowly*): Yes, it would be easier.

KAZYS: While we were still free, you asked me for the location twice. That seemed rather suspicious to me, Pranas.

PRANAS: I know. I speak with a slavic accent, but I said I'm from Panevežis where the landowners speak with a slavic accent and you were never able to check that. But I was recommended by Galinis.

KAZYS: That's why we tried to trust you.

PRANAS: But nevertheless they never did. And they still don't. "They"— is you. Our leader. I see you're looking at my beaten face and still you don't believe in me. You know, I'm not as strong as you. You know, I could fight ten men by myself but I couldn't stand waiting for months to die. I could strangle a few of them with my bare hands, yet I'd tremble if the jail was being bombed. I'm brave and I'm cowardly. You know that and you have to help me. You're my leader.

KAZYS: There's another possibility. When they take you again, tell them the truth; tell them I'm the only one who knows the location. Tell them everything honestly, you won't hurt our cause. Perhaps they'll leave you alone.

PRANAS: Do you want me to be a coward?

KAZYS: Your logic is twisted. I could tell you the wrong location and you'd be at peace, but I won't do it. I can't help you. You joined us knowing what awaited you. (*He starts whistling his mother's song.*) People like you should be spiritual leaders of the revolution. (*Whistles.*) Their work is useful but they die as sceptics of the revolution. (*Whistles.*) They don't dare drink black coffee day and night to keep a fighting spirit, because when the coffee runs out, defeat comes. (*Whistles.*)

PRANAS: I don't drink black coffee.

KAZYS: I had in mind an emotional exaltation. (*Whistles a little longer.*) Is this interrogator logical?

PRANAS: He doesn't talk much, but his words are aimed well. You either answer his questions or keep quiet. If you keep quiet he orders you to be beaten and watches you quietly, without anger, as though he were lazy.

KAZYS: Is he Lithuanian or did he learn the language?

PRANAS: I don't understand you very well.

KAZYS: Is he a native or brought in from Russia? Well, does he talk the way I do or the way you do?

PRANAS: Don't be insulting.

KAZYS (*surprised*): Pardon me. I was only comparing.

PRANAS: He's a native.

KAZYS: Now I should be insulted.
(*Smiles.*)

PRANAS: He's called Karnavičius. Comrade Karnavičius.

KAZYS: Karnavičius... What does he look like?

PRANAS: Medium height, moves slowly, talks with his mouth half closed. He opened his mouth a few times and I noticed...

KAZYS (*hardly sustaining his laughter*):... and you noticed his front tooth was missing?

PRANAS: That's right. The upper front tooth.

KAZYS (*bursts into laughter*): Oh, my Lord! If this isn't too insane. My friends... (*Laughs.*) I could really go mad. (*Laughs.*) He never did replace that unfortunate tooth. (*Calms down a little.*) Excuse me, sirs. It's not decent to laugh in jail. But this jail is a rather poor theater. And the play in which I have an important role is no tragedy. The first few pages smelled of nobility, but now... it's a run-of-the-mill triangle plot. (*Calmed down.*) Pijus Karnavičius was my classmate. For four years we sat at the same desk up to the final exams, and we competed for my wife Elena since the eighth grade until I finally won. It was a sentimental play for the young and now someone tacked on a last act. Pijus Karnavičius... Pijus... (*Suddenly.*) Were his ears clean?

PRANAS: I didn't notice.

KAZYS: Perhaps you noticed his hands?

PRANAS: Yes. He bites his nails.

KAZYS: So he hasn't gotten rid of his youthful habits. When he couldn't solve a problem in analytic geometry he bit his nails furiously. I had to solve it for him. When he wasn't able to charm Elena, he bit his nails again. And Elena became mine. Now he'll bite his nails again and what if I win for the third time. In fairy tales you win three times. You know, Pranas, we spent evenings arguing and never convinced one another, yet we were friends.

PRANAS: What did you discuss?

KAZYS: You're so curious. Curiosity will destroy you. All right, I'll tell you this time. Pijus belonged to an anarchist group.

PRANAS: He wasn't a communist?

KAZYS: He cursed them violently. He was a nihilist. Pijus was a nihilist because he enjoyed it. Pijus tortured himself because he enjoyed it. His atheism was completely saturated with a fear of religion. During his childhood, Pijus was religious. Every Saturday he went to confession. He used to talk about it ironically. He was afraid to believe, and fear—a step towards religion. I thought he would join a monastery. But he finally came to believe in communism and he was lucky enough to become an interrogator. But... did he really believe? Pijus Karnavičius...

PRANAS: You think he's not a true communist?

KAZYS: True or false—what's the difference? He's the interrogator and he's interrogating us. You're naive, Pranas. This system doesn't recognize classmates and close friends. He's interrogating—that's all.

PRANAS: And what if we try to analyze him? So that he won't feel as secure?

KAZYS: He'll interrogate us even more cruelly.

PRANAS: Besides you, are there many witnesses from his past?

KAZYS: From the anarchist group one became a missionary, one was shot at the very beginning by the bolsheviks for patriotism, and two hold high posts in the communist regime. Sereiva and Katkus. (*Suddenly.*) Why do you need this information? (*PRANAS is silent. KAZYS laughs.*) Are you thinking of informing on the N.K.V.D. interrogator to the N.K.V.D.? You really are naive, Pranas. (*Silent for a moment.*) Now I shall have to ask you for a little quiet. I have to think of what I'll say to my classmate.

(*Silence. PRANAS walks over to F. ANTANAS who is sitting on the stool. F. ANTANAS' lips are moving silently.*)

PRANAS (*quietly*): Are you praying?

F. ANTANAS: Yes.

PRANAS: Forgive me, but it's hard for me—the silence.

F. ANTANAS: I understand. We can talk. I'll finish my prayers later. Only more quietly—he asked us to.

PRANAS (*whispering*): Did he confess to you?

F. ANTANAS: He doesn't need a confession. He's an agnostic.

PRANAS: I know. But I thought, before dying...

F. ANTANAS: No, he didn't have a last confession.

(*His lips move silently, again.*)

PRANAS (*out loud*): Your wife is here.

KAZYS (*turns around and doesn't quite understand the words at first*): What?

PRANAS: Your wife is here.

KAZYS (*jumps towards PRANAS and grabs him by the lapels*): You saw her?

PRANAS: For a moment. When they brought me in to Karnavičius the door to the next room was slightly open and she was standing there— Elena. Her back was to the door, so she didn't notice me and Karnavičius closed the door quickly.

KAZYS (*slowly*): Was she... You saw... Did they start?

PRANAS: No. She looked fine. She was wearing a green coat, brown hat and I noticed that she wore lipstick.

KAZYS (*lets go of PRANAS*): She likes that green coat very much. That green coat—she likes it very much. And the brown hat fits the green coat. (*Walks over to F. ANTANAS.*) I'm guilty Father, that she's here. I couldn't convince her. I was too easy, Father. I asked her so many times to leave for the country but she wouldn't. I was too easy.

F. ANTANAS: Is your wife strong-willed?

KAZYS: In the morning she makes tea while I'm still in bed. And she hums Argentinian tangoes. She loves these little nothings. She also likes striped pajamas, bright colored coats, Gary Cooper, and sweet liqueurs. She doesn't belong to the underground. She's still a beautiful woman—and my wife. Her eyes are large and moist. She knows how to look through them. She's like a lazy cat. I called her "kitten". Perhaps that's why I love her, Father.

F. ANTANAS: And she?

KAZYS: She says so and... she would have left.

F. ANTANAS: Perhaps her strong love will help her through.

KAZYS: Those are just words Father, empty words. You don't know Elena. She is a woman, nothing more. Now they're ready to begin. (*He looks at PRANAS for a long time. PRANAS has moved against the wall. KAZYS walks over to him slowly and pronounced his words deliberately.*) Why did you tell me just now that Elena was arrested? (*PRANAS is silent.*) You heard when I whispered to her "run". You were standing next to me. (*PRANAS is still silent.*) The N.K.V.D. took us out, put us in the car and got in with us. All of them.

PRANAS: Perhaps we didn't notice one hiding in the street.

KAZYS: You think so? Maybe. (*Grabs PRANAS by the arms and pulls him towards himself, then looks into his eyes.*) Why don't you answer my question? I want to know, why did you tell me just now?

PRANAS: I don't know. They beat me up. I was concerned with myself and remembered just now.

KAZYS: Just now. You were distracted, were you?

PRANAS: Yes, distracted.

KAZYS: But rather coherent and logical during our whole talk. And curious—which doesn't fit distraction. (*PRANAS is silent.*) Your eyes are strange. They're colorless. Neither gray, nor green, nor blue. (*Suddenly.*) What color were your mother's eyes?

PRANAS: My mother...

KAZYS: You told me you loved your mother very much. Your mother liked Turgenev, and did something else. Do you remember the color of her eyes?

(*In the corridor footsteps are heard and a woman's long scream. KAZYS lets go of PRANAS' hands. F. ANTANAS gets up from the stool. The footsteps are closer. Sometimes they stop when the woman talks. The other steps overpower and drag her on. Her first words are hard to understand. Only a few reach the cell.*)

WOMAN IN CORRIDOR: ... all right? I'm asking you, listen, please... Don't break my hands... all right?... And into the street... No, no I'm not biting you... all right? It hurts, don't take me there... Dear friends, I don't want to, all right? I don't want to, all right? I don't want to. (*The footsteps stop and the woman is quiet. F. Antanas kneels in the middle of the cell. KAZYS kneels in front of the door. PRANAS sits on the stool. The woman manages to stop in front of the door. The sound of someone falling is heard, then words. They can be heard clearly.*) I'm not going any further, I don't want to. Let go of my hands, dear friends, for a minute, please. I'll rest, all right, don't crush me, I won't go I said—I won't go, all right, don't take me there, I don't want to, don't take me, I don't want to, don't want to,

don't take me, all right? don't want to, don't want to, all right?...
(*The words turn to screams, the footsteps take over and drag the
woman on. The screaming disappears beyond the door.*)
F. ANTANAS: Soon there will be shots.
KAZYS: I'm afraid, Father. I'm very much afraid.
(*The light bulb goes out slowly, and the cell is dark.*)

LA CUMPARSITA

(*When the light is turned on, ELENA is seen standing. She is wearing a
green coat, brown hat, and lipstick. A large room is lit up slowly: two
windows are draped in heavy, dark red curtains. A large portrait of a
smiling, benevolent Stalin is hung between the windows and underneath it
stands a polished desk. On the desk is a telephone, pens, pencils, papers,
and an ashtray. Behind the desk is a chair and opposite are two other
chairs. A radio with a phonograph stand in a corner near the desk. PIJUS
is standing next to the desk. The room has three doors. One leads to the
corridor, the others to the neighboring rooms. Next to the corridor door,
PIJUS' winter hat and coat are hung. There is a dark, red rug on the
floor.*)
PIJUS: Won't you take off your coat? It's warm in here.
ELENA: Yes, it is warm, and light—but somehow uncomfortable.
PIJUS: What can you do. It's an office. (*Takes off her coat and hangs it
on the back of the chair.*) Please sit down, Lena.
ELENA: Will we have a long talk?
PIJUS: We'll have a talk.
ELENA: Are you going to interrogate me?
PIJUS: We'll have a talk. Please sit, Lena. (*She sits.*) Don't be afraid.
ELENA: I'm not.
PIJUS: When I was taking off your coat, you were trembling. (*Smiles
with his mouth closed.*) I won't hit you. (*Smiles again.*) Were you sur-
prised to see me here?
ELENA: Very.
PIJUS: How many years since our separation?
ELENA (*thinks*): About eight.
PIJUS: Eight years and six months. We parted in the spring. I walked
into the garden and you were kissing Kazys. You didn't close the

123

curtains. They were like the ones here, perhaps lighter.

ELENA: Lighter. I didn't have time to close them. Kazys kissed me suddenly.

PIJUS: I saw you twice again—that same spring on the Boulevard. You were carrying a bunch of gladiolas and stopped near a meat market. You looked in the window for a long time and your face was hesitant. Like now. Then you went inside. That was the first time. The second time I saw you from a jail window. That was two years later. I was sent there for being a communist, and I watched the passers-by on the street from the third floor. I wanted you to look up, but you didn't. Some of the people did.

ELENA: I didn't know you were in jail and didn't notice you in the Boulevard. You disappeared so suddenly.

PIJUS: I joined the communists two weeks after you kissed Kazys. That time on the street—you were wearing a fur coat and walked hurriedly. It was rather cold then. Do you still have the fur coat?

ELENA: Yes. But... it's in the closet. You understand...

PIJUS (*nods his head*): It's too rich for our regime. I understand. It's still too bad you didn't wear it today. You see, I thought a lot about you in jail: what you do, what you think, how you love. Especially—how you love. We devoted a lot of time to thoughts like that in bourgeois jails. But they fed us well.

ELENA: Have I changed?

PIJUS: You've changed. You're not a slim girl any more; a naughty girl teasing your sighing admirers. Oh, a thousand pardons, you're still well built and pretty. You're a woman and I'd gladly go to bed with you. And afterwards I'd go to a bar, have drinks and talk with the other men. After lovemaking like that, it's pleasant to drink with men. Would you like a glass of liqueur?

ELENA: Are you interrogating me psychologically?

PIJUS (*smiling*): Yes, psychologically... Who put such ideas into your head? Kazys and his confederates?

ELENA: I'm not one of his confederates, I'm...

PIJUS (*interrupts*): I know. I don't require a confession or demand anything from you. We must have a talk. I'm busy. I really didn't have time to visit you so I've asked you here. Now we shall both have some liqueur. It's good—still made in the old bloody times. (*Opens a drawer and takes out a bottle and two glasses.*) Please try to forget all the atrocities you've probably heard of. The drink is all right, I haven't added any chemicals. (*Pours the liqueur into the glasses and hands one to LENA.*) To your health, Lena. (*They drink.*) Well, how do you like it? It smells of the past, doesn't it? Would you like a cigarette? I'm sorry, but I don't have any of the old kind. But these are also good. They're called "Moscow" and one can get used to them rather easily.

ELENA: I rarely smoke.

PIJUS: Forgive me. I had already forgotten. (*Lights up a cigarette.*) And I, have I changed much?

ELENA: Not too much. Those two wrinkles are deeper, and you still cut your hair short.

PIJUS: Only I wash my hair more often. I'm cleaner now, Lena.

ELENA: But you still smile with your mouth closed.

PIJUS (*shows his teeth*): I never changed my front tooth. As you see, I've remained a conservative. I hate dentists, ties, and manicures. I still bite my nails. Give me your glass. (*ELENA hands him her glass.*) Are you more used to this room now? (*Fills her glass and gives it to her.*)

ELENA: I've stopped shivering. The liqueur warmed me up. To your health, Pijus. (*Drinks.*)

PIJUS: To your health, Lena. (*Drinks his liqueur.*) To your health, Pijus... It's a long time since a woman said: Pijus...

ELENA: You didn't associate with women?

PIJUS: When I left the jail, I visited prostitutes. I never told them my name. You know, Lena, I got used to prostitutes and even liked them fat. I don't know if I'm still capable of loving a woman. Would you like another glass?

ELENA: Thank you, no. My head is spinning.

PIJUS: You still speak the way you did eight years ago. My head is spinning... Do you remember that phrase?

ELENA: I remember everything. Do you want revenge now?

PIJUS: Oh, what a primitive solution. I'm just remembering and asking you if you remember also.

ELENA: Kazys kissed me and you watched from the garden, and before that, I kissed you and said: my head is spinning. You want to know why it happened?

PIJUS: I'm remembering, I'm only remembering.

ELENA: You want to know why it happened. (*Nervously.*) It's hard for me to explain. I kissed you first. You were not good looking, your hair was atrocious and you had dandruff and a black hole in your mouth. And dirty, bitten fingernails. And a wrinkled collar turned inside out. And I kissed you first and my head was really spinning. Your lips were weak and chapped. You didn't answer, you became sad and left quickly. I waited for you to return. You didn't.

PIJUS: I wandered around your house for a few hours—until your light went out. It took you a long time to fall asleep that night.

ELENA: Kazys kissed me first. His eyes shone and the tango he found was my favorite: La Cumparsita. And the evening; you know what kind of evening it was if you were in the garden. Everything resembled a movie and Kazys was like Gary Cooper: quiet and aggressive. He won and I forgot about you. When he kissed me my whole body felt that he was mine, that he had been mine for a long time. My head was clear, but my body felt that he was mine. I don't know what would have happened if you had embraced me.

PIJUS: I came that evening to embrace you. And to ask you to be my wife.

ELENA: You came too late. Where were you those two weeks?

PIJUS: I wandered around. I wanted to formulate one sentence. It had to sound clear, so that you would believe me. Be my wife, be my wife. I couldn't repeat it very well. I said it a hundred times to the sun, the stars, water, trees, the back of a dozing fisherman. Be my wife, be my wife. Then came that charming evening. (*His fingers clutch a match box.*) The cigarettes are really not too bad. Try one.

ELENA: I'll have one. (*Light it.*) I'm very sorry it happened that way. (*PIJUS bites his nails.*) You're biting your nails.

PIJUS: Forgive me.

ELENA: You used to bite your nails when you wanted to say something serious.

PIJUS: That's true. We'll talk about serious matters. (*Coldly.*) Kazys is sitting downstairs. Nothing's happened to him yet. I'm interrogating him soon. If you help me, I'll try to save him.

ELENA: Me?

PIJUS: Yes, you. That's why I asked you here. I don't know about your present relationship, but he's your husband and you probably want to save him.

ELENA: I do.

PIJUS: Fine. Kazys is in pretty deeply. Your apartment was a meeting place for conspirators. They discussed methods of overthrowing the Soviet regime in Lithuania. The talks themselves would have been child's play, but they collected weapons and stored them in a secret place. We want to know the location of this place and we will find it out.

ELENA: You expect to get the location from him?

PIJUS: I said—we. I'm not in charge here. I don't work alone, but I'm very competent, my suggestions are listened to and if I suggest leniency, it will be accepted. I'm speaking realistically, Lena. He won't leave right away, I can't promise you that. It would be a lie.

We'll send him to jail. He'll stay there a few months, perhaps a year. You can send him food—they'll give it to him and when Kazys is forgotten, I'll let him out. I haven't seen him yet, Lena. I wanted to talk to you first. I know Kazys. He's a tough guy. I doubt whether he's changed. He's probably become even tougher working on this. He'll defend it, I know he will. His self-respect won't let him inform. He always won over me, Lena. I admit it. He used to solve my math problems, he used to take me home when I was too drunk to walk, he took you.

ELENA: You're afraid to lose?

PIJUS: I won't lose, Lena. This time he will lose. I don't want revenge and that's why I've asked you here. For both your sakes, I asked you. Tonight defeat is impossible. You understand me? I am a N.K.V.D. interrogator and I use different means. There are quite a few and the strongest men confess. Confession—it's only a question of time and the strength of the means. You understand me?

ELENA: I understand. You'll torture him.

PIJUS: You'll talk to him. And if you're successful the three of us will finish drinking this old liqueur. Just like old times when we visited you.

ELENA: I won't know how, Pijus. I don't know how to talk to him. I tried once, you know him, Pijus. He kissed me. When they came, he made me go to the kitchen where I made them coffee and Kazys himself would bring it out. I couldn't even tell you who came to our house. I was his wife, only his wife, Pijus. I was "kitten" to him. He called me that. What can I say to him? (*Suddenly.*) Oh, yes, once he asked something of me.

PIJUS (*quickly*): What did he ask you?

ELENA: He wanted me to leave for the country. I didn't agree.

PIJUS: Good, very good. You say "kitten"... you go ahead and speak like a kitten. You didn't go to the country because you were his kitten?

ELENA: Yes.

PIJUS: If I gave you arguments to use, he'll understand they're not yours. He's smart enough. Try to talk him into sacrificing himself for you. Don't try convincing him, Lena, because he'll overpower you. Be a woman, Lena, but then, you are a woman. Soon I'll order him to be brought in, but I won't show myself. I'm going into this room. Open the door when you've finished and call me. (*Points out a door in the room. This door can be called One.*) He'll come through these doors. (*Points to door numbered Two.*)

ELENA: Does he know I'm here?

PIJUS: No. (*Starts to leave. ELENA stops him.*)

127

ELENA: If perhaps...you understand...I'll try to. Pijus, believe me I understand and I want to, but if he... I don't trust myself. (*Starts to cry.*) What then, Pijus? (*A pause. PIJUS walks over to the phonograph and stops.*)

PIJUS: I remember the record that you played that evening. La Cumparsita. Sometimes when I have time off I listen to La Cumparsita. (*Opens up the phonograph and takes out a record.*) Here it is. A temperamental tango. It promises a long night and a desired woman's love. A body that you're drawn into first. You didn't have any lovers before us, did you, Lena?

ELENA: Why do you ask?

PIJUS: I demand an answer, Lena.

ELENA: Kazys was the first one.

PIJUS: In other words, I was right. Was it that same night?

ELENA: The same night.

PIJUS (*smiles*): I'm a lover who was too late. The late lover. Not a bad title for a farce, eh Lena? (*Puts a record on and closes the phonograph. Then hides the bottle in the drawer.*) Tell me truthfully, do you love Kazys? But please don't lie. Lying is unnecessary now.

ELENA: I love him. He forced me to love him and now my head spins when he holds me.

PIJUS: Fine. Have you heard about the N.K.V.D. methods of torture?

ELENA: Yes.

PIJUS: It's all true. And worse. If you don't succeed I'll have to force him to tell me the location. I'm the interrogator, I believe in my job, and I will torture him. For my belief. Without mercy, you understand? And you... there's a car downstairs, the same one that brought you here. It's awaiting my orders. Look out the window. It's there. You'll go home. And soon after, you'll disappear from the city. Someplace in the country, I don't know where. We won't look for you. But when you leave remember everything you've heard about us. Good luck, Lena. (*Goes out through the first door. ELENA stands withoug moving for a minute, then walks towards the window, opens the curtains and looks down. Then she opens her pocketbook, takes out a mirror and looks at herself. She takes out a handerchief and wipes her lipstick off, puts everthing back into the pocketbook, closes it and walks over to the radio. The second door opens and KAZYS walks in. He doesn't close the door, but someone else quietly closes it. KAZYS walks towards ELENA, embraces her and kisses her. The following words he says quietly, next to her lips.*)

KAZYS: My kitten... they brought you here... did they hurt you?

ELENA: They were polite. Your cheek is bruised. Did they hit you?

KAZYS: No. I haven't been interrogated yet. They pushed me into the cell and I bumped into something. But it's not bad in our cell. There's a pleasant priest and Pranas was brought in not long ago. Did you talk to him?

ELENA: I talked to him.

KAZYS: What does he want? (*ELENA presses her whole body against his.*)

ELENA: He wants to save us. (*KAZYS lets go of her and looks at her.*) Why are you looking at me that way? I said he wants to save us. He remembers our friendship. (*Now KAZYS walks around the room.*)

KAZYS: This is a dreary room. If it weren't for Stalin's smiling face, it would be even drearier. (*Walks towards the window and opens the curtains.*) The second floor. Is that the garage? So, our cell is downstairs a little to the right. (*Let's of the curtains.*) Oh, he likes music. A new characteristic. Which door did you come in through?

ELENA: This one. (*Points to the corridor door.*)

KAZYS: What's beyond them?

ELENA: A corridor which leads to some stairs and then a vestibule.

KAZYS: Are the guards in the corridor?

ELENA: I passed about ten.

KAZYS: So. (*Nods his head towards the second door.*) I know that entrance. Where did he go?

ELENA: Here. (*Points to the first door.*)

KAZYS (*walks towards the door*): Wait here. I'll try to find him, if possible.

ELENA: First we'll talk.

KAZYS (*stops*): Is that his order?

ELENA: He gave me no orders.

KAZYS: No?

ELENA: No.

KAZYS: I'm listening. (*Pause.*) I'm listening.

ELENA: He was pleasant. He offered me good liqueur. (*Looks at KAZYS. He's silent.*) I drank two glasses. Then we remembered the past. He told me that he thought about me. Did you know, Kazys, that he was in the garden the evening we played La Cumparsita and he listened and saw you kiss me. Two years later he saw me in the street from a jail window. He remembers my fur coat. It seems, he loved me. That evening he came to propose to me. (*Looks at KAZYS. He's silent.*) He spoke sincerely. He wants to save us for the sake of our friendship. He won't let you go today—you'll have to stay in jail for about a year and I'll send you food and then later on, his superiors will forget about you and he'll let you leave. (*Looks at KAZYS. He's silent.*) I told him I wouldn't know how to explain it to you and he said: If he gave me some arguments to use you would understand that they're not mine. Are you listening to what I'm saying?

KAZYS: I heard you.

ELENA: Well, say something if you heard. Say something!

KAZYS: Will he let you go?

ELENA: He promised to. The car that brought me here is still waiting downstairs. When I leave here I'm going to go away someplace and he won't look for me. (*KAZYS looks out the window.*]

KAZYS: The car is there with a driver inside. (*He turns around and spies the ashtray.*) Here's a longer butt and I want a smoke badly. (*Takes the butt and looks at it.*) Did you smoke this?

ELENA: Yes.

KAZYS: The cigarette butt has lipstick on it and your lips are clean. Why did you rub it off? You came here with lipstick on. Pranas told me. Why are you trying to fool me, kitten?

ELENA: I'm not trying to fool you dearest. Really, I'm not. Yes, I took the lipstick off because I thought you wouldn't like it. And I had to look well for him. I'm a woman, dear. (*KAZYS walks to ELENA and puts his arms around her.*) Are you mad?

KAZYS: Is this the time for getting mad? What do you want from me, kitten? Why do you ask the impossible from me? You understand— it's impossible. You didn't pronounce the most important sentence: tell Pijus the location of the warehouse.

ELENA: I can't lose you, do you hear me? You're mine and I don't want to lose you. He'll torture you, do you understand? He told me so. "I'm the interrogator and I believe in my job." And then he said, "I'll get the address, it's only a question of time and means." Do you hear me? And I'll leave for the country seeing you here...I'll have to see you, and how long he tortures you and I won't even know when you've died. They say the N.K.V.D. tortures for months. I'll always see you and I won't sleep nights, you know I'm afraid to sleep alone and I'll see your beaten face, and eyes, and hands, and everything, and I won't feel you and I won't hear your pleadings... are you listening, do you hear?

KAZYS: I hear you kitten. And do you remember one morning when I said: I'm going to work on something important, please don't interfere. And you kissed me and answered: I always knew you were an important man, that is why I'm going to give you an important kiss.

ELENA: But that was in the morning, understand? You were walking around without your pajama top, I saw your muscles and thought— you're very strong. You explained it to me so lightly and now suddenly you want to die.

KAZYS: I didn't want to frighten you, that's why I told you in the morning. I can't love you any longer, I have to die. Once in your life an incomprehensible word—die—bursts out and becomes real. Think of it this way kitten, it just happened that I have to die earlier. It just happened that way. Even Pijus Karnavičius, friend and grand inquisitor isn't necessary for this unexpectedness. Don't think about the torture. Think: Kazys came and went—like a prince who after eight years had a spell cast over him by a wicked witch. I would be happier if you remembered me that way. It would be easier for me to walk those few steps toward that door. I already know that door. I'm asking you, my kitten and joy. There was a prince named Kazys. We were pleased with that fairy tale with the unhappy ending. Remember your words: the prince won't return, but they were happy for a few years. And we had a happy eight years, when we read fairy tales and then drank coffee and made love, when you were mad at me for taking too long in the bathtub. All eight years, do you hear, each and every moment. And now the witch has waved her broom and the prince named Kazys has to die. That's the end of the fairy tale and the ending is right. But you won't forget me, I know. And remember that I wasn't such a bad prince after all. Remember it that way, I beg of you, please I beg you, remember it that way, remember it that way, I beg you, remember it that way. (*Wants to kiss ELENA, but she moves away from him.*]

ELENA: I can't, I can't, I'll scream, I'll die right now, here, I'll die before you. (*Controls herself.*) You're being silly, you don't even believe what you say. I saw your lips trembling. You want to quiet me and you don't have any words left. You don't have any so you tell me fairy tales. To a little girl. And why am I a little girl? You're to blame. It's easy for you to throw me out, because you've sacrificed yourself for a job I know little about. You're to blame that I know little. "Make some coffee, kitten. Go for a walk, the air is nice, kitten." And all of you crouching in the living room and whispering. Why didn't you call me in? Did you want to protect me? You destroyed me trying to protect me. Why didn't you call me? Perhaps I could stand it better. You are my husband and a husband shares with his wife. No, you're not my husband, you're just a lover and I only know how to make love. And now the hero stands there and tells his mistress to dream about a prince. It seems... no it doesn't seem, I'm beginning to hate you, you hear that, prince? (*A pause.*) Naturally, you're not telling the address.

KAZYS (*quietly*): Lena...

131

ELENA (*strongly*): I don't want to listen to you. Not another word. Answer me, are you telling or not?

KAZYS (*softly*): No. (*ELENA opens the first door.*) Pijus! (*A few seconds pass and PIJUS appears. They stand looking at each other.*)

ELENA: No?

KAZYS: No.

PIJUS: All right. Wait there. Sit on the sofa in the corner. (*Mouthing it.*) I'll try again. (*ELENA leaves. PIJUS closes the door carefully and locks it.*) She can't hear. We can speak. (*He goes behind the desk, sits and fingers some papers.*) Sit, if you like. (*Turns the pages. KAZYS stands.*) There are cigarettes on the table—have some. (*KAZYS remains standing.*) Don't play the role of the silent and noble tsarist revolutionary.

KAZYS: I'm waiting. (*PIJUS looks questioningly.*) I'm waiting for the end.

PIJUS: We didn't start yet. (*Leafs through the papers.*) Are you prepared?

KIZYS: Yes.

PIJUS: I have assistants in the other room. They are also prepared. (*Reading a typewritten report.*) They're talented in their field. Their sweeping imagination is amazing. Especially when the victim faints. The victim faints more often than hysterical women in old novels. (*Writes something in the corner of the paper*) My good manners come first. When you want to, sit down and smoke. (*Puts the paper in an envelope and seals it.*)

KAZYS: If your assistants are waiting, there's no point in sitting down.

PIJUS: They'll wait as long as we want them to. I've allotted you enough time.

KAZYS: My heartfelt thanks. (*Sits on the edge of the desk.*)

PIJUS: You've kept your old habits. I remember how you sat on the edge of the desk when you solved my problems. You don't lose confidence in yourself when you sit that way, isn't that so, Kazys? (*Writes an address on the envelope and puts it in the drawer.*)

KAZYS: I see you've learned basic psychology. Congratulations, Pijus.

PIJUS: In my profession any kind of psychology is useful.

KAZYS: Are you satisfied with your profession?

PIJUS: I'm satisfied. (*Takes out another paper.*)

KAZYS: Do you think this gimmick with the papers will prepare me for the interrogation?

PIJUS (*puts the paper aside*): My God, how naive you all are. This is an

PIJUS (*puts the paper aside*): My God, how naive you all are. This is an office, the same as any other. And the client thinks his case is the only one. Right now this office worker has a batch of cases. I want to finish off these papers so that we will have more time to talk. (*Takes out another paper and reads it.*)

KAZYS: May I ask you something?

PIJUS (*reading his papers*): Go ahead.

KAZYS: Will you let my wife go?

PIJUS: I'll let her go after we agree.

KAZYS: I doubt that we'll agree.

PIJUS: We'll agree in any case. Either you will return to your cell and go to a jail tomorrow or you'll go to the other rooms. I repeat, I'll let your wife go after we agree. The car that brought her here is still waiting. Look out the window. (*Crosses out some sentences and writes in his own.*)

KAZYS: I saw it. I want to believe you.

PIJUS: You won't be mistaken. (*Takes out a paper and clips on another piece.*) Well, it's done. (*Gets up and walks around.*) You know, I don't have time to take walks any more. We're overworked. I don't get a chance to breathe fresh air unless it's through a car window on the way home. It's two months since I've had a holiday. My co-workers say I look awful. And the promised holiday is put off indefinitely.

KAZYS: You must be a good executioner.

PIJUS: I'm a conscientious interrogator. But actually, you're wrong. I only head the interrogations. The physical acts are performed by others.

KAZYS: You should do them yourself. Physical exercise speeds up the circulation and would partially make up for the lack of fresh air. If you're interested in your health, beat up the faces yourself.

PIJUS (*smiles*): Now I can remember the bars in the Old Town, I remember the dirty Gluchas tavern we both liked. The booths with wooden doors, sawdust on the floor, dirty glasses, sour herrings and a bottle of whisky. Your comment reminded me of Gluchas. When I tried to be sincere you used to cut me down with sentences like that.

KAZYS: That was well said. You tried to be sincere and you weren't. You used to contradict what you had said a half hour before. If I caught you, you wouldn't agree, you would try to get out of it somehow because your nihilism would waver.

PIJUS: I like you this way. I'm sorry this isn't Gluchas and I don't have herrings and Lithuanian whiskey, but I can offer you some old liqueur.

KAZYS: I don't need it. I don't drink in jail. The few words of wisdom I have I'll give you while I'm sober.

PIJUS: Thanks. Unfortunately, your wise words can't harm me. I can listen to them, we have time. Sure, I'll listen to your wisdom, tell me your wise words, but don't think that they'll harm me.

KAZYS: You're the interrogator and each interrogation is based on provocation. Why provoke me? You have your basic aim and in order to reach it you choose a variety of tricks. But I don't need your tricks. I can see right through them. Tell me openly what you want from me and I'll answer. (*Jumps off the desk.*) Perhaps you shouldn't ask, you know my answer.

PIJUS: You know very little about N.K.V.D. interrogators. The N.K.V.D. doesn't work that way.

KAZYS: A former friend isn't interrogated every day. In this case you don't have a system. That's why you're groping.

PIJUS: That's why I'm sincere. I told Lena, I want to help you.

KAZYS: And you want to win. You don't have the right to lose. N.K.V.D. interrogators don't have the right to lose.

PIJUS: I won't lose. (*Takes out the bottle of liqueur and a glass from the drawer. Pours himself a half a glass and drinks it.*) You say—provocation. I'll prove to you that there's no provocation. I'm doing the same thing you are. You want to win also. How do you differ from me? You also have a belief. That's why you strive to endure everything for the sake of your belief. You're thinking, I'm right and he's not, and I think the same way. How do we differ?

KAZYS: Now you are provoking well. The drink has loosened your tongue. Those questions require an answer. If you're not interrogating me, I'd like to ask you first. Why are you sitting here? For the sake of your beliefs? Or for the sake of your instincts? Are you only a N.K.V.D. interrogator or could you just as well be a Gestapo interrogator? Or perhaps you've involved yourself too deeply like many and can't get out?

PIJUS (*takes the empty glass and looks at it for a moment*): I chose the truth. It is new and powerful. It encompasses all. Other truths are limited because they obstruct their direction with such nonsense as morality and Christian love. Our truth has only one moral: everything to win. The only love is for communism. That's why we're so powerful. We unite man's complete soul into our system. We don't distinguish bad from good. Both bad and good serve our ideas. We murder millions and conquer new ones, we destroy romantic farms and set up collective ones, in our system a son betrays his father and knows—it's right, an interrogator methodically and precisely disembowels a virtuous enemy and the same enemy screams in court—I'm guilty. Our system is life itself. An all-encompassing life. In life there are no weaknesses such as humanism or neighborly love.

Life, when it has to—despises; when it has to—caresses. The sun enables the most gentle flower to grow and the sun burns out prairies. It's the same with water, with fire, and with the whole earth. In our system, man obtains an immense treasure: complete objectivity. He will be God and rule worlds. I say, will be, because not all the communists comprehend the true essence of communism. That's the secret of the blessed and the blessed know that they can't destroy all the weaknesses immediately. That is why they tolerate goodness and patriotism and mercy and love and many other sentimentalities. (*He fills his glass one-third full.*) You and your friends are merely our shadows. You use only a few of our weapons. You don't have a clear aim. You are knights—with bound hands and wearing blindfolds. That is why you lost here and why you will lose everywhere in the world. (*Drinks.*)

KAZYS: You've become smarter during those eight years, and learned grand monologues. But my dear Pijus, you didn't change. Before, you stood on your feet rather weakly, now you stand on your head and think: I'm standing very firmly. Wait until the blood goes to your head. You negated everything before. Today you decided to affirm something. You were more profound when you negated. Better to walk weakly than to stand on your head firmly. You enjoyed being a demon. Now you're a mystic, a mystic of materialism. And you imagine yourself perfect; that you understand the essence of life, and that you know yourself completely. But you're not dull, nor stupid. That's why it will be sad to look at you when all of your blood rushes to your head. Only then will you remember: I am human. (*Stops. His glance catches Stalin's picture.*) Let's say that one day this pleasant uncle through his helpers decides to destroy you in the name of this great, noble idea. What then, comrade Pijus Karnavičius?

PIJUS: Then I shall bow to his will.

KAZYS: And beat your breast and scream in a loud voice: Pijus Karnavičius is a beast, Pijus Karnavičius, a traitor to communism. That's abnormal, my former friend. Your so-called life doesn't like abnormalities. Now I shall take a cigarette. (*Smokes.*) I didn't know you would be here. We only knew the name of the head of the N.K.-V.D. in Vilnius—Ignatov, the Russian. Isn't that so?

PIJUS: Yes. Comrade Boris Ignatov, head of the Vilnius N.K.V.D.

KAZYS: Is he your direct superior? (*PIJUS nods his head.*) Well, I wonder if his outlook is as grand as yours?

PIJUS: We don't discuss our views. But we use the same methods.

KAZYS: Many opposing views use the same methods. Does he trust you?

PIJUS: He trusts me. You say you didn't know I was here?

KAZYS: No. Pranas told me.

PIJUS: Pranas told you?

KAZYS: Yes, in our cell. He was pushed in after being lightly beaten. He could still talk.

PIJUS: Pranas is in your cell... (*The glass slips from his hand, but he manages to catch it and put it on the table.*)

KAZYS: Didn't you know he was in the same cell?

PIJUS (*quietly*): There's been a mistake. They put him in the wrong cell. You're right, we interrogated him gently. That was only the beginning.

KAZYS: It was useless. He doesn't know. I'm glad he's in my cell, I found out that Lena is here and he told me about you.

PIJUS: So. And you told him about me? So that he would know how to conduct himself? (*Bites his nails.*)

KAZYS: Is something bothering you, superman Pijus Karnavičius?

PIJUS: I'm not worried.

KAZYS: Yes, you are. You're biting your nails. You're worried because you can't find something out. It's a habit from your childhood.

PIJUS: It's remained a habit. I bite my nails because I can't get rid of the habit. Thank you for the observation. (*Pours himself some more liqueur.*) You've digressed. You promised to answer me.

KAZYS: It's very hard for me to answer you. Really, Pijus. I've always avoided strict views. They destroy a man. They create distant and noble aims and man can't carry them out. Sometimes man sees his salvation and thinks: everything is clear now. There remains only to seek it, right, Pijus? It doesn't matter how. So he concocts dogmas and he points out a way, but he doesn't notice that his dogmas are twisted and his way crooked. And then his own creation destroys him. When a strict belief rules this world it is destroyed by the same evil against which the belief fights. And those walking the crooked way can't turn back. Perhaps there's no need for a road to salvation? Perhaps it's enough to turn around oneself, or to walk in a circle a few inches in diameter?

PIJUS: You too search for salvation.

KAZYS: That's true. I search. I, a man named Kazys, search within myself. You're right. I'm a knight with bound hands and wearing a blindfold. You're fine when someone else is fine, and you're troubled when someone else is troubled. The salvation is extremely simple, we carry it within ourselves, but the difficult part is agreeing that we've carried it within ourselves for a long time.

PIJUS: Your organization has hidden weapons. Weapons kill people. You contradict yourself. You, wanting to save people, would be killing them. And you would also employ brutal methods in the name of an honorable aim.

KAZYS (*quietly*): I am disgusted by these methods, but I have to use them and now I have to suffer for them. There is a balance in this world. It will destroy you, it will destroy me. We both carry a curse within us. I thought perhaps I should wait, but this system does not allow waiting. It demands choosing for or against. But I had to choose and I chose against. It's very hard for me, Pijus, very hard. The fighter doesn't have to ponder. He knows he has to destroy communism and start again from the beginning. And he himself must die. That's the way the balance works. And those who follow, will be tired of the killing and therefore will be kinder. And relatively happy. And when they've rested they'll think up a new system or a new religion. Perhaps it's enough to circle around oneself and that's that. Now I'd gladly drink if you offer me some, Pijus. (*PIJUS takes a glass out of the drawer and pours the liqueur.*) That's enough, Pijus. (*Drinks it in one gulp.*) It seems we've talked enough. Further arguments will only confuse us. Shall we act instead?

PIJUS (*with difficulty*): Is your decision final?

KAZYS: It's final.

PIJUS: You forget Lena... you're determined to sacrifice her...

KAZYS (*cuts him off*): I said, further arguments are useless. I was wrong. We should have included Lena into our group, but now it's too late. It's night already, Pijus. Order her to be taken home. You're not completely emotionless yet. Then start the interrogation.

PIJUS: Wait. One more question. The question does not concern us. It only concerns me, believe me. Please answer it.

KAZYS: If I can—I'll answer.

PIJUS: Pranas was in your cell. He asked about me. He... (*The door opens and PRANAS walks in.*)

PRANAS: The door was open. I heard the last sentences.

PIJUS: You should have stood there a little longer, or else peeked through the keyhole. This house is like an old castle, it's full of keyholes. You haven't caught on to my system of interrogation yet. (*To KAZYS.*) Pranas is with us.

KAZYS: From Russia?

PRANAS: From the Soviet Republic. You were chatting rather cosily. Like school friends. Does liqueur belong to your system of interrogation, comrade Karnavičius?

PIJUS: Don't be sarcastic. Liqueur does belong to my system of interrogation. (*To KAZYS.*) Pranas was born, grew up and sat in Lithuanian jails. He went to the Soviet Republic ten years ago, as an exchange war prisoner and came back this year.

KAZYS: My suspicions were right.

PRANAS: I learned what I needed. (*Glances at PIJUS.*) And I'll learn more.

PIJUS: You're trying to be mysterious. If you want to talk to me I'll send him out of the room.

PRANAS: There's no need. I have nothing special to say to you.

PIJUS: Then I have something to say to you. I asked you not to enter the cell with your beaten mug. I'm conducting this case.

PRANAS: Comrade Ignatov will call you soon.

PIJUS: You got in touch with comrade Ignatov?

PRANAS: I called him. He agrees with me.

PIJUS: About what?

PRANAS: Comrade Ignatov will tell you over the phone. (*Pours himself a drink into KAZYS' glass and drinks it.*) Sweet stuff. (*To KAZYS.*) How did you like my bourgeois psychology in the cell?

KAZYS: It's outmoded. You smelled of the last century. You impersonated an intelligent hysteric. Even when I was free I sensed the lie.

PRANAS: Very good. I'll write a report to Moscow concerning this subject. I think we'll have to use newer methods in the bourgeois countries.

KAZYS: I would advise it.

PRANAS: Nevertheless, I learned something.

KAZYS: That may be. What happened to Galinis? The one who recommended you?

PRANAS: A week ago... I think it was a week, he was liquidated.

KAZYS: You mean he was already in your hands?

PRANAS: Yes.

PIJUS: Now I'd like to speak with you alone. Kazys...

PRANAS: There's no need. (*A pause, during which PIJUS and PRANAS look at each other.*) There's no need. I said: There's no need. Do you understand? (*To KAZYS.*) You're a clever guy. It will be very interesting interrogating you. Is your wife still here?

KAZYS: She's here, but...

PIJUS: I promised to let her go. I don't need her. She's leaving soon.

PRANAS: She won't leave. She'll be needed.

PIJUS: Look, comrade Pranas. This is none of your business. Do you hear, comrade Pranas? Leave my room. Is that clear?

PRANAS: I hear you, comrade Pijus. And I'm not leaving your room until comrade Ignatov calls. And Madame Elena is not leaving. She'll wait until comrade Ignatov calls. Is that clear?

PIJUS: Leave or I'll throw you out!

PRANAS: I'm staying here until comrade Ignatov calls. By the way, I gave orders downstairs for no one to leave.

PIJUS: In whose name?

PRANAS: Comrade Ignatov's. (*Pause.*)

PIJUS: There's been a small misunderstanding, Kazys. We'll have to wait for the phone call. (*Smiles.*) You see the N.K.V.D. can't avoid intrigues either. (*Smiles.*) We're in an office.

KAZYS (*quietly*): We're in hell, and hell is also an office. May I see Lena?

PRANAS: No.

PIJUS: You may see her. Let's go. (*They start going and PRANAS blocks their way. The phone rings. PIJUS walks towards the desk, sits down and picks up the receiver.*) Zdes Pijus Karnavičius... Ja slusaju... (*He listens, raises his left hand and closes it into a fist, then bangs it on the table.*) Ja ne mogu, ja ne mogu slisis tovarisc Ignatov... Pozvolte vam raskazat... (*He stops talking and listens.*) Tovarisc Ignatov... (*He yells into the receiver although it is clear to everyone that Ignatov has hung up. PIJUS puts the receiver down on the desk. He gets up and walks around the room aimlessly. PRANAS walks towards the desk and replaces the receiver. PIJUS turns around and walks towards PRANAS.*)

PIJUS: You...you...you...you...you are to choose the method. I want to know which method you are choosing. I want to know which method. I want to know very much. Do you hear? I want to know right now.

PRANAS (*peacefully*): I'm choosing the "psychological" method. It was quite effective for Vaineikis two weeks ago.

PIJUS: You bastard, bastard, bastard, bastard...

PRANAS: That liqueur is harmful. Drink vodka, it doesn't hit as hard. I'm leaving, comrade interrogator. And I'll come back to find out the results.

(*Goes towards the corridor door. PIJUS stands in his way.*)

PIJUS: You're not leaving. You're a bastard, do you hear me? A plain ordinary bastard. You want to liquidate me. That's what you want. Stay here and sit down. Sit here, you bastard.

PRANAS (*quietly*): I'll come back to find out the results. Control yourself, comrade interrogator. Your youthful anarchy is showing. I wonder what your former anarchist friends, industry commisar's aide Katkus and university lecturer Sereiva, can tell about you.

PIJUS: You know already.

PRANAS: Yes. (*Gently.*) Control yourself, Pijus. Comrade Ignatov is testing you. All communists are tested. Conduct the "psychological" interrogation and win. Find out the address. We'll forget the past.

PIJUS: But why this method? Tell me, why this one? We have better ones, I can get the same results...

PRANAS: Don't criticize comrade Ignatov.

PIJUS: And what if I fail? Stay here, you'll see how difficult it will be. This case is out of the ordinary. You know it, so you're leaving. I want you to be a witness, and if I lose...

PRANAS: If you're thinking this way already, of course you'll lose. In other words, you're an incompetent interrogator. And you're incompetent because you haven't completely lost that bourgeois sentimentality. If you're rotten inside, you can't be a N.K.V.D. interrogator. That's comrade Ignatov's opinion. I wish you luck, Pijus. (*Walks towards KAZYS.*) I like you, Kazys. I'm sorry you're not one of us. I'm curious to know what you will look like after the interrogation. (*Near the door.*) Perhaps you won't need an interrogation. Perhaps you will agree in a friendly, bourgeois manner while sipping liqueur. (*Goes out into the corridor. PIJUS walks over to the desk and bends over it.*)

KAZYS: What is the method? (*PIJUS straightens up and says nothing.*) What is the method?

PIJUS: You're worried about the psychological method?

KAZYS: Yes.

PIJUS: I have helpers. They will rape Lena one by one and you will watch. You will watch for a long time. If you don't reveal the address. (*Shows him the second door.*) It will be done in this room and you'll hear and watch through the open door. You will see everything and hear everything. You will look, look and finally you won't be able to go on. Now is it clear why you must reveal the address?

KAZYS: You promised to let her go. Remember, Pijus? You promised. And now you decided to interrogate against your will. All three of us have to leave here. Or else we are lost together. Don't you understand? I told Pranas; he provoked me. I told him you were an anarchist. They decided to destroy you. Everywhere, they are destroying their followers. They trust only their own—only Russians.

PIJUS: We can't leave here. Ignatov gave orders—this building is closed until further notice. You're wrong, Kazys. This is not the first time they're testing me. This test is the hardest one and, I believe, the last.

KAZYS: You want to fool yourself. Didn't you see through Pranas? Listen and I'll tell you how he acted when we were free and in the cell.

PIJUS (*screams*): Quiet! I don't want to! Quiet!

KAZYS (*paces the room. Stops suddenly*): I found a way out. Order us to be shot... or shoot us yourself. I'll make a scene, you'll get mad and

shoot us in front of witnesses. (*PIJUS sits, not hearing.*) Pijus, I beg
of you. Pijus, my old dear friend! I'm begging you!
PIJUS: If you won't reveal the address, I'll start the interrogation.
KAZYS: Start with me. All right? I'll try not to give in, but this will be my
first encounter with your methods. Perhaps I won't last, perhaps the
torture will force me to speak. Start with me. Pijus, start with me,
Pijus please, I beg of you, do you hear me, Pijus, do you hear me?
PIJUS: If you won't reveal the address, I'll start the interrogation.
(*KAZYS picks up a chair and throws it against the wall. It shatters.
PIJUS doesn't move.*) Will you tell me the address? (*KAZYS is
silent.*) The address?
KAZYS: No. (*PIJUS walks towards the first door and unlocks it.*) I want
to see Lena.
PIJUS: No.
(*Leaves. Closes the door. A key scrapes in the lock. Voices are heard
but they are not clear and although KAZYS strains to listen he can't
hear ELENA's voice. Suddenly it's quiet and ELENA screams, but
stops soon after, as though someone has put his hand over her mouth.
KAZYS jumps towards the first door and bangs on it, but without any
results. Then he jumps towards the second door and opens it. PIJUS
stands in the doorway.*)
PIJUS: Stop banging around. If you won't stay still they'll tie you up and
you'll have to watch anyway. There's no hope. (*Walks towards the
desk. Stops near the phonograph for a moment, then looks at KAZYS
who is still standing near the open door.*) There she lies ready for the
interrogation. They stuffed her mouth, but later on they will let her
talk to you. You see those faces. They are all quiet, I told them to be
quiet at first. This one will start first. I'll raise my hand and he'll
start. Tell me when, and I'll raise my hand. Tell me, Kazys.
KAZYS: Are you a human being?
PIJUS: Now I am a N.K.V.D. interrogator. And you?
KAZYS: I want to be a human being, I want very much to be a human
being, a human being, a human being, a human being, a human
being, want to, I want to, a human being. (*His face crumples and he
cries, a croaking sound in this throat.*)
PIJUS (*yells*): Raise her head. That's it. And hold it. (*To KAZYS.*) Now
you can see her eyes. Look into her eyes. Kazys, look. Look into them
well. Ask her and her eyes will answer.
KAZYS: Lena... I want to be a human being, do you hear me Lena, Lena,
my kitten, Lena, I can't, I want to, I can't, I want to, you understand
me, Lena, I'm afraid to be afraid, don't look that way, Lena...
PIJUS (*at the same time he starts the phonograph, takes out a record and*

puts it on): La Cumparsita... eight years ago, do you remember? It was a lovely evening, the phonograph was playing, the moon was shining, you kissed, and then... She is lying there now and she's not yours, but if you reveal the address, it won't happen... Reveal the address, reveal the address. (*He puts the needle on the record and La Cumparsita is heard throughout the rooms.*) I'm asking you for the last time, will you reveal the address? (*KAZYS is silent.*) I'm waiting. (*KAZYS is silent. PIJUS raises his hand.*)

KAZYS: Stop it, stop it! (*Jumps towards the door. Suddenly it's dark. La Cumparsita is playing loudly and constantly returns to the first bars as though the record was being played over and over.*)

THE AWAKENING

(*The same room is lit. The doors are still open wide to the other rooms. It's dark in there. The phonograph needle is scratching on the record. ELENA is lying on a rug in the corner of the room. She has been hurriedly dressed. PIJUS stands next to her for a moment. Then he kneels down, picks up her hand and feels her pulse. He passes his hand over her throat, lips, eyes and temples. He stands up, walks over to the coat rack, takes off a fur coat, hat, and takes a pair of fur gloves out of the pocket. He walks back to ELENA, kneels down again, puts the gloves and hat under her head and covers her with the coat. He stands up and listens for a while until he realizes that the sound comes from the phonograph. He walks to the phonograph and turns it off. Then he sits in the chair, takes a bottle and seeing that it is empty, puts it back. PRANAS walks into the room from the corridor. PIJUS pays no attention to him...*)*

PRANAS (*glances at ELENA on the floor*): What's the matter with her?

PIJUS: She fainted.

PRANAS (*hesitantly*): A... (*inquiringly*) What are the results?

PIJUS: She fainted.

PRANAS (*walks to the second door, goes in and comes out soon*): Where are the others?

PIJUS: I sent them downstairs. I don't need them anymore.

PRANAS: You're finished?

PIJUS? I'm finished.

PRANAS: Where's Kazys? (*PIJUS is silent.*) Comrade Ignatov ordered you to call him right away.

PIJUS: I'm not calling Comrade Ignatov.

PRANAS: Just as I thought. That's why I drove over to see him and got specific instructions.

PIJUS (*as though awakened*): You got specific instructions without knowing the results?

PRANAS: I still don't know the results.

PIJUS: What instructions did Comrade Ignatov give?

PRANAS: You're under arrest. I was told to watch you until he comes here and conducts the first interrogation. At the moment he's conferring with Comrade Dekanocov. The conference will be over in about an hour. If you don't believe me—call.

PIJUS: I'm under arrest and Comrade Ignatov will conduct the first interrogation... and if I got the address of the warehouse? What then?

PRANAS: You're still under arrest. This circus was only an excuse.

PIJUS: In other words...The results aren't important to you.

PRANAS: In part, perhaps...but not essentially.

PIJUS: Not essentially...what is essential then?

PRANAS: I'll answer you. But first tell me the interrogation method. Briefly, please. (*Looks at ELENA.*) She's taken care of, I see. And you covered her so she won't be cold. There was no need, the radiators are warm. Where's Kazys?

PIJUS: I shot him a few minutes ago. And then she fainted. She stood it all till the end. She fainted when I shot Kazys.

PRANAS: Why did you?

PIJUS: She screamed at the beginning only and then we stuffed her mouth. I executed the "psychological" method correctly. Naturally Kazys jumped towards the room so we tied him to a chair and he watched them, one by one, as they... I saw Kazys age each second. His cheeks sank in, dark circles formed under his eyes and wrinkles suddenly appeared on his yellowed face and his lips narrowed. Suddenly he became very old. I watched his eyes, they didn't blink. His face died. Then we took the rags out of Lena's mouth and she didn't scream, she only said: Don't tell them the address. And she kept repeating: Don't tell them the address. And when they finished—I started to interrogate Kazys. He screamed like an animal, and she kept repeating: don't tell them the address. Then I shot him.

PRANAS: Why?

PIJUS: I don't know. It's not clear to me.

PRANAS: You shot Kazys out of mercy.

PIJUS: Perhaps.

PRANAS: In other words, you didn't get the address.

PIJUS: No.

PRANAS: I'll have to get it.

PIJUS: It's impossible. Kazys is dead.

PRANAS (*laughs*): Now I'm fully convinced. You're a naive interrogator. I'll arrest his co-workers; two know the address. I think they'll talk.

PIJUS: You're taking my place?

PRANAS Yes. Comrade Ignatov appointed me.

PIJUS: Congratulations. Now, explain...

PRANAS (*cuts him off*): It's very simple. I was your aide and you assigned me to arrest members of that secret meeting. I was supposed to arrest them all.

PIJUS: You said only Kazys knew the address.

PRANAS: I lied. Two others know it also.

PIJUS: It was a trap.

PRANAS: It was the beginning of a liquidation.

PIJUS: When was my liquidation decided on?

PRANAS: I decided it a few months ago.

PIJUS: You wanted this place?

PRANAS (*cheerfully*): Of course. But I needed your sins. I must admit, it was hard digging them up. But somehow I sniffed out your friendship with Kazys. I was devilishly lucky. Today Kazys told me in the cell: you belonged to an anarchist group once. That was enough. If you didn't admit it—others would: Sereiva and Katkus. You understand, dear friend, this interrogation was your own interrogation. If you had gotten the address, I would have grabbed you for the past anyway. But you broke down during the interrogation. You didn't get the address and shot Kazys out of mercy. I used the psychological method and I was right. That's how you lost, dear friend. You're not an honorable interrogator.

PIJUS (*quietly*): You say, I'm not an honorable interrogator. (*Takes a folder off the table, looks through it and takes out a sheet of paper.*) This is the list for a half year. (*Reads quietly for a moment.*) During half a year I interrogated one hundred and ten people. In that room. My aides and I. I listened to a variety of screams. A falsetto squeal, when a man can still control himself; a shrill howl, when he can't stand the suffering; and a hoarse croak from the stomach when he's beginning to lose consciousness. People kissed my feet, they tried to beat me, and (*looks at the paper*) fifteen went mad. One hundred and ten corpses during a half a year. I slept four, five hours, ate, the devil knows when, lost my appetite and weight. I feel like an ascetic, like a medieval inquisitor. I don't have a personal life. I only serve. I serve the holy idea of communism. And you say I'm not an honorable interrogator?

PRANAS: And yet, you can't be a N.K.V.D. interrogator. You fulfilled your mission and now you must step aside. And N.K.V.D. interrogators don't retire with a pension. They die.

PIJUS: Buy why, tell me why?

PRANAS: You are an amateur interrogator. True, you showed high qualifications and for a time you were accepted, while we were still new in this country. But now the amateurs will be replaced by professionals. And professionals can only be Russian, or brought up on Russian communism. You're not one of them. You grew up in a bourgeois Lithuania and you were attracted to communism by literary romanticism. You recognized the aims of capitalism and visualized a salvation in us. And denying certain emotions and ideas, you conscientiously served us. But it was enough for your boyhood friend and sweetheart to show up and suddenly you capitulated. It's unimportant if you would have won. Sooner or later you'd lose. The remnants of your youth came through. You were an anarchist, you negated emotionally and today you negated your duty. That's why you're under arrest and that's why it is necessary for you to step aside.

PIJUS: Does Ignatov know of your provocations?

PRANAS: You want to wriggle out by unmasking me. Don't bother. These provocations are permitted in our profession. In this profession one provokes another. The results are important. I obtained results and I won. I'm better trained than you. I'm without emotions... Yes, I'm an egotist and I'm building a career, but my egotism is legal. My egotism serves the great idea of communism. (*Pause.*) You're not a bad guy and I'll try to make your dying easy. We'll take your work into consideration. Truthfully, a hundred and ten liquidated speaks in your favor. I'd gladly drink with you, but not this sweet mush. I'd gladly drink some vodka with you. (*Walks around the room.*) Oh, dear friend, today I feel a great upsurge. The bourgeois term is spiritual ecstasy, isn't that so, dear friend? As though I'm in the Kremlin again. We'll win, Pijus; we're winning on all fronts. Lithuania, Latvia, and Estonia are ours; tomorrow Poland, the day after—Germany. Our people are all over the world and it is full of literary dreamers like you. They sweep the way for us, and wait for us. For us—The Russian communists. And we'll come. We'll go everywhere. (*Stops in the middle of the room in front of the desk and Stalin's portrait. Looks at it for a moment.*) A great national leader—

Comrade Stalin. I saw him once in the Kremlin. He invited us before the invasion of Lithuania and granted each one of us a few words. He said to me: "I hear you're clever. Hold on and don't stumble." And I won't stumble, Comrade Stalin.

PIJUS: You think you won't?

PRANAS: No, Pijus. (*PIJUS opens a drawer and puts both hands in it. At the same time PRANAS takes out a pistol from his pocket and aims it at PIJUS.*) What are you looking for?

PIJUS (*calmly*): Vodka. Why are you so frightened, Comrade Pranas? You wanted vodka. Here it is. (*Takes out the bottle with his left hand and puts it on the table.*) We'll both have a glass.

PRANAS: Forgive me, but we're on guard.

PIJUS: I forgive you. I think it's ordinary nervousness. (*PRANAS lowers his pistol.*) With vodka one must eat. There's canned fish in the drawer.

(*He puts his left hand in the drawer again. Suddenly there's a gleam from a pistol in his right hand and almost at the same time two shots ring out. PIJUS' bullet hits PRANAS in the chest and he falls. PRANAS shoots too late, his bullet hits Stalin's face. The glass shatters, the bullet tearing the canvas where the nose was, making the good natured face look like a skull. PIJUS puts the pistol back into the drawer, walks towards PRANAS, kneels near him and looks at him for a few moments.*)

PIJUS: You stumbled anyway, dear friend. You stumbled and you can't get up again. Even genuine communists die. (*Lifts PRANAS and gets up holding him.*) You are number one hundred and eleven. I'd like to ask you—why did you lose? After all, your victory was—life. An unfortunate accident? Are unfortunate accidents counted with the communist triumph? (*Carries PRANAS out into the first room. Comes back soon, walks to the desk, uncorks the bottle and pours himself a drink.*) I lied. I don't have any canned fish. I drink without food to your unemotional soul, Pranas.

(*Drinks. ELENA wakes slowly and PIJUS doesn't notice when she brushes off the fur coat and sits up on the floor. She sighs deeply and heavily. Then PIJUS turns towards her.*)

ELENA: I'm alive? (*PIJUS pours some whiskey into a glass and hands it to her.*)

PIJUS: Drink. (*ELENA drinks it. PIJUS takes the glass from her, walks back to the desk, pours himself some more and drinks again.*) I think I'm getting drunk. My head is spinning. You hear that Elena? My head is spinning. (*ELENA gets up. PIJUS walks over and offers his hand.*)

ELENA: Don't touch. (*She gets up heavily, walks to the desk and sits down.*) Did I hear a new shot, or was it... (*She moves nervously in her chair.*)

PIJUS: Sit still, Lena. You heard a new shot. There was Pranas...

ELENA (*looks at the open doors nervously*): They're in there?

PIJUS: No. I sent them downstairs. We're alone, Lena.

ELENA (*quietly*): I'm alone...where's Kazys?

PIJUS: Lena...

ELENA: I remember. Where's his body?

PIJUS: Downstairs, in the cellar.

ELENA: I want you to order his burial. You'll give his body to his sister. She lives...

PIJUS: I can't give any more orders. I'm through. I can't leave this building. I'm under arrest and I'm waiting for them to take me.

ELENA: You didn't get the address?

PIJUS: Not only because of that. They decided: I'm unnecessary.

ELENA: Oh, I understand. The master hangs his old dog.

PIJUS: Don't joke, Lena. We have little time left. Soon we'll both die.

ELENA: I don't want to die with you. I'll die alone.

PIJUS: You'll die before me.

ELENA: Thank you. You'll shoot me?

PIJUS: No. You heard the last shots. I've hidden a cyanide tablet. I took it from someone I interrogated. Why did I hide it then? I'm not sure. Premonition? Perhaps. I'll divide it in half. There's enough for us both. (*Pours some whiskey and drinks it.*) Now I'm drunk. Soon I'll be as drunk as a pig. (*Smiles.*) For a half a year I couldn't get drunk and now I won't be able to sober up until I die. The law of balance according to Kazys? This side of the scale weighs only a few grains and the other weighed tons. A thousand tons.

ELENA: Is your conscience troubling you?

PIJUS: No, I am empty, and drunk. I am no longer I. Something left and won't return. Perhaps Karnavičius, the interrogator evaporated and Pijus, the youth remains? I feel the way I did once at Gluchas' tavern when I used to dream about you. No, I wasn't empty then. Perhaps I'm lying, Lena? Perhaps I'm only drunk. And if I sobered up...(*Smiles.*) But I'll never sober up. I will be eternally drunk. (*Takes the bottle.*)

ELENA: It seems to me, you're afraid.

PIJUS (*puts the bottle down*): Afraid? Of what?

ELENA: You're afraid of me.

PIJUS (*looks at her for a long time*): Of you? (*As though learning it.*) I'm afraid of you, I'm afraid of you, I'm afraid of you...

147

ELENA: What did you feel when you interrogated us? Why are you silent? Answer me. Answer me, I ask you. When they to me and you to Kazys? Answer me, what did you feel? And when you played La Cumparsita. What did you feel? (*PIJUS takes the bottle.*) Don't drink, I want to talk to you sober. And you'll die sober; you'll die afraid. Don't drink, Pijus, don't drink, Pijus, don't drink. (*Walks towards the desk, takes the bottle out of his hand.*) Is there any water here? (*PIJUS nods his head.*) Is this the last bottle? (*PIJUS nods his head. ELENA suddenly turns the bottle over and spills the whiskey on the rug.*) So, you no longer have an aide. You have only me, only me. And I won't say a word to you, Pijus. I'll keep quiet and I'll look at you, and you won't be able to close your eyes. How much time do we have?

PIJUS (*heavily.*): Perhaps a half an hour.

ELENA: That's a long time, a very long time, Pijus. For a half an hour I won't take my eyes off you. And when you start to break the pill in half, I won't lower my eyes, and when you pour the water I won't take my eyes off, and I'll drink it and fall, and you'll bend over me and I won't take my dead eyes off you. You'll have to bend over, Pijus, I'm ordering you to, you'll kneel over me and looking into my eyes you'll drink your water. And when you lose consciousness the last thing you'll see will be—my eyes. And you'll be sober, completely sober. You're sober now, aren't you, do you hear, I'm ordering you.

PIJUS (*screams*): Stop, stop! Lena, stop!

ELENA (*breaks into a long laugh*): How weak you are, Pijus, my God, how weak! You boldly tortured so many people and suddenly my chatter frightens you. Don't worry, little one, I won't look at you, I'll let you close your eyes. And if you want to break the tablet now, I've shortened the term. I'm very sorry I spilled your whiskey. (*PIJUS looks at her with a fixed stare.*) Don't stare, there's no need. If I hated you, you'd suffer for it. But I feel only pride, for Kazys and myself. We are the winners and we are granting you amnesty. Too bad you can't run away. I want you to live. If you hadn't killed, you'd be alive.

PIJUS: We can't run away, Lena. They won't let us out of this building.

ELENA: I wouldn't run away. The winners don't have a right to live. They win and die. And if they live—they become comical. You're probably amazed that I've learned to talk. I learned in the other room. It was horrible for me at the beginning, very horrible, Pijus. Then I saw Kazys' face and only his face. And then I felt another fear, an overpowering fear that he would confess and I couldn't say anything; you stuffed my mouth. And my eyes screamed "Don't give the address" and when you removed the rags, I knew only those words: "Don't give the address." And I didn't feel it when they... and it wasn't disgusting anymore... I didn't think of myself in this room. I thought about him and I felt stronger, perhaps even stronger than he. And when you were breaking his bones and put out your cigarette in is face, and stuck needles under his nails and when I heard him screaming, I knew only "Don't give the address" and I saw Kazys' eyes and understood he's screaming only in pain, he's not afraid, and we don't have to talk and I don't have to repeat "Don't give the address" without stopping. And when you grabbed the pistol from someone's belt and stuck it in the back of his head, I understood: Kazys and I won. We didn't give the address.

PIJUS: They will find out anyway.

ELENA: But *we* didn't give the address. That's why we won. And you lost, Pijus. I don't envy you. Having lost, it's not easy to die.

PIJUS: I'll die with you Lena. Perhaps I don't need anything else. (*To himself.*) I'm sober and I have a headache.

ELENA: And I'm to replace the whiskey. Don't fool yourself, Pijus.

PIJUS: You won't replace anything. You are you and I love you. And I'll never kiss you, and I'll never have you. And I thought of it always. And now we've met before dying. Like terribly close people. I lost, Lena. When I saw you in this room I lost already. I interrogated you needlessly. Whether Kazys told the address or not the results would be useless. I lost because I dared to interrogate you two. I didn't have that right because I loved you both. (*He takes the empty bottle from the table and puts it in the drawer. He bites his nails.*)

ELENA: You're biting them again?

PIJUS: I'm biting them... I don't know how to... without fear, without hope, without anything... the tablet broken in half, put into a glass of water... say, a half of a glass and... (*His glance falls on the papers on the desk. He picks one up.*) Once I handled a prayer book. Everything was written in there.

...God, the Father...the Son...honor your father and mother, fast, observe the sabbath... Holy Mary, pray for us, Sacred Heart of Jesus, have mercy on us... (*stares at one paper*) Everything is written here also... cell number 11, Juozas Girdeikis and a note—be lenient and send him to Siberia if he signs our dictated confession... Cell number 12... Albinas Matulis... liquidate after a long interrogation... Cell number 14... (*Wants to throw the paper, but stops himself and looks again.*) There's a priest in Kazys' cell. (*Reads.*) Got there by mistake, liquidate him. (*Puts the paper on the desk.*) Do you need a priest, Lena?

ELENA: No. But if he was with Kazys, I'd like to see him. No, I don't want to see him, I... (*Starts to cry. She sobs like a small child.*) I can't, I don't want to see anyone. Really, I'm very strong and...I'm crying. The victors should die right away, otherwise—they cry. But, I'm very, very strong...

PIJUS: Lena! (*ELENA looks at him.*) Lena, I know I don't have the right, but... have mercy on me. Let me die with you. I can't, I don't know how to do it alone. (*ELENA looks at him, doubtfully.*)

ELENA: Give me the tablet and bring in the priest.

PIJUS: Will you wait for me?

ELENA: The tablet! (*PIJUS unbottons his jacket, pulls out a wallet from the side pocket and takes out a tablet wrapped in paper.*) Give it to me. (*PIJUS gives ELENA the tablet.*) The glass is on the table. Where's the water?

PIJUS (*points to the second door*): In that room. The sink is next to the window.

ELENA: I remember the sink, only... it's dark in there.

PIJUS: The switch...

ELENA: I don't need electricity.

PIJUS: Open the curtains, the moon is shining outside.

ELENA: Good. Bring me my handbag. (*PIJUS leaves the room through the first door and comes back right away with ELENA's pocketbook. He hands it to her.*) Thanks.

PIJUS: Will you wait for me?

ELENA: I'll be in the other room. Kazys' room. Don't disturb me for a moment, you two.

PIJUS: I understand.

ELENA: Go. (*PIJUS goes out into the corridor. ELENA opens her pocketbook, takes out powder, a mirror, lipstick, and a comb. She combs her hair, powders her face and puts on lipstick, then puts everything back into the pocketbook and straightens her dress. She takes the glass and goes into the second room. The sound of curtains opening is heard. The second room is lit up by a green light. Then silence. After a few moments PIJUS and F. ANTANAS come in from the corridor.*)

F. ANTANAS: You say, in this room...(*Looks at the room carefully as though it were in a fog.*)

PIJUS: Here and in there, Father. (*Points to the second room.*)

F. ANTANAS (*to himself*): And nevertheless Kazys held out. He didn't give the address?

PIJUS: No.

F. ANTANAS (*to PIJUS*): Where is she?

PIJUS: In the other room. She asked for a moment to herself. Perhaps...she's saying goodbye to Kazys? When she's through—we're going to die. (*Pause.*)

F. ANTANAS (*looks at the phonograph*): Were you playing this?

PIJUS: Her favorite tango. La Cumparsita.

F. ANTANAS: You played it while interrogating?

PIJUS: I interrogated with love.

F. ANTANAS: You remind me of one who made the same mistake. In the garden house (*to himself*) I'm beginning to understand some things. To hold on, to hold on. My God, forgive me, help me, let me hold on. (*Pause.*)

PIJUS: Why is it so quiet in there? (*Quietly.*) Lena... (*A little louder.*) Lena! (*Runs into the second room. After a moment*) Father! (*F. ANTANAS goes in. The light is turned on.*)

F. ANTANAS' VOICE: Turn it off! (*The light is turned off, and only the moonlight is seen in the room. PIJUS comes in supported by F. ANTANAS.*)

PIJUS: She tricked me. She didn't wait to take it together.

F. ANTANAS: She tricked herself. She didn't dare hold on. Merciful God, don't condemn her. Forgive her for her unearthly pain.

PIJUS: She fell alone. You saw Father—she fell. I kissed her lips. They're still moist and warm. We kissed one another, and we never kissed. (*Frees himself from F. ANTANAS' grasp and paces about.*) I'm alone, alone.

F. ANTANAS (*looking at PIJUS carefully*): Perhaps you can liquidate me also?

PIJUS: You? No, I can't. I can't even liquidate myself. There's a loaded revolver in the drawer. If you want to...

F. ANTANAS (*interrupts*): You're not capable?

PIJUS: No. I'm a name, muscles, thoughts, but I am no longer. Perhaps you can help me, Father? Order me, command me.

F. ANTANAS: Once I thought that a great belief allows a strict command. But I was wrong and my God has forsaken me. I commanded my sister and she died. I can only answer for myself. Now I understand the great hermits. Nothing around you and your God inside of you. And when you feel Him, your faith will melt words and commands, and there will be only love. You will love Him, yourself, and your fellow man. Ask for His grace. A great light descended upon me when I found out that Kazys held on and I am calmer, and I want to pray, and I don't hear the footsteps any more. My God, help me to hold on! (*To PIJUS.*) If you want·to—you may follow me—if it will help.

PIJUS: I want to, Father.

F. ANTANAS: Good, we'll pray for them.

PIJUS: We'll pray.

F. ANTANAS: You said that record was her favorite?

PIJUS: Yes.

F. ANTANAS: Put it on quietly. (*PIJUS starts the phonograph. La Cumparsita is heard softly.*) Our Father, who art in heaven...

PIJUS: Our Father, who art in heaven...

F. ANTANAS: Hallowed be thy name...

PIJUS: Hallowed be thy name...

F. ANTANAS: Thy Kingdom come...

PIJUS: Thy Kingdom come...

F. ANTANAS: Thy will be done, on earth as it is in heaven...

PIJUS: Thy will be done, on earth as it is in heaven...

CURTAIN

MAD CHRISTOPHER, MAD

A Northern Legend
in seven scenes

by
Mārtiņš Zīverts

Adapted from Latvian by
Alfreds Straumanis

Introduction to
Mad Christopher, Mad

Mārtiņš Zīverts has endowed Latvian drama with works that not only have established him at the forefront of Latvian dramaturgy but can also vie for recognition with the best representatives of dramatic art. "About the author of my plays," Zīverts volunteers, in his typical ironic manner, some dates and facts: "Born: January 5, 1903. Height: 173 cm (without shoes). Weight: between 57 and 67 kg depending on the availability of food. Face: oval, unfriendly... Level of intelligence: somewhat below normal... Health: labile. For more than thirty years I have been living only for the sake of spiting death." Zīverts was born in the provinces, and his father, among his many other pursuits, was also a gravedigger. Zīverts admits that some of the macabre sights in his plays are not products of morbid fantasy but are based on recollections from his youth. The early deaths of his two younger sisters from tuberculosis left another indelible imprint, and later he himself succumbed to the "skeletal lady." After high school, Zīverts takes a vagabond trip to sunny Italy. Upon his return to Latvia, he pursues psychology studies at the University of Latvia and to keep body and soul together teaches part-time and dabbles in journalism. His first produced play, Naphtha, in 1931 gains scant popular notice, but five years later, with the success of a very taut drama, Tīrelpurvs (name of a swamp near Riga, site of fierce battles during World War I) come consulting positions with the official theaters and popular recognition. The war and occupation years of 1940-45, spent in anxiety and uncertainty, disrupt many a project. In November 1944, after perilous waiting, Zīverts reaches Sweden in a fishing boat. He works successively as a librarian, archivist, stage hand, and waiter. Presently, although retired and his health impaired, he continues to lead an active cultural life. He has traveled to the United States, Australia, and Soviet Latvia. His travels and other personal experiences have always enriched his work: "The most important seem to be the events that I have watched from the sidelines... From them, I 'make my plays.' I have such poor fantasy that it is not worth bothering about it. I have to build my plays from what I have directly seen and experienced."

157

Perhaps Zīverts' concern with his most immediate reality focusing on human relations explains why he is seldom tempted by the great philosophical themes of our times. But his work has never exploited the popularity of ephemeral fads, nor has it ever stooped to embrace the facility that the eupeptic theater goer seeks for his after-dinner enjoyment. Zīverts has written some fifty plays that vary considerably in texture and span a wide range of topics. In addition to the traditional designations such as comedy, tragedy, etc., some works bear subtitles like detective story, mime, modern fairy tale, dialogued anecdote, contemporary circus act, etc. There are experimental one-acters and full-length historical plays, like *The Court Jester, The Marriage of Munchhausen, Might*, etc. Most frequently Zīverts contemplates with irony and compassion human relations in situations that test the authenticity of our feelings toward other human beings. Love, family bonds, affection, and friendship are constantly comically warped by our potentially tragic drives and acquire a high degree tensity in the Zīverts' play. War, refugee life, exile, when absurdities of fate and accident seem to subject human lives to gratuitous punishment as well as to afford unmerited impunity, have also provided settings and characters for many of his plays. The greed for power with its concomitant conflicts is probed in the historical tragedy, dealing with the downfall of the Lithuanian King Mindaugas. Whatever the form or the topic may be, Zīverts has proven himself a master of dramatic techniques. Most of his plays have tightly constructed plots that are skillfully developed from the engaging exposition, through a series of peripeteias that bring about suspense and contrasting changes of dramatic situations, to the final denouement that always hides some unexpected resolution and drives home some compassionately ironic observation.

In the above mentioned war drama, *Tīrelpurvs*, the three characters of the eternal love triangle are tied together and immobilized by multiple bonds. On the edge of the almost impassable swamp, they are surrounded by the invading Germans who watch their every move with suspicion. Their temperaments are poorly suited to tolerate the siege and the feeling of powerlessness and interdependence. In addition, the besieged must also find an exit in their emotional impasse where opposites such as duty and inclination, love and jealousy, admiration and hatred, entangle their relations in psychological Gordian knots. The husband, chained to his invalid's chair, is at the mercy of the lovers for his physical wellbeing, but their guilt places him in a morally superior position. For a while, he is much tempted to break out of this impasse by betraying to the Germans his rival who is a Russian officer. Finally, however, magnanimity and duty gain the upper hand over inclination and self-assertion. Knowing that this act will cost him his life, the husband permits the lovers to escape through the swamp and thereby to transmit valuable military information which will save Riga. Again, Zīverts asserts man's intrinsic freedom to be the master of his fate if he resists the enslavement to his baser impulses and listens to the clear voice of reason and moral integrity.

The action of *Fiasko*, another war drama, is set in those days of terror when military power hangs in the balance and madmen can indulge with impunity in vindictive homocide. The central character, Fiasko, a recurrent personage in Zīverts' theater, is a philosopher-clown, the illusionist who makes life bearable for others but himself is cured of all illusions and idealism. In the final act, Fiasko and his companions are imprisoned in a cemetery chapel waiting to be executed. When Fiasko finds out what is in store for his fiancee before she dies, he inveigles her into swallowing the poison he had intended to use on himself. But here again, in a scene with high dramatic potential, very much reminiscent of the ending in Malraux's *La Condition humaine*, Zīverts orders a *deus ex machina* to reverse an irreversible situation in order to prove that one must never despair of life. The terrorists are driven away in the nick of time, and the girl even does not have to be resurrected because she only swallowed an innocuous medicine with which she had secretly replaced the poison the previous day. Zīverts absolves the characters from their predicament and springs the prison door open because at least one human being had absolute faith in life's value. The spectator, however, may wonder if in the Zīvertian universe man is really free. Irrespective of the human condition, a providential design seems to unfold to assure man that higher moral principles will justify life. But is it not perhaps in the very absence of clear signs and under the ubiquitous shadow of uncertainty and ambiguity that accompany human acts that man's freedom acquires its true meaning?

Mad Christopher, Mad was first published in 1954 under the original title of *Rūda* and first produced in Melbourne, Australia, in 1960. An English translation by Alfreds Straumanis was published in Sydney, Australia as *The Ore* (literal translation of *Rūda*) in 1968. The present version, *Mad Christopher, Mad*, is an adaptation of the first translation. It is closer to the American idiom, and was produced in 1969 at the New York State University at New Paltz. The original designation of the play is a northern legend, but in his remarks Zīverts has referred to it as a grotesque tragedy. The setting of the play is obviously of Scandinavian inspiration, with its romantic background of aurora borealis, polar summer midnights, trolls, as well as with its colorful secondary characters, like the Prime Minister, the Secretary of the Academy of

Science, the Manager of the insane asylum, who all possess a facet that can be termed Swedish. On the other hand, these very same characters and the protagonist and the conflicts they confront surpass national geographic boundaries to acquire timeless dimensions of universal significance, as a legend or a tragedy would have it. From a certain point of view, the action of the play consists of a series of confrontations that pit the individual, Professor Christopher, in his quest for knowledge and better life, against inflexible tyrannical systems that too were originally designed for the purpose of improving the quality of human existence. The Academy of Science, supposedly the fount of all knowledge, exercises tyrannical power over its members, persecuting unorthodox deviation from procedure, stifling all inventiveness and originality. The government has become oblivious of its original charge to protect its citizens and pursues those who in their quixotic idealism endanger the good public image of its politicians. When Christopher's discovery of the mountain of superior iron ore becomes known, the Prime Minister dreams of advancing the rank of his nation among the global powers by undermining existing international markets and making huge profits from the cheap iron ore sales. Parenthetically, it can be pointed out that Zīverts in this play which was written some twenty years ago, envisages the possibility of an international economic tyranny of yet unknown proportions that threatens the world markets today. Since Christopher refuses to play along and to be an accomplice in the perpetuation of these systems, he is neutralized by being sent to an insane asylum, "where everything is defined by authority," the Manager reigns supreme over the inmates. His presence drives away the sunshine and stops the birds from singing. "He has seized all power, employs a thousand spies and body guards." The inmates are trapped in a system that can only justify its existence by abnegating its essence, since to maintain his managerial empire, the Manager must make sure that the inmates are never cured enough to leave the institution. Within this empire, there is the kingdom of the mad King of Madmen whose reign is not less ambitious than the increasingly more monstrous tyrannies outside. The mad King's dream is to gather all madmen of the world in one mighty International, "united in a beautiful and mighty idea of madness," and to breed, through evolution and selection, a superior class of madmen "from which all nations will draw their princes and their regents."

Professor Christopher, having suffered at the hands of those who have usurped power and turned authority into tyranny, decides to remain in the insane asylum with the minority of men gone mad, because he is a man of compassion who sides with the oppressed, the underdog, the servant girl instead of the mistress, the King of madmen instead of the

Prime Minister and the Secretary of the Academy of Science. The conclusion of the play seems to suggest that there is no escape from the various forms of tyranny as long as men are hypnotized by power, greed, selfishness. The real treasures of priceless ore lie in their hearts. As Christopher exhorts: "Clean away the refuse of selfishness... so that the divine metal becomes pure and sonorous—let your spirit be free!" Christopher returns to the madhouse, but the message Zīverts leaves with the spectator has timeless qualities that all men who care about freedom can value.

Juris Silenieks

MAD CHRISTOPHER, MAD

CHARACTERS

CHRISTOPHER—a geology professor
THOMAS—his assistant
HANNA
SECRETARY of the Science Academy, Hanna's father
KARIN
JONATHAN SIMS—the police inspector
PRIME MINISTER
MANAGER OF A MADHOUSE
KING OF ALL MADMEN
1st COMMENTATOR
2nd COMMENTATOR
A TROLL

ORDERLIES, MADMEN, JOURNALISTS, PHOTOGRAPHERS, AND FANFARISTS

SCENE ONE

HANNA: (*sits and drinks from a square mug.*)
KARIN: (*with a remote control switch searches for news on a super modern screen. On the screen little scenes, probably just headlines relative to the happenings in the world now, only the time and places are changed. They can be narrated or superimposed by teletype letters. In order to insure fast action, two similar "screens" could be used.*)
HANNA: Can't you get something better?
KARIN: I'm trying.
HANNA: Try harder!
KARIN: (*switches the stations once more.*)

COMMENTATOR: We are listening to the latest work by the Bushmen composer, Wauchaubum, which will be played tonight by the author on the Satan's organ at Beethoven Auditorium. During Wauchaubum's last concert in Vienna, the public expressed its delight by breaking two of his ribs and fracturing his skull. In spite of the brain damage he suffered...

HANNA: Enough of medicine!

KARIN: (*switches to another station.*)

2nd COMMENTATOR: Arriving in our city this morning was Mr. Hopalong who is the world champion in the backward jump. We proudly salute him and wish the best of luck in trying to improve his record in our stadium. This new sport star...

HANNA: Enough of astronomy!

KARIN: But there's nothing else... (*Switches station.*)

COMMENTATOR: And now to our national news. In its last session, the Council of Ministers, appointed Mr. Jonathan Sims as the new police inspector.

HANNA: Finally.

COMMENTATOR: The new police inspector has honored us with his presence and will make the following statement:

SIMS: (*his still picture on the screen.*) I have decided to radically change the methods of the police and to adapt them to demands. In the future we shall keep ourselves ahead of the crimes so they can't happen at all.

HANNA: Do you understand that?

KARIN: No.

SIMS: With this ingenious formula, I have abolished the prejudice that was obsolete for so long. In the future we will not be prevented to use prisons as nursery schools and the nursery schools as homes for beggars.

HANNA: He bores me with his prisons and beggars.

KARIN: (*switches the station.*)

2nd COMMENTATOR: We interrupt our program to inform you about the greatest science sensation of today: Professor Christopher starts an expedition into the Northern Mountains. Our special correspondent will have a full report on... (*Picture continues without sound which is turned off by KARIN as soon as HANNA talks.*)

HANNA: That can not be! Without my knowing it? The professor seems to have forgotten that my father is the secretary of the Science Academy.

KARIN: (*shrugs her shoulders and turns up the volume.*)

2nd COMMENTATOR: ... however due to the unfortunate situation created by the crossing of the North African mule with the Dutch cow, we should not expect a rise in milk prices for more than ten percent...

HANNA: Get something more on Christopher!

KARIN: (*switches stations.*)

COMMENTATOR: Professor Christopher has planned this expedition for a long time. The esteemed professor, the highest authority in mineralogy today, is very much interested in abberations of the magnetic pole and is convinced that this expedition will supply all sciences with invaluable facts. Professor Christopher has petitioned the government six times for financial aid. Not long ago the Council of Ministers considered this petition once more and, due to a memorandum from the Science Academy, rejected it completely. It is interesting to note that the memorandum contained only two points: 1) the organization of such an expedition would take ten years; and 2) such an expedition can be organized only by the Science Academy that unites all sciences in a concentric complex of knowledge.

HANNA: What does that mean in our language?

KARIN: (*who has turned off the volume.*) It means the Academy is standing in its place like a rock and doesn't want anybody to meddle in its affairs.

HANNA: I told the professor to be friendly with the Academy. But he's so obstinate, and now he'll lose his job!

KARIN: He doesn't care about the job.

HANNA: But the salary?

KARIN: Nothing is ever left over from it.

HANNA: Because he throws every cent of it into his laboratory...

COMMENTATOR: But destiny kept its biggest surprise for that moment when the professor needed it the most. The same day he received the letter from the government telling about the rejection of his petition, another letter came from the inheritance court stating that an old case has been decided in Christopher's favor. In a few days he'll be eighty thousand dollars richer. (*Karin switches the volume off.*)

HANNA: What? He finally got the money!

KARIN: So they say.

HANNA: In that case, my father can't grumble any longer about Christopher not being able to support a wife.

KARIN: Today the professor is the most eligible bachelor on the market.

HANNA: He belongs tc me! He has visited me once a week; and these visits were scheduled for a whole year in advance. But he always brings violets, never a bouquet of noble roses. That, as father says, is below my dignity. And last week he didn't come at all!

KARIN: I'm sure he'll be here today.

HANNA: Never be sure about a man, especially if he's a professor.

KARIN: He'll bring you a bunch of roses, so big his assistant will have to carry it.

HANNA: Ah, his assistant! Christopher knows very well that I hate that sneering man, yet he can't spend a minute without him. I'm afraid that even on our wedding night he won't be able to manage without his assistant! But as soon as we're married I'll forbid this scoff to enter my house. You tell him that! No, I'll tell him myself! I think today I'll put on my yellow dress.

KARIN: I've laid it out in your bedroom

HANNA: Which earrings should I wear today? The pearls in platinum?

KARIN: No, today you should wear your amethysts.

HANNA: But they look cheap and remind me of violets.

KARIN: The professor is in love with your amethysts. He can't take his eyes off them. Didn't he once tell you that they were the most beautiful crystals he's ever seen?

HANNA: Then, amethysts it will be. I'm going to change.

(*KARIN turns on the volume. HANNA stops to listen.*)

COMMENTATOR: During the last interview professor Christopher stated very energetically that he has not changed his idea to explore the Northern Massif, and he'll do it this very summer. The esteemed scientist said very resolutely that he has no need for private or government contributions. He has enough of his own in order to organize the expedition.

HANNA: How? With the eighty thousand?

KARIN: Maybe something will be left over...

HANNA: Something! But he swore to me that we would be married as soon as the inheritance came through. And now he'll throw his money in the Northern Mountains! That's how much my happiness means to him. I'll never forgive him for it! Never! At least, not soon. When he comes tell him that I'm not at home. No, tell him I'm home, but don't wish to see him! No, better make him wait for a whole hour!

KARIN: But if he doesn't wait?

HANNA: Then let him in immediately... I'm going to change.

(*Exits.*)

KARIN: (*arranges the room. The door bell rings. She exits into the ante-room and lets in a visitor.*) Mr. Inspector. Please come in!

SIMS: Thank you, thank you.

KARIN: You were not expected, but please come in. May I take this opportunity to congratulate you on your new position.

SIMS: Thank you, thank you... Are you expecting someone else? Professor Christopher?

KARIN: Mr. Inspector shouldn't ask what he already knows. And he knows everything.

SIMS: Thank you, thank you. Why does the professor come here so often?

KARIN: Mr. Inspector knows why, therefore, any explanation is unnecessary.

SIMS: Now there's a good quality that one encounters nowadays as seldom as a timely paid bill. Where are you going?

KARIN: To announce you, Mr. Inspector.

SIMS: Thank you, thank you. But I would like to exchange a few words with you alone.

KARIN: Thank you.

SIMS: Tell me, what kind of person is the professor?

KARIN: A nice person.

SIMS: I don't want your personal opinion, please. I'd like to know what you think about the wild rumors that are going around. Everybody talks, you know, about the professor going North to look for gold.

KARIN: The professor knows what he's doing.

SIMS: I'm sure of that. But I'd like to know what he thinks. It's very peculiar that he has never mentioned a word about the goldmines. His assistant spreads the rumors. I'm interested in knowing whether the professor believes these rumors. At this time I don't want to start an official inquiry. That's why I'm talking to you. Don't you talk to the professor sometimes?

KARIN: I would, but he only talks with stones.

SIMS: You mean, about stones?

KARIN: With and about.

SIMS: Does he talk about gold?

KARIN: Yes.

SIMS: What does he say?

KARIN: That it's a heavy yellowish metal; does not corrode in acids; therefore, is very valuable and irreplaceable in many manufacturing processes.

SIMS: Thank you, thank you. I'm looking for the truth. Do you remember how the professor once started to ask for donations? That proves he needed money for his expedition. I saw at once that it would fail. Luckily nobody donated, and the police had no reason to stop this affair. But now, because of the rumors about the goldmines, I hear he is getting plenty of donations.

KARIN: It's understandable. But it is certainly only paper money.

SIMS: Legally it's the same. But I have to ask you one more question.

KARIN: In a minute, please. First, let me announce you. Miss Hanna heard the bell, and she's not used to waiting so long. (*Exits.*)

SIMS: (*left alone he can't resist his professional weakness. He inspects the coffee cup and the lipstick on it with a magnifying glass. He looks at the spoon. From a corner of the sofa pulls out a bra, bashfully hides it again. Under the sofa he finds a fragment of a rock and investigates it very carefully. The door bell rings, and he hides the fragment in his pocket, but forgets the magnifying glass on the table.*)

KARIN: (*returns.*) Miss Hanna is waiting.

SIMS: Thank you, thank you. (*Arranges his necktie, nobly starts to go, then turns back.*) I consider it my duty to tell you that thirty-six seconds ago the door bell rang twice very briefly and abruptly. It means that a nervous person is standing outside.

KARIN: Thank you. (*SIMS exits.*)

KARIN: (*has opened the door.*) Mr. Professor! Good morning! The same to you, Mr. Assistant. May I take your hat, Mr. Professor? Your gloves, Mr. Assistant? Thank you! Please enter.

ASSIST: Talk less and not so loud, Karin! The professor just entered the third circle of concentration.

KARIN: Don't frighten a weak woman! I sensed something like that. But what is this?

ASSIST: (*shows her a bunch of roses.*) What does your nose tell you?

KARIN: Twenty cents a piece!

ASSIST: Thirty.

KARIN: Then I must announce you immediately! (*Exits.*)

ASSIST: That's it, Christopher! Wouldn't it be wiser to leave you alone with your misfortune? I can't understand why I should be here.

CHRIS: It's safer with two.

ASSIST: For over a year now you've been teaching your future wife the elements of mineralogy, and still she can't distinguish between marl and gneiss. Why do you need an assistant? I'll wait for you downstairs.

CHRIS: You'll stay right here!

ASSIST: I could play Chinese checkers with Karin while you discuss your marriage.

CHRIS: Who's Karin?

ASSIST: The maid who let us in.

CHRIS: Is she suitable for such a pastime?

ASSIST: More suitable than Miss Hanna for your pastime. Ssh! Here she comes. Soon she'll invite you into the guest room, but will entertain

me here by herself.
CHRIS: Give me the flowers. Take the paper off them...
KARIN: Mr. Professor...
CHRIS: Right away!
KARIN: Miss Hanna asks you...
CHRIS: I'm coming, I'm coming.
KARIN: ... to wait.
CHRIS: Wait?
KARIN: She has a visitor in there, and he might stay for quite a while. I hope you won't have to wait more than an hour. Please sit down. Make yourself at home. (*Awkward silence.*) Here's an ash tray, in case you want to smoke. It's a beautiful morning. Would you like the window open? (*Silence. KARIN tries hard to humor them.*) Would you like to read the newspapers? There's a whole column about you... a picture too... A very good picture... I'll find it for you...
CHRIS: Tell that magpie to be quiet!
KARIN: I understand Mr. Professor is not satisfied with me. I don't know how to talk to gentlemen... And now Mr. Professor looks at me in such a way that I wish I could crawl in a hole... But I have to stay here.
CHRIS: No tears, please! Go away!
ASSIST: Try to understand and forgive him, Karin. This situation is unbearable to the professor.
KARIN: I understand. It's unbearable for me too. But what can I do?
ASSIST: Leave us alone.
KARIN: Please. I'd like nothing better. But I can't go.
ASSIST: Why not?
KARIN: Miss Hanna sent me to entertain the professor until she'll be able to receive him... That's why I have to stay. But Mr. Professor won't talk to me... He doesn't even look at me... How can I entertain him?
CHRIS: What? Did you hear that, Mr. Assistant? She sends her maid to entertain me! A maid! As if I've come to sell vacuum cleaners or repair refrigerators. To entertain me! Ah! (*Sits on sofa. Takes out a handkerchief and dries his forehead. In doing so he drops a fragment of rock.*)
ASSIST: Your presence makes Mr. Professor nervous. Have some respect for his suffering and go away.
KARIN: I'm going. But Mr. Professor dropped something. I'll pick it up.
CHRIS: Give it to me!
KARIN: Right away. Just let me look at it for a second.
CHRIS: You like it?

KARIN: It's like a work of art. These reddish lines interchanging with the olive green... they look like an April-evening sky...

CHRIS: Good comparison, hmm... It shows you can sense the soul of a mineral. Do you know the name of this stone?

KARIN: It's a gneiss.

CHRIS: And what is a gneiss?

KARIN: Gneiss is... a coarse-grained, metamorphic rock... resembling granite, consisting of alternating layers of different minerals...

CHRIS: Right. And further?

KARIN: Such as feldspar, quartz, mica, and...

CHRIS: And?

KARIN: ... hornblende, and...

CHRIS: (*looks at his assistant, astonished*)

KARIN: ... the structure might be granular or conglomerate.

CHRIS: I'm surprised for the first time in my life, I think. And this man tried to persuade me that all women are the same. But please tell me, Miss, how do you know so much about mineralogy?

KARIN: Mr. Professor usually tells Miss Hanna about it.

CHRIS: And you remembered it? In that case I'll give you my *Handbook in Mineralogy* as a present.

KARIN: Thank you Mr. Professor, but I already have it.

CHRIS: But do you read it too?

KARIN: Everyday. And nights I keep it under my pillow.

CHRIS: You didn't have to buy my book. You could have asked me for a copy.

KARIN: I didn't buy it. Miss Hanna gave the copy you sent her on her last birthday.

CHRIS: So, so... I am happy that my book has landed in good hands. Please, don't stand. Don't be afraid to sit beside me. There's enough room here. Please! You are not like other women. What's your name?

KARIN: Karin.

CHRIS: Karin. A nice name. Have you lived here long?

KARIN: Yes, Mr. Professor. I always open the door when you ring the bell. I am the maid.

CHRIS: Yes. I knew you. I just couldn't remember where I'd seen you before. Sit down. I'll entertain you. Here's a magnifying glass. Take it and look at that stone. Its formation is sedimentary, therefore, it is a paragneiss.

ASSIST: (*jumps up*) What?!!! Don't listen to nonsense, Karin. From the first glimpse I could tell it's a pure orthoclase.

CHRIS: One should not wonder about his peculiar conclusions. He could mix up a gneiss with a vulgar silicate.

ASSIST: But yesterday when I said it's a paragneiss, you insisted upon orthoclase.

CHRIS: That was yesterday. Last night I couldn't sleep. I thought it over and came to the conclusion that you were right. You see, Karin, orthoclase developed at the time the rocks were in liquid form. While they cooled...

ASSIST: She's not interested in that.

KARIN: I'm very interested.

CHRIS: I brought this little fragment here for Hanna to see. My greatest love is quartzites. In those the quartz granules are bound together by secondary quartz in contrast to simple sandstone where the bounding agent is opal.... As you may know, the quartzite family is very large, therefore, I carry only the latest samples because I enjoy looking at them anywhere—while riding the bus or even at the dinner table. If you would visit me at home, I'd show you a very complete quartzite collection.

KARIN: I accept the invitation.

CHRIS: But there is something I can show you right here. This, as you see, is pure quartz, the aristocrat of minerals. Noble and cool, a ray of light shines through it without touching it. This blueish pink...

KARIN: Like a violet breaking into blossom is amethyst. I can feel its fragrance.

CHRIS: Yes. And here is a beautiful crystal in which you can see something like frozen smoke signals. Do you know its name?

KARIN: Yellow topaz.

CHRIS: Right! This black one is morion, or, as Pliny called it, mormorion. This pink fragment I got from Finland, this dark red came yesterday from Spain. And this yellow one with silver lining is aventurine.

KARIN: How they glitter and shine together!

CHRIS: Like your eyes, Karin.

ASSIST: Congratulations, Karin!

ASSIST: The professor already knows your name by heart. Until now he got excited only over minerals. Now he adds your eyes to them.

CHRIS: I just wanted to say that Karin is the first woman whose eyes sparkle when she talks about minerals. And in her excitement she's even beautiful. Yes! She's the most beautiful woman I've ever seen!

KARIN: Not so fast, Mr. Professor. You haven't given me time to blush.

ASSIST: And five minutes ago you called her a magpie.

CHRIS: What? I don't believe you, though I remember using such a word. But then I was very angry. Look! I came to ask for a woman's hand

and she sends a maid to entertain me! Isn't that an insult? I was angry; and I am sorry I took my anger out on you. But I did not know you then. Now I don't know how to get out of this mess.

KARIN: This mess is buried and forgotten.

CHRIS: Then let's put these flowers on the grave.

KARIN: Should I take them to Miss Hanna now?

CHRIS: No. They are yours.

KARIN: Mr. Professor! I'm the maid.

CHRIS: If you aren't willing to accept them...

KARIN: Oh, I accept! Yes! I just don't know how to thank you.

ASSIST: Don't rush your gratitude, Karin. Give the professor enough time to come to his senses. Let him figure out what he'll have for Hanna if he gives these roses to you.

CHRIS: I've thought about that too. You'll run downstairs to get more roses.

ASSIST: All I have is enough money for the bus.

CHRIS: That's enough. There's a girl on the corner with violets. Buy a bunch as usual.

KARIN: God, save us!

ASSIST: If Karin would be more reasonable than women usually are, she would refuse the roses...

CHRIS: What's given, is given.

ASSIST: But if she does not take them?

KARIN: Why won't she?

CHRIS: Don't stall. Hanna might call for me right away and I wouldn't even have violets to give her.

ASSIST: I'm going. I just wish I didn't have to come back.
    (Exits.)

CHRIS: Karin, keep an eye on that man from the window. I'm afraid he'll really run away.

KARIN: If he does not come back with violets, I'll help you out with my roses... Shouldn't I open the window?

CHRIS: Maybe you'd better. The air seems quite heavy in here.

KARIN: Really? I'm sorry!

CHRIS: Not really. Actually it's another thing.

KARIN: Aren't you well?

CHRIS: Everything is new to me, you understand? I've never proposed before.

KARIN: I understand you perfectly. Nobody has proposed to me either.

CHRIS: Our destinies are very similar. But I don't know how I should behave.

KARIN: Neither do I.

CHRIS: Have you read novels that tell about similar situations?

KARIN: Yes! The hero presents the lady with flowers and says something like: Dear Miss Hanna, make me happy by accepting these roses that glow like...

CHRIS: ... the rubies of Transvaal and that smell as sweet as carbonic...

KARIN: No! Better not say that. Try to dispense with chemistry.

CHRIS: But in case they are violets?

KARIN: Then find another comparison.

CHRIS: Should I fall on my knees?

KARIN: It would be a good effect. But on one knee. And then you have to say: Dear Miss Hanna, be my wife. When she hears that she'll be perplexed... for a while... then she'll flush up to the ears... you have to wait till her confusion is over. Then she'll put her arms around your neck...

(*They act out what they are saying.*)

CHRIS: I imagined something like that. But now the solemn feeling is gone. I've lost my temper and can't find it again. I'm sure Miss Hanna insults me intentionally. I'm not as stupid as I look, though I am a professor. I thought it over, it's better for you to keep the roses. It would look suspicious if I gave them to Hanna. Violets are more ordinary flowers. Where does that idler keep himself?

KARIN: He is still talking to the violet girl. It looks like he's bargaining.

CHRIS: He should be ashamed!

KARIN: Maybe he wants to buy the violets and still be able to pay the bus fare.

CHRIS: He's saving for the expedition.

KARIN: When will it begin?

CHRIS: We must start without delay, because we have to walk five hundred miles from any civilized place and carry all supplies on our backs. There are no roads, no paths. It would be a catastrophe if the rains would start early in the fall.

KARIN: Why?

CHRIS: We have to cross ninety-six mountain streams, maybe more, because the maps are still very primitive. In the summer the streams are dry, but in the fall they turn into billowy rivers over which only birds can fly. If we have to stay there over the winter, we'll freeze to death.

KARIN: You'll have to take fur coats with you.

CHRIS: Who'll carry them?

KARIN: How many are there in the expedition?

CHRIS: My assistant and I.

KARIN: Only two?

CHRIS: Yes, one and one is two. I could not find anybody else who'd risk his life. At the beginning there were two academicians, but they insisted upon stretchers, mosquito nets, a learned cook, and many other things. I could not promise such things, so they resigned.

KARIN: Who'll cook for you?

CHRIS: We'll take only biscuits with us. We'll find fish and partridges there.

KARIN: They have to be cooked in order to be swallowed. I doubt if your assistant or you can cook.

CHRIS: I doubt it too... Where is my assistant?

KARIN: He's coming.

ASSIST: Here's your proposal bouquet, Professor. Please accept it. It's the cheapest I could get. I used ninety per-cent of my eloquence in order to get five cents off the price. I have done my duty honorably, please don't count on me in the future. Good-by!

SIMS: (*enters and stiffly greets the gentlemen*) Miss Hanna requests Professor Christopher to enter if he happens to be here.

CHRIS: Yes, I happen to be here.

SIMS: I regret not having had the opportunity to know you better—as well as the fact that I don't have time now.

CHRIS: As far as I'm concerned, I regret neither the first nor the second.

SIMS: I'm sure such an opportunity will come. But, before you leave, please return my magnifying glass that you just put into your pocket. I am a criminal inspector, and this thing is a tool of my trade.

CHRIS: With your permission, I'm a geology professor, and I can use this glass myself.

SIMS: But it's mine.

CHRIS: To prove the fallacy of your argument, I will take it out of my pocket.

SIMS: You just put it in there.

CHRIS: But did not take it out of yours.

SIMS: I left the glass on the table and you appropriated it while I was with Miss Hanna.

CHRIS: Did you come on official business?

SIMS: I don't have to answer that.

CHRIS: But you'll have to answer other questions. Let us assume you lost this glass and I found it. In that case you have to describe the lost object.

SIMS: It magnifies three and a half times.

CHRIS: What else?

SIMS: It can be held in my hand...

CHRIS: In which one?

174

SIMS: Both.

CHRIS: Wrong. It can be held by only one hand.

SIMS: First in one hand, then in the other; I did not express myself very precisely.

CHRIS: And you insist you are a criminal inspector?

SIMS: I refuse to answer any further questions. But I categorically insist that you appropriated my property which is indispensable to me in fulfilling responsible tasks. To take possession unlawfully is a criminal case. Such an attempt can be prosecuted.

ASSIST: Let me see the glass, Professor. (*Examines the glass.*) Sorry, but it's not yours.

CHRIS: What do you mean?

ASSIST: I know yours very well; you appropriated it from me.

SIMS: Very interesting.

ASSIST: Mr. Inspector, it was a misunderstanding, and this tool of the trade goes back to its lawful master. Here!

SIMS: I don't see why I should thank you for it.

CHRIS: And I don't see why I should remain here any longer. We'll discuss this happening some other time.
(*Exits.*)

SIMS: I'm sure of that.

ASSIST: He'll forget it in two minutes.

SIMS: But I won't!

ASSIST: Insulted, Mr. Inspector?

SIMS: My position forbids me to be insulted. But this incident is very indicative. Does this professor call things that belong to others his own very often?

ASSIST: Very often.

SIMS: Thank you. That is interesting.

ASSIST: This time it was a trifle. I would not be surprised to hear the professor call your wife his and *vice versa*.

SIMS: I am not married.

ASSIST: But it can happen, to you as well as to him.

SIMS: Only to one of us.

ASSIST: It was only a comparison.

SIMS: Not very well made, though.

ASSIST: But right to the point.

SIMS: Mr. Assistant, I don't like impudent people, but you are an exception.

ASSIST: Please forgive me, but I can't say the same about you!

SIMS: Thank you, thank you. You are lifting your nose too high too soon. You haven't found the goldmines yet.

ASSIST: Mr. Professor is searching for them this very instant.

SIMS: (*bows deeply*) I understand you perfectly.

ASSIST: (*returns the bow*) It's mutual.

KARIN: (*enters hastily*) Your hat and gloves, Mr. Professor!

CHRIS: (*hastily*) We have to run in order to catch our bus.

HANNA: (*follows them both. Throws the violets at the professor.*) Run, Professor, run! Take the bouquet with you; you can present it to the next woman. You can present them to my maid, if you wish.

ASSIST: I better take them back to the violet girl.

HANNA: Mr. Assistant is here too?

ASSIST: Why not? I did not have the chance to extend my greetings...

HANNA: Now you have a perfect chance to say good-by.

ASSIST: I'll use it immediately. I have the honor!

HANNA: (*sees the roses*) Professor, wait! Please! I acted too hastily. What about those roses?

KARIN: Mr. Professor brought them.

HANNA: How sweet and fresh they smell! As if they had budded this very instant. Why didn't you bring them to me at once? I know that the actions of our professor are quite peculiar and always end in misunderstandings. Dear Professor, I beg your forgiveness for my sluggish maid's actions!... You don't answer? Alright, I beg forgiveness in place of my maid!

CHRIS: Miss Karin needs no forgiveness. She acted correctly. She kept the roses because I gave them to her.

SIMS: Ah!

CHRIS: Point well made, Mr. Inspector. Miss Hanna will repeat it presently with two exclamation signs.

HANNA: Ah!!

CHRIS: Thank you, and good-bye.

HANNA: You will regret this visit, Professor Christopher!

CHRIS: I've regretted it already!

HANNA: You have made me a laughingstock in my own house, not only in front of my friends but also my maid. I am not used to such things.

CHRIS: I am not used to being slapped, even by the daughter of the Science Academy's Secretary.

HANNA: Nobody saw it!

SIMS: It's an important circumstance.

KARIN: I saw it.

HANNA: You snake in the skin of a woman! I give you five minutes to get your things. I'll pay you off! I don't want to see you anymore. I don't want to see anybody! Out all of you! Out! Out! Out!

SIMS: I can't leave you alone in such a state of mind. May I stay and

comfort you?
HANNA: You may...(*Both exit.*)
CHRIS: I'm sorry for this inconvenience, Karin.
KARIN: I'm only sorry that you won't be able to inconvenience me anymore, Mr. Professor.
ASSIST: We leave in a few days.
CHRIS: I hope to see you again, Karin.
KARIN: One more thing, please.
CHRIS: Yes?
KARIN: Do you have place in your expedition for any more?
CHRIS: For as many as wish.
ASSIST: Who wants to join us?
KARIN: I do.

SCENE II

The Northern Massif. Nothing but stones. The rock is covered with snow in places. The snow changes its color from time to time from red to blue and purple. There is something unreal in the sunlight. Time: around midnight. A tent near a big rock.
CHRIS: (*sits on a rock, breaks stone fragments with a hammer and scrutinizes them through a magnifying glass.*)
ASSIST: (*has a stick in the ground. Looks at his watch and the shadow cast by the stick.*)
KARIN: (*enters from upstage, sees both men, rubs her eyes in wonder, then goes to the campfire and throws some sticks and grass she has gathered onto the fire.*)
CHRIS: You've been away a long time, Karin. It will soon be midnight.
KARIN: I've had to walk around for miles in order to find some kindling wood. The only wood I've found looks more like grass than bush.
CHRIS: *Betula nana.*
KARIN: You can't make fire with a Latin name. In the future we'll eat raw patridges and the fish will be smoked in the wind.
CHRIS: Your imagination expresses itself in a search for new ideas.
KARIN: My duty is to keep us at least half alive as long as possible. On our way back each of us will have to carry about half a ton of rocks.
CHRIS: At least!

177

KARIN: And five hundred miles!

CHRIS: Even more if we get lost.

KARIN: And it's certain we'll get lost. This area is cursed. Even the rocks move from one place to another.

CHRIS: What are you talking about?

KARIN: I shouted and screamed for help. Why didn't you shout back?

CHRIS: We heard nothing.

ASSIST: Why did you scream for help?

KARIN: I was lost. Although I kept my eyes upon this rock all the time, I got lost. I knew I hadn't walked far. I screamed so you could hear me. When you didn't answer I thought I was lost and would perish here alone. I walked and walked, until my strength was gone. I decided to climb a little hill and die on top of it. And there you were. Still I'm not sure that you are where I see you.

CHRIS: All of us here fight with hallucinations. But if you think that I am a hallucination, I protest.

KARIN: Then tell me what's happening around here.

CHRIS: It's simple. We haven't eaten regularly for four weeks. We have not slept either. How could we with the sun in our eyes at midnight? That's the reason for the nightmares when we're awake. You see things where they aren't. This is an entirely different world we're in now.

KARIN: Could we have stepped into the other world?

ASSIST: By Jove, I've had this suspicion for quite a while.

CHRIS: You better keep quiet and pay attention to the points of culmination. You can't stick a pin in the sky as easy as in your drawing. The day before yesterday you mixed up the zenith with the azimuth. Yesterday you drew the meridian right where the local parallel goes. I'm anxious to know what you will do today.

ASSIST: The day before yesterday I made a mistake, but only between the upper and the lower culminations. Let us not talk about yesterday. There was no sun by which I could have proven my...

CHRIS: ...mistake.

ASSIST: No, by devil! My computations have always been right. The mistake is someplace else.

CHRIS: Where, for instance?

ASSIST: In your compass.

CHRIS: Our compasses were tested in the laboratory of magnetophysics. It was done by a professor who is the best authority on such matters, not to mention the fact that he's my friend. Are you suggesting he does not know how to test a compass?

ASSIST: Are you suggesting that I don't know the difference between a meridian and a parallel?

CHRIS: It looks that way. How else can we explain what has happened to us the last three days?

ASSIST: The explanation is simple: the devil is in our company.

CHRIS: There is no such thing in physics.

ASSIST: But he's here! Certainly incognito. He's hiding behind an assumed name.

CHRIS: As soon as we reach home I will examine your mental capacity.

KARIN: If we ever reach home. I don't doubt it anymore; the devil haunts us.

CHRIS: What? You too believe in ghosts?

KARIN: I believe what I see.

CHRIS: Did you see a ghost?

KARIN: Yes.

CHRIS: Maybe it was the devil himself?

KARIN: Maybe.

CHRIS: When did you see it?

KARIN: Just a while ago.

CHRIS: Where?

KARIN: Down there.

CHRIS: Are you sure about it?

KARIN: Are you sure that, except for us, there are no beings around that look like humans?

CHRIS: I am sure there are none.

KARIN: But I just saw one. He crawled between the rocks, and he followed me. When I looked at him, he stopped and changed into a rock. Very sly! But I noticed that craftiness at once. I pretended that I was looking in another direction. Then, suddenly, I turned my head, and there he was. But as soon as he saw me looking at him, he turned into a stone.

CHRIS: Is that all?

KARIN: You are impatient! I almost died of fear, and it's nothing to you. (*Takes a fragment from her pocket.*) Then is this nothing to you also?

CHRIS: What is it?

KARIN: A rock. From looking at it one would say it is a gray granite.

CHRIS: That gray granite is all around us. Why did you bring it here?

KARIN: Because it seems to be much heavier than it should be.

CHRIS: Let me see it.

KARIN: That's why I brought it here. Do you recognize it?

CHRIS: I think so.

KARIN: What is it?

CHRIS: Ore. Iron ore with a very high metal percentage, at least eighty.

Is that all you found?

KARIN: Eighty percent, and you are not satisfied! How much did you want?

CHRIS: I am not interested in ore. Everybody knows of its presence here. I've seen such fragments before.

KARIN: But it's a fortune!

CHRIS: (*throws the fragment away*) It's nothing. The ore here can be found in small quantities and is not worth exploiting.

KARIN: And you simply throw it away.

CHRIS: What else should I do? Do you want it as a souvenir? No? Then I will put it in my pocket as a present from you. Thank you! You feel insulted? You are getting nervous. You should sleep more. Take a look at the assistant. He sleeps while researching. I also would like to take a nap...if only the sun wouldn't shine straight in my face.

KARIN: I'm really tired. (*Sits down at the campfire and tries to sleep.*)

CHRIS: Try to rest a while. I'll stop hammering and work with the glass.

KARIN: Just a short while.

CHRIS: (*investigating a mineral fragment leans against a rock. The rock starts to move. CHRIS pulls himself away, but due to his amazement forgets to stand up. The rock stands up and it is half human—the TROLL.*)

TROLL: Get up! Tell me what right do you have to gad about here? Not enough work down there?

CHRIS: Please. I expect more courtesy! Better tell me why you gad about here.

TROLL: I live here.

CHRIS: And I am visiting here, as your guest.

TROLL: An unwanted guest.

CHRIS: For an unkind host all guests are unwanted.

TROLL: If you had come alone, but you've brought a whole group with you. No peace here anymore. A while ago that woman screamed with a voice that stuffed my ears forever.

CHRIS: It was you who ran after that girl? Shame on you! At your age...

TROLL: I did not expect her to be so naughty.

CHRIS: What are you doing here?

TROLL: I'm guarding the stones. And you?

CHRIS: I'm looking for them.

TROLL: A thief.

CHRIS: I think I'd better wake up the others so you can get put in your place.

TROLL: I don't need to be put in my place.

CHRIS: What do you actually want?

TROLL: Return that stone you just put into your pocket.

CHRIS: Do you need it?

TROLL: I need it.

CHRIS: Why?

TROLL: I have to watch that everything stays exactly as it was before you came.

CHRIS: But now I'll keep it because you are impolite.

TROLL: Give it back without a fight.

CHRIS: I'll keep it!

TROLL: I repeat once more. You will not carry this fragment with you.

CHRIS: I'll do exactly that. And not only this fragment, but the whole heap.

TROLL: You'll ruin me!

CHRIS: So what?

TROLL: So what? For one hundred million years I guarded my stones. Suddenly a spook comes and says, "So what?" No, mister, not I, but you'll be ruined. And I'll still be here when your town is nothing but dust.

CHRIS: Be arrogant, but don't shout.

TROLL: For the last time I am telling you. Not a stone will be carried away from here. You heard my warning. If you still try to take what's mine, you'll be ruined.

CHRIS: Now you are threatening me quite disrespectfully. I better show you who I am.

TROLL: A city spook!

CHRIS: I'll put some respect into you. I'll grab you and shake the arrogance out of your guts. (*Tries to catch the TROLL, but misses.*)

TROLL: Caught the wind?

CHRIS: Quite dodgy, aren't you? But I'm the best fencer in the country, and you'll see what I mean. (*Knocks himself against a rock.*)

TROLL: Didn't you want to catch me?

CHRIS: Just a little error on my part. But now I know your war ruse, and you won't get away anymore. One, two, and...I've got you! (*He's caught his assistant.*) Now we'll see who's the master!

ASSIST: Help! I'm being strangled!

CHRIS: I'll kill you without any help, you shameless ball of tatters.

ASSIST: He'll kill me. Help me, Karin!

KARIN: Professor Christopher!

CHRIS: (*as if just awakened. Looks from one to the other.*)

KARIN: Why did you strangle the poor man?

CHRIS: I just wanted to wake him up. He has to watch the culmination, but he's sleeping.

ASSIST: Was I really asleep? (*Looks at his watch.*) But I'm not late for the culmination. It'll be here in a few minutes.

CHRIS: When it comes send it away again. We won't need it anymore.

KARIN: What does that mean?

CHRIS: That we are going home immediately...before we've lost our senses completely. To tell the truth, I'm disappointed in this expedition. We've found nothing unexpected.

KARIN: But the iron ore?

CHRIS: It is scientifically and practically insignificant. The iron ore deposits here are sporadical. Unless these deposits would reach millions of tons...

ASSIST: I've got it!

CHRIS: Again? What did you catch now?

ASSIST: The meridian.

CHRIS: Let it loose and dismantle the tent. We are leaving this very hour.

ASSIST: Good! But before we leave I'll force you to admit that my computations have been correct all the time. Come, check the situation. Don't use your compass! Here's my chronometer. It's exactly twelve o'clock. Is it the same as yours?

CHRIS: Exactly.

ASSIST: So we can assume that the time is almost correct?

CHRIS: Not almost, but exactly.

ASSIST: In which culmination is the sun now?

CHRIS: In the lower, if you don't mind.

ASSIST: I don't mind.

CHRIS: But it's unimportant; both culminations are above the horizon.

ASSIST: Do we agree that it is midnight?

CHRIS: Do you test me in elementary cosmography?

ASSIST: Is my sextant on the meridian?

CHRIS: Any fool could see that.

ASSIST: Thank you! Now take your compass and check it once more.

CHRIS: You are unbelievably stubborn. Alright! I'll check it. (*Puts his compass down and indicates the needle in triumph. Suddenly realized that the needle is not parallel to the meridian.*)

ASSIST: Will you still insist that there's no devil in the compass?

KARIN: How does he manifest himself?

ASSIST: Yesterday the needle turned toward the East...

KARIN: And today?

CHRIS: Toward the West.

KARIN: Though scientifically this is incomprehensible, it's simple to me. Because I look only as far as I can see.

CHRIS: Are you trying to tell us that yesterday, when we were on the other hill, the needle did not indicate the East?

KARIN: It did not indicate the East.

CHRIS: Therefore, you say that today the needle does not indicate the West?

KARIN: No, it does not indicate West. All the time it indicates one and the same point.

CHRIS: And which point, if I may ask?

KARIN: There, that mountain.

CHRIS: Your empirical observations seem to be logical, but without a scientific basis. In order to turn the magnetic needle one should have an immensely huge metalic mass.

KARIN: In that case it is there. Maybe a million tons.

CHRIS: Karin! There must be hundreds of millions tons...at least!

SCENE III

A secret conference between the PRIME MINISTER, the SECRETARY of the Science Academy, and Inspector SIMS. A scribe sits beside the PRIME MINISTER.

PRIME MINISTER: With three strokes of this hammer I declare the conference open. Ladies and—no, only gentlemen! Although I just declared this conference open I have to emphasize that it is a closed and highly secret session. Because what we shall talk about is a matter of our conscience, nothing will be recorded. I feel heavy clouds thickening over my head. The primordial powers of the masses can throw the lightning at me any minute and smash our government to pieces. In order not to create panic I did not ask the ministers to attend this meeting, but only you, gentlemen, who I don't doubt will be able to endure the blows we might receive. Before I reach my decision I've also decided to consider your opinions. And I do it with sincere hope that you will take the most of my responsibility upon your shoulders. The events descend upon us like an avalanche, and, in case we cannot find other victims, it will break our own skulls. Mr. Criminal Inspector will inform us about this possibility. Will you speak?

SIMS: Thank you, thank you! Excellencies and gentlemen. I'll be concise, because conditions get more and more complicated. What might have seemed important half an hour ago, might be nothing in thirty minutes from now. The immediate conditions are known to everyone, although I doubt there are many who sense the real danger of implications. When Professor Christopher returned from his expedition, he and especially his two accomplices excited the whole country with fantastic news that threw the whole nation out of balance. It's not enough that the professor has given many interviews and has talked at many meetings—openly and secretly—he intends to go further. He is organizing a stock company, but he refuses to sell any stock to the government. Why is that? Although the geographical location of the ore deposits are not known to anybody, he promises fantastic dividends. Why? But I have the information that he gets unconditional offers in cash and securities. Why is that?

SECRETARY: Why do you always ask, "Why?"

SIMS: I'll go on asking, "Why?" Primarily, what has happened since the professor returned from the Northern Mountains? Our stable stock-market is shaky. Many mining companies stand with one foot over the abyss of bankruptcy. If they crash—and I'm certain they will—two hundred thousand workers will be without jobs and bread. Do you, gentlemen, understand what that means?

PRIME MIN: A revolution.

SIMS: Therefore, I ask: How far can it go? As a criminal inspector I don't have to bother with the economic stability, but I must watch that the chaos we anticipate is not used for private gain. And I have definite suspicion, that when a sufficient amount is collected, the professor will disappear in the jungles of South America as many swindlers did before I became inspector. And, because I fight crime before it even happens, I've ordered the professor to be isolated—in other words—arrested.

PRIME MIN: I think I shall have to thank you for the next interpellation by which the opposition will get the reins of the government.

SIMS: I am aware of the seriousness of the present situation, Excellency. That's why I asked you to look after it personally. If Professor Christopher is successful in his plan, you'll have to answer ten interpellations. He's waiting in the next room. I'll interrogate him in your presence, and all circumstances will be clear to you. You may then make the decision as to what to do next.

PRIME MIN: How kind you are to shift the responsibility to me!

SIMS: Somebody has to take it.

PRIME MIN: Then you take it!

SIMS: Thank you, thank you! But we are not dealing with ordinary crime. It concerns the whole nation. In order to take the responsibility I have to have your permission.

SECRETARY: But why do I have to be here? Do you want to give up the responsibility in my favor? Please, don't mix the Science Academy in this matter!

SIMS: We need an authority. And because I don't know anybody who is so learned as you...

SECRETARY: In that case, I'll stay.

SIMS: Thank you. Can we start?

PRIME MIN: Please.

SIMS: (*into microphone*) Show Professor Christopher in!

CHRIS: (*enters and observes coldly those present*)

SIMS: Please sit down!

CHRIS: I have been sitting for three days.

SIMS: To be more precise—seventy-one hours. I am permitted to keep you only seventy-two hours. Therefore, in an hour your state of isolation will end either by an arrest, and then you'll land in a prison, or by regaining your freedom.

CHRIS: Now you are talking sense. Therefore, I'll answer in the same manner—in an hour I'll regain my freedom and you'll land in a prison.

SIMS: Although it's against my principles, I'll give you some friendly advice. Don't insult me while I'm on official duty. Would you kindly answer some questions?

CHRIS: No!

SIMS: Does that mean you are not going to answer?

CHRIS: I'm going to answer, but not kindly! First I want to know on what grounds you keep me here. Do you have any evidence against me?

SIMS: I have no evidence, but I'm going to get it presently. If you would only help me a little...

CHRIS: With pleasure.

SIMS: Thank you, thank you. You still maintain having found ore deposits?

CHRIS: Yes.

SIMS: And is that ore of a high quality?

CHRIS: As I said before—at least with eighty percent metal.

SIMS: Did you have instruments with you by which you could determine the percentage?

CHRIS: No.

SIMS: How then did you determine it?

CHRIS: By the specific gravity of the ore.

SIMS: Did you determine the specific gravity with instruments?

CHRIS: No.

SIMS: But you determined it?

CHRIS: Yes, by the pressure the fragment of ore exercised upon the palm of my hand.

SIMS: Mr. Secretary, is it possible to determine the metalic contents in an ore by such a method?

SECRETARY: No.

CHRIS: I say yes! An expert geologist can do it by weighing the ore in his hand, at least approximately.

SIMS: But you did not say approximately.

CHRIS: Then I say it now.

SIMS: You also maintained that the quantity of ore in the deposits you've supposedly found reaches into the hundreds of millions of tons...

CHRIS: I still maintain it.

SIMS: Did you have drilling machinery with you that helped to estimate or trace the spread of the deposits?

CHRIS: No.

SIMS: Then how did you estimate the quantity?

CHRIS: By the intensity of the inclination of the magnetic needle in my compass in a given distance from the ore deposits.

SIMS: Mr. Secretary, is it possible to determine the quantity of ore in a deposit by such a procedure?

SECRETARY: No.

CHRIS: It is possible. Not precisely, perhaps, but certainly in approximation.

SIMS: You did not say in approximation before.

CHRIS: Then I say it now.

SIMS: Thank you. Can you indicate these deposits on a map?

CHRIS: No.

SIMS: Why not?

CHRIS: That area on geographical maps is nothing but a white speckle without any legend whatsoever.

SIMS: Didn't you prepare your own map?

CHRIS: Very carefully.

SIMS: Can you show us your map?

CHRIS: No.

SIMS: Why not?

CHRIS: I don't have it anymore.

SIMS: Where did you put it?

CHRIS: I lost it.

SIMS: What a pity! It was a very important document. Why were you so careless with it?

CHRIS: I kept it very carefully—in the inner pocket of my jacket. But we remained up there longer than expected. We were caught by the rainy season, and during our return trip we had to wade through many streams, often through water up to our armpits.

SIMS: In other words, the map got wet?

CHRIS: While crossing the streams I kept it over my head. But in a deep spot I stumbled, got under the water, and the map floated away.

SIMS: What a pity! It means that the ore deposits are lost forever?

CHRIS: On the next expedition I'll find them again.

SIMS: Are your two partners able to find them again?

CHRIS: They are able to, but they don't want to.

SIMS: Do you have special reasons for not revealing the place of the ore deposits to the government?

CHRIS: I have no reason to calm the curiosity of the government.

PRIME MIN: The government represents the country.

CHRIS: The country should not stick its nose into such matters.

PRIME MIN: The territory where you found the ore belongs to the state.

CHRIS: Then let the state exploit the deposits.

PRIME MIN: How can we exploit them not knowing where they are?

CHRIS: I know where they are.

PRIME MIN: You know, but won't reveal!

CHRIS: At the beginning it was my intention to find the treasure that belongs to the country so that the country could profit by it. But the country didn't allow me a cent to cover my expenses.

PRIME MIN: That's another matter.

CHRIS: Not to me, though. If the state wanted to profit, it had to take a

CHRIS: Not to me, though. If the state wanted to profit, it had to take a risk. Now, after I've risked alone, I'll keep the profit alone.

PRIME MIN: You'll have to share.

CHRIS: Certainly, but only with those who please me.

PRIME MIN: And the state will not be among them.

CHRIS: No.

PRIME MIN: It's a larceny! You rob from the state! I won't tolerate such things!

CHRIS: Mr. Prime Minister, if you are going to abuse our Constitution, tread upon it with your feet, I shall have to assume that you're a traitor to our nation, and I will have nothing to do with such.

PRIME MIN: What? I abuse our Constitution? Tread upon it with my feet? A traitor to our nation? Do you hear that? ... put it in the record, put it...(*The scribe starts writing.*)

SIMS: I'm sorry, your Excellency, please be reminded that, according to your order, this is a highly secret session and no records are kept.

CHRIS: You can consider yourself lucky, your Excellency. If such a record would exist you would have to exchange places with me in prison. The law states that in uninhabited districts the land belongs to everyone and all who care to make any use of it. Therefore, the moment I start to exploit the ore deposits, the surrounding land will belong to me. Certainly, the state can start the exploitation before I'm able to do so. Especially now, while I'm under arrest, it can easily be done.

PRIME MIN: He does not stop at insults; now he ridicules me. Therefore, I protest!

SIMS: Excellency, for the good of our cause, please sit down!

PRIME MIN: I'll try. But for the last time.

SIMS: Thank you. As we all know, the law is just, and this time it's on Professor Christopher's side.

CHRIS: Thank you, thank you!

PRIME MIN: The Parliament will repeal this law!

SIMS: The next session of Parliament will not start for five months. And until then the law is in force. Therefore, Mr. Professor, let us assume that the ore deposits will belong to you. But what then? Do you have the necessary capital?

CHRIS: I am looking for it.

SIMS: With any success?

CHRIS: It looks very bright.

SIMS: How much?

CHRIS: It's a secret.

SIMS: The security institutions can't accept the fact that you collect money for a venture that... that still hangs in the air.

CHRIS: The ore deposits don't hang in the air. They are in the ground.

SIMS: As far as I know, you've stated exactly the opposite: that you've found mountains of ore.

CHRIS: That's right.

SIMS: Does that not mean that the ore is above the ground?

CHRIS: Just partly. The main mass is in the ground.

SIMS: As far as this matter is concerned, I've asked for a report from authorities. Mr. Secretary, would you kindly proceed.

SECRETARY: The Science Academy in its last session discussed this matter and unanimously agreed that: 1) It has never been established that on this planet the deposits of iron ore would form mountains high above the sea level. It is understandable, because the layers that contain iron ore, due to their specific gravity, sank during the time our globe was in liquid state. Therefore, 2) in the Northern Massif such iron ore mountains can't exist.

SIMS: Thank you, thank you.

CHRIS: It's lucky that the existence of the iron ore mountains can't be influenced by the resolution of the Science Academy.

SIMS: But you have to prove it. You have to prove that such ore deposits as you describe them really exist. I am sure you brought some samples with you?

CHRIS: Certainly we took samples with us, and quite a lot.

SIMS: Could you hand these samples over for a scientific analysis.

CHRIS: No.

SIMS: Why not?

CHRIS: I don't have them anymore.

SIMS: What happened to them?

CHRIS: I lost them.

SIMS: All?

CHRIS: All. The last fragment.

SIMS: What a pity! Where did that happen?

CHRIS: While crossing the mountain streams we lost all of our bundles, one after the other. We saved our naked lives only.

SIMS: You want me to believe that?

CHRIS: If I had not saved my life, I would not be here and would not be able to talk this nonsense with you.

SIMS: Now you admit that you talk nonsense?

CHRIS: If you want to believe, do so, if not, no one is forcing you.

SIMS: Thank you. Would Mr. Professor be so kind as to wait in the next room until the end of this session?

CHRIS: With pleasure. Only may I point out that my seventy-second hour is coming to an end.

SIMS: Gentlemen, I think we heard enough to be able to evaluate the situation.

PRIME MIN: We heard barefaced impudence to which I'm not used to listening. This man is a swindler without shame.

SIMS: Or a shameless swindler.

PRIME MIN: He has found mountains of ore and wants to take them away from the state, and, on second thought—such mountains of ore don't even exist!

SIMS: That's exactly what I think.

SECRETARY: Certainly they don't exist in accordance with the Science Academy's report I had the honor to deliver.

SIMS: We cannot be sure the professor does or does not have the ore mountains, but we can be sure we are in trouble. In case he has the mountains and takes them away from the state right under its nose, the consequences will be scandalous.

PRIME MIN: In that case, my government will go down in history as the silliest political creation of all times.

SIMS: On the other hand, there may be no mountains of ore, and, in my opinion, based upon the report of the Science Academy, there are none. The professor could not give any proof. The simple reason he's "lost" it is too weak to hold up. Such cases are very common in criminal history. The uncommon thing, however, is that this affair has been splendidly started and we lack the means to stop it.

PRIME MIN: We appointed you as a criminal inspector and you have to stop it.

SIMS: But how? It's not possible. The only thing I could do was to isolate the professor for seventy-two hours. Now I have to release him.

SECRETARY: Why do you have to release him?

SIMS: Because the prosecutor's office won't give me a warrant of arrest without material evidence. And I don't have it. This swindler is so crafty that my men haven't been able to discover one instant when he had taken money from somebody. But I'm convinced he'll do it the moment we release him. He's so impudent, he doesn't even deny it. He's going to create a stock company through which the whole nation will become the owner of these ore mountains! Have you seen a man who's so stupid and thinks about the good of others without profit for himself?

PRIME MIN: There's no such man!

SIMS: I agree! But there's no law that forbids the establishment of stock companies either.

SECRETARY: That's good. You would have to imprison at least half of our nation if there were a law against stockholders.

PRIME MIN: And that's impossible. In such a case we would have to ask for a foreign loan. Where will we find an international bank which would advance money for the building of prisons?

SIMS: There are no such banks. Therefore, it's better to isolate one dangerous individual who's liable to put half of the nation in prison. I suspected Professor Christopher for a long time. Once he tried to steal my magnifying glass. Yes, the glass of a criminal inspector! And now he shows the tendency to enlarge his cleptomania to wider horizons. Now he wants to steal from the nation, from the state; and he'll do it while looking us straight into the eye.

SECRETARY: Oh, this mad professor!

SIMS: What did you say? Mad professor? Wait a minute, wait a minute! Such an outlook puts the matters in entirely different light. Cleptomania is not a criminal but a pathological phenomenon. Every normal human being has it in a light form, like the thyroid gland which becomes the symptom of a sickness only when enlarged. Cleptomania is not only a pathological, but a psychopathological occurrence that suggests a disturbance in one's mind. And when we analyze the actions of Professor Christopher in detail, we have to admit they are peculiar, not to say more. Would a man in his right mind propose to a lady and then give his bunch of roses to her maid? Would such a man use his whole inheritance to finance an expedition on which he has no hope to find iron ore, not to mention gold mines? What man in his right mind would revolt against the state in such an open manner as Professor Christopher does? And what man in his right mind would think about others while gaining nothing for himself? To sum up all these indications that compromise our suspect to the utmost, we have to come to the conclusion that Professor Christopher is... to put it mildly...

PRIME MIN: Mad!!

SIMS: Excellency, that wasn't I who said it. As a criminal inspector I need a doctor's certificate in order to repeat it in a form that would be legally appropriate. My duty is to see that the mental capacity of the professor is carefully tested. And, as I am always prepared for all possible emergencies, two orderlies were asked to wait in the same room with Professor Christopher. If Excellency has no objections...

PRIME MIN: None whatsoever. That's a perfect solution. The main thing is to give time to my government to consolidate the *status quo.* Mr. Inspector, please accept my gratitude in the name of the nation. Your fast and firm action saved the nation from disgrace and financial disaster. Furthermore, I'll order the Minister of the Interior to present you for a decoration.

SIMS: Thank you, thank you! I'm only doing my duty to the nation. Therefore, (*In microphone.*) will Professor Christopher kindly re-enter? Thank you. Gentlemen, as all suspicions of Professor Christopher are cleared away, he should be honored with our deepest sympathies.

CHRIS: (*enters*)

PRIME MIN: My apologies that a while ago I was worried too soon! Concerned with the security of the state I sometimes forget... yes, what do I forget? I am happy to say that we find you above all suspicions and that you are freed from your confinement.

SECRETARY: Professor Christopher, I attest that I consider you still my best friend, although I had to express the opinion of the Academy which is contrary to yours. As you know the scientific truth is merciless. Therefore, I hope you'll forgive me. (*CHRISTOPHER looks at the three with growing suspicion.*)

SIMS: I'm truly sorry about the misunderstanding that kept you in isolation for seventy-one hours and fifty-nine minutes; and now I will return to you the identification papers. Would you kindly sign here, certifying your release from confinement? (CHRIS *signs the paper, but while looking up, sees the two orderlies that have entered the room.*)

SIMS: Thank you, thank you. Now you are again a free and honorable citizen.

SECRETARY: From now on I'm sure the Academy will be able to mention your name with respect.

PRIME MIN: But, because the last events have asked a lot from your mental reserves, the state has granted you a free-of-charge sojourn in a rest home. A car is waiting for you at the door and these two gentlemen (*Both orderlies stand close to CHRISTOPHER.*) will guide you.

SCENE IV

(*The garden of an asylum for mentally ill. A sunny morning. In this garden nothing is normal. The blossoms on the bushes are oversize, the birds are singing in a rhythmic fashion as an invisible orchestra, the mad inhabitants of the asylum are walking in the garden half dancing to these rhythms. Unexpectedly the MANAGER of the asylum appears. He's a tiny man with a white goatee, dressed in black. Two stocky orderlies follow him in the distance. With his appearance everything suddenly changes. The sunshine disappears, the birds stop singing, and the madmen vanish. When this procession walks off, everything returns to "normal." The KING OF ALL MADMEN runs across the stage pulling with a string a bundle of old newspapers, growling madly. PROFESSOR CHRISTOPHER enters slowly and fearfully, sits down on a bench and breathes the fragrant air. The KING runs back growling. CHRISTOPHER, scared, hides himself behind the bench. For a while they observe each other distrustfully, CHRISTOPHER waves his hand, the KING answers in the same fashion. They move closer to each other, both prepared to run at any instant.*)

CHRIS: What do you have on the leash?

KING: If you take a look, you won't have to ask.

CHRIS: Because I'm blind, it seems it's a dog.

KING: A lion.

CHRIS: Right. I've never seen a lion, but recognized him from his mane at once. What's his name?

KING: Fifi. Spelled with two "r's"—the same as Mimi.

CHRIS: A terrific name. Doesn't he bite your legs?

KING: It seems you don't know to whom you are talking.

CHRIS: No, because I'm mad.

KING: Down onto your knees! The King of All Madmen stands before you. Our majesty Doremifasolasido the First and the Last.

CHRIS: I degrade myself at your feet, your Majesty.

KING: I'll upgrade you again. Stand up! The sun of my mercy will shine upon you. But I have to know if you are trustworthy. Can you keep silent?

CHRIS: I'm a deaf mute.

KING: But you talk.

CHRIS: I just pretend I'm talking.

KING: Madly clever! But aren't you a wise guy who pretends to be mad.

CHRIS: I'm mad, but pretend to be a wise guy.

KING: And that's better than the other way round. How long have you studied madness here?

CHRIS: A couple of months.

KING: It's strange that I have not seen you before. But my kingdom is so big and I have so many subjects, not only here but all over the world, that I can't know everybody.

CHRIS: I understand.

KING: That's our password: I understand. I don't doubt it anymore that you are one of us. But why did you come here? Isn't there any space left outside?

CHRIS: There's still a little, but the big shots wanted to live more comfortably. And because they have the power...

KING: I understand. (*Suddenly he starts to pull the leash and to growl terribly.*)

CHRIS: Why does the beast growl so terribly?

KING (*mysteriously*): I'm growling.

CHRIS: I'm not so mad that I could believe that.

KING: My word of honor! And that's not a lion, just a simple bundle of newspapers.

CHRIS: I don't understand you.

KING: No, they don't understand me. Not only those who call themselves wise. There are also many madmen who don't understand these ideas of mine. It seems, the ideals I've set as the goal of my life are too high.

CHRIS: The higher the goal, the easier one can reach it. What's your ideal?

KING: To unite the madmen of the world in one might Internationale. There have been many Internationales: the first, the second, the third, the fifty-ninth, and the sixty-eighth; there's a women's Internationale, the Internationale of Esperanto... but mine will be the true and only one! Therefore, I call upon you all: the madmen of the world unite!

(*The MANAGER of the asylum appears in a solemn procession. The KING hides himself immediately behind a bench, CHRISTOPHER stands still. The MANAGER stops surprised, looks scornfully to his orderlies who start to tremble.*)

MANAGER (*looks at CHRISTOPHER, firmly*): So, so, so...What do we have here? (*Walks around CHRISTOPHER, observing him carefully.*) So, so, so...No reverence at all! (*To orderlies.*) And you call that order? Have you joined the madmen? So, so, so...(*To CHRISTOPHER.*) What are you doing here?

CHRIS: I cast a shadow.

MANAGER: I see that. But why do you cast it?

CHRIS: To find out how long I'm here.

MANAGER: A new one, eh? So, so, so...What's your name?

CHRIS: Christopher.

MANAGER: Born?

CHRIS: I think so.

MANAGER: How old?

CHRIS: Professor.

MANAGER: So, so, so...Are you or do you pretend?

CHRIS: I pretend that I'm pretending.

MANAGER (*to his orderlies*): A very complicated case! Usually the personality splits into two parts, but this one is broken into four fragments. Why are you here?

CHRIS: In order to find out why.

MANAGER: Do you know where you are?

CHRIS: I'm not mad.

MANAGER (*to orderlies*): Did you hear it? Keep your eyes on this one! So you are not mad?

CHRIS: Not at all. I just pretend to be out of solidarity while talking to you.

MANAGER: Don't you feel any respect towards me?

CHRIS: None whatsoever. You gentlemen don't seem to be dangerous. You seem to belong to the peaceful inmates.

MANAGER: So, so, so...That's how it is! This comes from slackening the reins. Now you listen and don't ever forget. I am the manager here and the only one with power.

CHRIS: You don't seem to carry much of it.

MANAGER: They do. (*Points to his orderlies.*) They are my executive committee. Here everything is defined by authority, meaning me. And I ask that respect due to authority is shown to me. Therefore, the next time we meet, you'll try to escape from me or at least hide yourself symbolically as the others do.

CHRIS: Where should I hide?

MANAGER: Behind a blade of grass, if you wish.

CHRIS: But gentlemen...

MANAGER: Silence! Here everybody learns how to respect authority. People in your state of mind can be brought back to senses only through respect of authority. Keep that in mind till next time we happen to meet. (*Exits.*)

KING (*comes out of his hiding place*): I saw how expertly you deal with masses. That little one is very dangerous. Nevertheless, you got away without a scratch.

CHRIS: Although he tried to talk sense, I saw at once that he's out of his mind.

KING: He pretends to be the manager.

CHRIS: Such a madman!

KING: A saboteur, a traitor, a dictator! He has seized all power, employs a thousand spies and body guards. The best of us he has locked up in individual cells. Now he's looking for me. His spies have told him that I have delivered a manifesto to the madmen of the world. Have you read it?

CHRIS: It's maddening, but no.

KING: I'm hiding this historical document in the lion's tail. Listen! Simpletons, imbeciles, and the madmen of all continents! Your only and consecrated King, Doremifasolasido the First and the Last, talks to you saying: Throw off the oppression of the slyboots! Ready yourselves for the moment of reprisal. Who's in the majority in this world? With what rights does the minority of slyboots oppress us? We want to build the world according to our madness. Therefore, be ready! Set up secret arsenals, save bottles, pins, and fly-flaps...

CHRIS: But, Majesty, then there will be a fight!

KING: Yes! When the legions of the enemy will be crashed and the aristocracy of the madmen will have taken over the power, we'll open the cells of the insane in order to free the victims of the slyboots. In order to keep our race pure, we won't allow an interbreeding between a crazy girl and an insane man, because madness has to progress by natural selection and the posterity has priority over their ancestors. Therefore, the aristocracy of the madmen will always be the ruling class, with the masses of simpletons in a united front standing behind it. Those who do not want to stand can fall. From the aristocracy of the madmen will develop the most beautiful flower of evolution—a selection of madmen from which all nations will draw their princes and regents. We'll indoctrinate the clever ones in our way of thinking by putting them into individual cells, the balance will be reestablished, and nobody will see any change, because all men and animals will be united. United in a beautiful and mighty idea of madness!

CHRIS: Not so loud! Somebody's coming.

KING: They're from our camp.

(*Enter two men who constantly try to get in front of each other, as if throwing imaginary fishing lines.*)

CHRIS: Who are they?

KING: Separatists. Democrats by profession.

CHRIS: What are they doing?

KING: Fishing.

CHRIS: In a park? There's no fish here. What are they fishing for?

KING: Votes.

CHRIS: And what do they do with votes?

KING: It depends. With votes one can do many things. Play Chinese checkers, feed a cat, put in an album like pictures and show them to one's grandchildren. Otherwise those two are O.K.; they are our best standard-bearers.

(*The two exit.*)

CHRIS: Still, better that they passed by.

KING: Now you can tell me how you got here?

CHRIS: I got into an argument with psychologists. I tried to persuade them that I'm a madman who pretends to be normal.

KING: And they?

CHRIS: They insisted that I'm normal and only pretend to be mad.

KING: How cunning! And who was finally right?

CHRIS: I thought they were right, but they insisted I was.

KING: It was the same with me, only the other way around. But having come recently from the outside, haven't you seen Professor Christopher?

CHRIS: Are you waiting for him?

KING: Yes. He seems to be a very clever man. We need such people. We still don't have a chief of propaganda. The idea of madness still has to be carried by the masses.

CHRIS: You want me to carry the idea of madness?

KING: I'm sorry, Christopher. I did not recognize you! You've changed! I greet you!

CHRIS: What do you know about me?

KING: Everything. Come here, lion! Don't bite my hand! Look here! You were praised in all these newspapers that told how you got into the asylum. I have to admit your actions were very silly while you were outside.

CHRIS: What did I do that was so silly?

KING: Very silly! How dare you to revolt against the Academy about such a trifle as a mountain of ore? If the Academy says there are no mountains, there are none.

CHRIS: But there are!

KING: They shouldn't be there. And even if they are it's their fault, not that of the Academy. Why did you have to accuse the Academy of being mad because of such a trifle? You could have proven that the mountains that elevate themselves against the decree of the Academy are mad. The academicians would have felt flattered, the mountains would not be offended, everybody would have been happy. But you spit the Academy right in the eye. Is that sane? They all are on our side anyway. Our fifth column.

CHRIS: What?

KING: That's why the Academy sent you here. You have to re-educate yourself before you can become a member of the Academy. And you'll become a member as surely as I am mad. But here comes the usurper again. Let's hide. (*Both exit.*)

MANAGER (*enters escorted by his orderlies. Sits down on a bench, yawning. One orderly wipes the sweat from the MANAGER's forehead; the other opens his collar.*): So, so, so...After the walk I'll have a nap. Don't let the inmates near me! One is coming already. (*Orderlies are nervous.*) What's the matter with the discipline here? No respect for me anymore? Is she one of us? (*Orderlies shake heads negatively.*) Insane? (*Orderlies shrug their shoulders.*) And she comes right up to me!

KARIN (*stops and curtsies*): Good day, Mr. Manager!

MANAGER: She knows me. How do you know that I'm the Manager?

KARIN: Your imperious bearing shows it.

MANAGER: A very clever woman. What do you want?

KARIN: A job.

MANAGER: What kind of job?

KARIN: I just finished a course at the Department of Education. I learned how to work with simpletons, maniacs, schizophrenics, idiots...

MANAGER: But do you know how to teach respect? To drive it in and out?

KARIN: Exactly as needed.

MANAGER: Then make an application.

KARIN: I left it in the office.

MANAGER: We need a photograph also.

KARIN (*finds one in her purse*): If you please!

MANAGER: I'll keep it with me in order not to forget to accept your application. You'll receive the answer in a year's time.

KARIN: Can't it be done sooner?

MANAGER: Why sooner? There's no hurry here. Those who are mad will be so for a long time. But maybe we'll make an exception with you.

KARIN: Thank you!

MANAGER: I'll have to check your mental capacity, however. Don't be afraid; the test isn't hard. I'm convinced that everybody is mad to a degree. Those men as well as myself. That's the most modern point of view, and if you plan to work here, you'll have to adapt to it. Tell me, could you feel any respect out there toward somebody who's insane?

KARIN: No.

MANAGER: In order to win the sympathy of the insane, you'll have to pretend you are mad.

KARIN: I'll try my best.

MANAGER: One can establish authority only among his equals. That's why everybody fears me and likes me here. I never let my orders be questioned, not by the mad, nor the sane ones. In our times the authority can be found only in insane asylums. Here you'll serve the highest humanity.

KARIN: That's why I am here.

MANAGER: Then stay here for a while and breathe the air of the future. I'll look for a quieter place; I'm sleepy.

(*He exits accompanied by the orderlies.*)

(*As soon as the MANAGER is gone, the KING runs across the stage with his lion growling happily. KARIN, afraid, shrinks into a corner. When she hears steps behind her, she turns and confronts CHRISTOPHER. Both are surprised and an uneasy feeling inhibits their conversation at the beginning.*)

CHRIS: Is that you, Karin?

KARIN: Yes, Christopher.

CHRIS: I have been waiting for you—everyday.

KARIN: I thought about you too—everyday.

CHRIS: I knew it. I knew you'd come.

KARIN: I came—and often. But getting in here is as hard as getting out. I couldn't even talk to the guard at the gate. Today I climbed over the wall and now I'm here...

CHRIS: But how will you get out?

KARIN: The same way. I have a ladder hidden in the bushes. You can come with me. Let us flee, Christopher!

CHRIS: But if they catch me? They'll lock me up in an individual cell from which I'll never get out. No. Let me think it over...Why didn't you write beforehand so I could prepare myself?

KARIN: I wrote you a lot.

CHRIS: I haven't received one letter. But I wrote many to you.

KARIN: I didn't receive anything.

CHRIS: We have a tight censorship here. Do you know why? They are afraid of a madmen's revolution in the world.

KARIN: But Christopher!...

CHRIS: Now you think I'm crazy. Maybe it's true, but try to live here a week without going out of your mind and you'll see how hard it is. Anybody else in my place would be insane. How long have I been here?

KARIN: Over a year, Christopher.

CHRIS: And how much longer must I stay?

KARIN: I don't know. Nobody knows. You were legally admitted to this asylum, and then legally forgotten. It's convenient for everybody.

CHRIS: What's going on outside?

KARIN: I don't know. I'm not sure anymore who's living in a madhouse, you or I.

CHRIS: I thought it was a silly joke at the beginning. I was calm, because I knew I have friends outside who would help me in my misfortune. Now a year has passed, and you tell me that I'm legally forgotten.

KARIN: You are not forgotten by your friends, Christopher. But what can we do? We are trying to finance another expedition.

CHRIS: Why?

KARIN: It's the only way to get you out of here. In the eyes of the world you are either a crook or insane, and your mountains of ore are forgotten as well as you. That's why we have to organize a new expedition in which, this time, the geologists of the Science Academy will be asked to take part. This way we'll lead them to the mountains and say: "Here they are." Then you'll be justified.

CHRIS: Justified? What's my crime?

KARIN: There is no crime. But to prove it one needs a lot of money.

CHRIS: The truth is on my side, and you still want to buy it.

KARIN: The truth belongs only to the majority, Christopher. And the majority is the nation. You can't prove something to the nation it doesn't like.

CHRIS: The truth is not a beauty queen. But that's no reason to put it in a madhouse.

KARIN: In time they'll understand it, but now you have to flee. You can't stay here until the nation comes to its senses.

CHRIS: Should I help them prove I'm really mad? What would you think of a man who runs away from his own truth? No, Karin, I am staying here—until those outside recognize that my truth is the real truth. They'll come for me, the ones who put me in here. They'll come with a brass band to open the gates. Why should I climb over the wall now? No! I'll leave this place as a victor...or will stay here ...as a victor!

KARIN: You can't win against the mob, Christopher.

CHRIS: That's a lie! And the mob circulates this lie in fear of someone who can break its clay pedestal and throw the mob into the dust. I'm not afraid. Those who were not afraid in the past got crowns of thorns; today they are put in straight jackets. The sign of honor is different, but the symbol remains the same...and I'll fight for this symbol to the end! If only I could prove I'm not insane.

KARIN: The law permits you to be insane, but does not permit you to prove you are not insane. So far you are, Christopher. And why? You wanted to make the people happier and better by giving them knowledge, but they only wanted to become richer.

CHRIS: Unfortunately...

KARIN: You've always thought about minerals. You don't know people.

CHRIS: Isn't it the same? Karin, have you ever seen how a crystal changes in the hands of a master cutter? First the edges of selfishness are cut off. Then the cracks of conceit are smoothed over; quite often the crystal is split in two before it is polished. But when the work is finished you can't recognize the rough stone anymore. The tiniest ray of light can get through it. The whole world glimmers and shines in it. The whole world exists in order to shine for one moment in purity. Mankind exists in order to be polished. But a diamond can be polished only by its own dust. Therefore, we should not be afraid to crumble to dust, if it's necessary...if the master has to grind thousands of small diamonds in order to polish a big one...Do you understand why I'm staying?

KARIN: I understand, Christopher!

(*KING in the distance signals to CHRISTOPHER.*)

CHRIS: Come here, Majesty. Don't be afraid. She's on our side.

KARIN: From the light-minded section.

200

KING: A candidate? Greetings! We'll soon promote you to the half-insane, in case you have a good head. Now I'll show you what I've found. No, we'd better go someplace else. It seems there are too many nosy people around here.

CHRIS: They're on our side. Show us what you found.

KING: A knife! And a very sharp one! Look! If I only had it in my hand during the great revolt! The tyrant was under my heel, but I only had a pin in my hand...

KARIN: A knife! Be sure to cut with the backside.

KING: Why?

KARIN: It tickles very, very much.

KING: That's an idea! We'll tickle the usurpers to death. But here comes the saboteur with his bodyguards again. I have to run. (*Exits.*)

KARIN: I have to go too. I don't want the manager to see us together.

CHRIS: You're right, Karin. Go now! When shall I see you again?

KARIN: Soon, very soon! (*Exits.*)

(*The MANAGER enters with his orderlies. He stops and this time looks at CHRISTOPHER very angrily.*)

MANAGER: He still stands here and contemptuously provokes me to anger.

CHRIS: What should I do?

MANAGER: Flee or hide, as all others do. That's the only way to show respect to the only authority here—me. Don't stand still like a stake. You're destroying the existing order. You have to bend to our laws like the others!

CHRIS: But I'm not insane.

MANAGER: Did you hear that? That's the craziest thing I've ever heard! He's not insane! With what rights? You don't know! The sickness you have is called silent madness, the worst kind of insanity. Therefore, orderlies, you'll put this patient every night into a straightjacket and give him a nice cold shower.

(*Exits while the orderlies advance towards CHRISTOPHER.*)

SCENE V

COMMENTATOR: Attention, ladies and gentlemen! We are reporting from the government house. Very shortly you'll be witnessing an historic event. The Prime Minister will deliver a speech, the content of which is still a state secret. I can see patriots gathered here from all walks of life. In respectful silence and great expectation their eyes are turned towards a platform on which there is a table with three chairs. At this moment two servants are hurriedly covering the table with a dark red cloth. This is a very solemn occasion. Now two gentlemen enter. I recognize one of them—he's the Secretary of the Science Academy, internationally known, and his name brings honor to our nation. The other gentleman is younger. I have no idea who he is, but his presence here at this time speaks for itself. Both gentlemen are taking their places at the table and respectfully remain standing. It's evident they are waiting for his excellency, the Prime Minister. Yes, there he comes. His firm, energetic step and the deep earnestness in his intelligent face is known throughout the country. His Excellency takes his seat at the table. The assembly has stopped breathing. The big moment is here! Attention, attention! His Excellency, the Prime Minister!

PRIME MIN: My people! Hhm...With three strikes of this gavel I proclaim the beginning of a new era. The event I am going to acquaint you with has, until this moment, been kept in the greatest secrecy so that we could check and double check its importance. A scientific expedition to the Northern Mountains, organized by my government seeking nature's treasures in, until now, unexplored areas of our country, returned a couple of days ago. I have the honor to report that this enterprise of our government has been an unexpected success. This expedition found new deposits of iron ore in the Northern Massif. According to our preliminary calculations, it will supply the state with foreign currency and the nation with work and food for two hundred years. In two years we will become the second largest steel producers in the world. This means that the economical and political importance of our country will experience a rapid growth. As soon as this news is made known to the world, we shall advance to a honorable fourth place in a group of second rate countries politically. And that's only the beginning. We'll advance further and will become one of the Great Powers. According to the analysis of the samples, we've found iron ore of such quality that has never been known before. Because the ore is not underground but forms mountains as high as a thousand feet, its exploitation will be the cheapest in the world. That, in turn, will enable us to withstand the toughest competition, and our state treasury as well as the well-being of the nation will be ensured. Some of our men are still up North doing research and fighting the mosquitoes and other forces of nature. I salute these heroic pioneers with a hip, hip, hooray! Khhm! You see two of the responsible leaders of the expedition at my side. The first is Mr. Secretary of the Science Academy who led the expedition while sitting at his desk. He worked out the theoretical concept for the expedition without which there would not have been practical success. The other is our young and persevering research scientist, Dean Thomas, called Thomas the Skeptic, who guided the expedition to the Northern Mountains. He left the others there. He returned with some scientists and two mules to bring us samples of the iron ore. Since his return our ministers have been in session twenty-five hours a day. The government does everything impossible to bring our nation towards prosperity in the shortest possible time. Khhm! For their high public service and their daring, as the Master of the Order, I propose to grant them the title of knights, and as the head of our government I will decorate them with the Order of Legion of Honor.

SECRETARY: May I ask for the floor?...Excellency, ladies, and gentlemen! Being too moved because of the honors bestowed upon me, I'm afraid I won't be able to find words to express my gratitude. But I have to speak in order to tell you that this is the greatest satisfaction of my life. My scientific theory that was ignored, even defamed, for forty-eight years, has finally triumphed. Even as a young scientist I was interested in the angle formed by the terrestrial axis and the plane of orbit. Assuming that the specific gravity of the Earth is distributed comparatively evenly, after complicated computations, I found that this angle was not as had been calculated. But if it were not so, it would mean that the weight of the Earth is not distributed evenly and on one of the two poles there would be an unnecessary burden. Such a burden could be created, for example, by great chunks of metal that, for reasons unknown, have moved into the periphery of the globe. Now they are found; my theory has been proven correct. I wholeheartedly express my thanks to our clever Prime Minister. I've spoken. Thank you, thank you!

PRIME MIN: Will the factual leader of the expedition also say a word?

THOMAS: With pleasure. I'm not a speaker, Your Excellency, and I'm afraid that what I have to say will not be very pleasant. But at this moment I cannot keep quiet. To be present is a great honor and I am pleased. But it's not sufficient for somebody whom I represent.

PRIME MIN: I beg you not to deviate and talk only for yourself.

THOMAS: About the ore mountains?

PRIME MIN: Please!

THOMAS: It was easy to find these mountains, because they were already found two years ago. At that time I was a member of an expedition as the assistant of Professor Christopher. When we returned the newspapers wrote about it. The whole nations talked about it. But in a couple of months everything was forgotten. And tonight carefully listening to the solemn speeches I was surprised not to hear the name of Professor Christopher. Nor have I seen him lately either, although he's the one who should be present here tonight. Therefore, Excellency, gentlemen, and the nation—I ask you now: where is Professor Christopher?

PRIME MIN: Professor Christopher? Excuse me! It seems I've heard this name before. You say he was the first who found the ore mountains? In that case it's a *faux pas*, I mean, his not being here today. Mr. Professor, please take your place at this table! You have to understand that I cannot keep in my mind all the details in the middle of such great events. Is he not here? Isn't Professor Christopher here? He isn't. Where's the police inspector?

SIMS: Here!

PRIME MIN: Come here!

SIMS: At your service, Excellency.

PRIME MIN: In the name of the nation I ask you: where is Professor Christopher?

SIMS: With your permission, Excellency, in the madhouse.

PRIME MIN: What is he doing there?

SIMS: With your permission...

PRIME MIN: Why do you say: with your permission? Did I put Professor Christopher in the madhouse?

SIMS: I did, with your permission, Excellency, to check his mental capacity.

PRIME MIN: Now I start to remember. There was that unpleasant matter some time ago...Why did you not give me a progress report in this matter?

SIMS: Until now there has been no progress.

PRIME MIN: What? You put a man into the madhouse and simply forget him?

SIMS: I cannot instruct the doctors in the matters of the length of a test.

PRIME MIN: But that's a scandal! If I were not the head of the government, I would not believe that something like that could happen in our country. A man is put into a madhouse and forgotten!

SIMS: When the expert of psychopathology is finished with his report...

PRIME MIN: I repeat, it's a scandal! To the devil with the expert! Now it is clear to everybody that Professor Christopher is a respectable and highly educated man.

SIMS: Exactly my opinion, Your Excellency! I have always thought so—
as a man. But as police inspector I have to do my duty, and duty very
seldom corresponds with personal wishes. And after the Secretary of
the Science Academy, by his testimony, had crushed Professor
Christopher not only morally but also as a scientist...

SECRETARY: I protest! That's a falsification of facts. I testified as the
Secretary of the Science Academy, not as a private citizen. I did not
express my personal convictions at all. As a functionary, I could only
quote the opinions of the Academy, and I did exactly that. As far as
my personal opinion is concerned, it coincides in the minute detail
with that of Professor Christopher. The best proof for that is my own
theory that was justified only by the practical application executed
by Professor Christopher...

SIMS: May I point out that I was misinterpreted? The words just said by
Mr. Secretary of the Science Academy are very gratifying to us all.
The only scientific basis upon which Professor Christopher was put
into the state of a madman was the memorandum of the Science
Academy. Ladies and gentlemen, tell me...would an insane man risk
his own money for mere scientific principles? And would an insane
man be so proud as to give the bouquet of roses meant for the lady he
was going to propose to after a trivial slap in the face to the servant of
this lady as Professor Christopher did? I'm deeply gratified that the
head of our righteous government has averted this misunderstanding
by allowing me to express my sincere convictions in the matter of
Professor Christopher.

PRIME MIN: With these three strikes by the gavel I ascertain that
Professor Christopher was victim of a misunderstanding and, as a
consequence, has suffered an injustice. Therefore, it's the sacred
duty of my government to rehabilitate him in the name of the nation.
An extraordinary situation asks for a firm action. As soon as the
government has finished lunch, it will convene in a special meeting to
discuss the steps to be taken in the matter of Professor Christopher.
The satisfication given to him has to represent our nation's best
sentiments. We'll work out a detailed plan for the manifestation of the
nation's spontaneous enthusiasm. But at this moment, and I hope
everyone agrees, I hail Professor Christopher, in the name of the
nation: hip, hip, hurray!

COMMENTATOR: The historical meeting has ended. The Excellency,
followed by his suite, leaves the platform, and the people, elated by
the victory of justice, disperse. Attention, attention! From here we
switch over to Beethoven Auditorium, and in a moment you'll hear a
solemn jazz concert conducted by the master-musician

Wauchaubum...

SCENE VI

(*A polar night in the snow-covered Northern Mountains. The Northern Lights flutter in the sky. The colors change slowly from one into the other. Everything seems to be unreal. The TROLL lies on a rock and warms himself in Aurora Borealis, while the mountains crackle in the cold. CHRISTOPHER, in his hospital gown, enters, looks around, and sits down beside the TROLL.*)

TROLL: You here again! Are you not satisfied down there?

CHRIS: I have a magnetic needle in my chest, and it always turns toward the North.

TROLL: Towards the mountains of ore? Enjoy yourself, just don't touch anything.

CHRIS: I don't need anything anymore.

TROLL: Finally you've come to your senses, only a little too late. I warned you once, you'll be ruined by taking what's mine. Why didn't you listen?

CHRIS: Because I'm a human being, but you're a stupid ghost.

TROLL: A wise guy from a madhouse! You've gotten so far and suddenly lost your way.

CHRIS: There's a way without a way. If you leave your footprints in the snow, others will find them; and it's a way. But someone has to be the first.

TROLL: Usually the first either freezes to death or declares bankruptcy.

CHRIS: Everybody goes bankrupt once. But the imprints remain.

TROLL: Very clever talk!

CHRIS: The truth does not mind how it is expressed. The footprints still remain.

TROLL: I'm afraid there are too many of your footprints here. Hundreds have followed you! Look down there—hundreds of tents. I crawl around them every night, hoping to find frozen corpses. But they're still moving. And when the spring comes, they'll really start to move. They are surveying land for railroad tracks and highways. They are drilling deeper and deeper and calculating the value of the ore in the millions and millions. With lust and envy their trembling fingers are groping around these clean mountains. They would sell the whole globe to the devil himself if he would buy it. I anticipated it all at the time you were here. That's why I decided to ruin you, and I've kept my promise. But your footprints remained. And others came to ruin me! You still have a madhouse for a shelter. I have nothing. Do you understand, what you've done, Christopher?

CHRIS: Yes, I understand.

TROLL: Hundreds and thousands of people will suffer and die here, filling graveyards and for payment they won't get as much as a wooden cross. Are you making the people happy? They already have everything in excess, the only thing they're missing is peace and clean air. Instead you rolled mountains of ore upon their shoulders.

(*Christopher remains silent.*)

TROLL: From the heights of your madness you can observe the results. See the posterity creeping between the ore mountains like the plague. Their own failure makes them creep!

CHRIS: Yes, our own failure makes us creep, but only because we are humans. Every animal is happier than we are, and yet there is not a human who would renounce the rights to fail.

TROLL: Christopher, until now I thought you got into the madhouse because of the stupidity of others. But now I believe it is the proper place for you. You're blaspheming life itself. Every creature runs away from misfortune and pain in order to exist.

CHRIS: And yet, no one exists. They all perish. Why run from misfortune and death, knowing full well you can't outrun them? Therefore, in order to find wisdom, a man has to renounce common sense.

TROLL: And you've done it splendidly. Congratulations, Christopher! Or should I say—to your misfortunes? I suppose you'd like that better.

CHRIS: It doesn't matter whether I like it or not. When man was created nobody asked his opinion. A legion of misfortunes with the field-marshal Death encircled him. In order to free himself from his misfortunes he had to solve thousands of riddles. In order to evade sickness he had to conquer it. In order to conquer Death, he had to use his thinking powers that lead him to the very source of reality. Tell me, what would a man be without his misfortunes? Only an animal has no misfortunes or isn't conscious of them.

TROLL: And you pushed mountains of misfortunes upon men—just to make them happy?

CHRIS: Not happy, but better.

TROLL: In order to make man better you had to come here and disturb my peace? Did you have to dig the ground in order to find misfortunes that would make men better? No, Christopher! You did not have to search in the ground, but (*Angrily pointing to CHRISTOPHER's heart.*) there!

SCENE VII

(*Wide stairs leading to the gate of the asylum.*)

SIMS (*in a gold uniform, girded with a sword enters*): Fanfarists here!

THREE FANFARISTS: Here!

SIMS: Take your places! Here, there, and there! More of a military bearing! Thank you, thank you! You are responsible not only for the success of the ceremony but also for the security of the excellencies. Be vigilant, keep your eyes open, and nothing will happen that I've not thought of. When I lift my hand, you'll make yourselves ready. When I lower my hands you'll let the flourish be heard. Understand?

FANFARISTS: Yes sir!

SIMS: Thank you, thank you! Who's coming?

SECRETARY: The Secretary of the Science Academy on special assignment.

HANNA: His daughter. On her heart's assignment.

SIMS: The second and third place on the right from the center.

HANNA: I've not slept for two nights because of the excitement. Where may I sit down?

SIMS: On the steps, but only temporarily until the Prime Minister arrives. There is no provision for seats in the solemn ceremony. To tell you the truth, your name is not on my list.

HANNA: Nevertheless, I came and I intend to stay. I have to see Professor Christopher because his way to the asylum started in my living room.

SIMS: You are right, but it isn't desirable to relate a private matter to that of the nation. Who's coming?

GENTLEMAN: The press and photographers.

SIMS: To the lower left corner. Do you personally know all of your people?

GENTLEMAN: I'm responsible for them.

SIMS: Your pass, please!

GENTLEMAN (*gives him a certificate*): The pass of the International

Federation of Journalists.

SIMS: Thank you, thank you! Who's coming?

COMMENTATOR: The producer of the largest news' media.

SIMS: And who's he.

COMMENTATOR: My assistant.

SIMS: What's he carrying?

COMMENTATOR: Cables and a microphone.

SIMS: Legitimize yourselves.

COMMENTATOR: A special pass.

SIMS: Thank you, thank you. Lower right corner, please.

COMMENTATOR: I have to be in the center of the solemn ceremony, at least the microphone does. Where will Professor Christopher stand?

SIMS: Here. I have marked it with a blue cross.

COMMENTATOR: And His Excellency the Prime Minister?

SIMS: Here. I've marked it with a red cross. I'll stand right here. Who's coming?

THOMAS: Professor Christopher's assistant.

SIMS: Your pass, please.

THOMAS (*pushes the Inspector aside*): Get lost!

SIMS: Thank you, thank you!

COMMENTATOR: Dear listeners, ladies, and gentlemen! Attention, attention! We are in a place that is quite hard to describe. I see a wide staircase that leads toward a magnificent gate. Beyond that gate starts a separate state within our state—a model madhouse. In there for two years has lived our national hero—Professor Christopher, isolated from the great events we live through at this time. I see people gathered here waiting for the arrival of the Prime Minister and, symbolically, the whole nation is here. Attention, attention! His Excellency has arrived for the solemn event.

SIMS (*reports to the PRIME MINISTER*): Your Excellency, as the director of this solemn moment I take the liberty to report that everything till now has proceeded as expected.

PRIME MIN: Where's Professor Christopher?

SIMS: At this moment still in there. According to the protocol, you'll await him here. Will you give the order to begin the ceremony?

PRIME MIN: Begin!

SIMS: Mr. Assistant, please accompany me to meet Professor Christopher.

THOMAS: I'll get him myself.

SIMS: Thank you, thank you!

(*THOMAS enters through the gate. A nervous waiting. SIMS checks around. PRIME MINISTER arranges his decorations, puts on an eye-glass. Photographers make themselves ready to shoot pictures. The Fanfarists are frozen to attention. The gate opens a little, and, followed by his assistant, Professor CHRISTOPHER comes out. THOMAS holds him at the elbow and reassuringly talks to him about something. Complete silence. We hear the clatter of the Professor's wooden shoes on the stone steps. CHRISTOPHER has arrived almost at the lower step when the Inspector remembers to give the signal to the Fanfarists. But at the sound of the fanfares, CHRISTOPHER, frightened, leaves THOMAS and runs back toward the gate. THOMAS catches him at the gates. The fanfares are silent now, and the Professor slowly comes back. He stops in front of the PRIME MINISTER.)*

PRIME MIN: Professor Christopher—and I don't have any reason to doubt that you are the Professor—listen to me! We who have come for you here are not alone. On these steps leading toward the madhouse stands the whole nation. And therefore, you have to know that a nation can wrong anybody, but it isn't unjust; it can do something incorrectly, but it never makes mistakes. This time—and it's the first time in our glorious history—the nation recognizes its mistake. The nation calls you back!

CHRIS: The whole nation? I did not see the nation when I was put in here. I don't see the nation now.

PRIME MIN: We came for you in the name of the nation. When you were carried away in a prison car, it was disagreeable to you. Now it's disagreeable to the nation, therefore, you'll return in triumph. The nation restores you honor and does it on the same spot where you met your disgrace.

CHRIS: Was it my disgrace?

PRIME MIN: And we highly appreciate the endurance with which you carried yourself through it.

CHRIS: My father was a lumberjack, Your Excellency!

PRIME MIN: From this moment on your father has never been a lumberjack, Christopher, because the Order of Chivalry by its imperious command has elevated all your ancestors and the ancestors of your ancestors into knighthood. *(The fanfares honor the new knight. A frisbee is hung around CHRISTOPHER's neck.)* Let us proceed. As the president of the local chapter of the Legion I have the honor to award you with the highest order of the Legion of Honor. Here it is. *(Puts on CHRISTOPHER the decoration. Fanfares.)*

SECRETARY *(comes forward)*: My noble friend! The world, as you well know, is not perfect, and doesn't even show its willingness to become such. You know that the road to the highest cognition is very hard. It does not lead us from smaller to greater truths; no, it leads us from bigger mistakes to smaller ones. The Science Academy went the same road when two years ago it signed a memorandum that suggested your isolation in a madhouse. But today, I, the Secretary of the Academy, and your best friend, have the honor to report that in its last meeting the Academy unanimously—as unanimously as it signed the memorandum—decided to accept you as its member. Now we are here to hand you the diploma of immortality and to dress you in the Academy robes. The hat is not quite ready yet, and you'll receive it through the mail.

(*Fanfares.*)

PRIME MIN: Professor, allow me to congratulate you.

CHRIS: Excellencies and gentlemen... as well as all decent people who are not present, I thank you. These are only words, but I beg you to forgive me. The two years I spent among the insane have impaired my nerves quite heavily. The only thing I'm able to say is... that I'm happy, not so much for the honor you've shown me, but because the truth has been victorious, and the ore I found will make the life of the people easier as well as make the people better. All this time that I was not able to work among you, I was thinking about the ore, and did not stop my research even here... Now my friends I can give you top secret information. I've found new treasures against which the mountains of ore are nothing but a speck of dust, a trifle.

JOURNALISTS/PHOTOGRAPHERS (*start their attack*): Please, a more precise statement. About what kind of treasure did you talk? New deposits of iron ore?

Where are they?

What kind of ore is it?

Will you create a new stock corporation?

Where is the stockholder registration?

CHRIS: Yes, my friends, I've discovered new deposits of ore. It is a brand new ore that science hasn't dealt with before. It doesn't even have a name, but it is such a valuable ore, it can't be expressed in monetary terms.

JOURN/PHOTOG: To honor the discovery I propose the name "Christopherite!"

What are its characteristics?

How about the exploitation of the deposits?

CHRIS: When I first found the mountains of iron ore I wanted to make all of you equal owners. But the state intervened and took everything for itself. No such problem will be created with the deposits of this new ore. Not a thief, not a robber, not even the state can take it away from you.

PRIME MIN: Mr. Professor, I have to point out that you are embittered, and I understand it. But my government cannot be made responsible for the wrongs inflicted upon you. The government did everything possible to exploit your findings. It is understandable that you were forgotten in the madhouse because everybody was preoccupied with your great discovery. When you come to the Industrial Department to take over its leadership, you'll be given the most detailed information about it. Please consider what I've just said before you make public any supplementary information about the new ore deposits. An invasion of foreign capital at this time would not be welcome nor desirable because a great percentage of the profits would flow over the border. We are rushing to finish the last section of the five hundred mile doubletrack railroad into the Northern Massif so that the ore can be loaded directly from the foot of the mountains into the freight cars.

CHRIS: What? Do you mean to quarry starting at the foot of the mountains?

PRIME MIN: According to the expert resolution of the Academy...

CHRIS: It's wrong! The mountains of ore should be exploited starting at the top. The ore, quarried at the top will roll on its own right down into the freight cars, but if you start digging away the bottom, how do you intend to later get at the top?

SECRETARY: The solving of this problem is the work of a genius. Why didn't we think about it? The Academy will certainly change its point of view accordingly.

MANAGER (*has come out of the asylum together with his attendants and has listened for a while*): I beg your pardon, excellencies and gentlemen, for my standing behind your backs unnoticed...

PRIME MIN: Who's he?

MANAGER: Excellency, allow me to present myself. I am the manager of this institution, and I'm quite honored to greet you.

PRIME MIN: So that's been you, who for the past two years, has given a refuge to our dear professor? You've earned the highest recognition. I shall present you for an award.

MANAGER: I'm just doing my duty, Your Excellency, and I'll do it in the future whether I get a medal or not.

PRIME MIN: In the name of the government I thank you!

MANAGER: I was so lost in my work that I did not notice your arrival. However, the fact that I was not warned beforehand, minimizes my guilt. Therefore, I can only express my regrets and ask you to end this celebration as soon as possible.

PRIME MIN: What did you say? Are you sending us away? But, man, do you know to whom you are talking?

MANAGER: I know, Your Excellency. But I'm used to great men. In there I've plenty of them. I'm honored that you've chosen to visit your colleagues who live in my boarding house. But you've come in such a number, with your own orchestra, that your celebration is much too loud and disturbs my boarders.

PRIME MIN: We did not come to visit Professor Christopher, but to take him with us. And we will leave more quietly than we came.

MANAGER: Thank you. So, so, so! But I doubt that we have cleared this matter at all. As far as the Professor is concerned, I have to point out that he can't go with you.

PRIME MIN: Why not?

MANAGER: Because he must stay here.

PRIME MIN: Tell me, dear Professor, is this man really the manager of this asylum? Isn't he one of the inmates?

CHRIS: I don't know, Excellency. Nobody knows. The only sure thing is that he impersonates the manager. But be careful, Excellency! Don't make him angry! You may repent it bitterly for a long time. Especially keep your eyes on those two men behind him. They are very dodgy, therefore, dangerous. In half a second they'll put you into a straitjacket and under a cold shower.

PRIME MIN: We'll try to dissolve this thing without a discord. Mr. Manager, you did not understand me correctly. This man is Professor Christopher, a very honorable and clever scientist. He was admitted to your institution because of a regretable mistake. He's not insane.

MANAGER: That's the reason he will not go with you. All he needs is peace and quiet; and he gets it here.

PRIME MIN: But you are insane, Manager!

MANAGER: In there everybody thinks that; that's why we understand each other so well. And I hope we'll come to an understanding with you too, gentlemen. Your dear professor will help me, won't you? You'll come with me back in there?

CHRIS (*looks at the attendants*): It seems I'll have to, either on my own free will or by force.

PRIME MIN: Manager, I represent the highest power of the state. And I order you to declare this man normal and sane this very minute and strike him off the list of your inmates!

MANAGER: Excellency, in the territory of this state of which I am an absolute monarch and in which you are an intruder, there is no such power that could take away an inmate against my will.

PRIME MIN: Not even the highest power?

MANAGER: It can change a lumberjack into a knight, but can't make a sane man out of a madman.

PRIME MIN: Inspector, put this man into irons and prosecute him as a rebel.

SIMS: I'm sorry, Your Excellency, you just gave an inconsiderate and illegal order. I can't execute it.

CHRIS: But gentlemen, think about your prestige! As far as I'm concerned, I'll have to remain here. Therefore, I thank you from the bottom of my heart for the visit, for the knighthood, for the medal, and especially for the robe. These things will be very useful to me in the carnival on the Day of All Madmen that will be soon celebrated. They will create quite a reputation for me among the maddest of the madmen. But I see the Manager gets impatient. It's a sign for me to leave now. Goodbye!

HANNA: Christopher!

CHRIS: Hanna! You've come too—with violets! Thank you. These amethyst flowers are the most beautiful. Where did you get them at this time of the year?

SIMS: From the flowergirl in front of her house.

CHRIS: Oh, Mr. Inspector! I'm glad to meet you. Your uniform seems to be very well fitted, and you have many more medals since I last saw you. Which one did you get for putting me in the madhouse?

SIMS: The third from the left.

CHRIS: Such a trifle! But then at that time I did not rank as high as today. To make up for the medal... (*Suddenly pulls out the Inspector's sword.*) this sword—oh! The steel seems to be quite good.

MANAGER: Disarm the inmate! He's having a nervous fit!

CHRIS: Two years have passed since I had a sword in my hand.

SIMS: But be careful! It is very sharp.

CHRIS: Surely so sharp that I could cut off one of your ears?

SIMS: So surely that there's no use to try.

CHRIS: Could I stick the manager on it?

SIMS: I doubt it, but you may try.

CHRIS: With pleasure!

MANAGER: The police inspector incites a madman to murder.

SIMS: Give me the sword for a while, I'll show you how to use it correctly.

CHRIS: You'll show me? The best fencer in the country! True, I have not used a sword lately, but let me have a little practice. Before I take on the manager I'll tickle his boys a little. They are trying to jump me from behind.

(*He strikes the sword against the stone steps; the attendants swiftly step back.*)

MANAGER: Please, Excellency! Here is your professor! I declare him normal and strike him off my list. Just go away and take him and the sword with you. Where are you running, rams? (*He runs after the attendants; his foot gets caught; he falls. In a jump, CHRISTOPHER is over him and puts his foot onto the manager's nape of the neck.*) So, so, so!

SIMS: Mr. Professor, let me point out that you are ready to accomplish a crime.

CHRIS: Not at all. I just want to stab him.

SIMS: But you stopped to think, and that's a crime.

CHRIS: What kind of crime are you talking about? I can do anything; because, I, gentlemen, I am insane!

COMMENTATOR: As far as I'm concerned, I'm neutral. I just ask for permission to put the microphone nearer to this group.

SIMS: You seem too clever to be insane.

CHRIS: The manager told you that I'm insane, and what he says counts. Now I'm going to stab him to prove that he was right!

COMMENTATOR: Mr. Manager, please... your last words directly into the microphone!

MANAGER: Help!

CHRIS: No one helps each other here. Everybody is neutral. They'll just look on and wait their turn. I must not let them wait too long....
(*Lifts the sword preparing to stab the MANAGER, but a cry from the gate stops him.*)

KARIN (*rushes out of the asylum*): Christopher! (*CHRISTOPHER stops suddenly.*) Throw the sword away! (*CHRISTOPHER lets the sword fall. The MANAGER uses this opportunity to run away. Stops at a safe distance.*)

CHRIS: Karin, what was it?

KARIN: Christopher, be calm! You had a sword in your hand. But it's over now.

CHRIS: It seems I've done something terrible, Karin.

KARIN: Nothing is more terrible than that which was done to you.

CHRIS: But it's over now... everything is over. I fought for my rights, and lost the fight. And in my anger I forgot that I can't fight for truth with a sword in my hand. That's why I envy you. They forced me to be here, but you came of your own free will.

KARIN: I'm here, where I'm needed.

CHRIS: Won't you regret spending your life in a madhouse?

KARIN: Is there a difference between here and the outside?

CHRIS: The majority is on the outside.

KARIN: I know. But I'm not in love with the majority; I'm in love with you, Christopher.

CHRIS: Do you know who found the mountains of ore? Not I, but you, Karin. Do you remember the beautiful day when our compasses turned into all directions as if the devil himself were hiding in them? In the morning they indicated West, in the evening East. I tried to define the directions, I lived in a fever, I saw ghosts... while you simply looked over my shoulder and said: "In my opinion the compass does not indicate East or West. It simply indicates that mountain there." Why hadn't I thought of it myself? Because we are looking for the truth far, far away when it is really right beside us. A human being knows much more about the stars millions of light years away than he knows about himself. Yet the truth is really within him. How strangely and silently everybody looks at me.... Shouldn't I say something to them before we leave?

KARIN: Say goodbye, Christopher!

CHRIS: My friends! It is time we part, and, who knows, we may never meet again. But before I say goodbye, I'd like to ask a favor. Forget what you saw. That was not I; that was the other me over whom I have no power. But now I'm myself again, and in parting I shall tell you something very important. I already mentioned that I have found invaluable treasures against which the mountains of ore are nothing but dust. I'll let you in on a secret. Write it down, put it in the newspapers. Let the whole world hear about it, because nobody can take this treasure away from us. This new ore is in every human soul. Start digging, my friends! Bring into light this divine ore that since the beginnings of mankind has slept in your souls. Clean away the refuse of selfishness, the oxides of envy; then with a flame of love burn away the phosphorus of anger and the sulphur of hatred... so that the divine metal becomes pure and sonorous—let the spirit be free!

(*With the sound of fanfares, CHRISTOPHER, KARIN, followed by the MANAGER and the attendants enter the asylum. The gates are closed.*)

CURTAIN

THE BLUE ONE

A drama in three acts

by
Gunārs Priede

Translated from the Latvian by
Andre Šedriks

Introduction to
The Blue One

Quite early in his literary career, Gunārs Priede was hailed as the Soviet Latvian playwright of youth *par excellence*. And indeed, some twenty years and twenty-three plays later, his work has matured considerably, but has aged very little.

Priede was born in Riga in 1928. During the war years his family moved to a provincial town where he finished high school. After the war Priede returned to Riga where he studied architecture. Upon earning his degree, he worked for various educational institutions in various capacities, but always preferring teaching that kept him in touch with today's youth and the ever so precipitous changes in youth culture. Parallel to his educational and professional activities, Priede took interest in writing. In 1953, his first produced play, *Jaunākā Brāļa Vasara* (The Younger Brother's Summer), scored considerable success, and his appeal to the general public has not waned since. In 1959 his widely acclaimed *Normunda meitene* (Normund's Girl) won him also official recognition. The present critical consensus tends to rank Priede among the best Soviet Latvian playwrights. Priede is also very active in the Soviet Latvian Writers' Union and presently serves as its First Secretary. In addition to playwriting, Priede has tried his hand at cinematography and has written a film scenario. To date, several of Priede's plays have been translated into Russian, Estonian, Rumanian, and other languages and produced not only at most leading theaters in Soviet Latvia but also in other countries. His closest association, however, remains with the Youth Theater in Riga where he has found his most congenial director, Ādolfs Šapiro, who has staged some of the best productions.

Priede's dramatic vision seldom encompasses the great universal philosophical and ideological problems that tempt many a contemporary playwright. His inquiry gravitates toward the moral complexities of human relations, especially as they affect the youth. Quite often the dramatic action concerns the passage from youthful unattachment to adult responsibilities. Priede's first play, *The Younger Brother's Summer*, deals with the initiation of restless adolescence into the routine of workaday life. The work ethic has ever since frequently surfaced in Priede's *oeuvre*. In one of his most recent plays, *Udmurtijas Vijolīte* (The

Violet of Udmurt), written during the author's convalescence in 1973 in a TB sanatorium located near a huge textile factory complex, Priede pursues a kind of documentary inquiry into the life of the Soviet factory girl, carefully balancing the monotonousness of useful and necessary productivity against the youthful attraction to adventure and escape from the prescribed. Quite characteristically of Priede's dramaturgy, the play runs the risk of becoming a testimony of local and ephemeral interest, if the larger perspective that projects in the individual certain dimensions of universal import is overlooked. And occasionally Priede has succumbed to temptations of topicality and instant success. Such was the case with *Normund's Girl*, subtitled "The Diary of a Harvest Helper," that enjoyed tremendous popularity not only in Soviet Latvia but also in other republics. One obvious objective of the play was to promote the various schemes under which students are required to help kolhozites harvest the fields. The play draws copiously from the grab bag of dramaturgical tricks and stock situations that never fail to elicit a laugh, such as the encounter between the sophisticated and assuming city dweller and the simple and astute country folk. What saves the play is Priede's psychological insights into various youthful types, evincing his gift for capturing subtle shadings of individuality.

Priede's early works tend to display a syndrome of moral righteousness and overt didacticism. In his more recent plays, however, the polarization of ethical categories is less distinct. Values carry no price tags, and idealism can turn out to be a gesture of expediency. As the barometer of future change, today's youth prompts Priede to read the future with a mixture of anxiety and confidence. A recent play, *Es jums piespiedīšu mīlēt Raini* (I Shall Force You to Love Rainis *), deals with the dialectics of coercion and unrestraint that develops when pedagogical responsibility taken too seriously turns into tyranny. But the author no longer intervenes to instruct his audience when the right to individuality must be measured against collective concerns. When Priede is in his most pensive moods, confrontations of opposing moralities remain ambiguously unresolved.

If the latter-day Priede is quite complex in his treatment of questions of morality, the dramatic forms of his plays are less diverse and most frequently follow the tenets of realism, which is the prevailing mode of expression for most soviet playwrights. His adherence to the principles of stage realism, however, is far from fanatic, and on occasion he is willing to insert an eerie flashback scene, ask a character to step outside its

---

* Rainis is considered the foremost classical author in Latvian literature. The study of his works is *de rigueur* in school curricula.

fictional reality to address the audience, or to perplex the spectator with multi-leveled dramatic realities. By Western standards these departures from the "fourth-wall" principles would appear quite timid, but in the context of prevailing aesthetic orthodoxies, these efforts should not be considered negligible. Quite recently, to the consternation of many drama critics, one of Priede's latest plays, *Aivaru gaidot* (Waiting for Aivars), was staged as an absurdist play where old ladies act like teenagers, words are contradicted by gestures and stage movement, and the sequence of events has very little to do with causality. The title and the non-arrival of the character Aivars, evoking parallels with Beckett's *Waiting for Godot*, must have inspired Priede's friend Šapīro to experiment with an avant-garde approach. The production may not have been successful for various reasons and may not be considered a landmark in the history of the Latvian theater. It may, however, point up the multifariousness of Priede, suggesting facets of classical universality in a period when single-track drama assures comfortable popularity. *The Blue One* represents also one of Priede's most serious and complex inquiries into contemporary society and human relations.

On the surface, though cast in an uncharacteristic mood of gloom and hopelessness, the play has a laudable didactic purpose, which is to condemn alcoholism and bourgeois materialism and oneupmanship. It is a play of remorse, castigating impetuousness and irresponsible self-centeredness as well as suggesting that only too frequently the absurdities of life vagariously determine the guilt or innocence of human acts. It is also a play that attempts to probe more deeply into human relations, beyond the surface of presumed social accords. In a way, Priede intimates that most human relations can be reduced to a sequence of dominances, perhaps not unlike the existentialist view which holds that a consciousness always strives to exert tyranny over the confronting consciousness, to deprive it of its liberty, to reduce it to an object. Thus, a strange possessiveness has seemingly always underlaid the relations of the family of Rasma, Juris, and the late father. The fatal accident, for which Juris senses indelible guilt and Rasma a mixture of shame and remorse, as well as relief, has ambivalently distorted the mother-son emotional reciprocity. Because of the accident, Rasma, who enjoyed being a kind of society woman, was forced to abandon her career and sell their family possessions to pay for Juris' rehabilitation. Guilt and revenge, not always surfacing to the conscious level, alternate their hold over her. Guilty for having neglected her son who, in the absence of maternal care, grew up a brat, she also resents the sacrifice of her ambitions. To make up for past neglect, Rasma's solicitude over her invalid son now verges on virtual tyranny and is ambivalently reinforced by her apparent desire to hurt her son who with his recklessness had destroyed her aspirations to a fuller life. Rasma's unrelenting oppresiveness has infected other human relations around her, whereby love, affection, and concern have turned into possessive subjugation of the other consciousness.

The Blue One is a typical late vintage Priede play that grows from a topical sketch on current social ills to a tragedy of universal import that reveals subtle psychological complexities in human relations. As a play of classical plotlessness where external motion is practically nil while behind this surface immobility emotions reign rampant, it exemplifies the recent deepening of Priede's dramaturgy that used to incur reproaches for focusing on thematic trivialities and simplicities. A Priede play can no longer be approached with a wearied *déjà vu* attitude. His characters defy preclassification, and in their emotional convolutions we discover novel insights of timeless qualities.

Juris Silenieks

THE BLUE ONE

CHARACTERS

RASMA
JURIS—her son.
LINDA
VIDVUDS

ACT ONE

(*Gagra, a town on the Black Sea. December. The nights here are cold now. On the other hand, during the days, the thermometer frequently climbs to 80°, and then sunbathing by the sea is possible. The eucalypti along the shore drive are standing green. Green also are the gardens on the hillside facing the sea, since they contain thujas, cypresses, laurels, oleanders, and other evergreen trees and shrubs found in warm climates. A little further up, beyond the houses and gardens, stands a forest. Still further on, beyond the forest, there is snow on the mountaintop. It is the only reminder of the time of year existing north beyond the mountain. We find ourselves in the courtyard of a house built at the very top of the terraced town and on the edge of the forest. Everything in this house is in miniature, the small rooms with tiny windows, the veranda on the south side supported on fragile posts facing the sea... The opposite side of the house is flat against the cliff. A street leads by the house at roof level, and the only way to get to the courtyard is down a set of steps, which are partially cut out in the rock and partially natural. The sky is a bright, sunny blue. Far below lies the sea. JURIS is sitting at a table on the veranda, leaning across the table with his head in both hands. A loud-speaker in the neighboring garden, hooked up to a radio, blares forth a*

225

lively Georgian song. RASMA climbs down the steep steps. She is dressed in a light summer coat, a black dress with a white lace collar. She is carrying two heavy packages which she puts on the veranda floor. She straightens herself, stretches her arms and looks at her son. JURIS is sleeping.)

RASMA *(quietly)*: Juris...

(JURIS does not react.)

RASMA: Juris! *(JURIS lifts his head slowly and looks at his mother.)* Here they are.... Finally! See? *(JURIS looks at the packages.)* I never thought the books would be that heavy. My arms are pulled out like.... And it's hot today. I tell you... I saved me a place in the line at the post office and went down to the sea. People were sunbathing again! A number of men and women in swimsuits. In December! While I was looking around there, nobody actually went in for a swim, although, the water looked so warm and inviting as.... Juris, aren't you at least glad? You were waiting so impatiently for this shipment.

JURIS: Yes, I... of course. Thank you.

RASMA: I'll unwrap it immediately.

JURIS: Please.

RASMA: Just let me catch my breath... I stopped twenty times coming up our hill; and if you knew how I envied those Georgian ladies! Each one who came up went right by, and with their shopping bags full. One even had a child on her arm...

JURIS: They're used to it.

RASMA: By now, I should be too; this is our second month here.... I'll unpack those books and trot on down to get something for lunch.

JURIS: Don't hurry.

RASMA: I saw some tangerines being sold in one of the streets. I'll pick up a couple of pounds for New Year's. Those trees looked quite funny without leaves, you know. The tangerines are hung in the bare branches like so many Christmas decorations.... *(As she speaks, she is observing her son closely.)* Juris! What happened?

JURIS: Nothing.

RASMA: Was someone here?

JURIS: No, only...

(Catches himself. The stage momentarily grows dim and then brightens again.)

RASMA: Only?

JURIS: Gro, papa, and Madame Schwahn... in a dream.

(RASMA's lively mood disappears at once and she sits down slowly on the veranda's steps beside the two bundles of books.)

JURIS: Gro, papa, and...

RASMA (*pulls herself together and interrupts her son*): I don't like your saying "gro."

JURIS: I know, but she liked it, because she colored her hair red and dressed like a young girl. The name "grandmama" didn't suit her. "Grossmutter" was more like it, "gro" for short.

RASMA: I'll unwrap the books immediately, and you'll have something to do.

JURIS: Mom, all three of them seemed alive; gro, dad and Madame Schwan, and they talked to me and even laughed, but I knew... as I looked at them in my dream... that they were dead... because I killed them. (*Momentary silence. Light music is heard through the neighbor's loudspeaker.*)

RASMA (*slowly, seeking for words*): You did not kill them. I've told it and repeated it time and time again to you, and all for nothing? They were at fault. They should have noticed that you were tipsy, and under no circumstances should they've let you drive. Why can't I drum that into your head?

JURIS: Because you don't believe it yourself.

RASMA: You were with them in the same car and could have ended up exactly as they. For a whole year you've been balancing between life and death.... Only down here in the south you are starting to look like a human being again and I won't let you.... (*Catches herself and starts to unwrap the books.*) Juris, here are the books you were talking about all the time.... They finally came.... Here you are! (*She puts the first volume of* **Latvian Dainas** *by Krishjanis Barons on the table and continues to unwrap the rest.*)

JURIS (*opens the book slowly*): **Latvian Dainas**.... Have you read them?

RASMA: To tell you the truth, no.... Here's the next volume.

JURIS: I never read them, although, they were there, in our dining room in a glass case, right in front of our eyes...

RASMA: It was common practice in the old days for every respectable Latvian household to own a set of **Dainas**, but I doubt it if anyone really read them.

JURIS (*reads*):   The pine and the spruce trees
Boasted to climb the mountain;
The poor little juniper
They pushed down the hill.

RASMA: Interesting. Guess I'll have to glance at them myself. I mastered the folk songs in my time when I lived in the country; my parents loved to sing, but for us the real thing to read was the novel, the thicker the better.... Here are all seven volumes! (*She stands up and gathers the wrapping paper and string.*)

JURIS: Thank you.

RASMA: I'm going now. (*Goes into the house and comes back after a while with a shopping bag.*)

JURIS (*reads*): Neighboring bullies
Set on my child,
Took his good clothing
Gave him back rags.

RASMA: Strange, really.... Rags.... Son, is it all right to leave you alone...

JURIS: Perfectly.

RASMA: Don't you need anything?

JURIS (*remembers*): Mamma, we are having a guest for lunch.

RASMA: A guest? Here?

JURIS (*looking at a volume of* **Dainas**): Title: "In Praise of Youth, Youthful Living, and Joyous Nature."

RASMA: Juris, please. Did you say a guest?

JURIS: I? Oh, yes, yes... Linda, right. Linda is coming.

RASMA: How do you know?

JURIS: She... She was here yesterday. While you were visiting the Rozanovs.... She lives here.

RASMA: In Gagra?

JURIS: No, further away, in Pikunda.... (*Leafs through the volume.*)

RASMA: Why didn't you tell me?

JURIS: I knew that you wouldn't like it... (*Reads.*) "Vices and virtues in human nature."

RASMA: It had to be Linda.

JURIS: Yes.

RASMA: Yes.... What more is there to say.... Juris, I'll go down to the store, I won't be long.

(*JURIS nods. RASMA climbs up the steps and disappears. JURIS lays aside the second volume and hopelessly stares at all seven of them one by one, obviously at a loss to find in them something that is very important to him. A pine cone flies down from above and hits the volumes. JURIS lifts his head. Loud laughter is heard and LINDA appears at the top of the steps.*)

JURIS: Come and help me!

LINDA: This is high enough to make my head spin. (*Climbs down in the courtyard.*) Couldn't find a place farther down, could you? Nearer the sea?

JURIS: Down below were only single rooms, but here I could rent a whole house.

LINDA: Short of breath, I was stumbling and falling all the way up... I mean these aren't mountain climbing shoes. I sat down behind some bushes for a minute while your mother went by, and there I had a chance to catch my breath... (*Hands JURIS a green branch.*) What do you call these shrubs?

JURIS: Haven't the faintest.

LINDA: Smells a bit like tansy.

JURIS: More like a southernwood.

LINDA: Aren't they the same?

JURIS: I don't think so.

LINDA: It's hard to get used to the fact, to say the least, that the grass is green and there's no need for an overcoat.... There's snow in Riga, real deep!

JURIS: Yes?

LINDA: Like this!

JURIS: That's a...

LINDA: Fact. What kind of bibles are those?

JURIS: "Dainas." Do you know their meaning? You must have read some!

LINDA: Listen chum, what do you take me for? Let's see.... Gothic letters, yech.... I can't make heads or tails out of that kind of print.

JURIS: There's not that much difference.

LINDA: Thanks a lot. No difference.... One has to be at his absolute wits' end to say the least. In Gothic letters, you got to be crazy. With anything in the regular print I often doze off after ten pages and then sleep like a log. I even forget to turn off the light, it burns all night.... Juris, why did you shout?

JURIS: I?

LINDA: You called for me to come and help you, and don't pretend you didn't.

JURIS: I have to find...(*Hesitates.*)

LINDA: What do you have to find? Where?

JURIS: In these volumes. Folk songs about cows.

LINDA: That does it.... You? About cows?

JURIS: There must be something about cows... verses about people tending them or something, but I have no idea how to go about looking for them among these thousands of songs.

LINDA: Well, I think you should look at the index. How do you find things in the telephone directory? You go down alphabetically. You should have something there, either an index or an alphabetical listing or something.

JURIS: Each volume has its own table of contents.

LINDA: It seems to me that there aren't all that many volumes.

JURIS: Seven.... Linda, have you heard of a cow called "Latvian Blue"?
LINDA: I know there is one called "Latvian Brown."
JURIS: Everyone knows that. Good breed, but suffers from undulent fever.
LINDA: And the blue doesn't?
JURIS: No.
LINDA: Have you seen one?
JURIS: Yes.
LINDA: With your own eyes? Interesting, where? (*JURIS appears to grow still, and dark waves roll over the stage. At one moment all light almost disappears.*) What happened to you?
JURIS: Nothing.
LINDA: That was meant as a joke, wasn't it? A cow can't be blue.
JURIS: Seems like it can.
LINDA: As blue as the sea?
JURIS (*looks down*): Over there, where that white ship is sailing, lies Turkey.
LINDA: Don't tell me...
JURIS: That's a fact.
LINDA: Far?
JURIS: Not too far.... No, of course not that blue. More grayish. You can almost say, bluish. Grayish-blue. Bluish-gray.
LINDA: And why do you think I'm here?
JURIS: You?
LINDA: Yesterday you told me to come over, but today you subtly shift the conversation to cows.... Should I interpret it as sarcasm or as a sign?
JURIS: What kind of sign?
LINDA: You called me in your letter and I came—think of the distance! You can almost reach Turkey with your hand!
JURIS: You should have come alone.
LINDA: From winter to summer, imagine!
JURIS: You should have come alone.
LINDA: To Georgia, no less. On my dinky salary.
JURIS: You should have...
LINDA: Stop repeating yourself, will you. It isn't very clever. You have changed a lot, among other things.
JURIS: Me?
LINDA: To say the least, don't you feel it yourself? It hasn't been that long, a little more than a year, but yesterday you... no. I recognized you by your looks, no question there, but when you started to speak, I began to wonder.

JURIS: C'mon now.

LINDA: I'm telling you this in all seriousness.

JURIS: But why?

LINDA: We girls, used to call you The Mumbler behind your back, because at parties you either didn't let out a peep or you would start in with some sort of animal noises. In other words, mutter and mumble. When you felt good, you grunted, and when you saw a bottle you began to cluck, but if you didn't like somebody, you...

JURIS: Linda, you know... drop it, okay?

LINDA: All right chum, I will, but still it's almost unreal to talk to you about... well, just to talk to you. A friendly chat, so to say... Tête-à-tête. You were such a...

JURIS: Mumbler, yes I know...

LINDA: To say the least! One summer evening when you visited us, you were being sarcastic left and right, not letting the other people express themselves, and one of the students, whom you impressed at first, later read to us from her notebook where she kept aphorisms from her favorite authors: "A real weirdo, brays like a poisoned jackass!"

(JURIS stands up slowly, though when he looks up, he sits back down immediately. LINDA also looks up and, startled, pulls herself back deeper under the roof of the veranda.)

LINDA *(in a whisper)*: Oh, God. Vidvuds is floating here through the clouds.... If he won't notice us maybe he'll go on by, he doesn't know the address. No sense in introducing him.... And I told him explicitly to sit and wait!

JURIS: Even here you couldn't come alone.

LINDA: Don't be childish. I with my superbright mind in Georgia? Even with Vidvuds at my side, all kinds of things are happening! Some boy behind a fence, when I looked at him closer because he really was cute, winked at me, and as soon as Vidvuds and I were past him, he even whistled!

VOICE OF VIDVUDS *(from up above)*: Hello! Are you the sick classmate?

JURIS *(gives a nondescript gesture; VIDVUDS appears on top of the stairs. He is a well-built, middle-aged man)*: So where's Linda? *(JURIS looks over to her side, but she presses a finger to her lips, and disappears into the house. VIDVUDS climbs down into the courtyard.)* You are Juris, if I'm not mistaken.

JURIS: Yes.

VIDVUDS: My name is Vidvuds. Last names aren't very informative and need not be mentioned. You really found a marvelous place here. The vastness of the Black Sea, like in the palm of your hand.... Beautiful. (*In the silence that ensues, because JURIS does not say anything, a radio announcer is heard, reading the news in Georgian. A female announcer takes over.*) Linda has told me about you. Yesterday she visited with a Latvian family where she accidentally found out about your illness and also got your address, but this morning at the breakfast table she was so upset, that I talked her into coming here. Our girl was only afraid that I would not be able to keep my boisterous nature in check at the patient's bedside, so she left me up there in a little meadow, but I really got bored waiting, and you, it seems, are not about to die.... By the way, where is she? Linda!

JURIS: She... will be here any moment.

VIDVUDS: Ah!... It's really beautiful here, unbelievably beautiful. It's not bad down by the sea, though, especially today, when those blue and white waves wash over the pebbles on the beach just like in summer.... Not bad at all, no, and yet it was worth climbing up here to your twentieth and something floor, honest. If only to experience this top-of-the-world vastness! The heights too—of course—look, even the helicopter is flying below us.... Is that a commercial air lane?

JURIS: Yes.

VIDVUDS: Which one?

JURIS: Adler—Gagra—Pikunda—Sukhumi—Batumi.

VIDVUDS: Adler—Gagra.... The words themselves sound like beautiful music.... Look, the helicopter's shadow glides over the green gardens at the same time when snow covers the frozen bay of Riga. I was still there just a couple of nights ago.... To return for a moment to summer, it's like in a fairy tale, don't you think so? Returning to summer is so fantastic as, let us say, returning to one's youth.... This is so unique, and so thrilling that all morning I've been wandering around as if in a daze and I keep humming to myself an old and precious tune... (*Sings.*)

> Come back, come back
> Just one more time
> My sweet and wondrous youth...

(*Stops, catching sight of RASMA on the stairs.*)

RASMA (*shopping bag in hand*): Who is in the courtyard singing, and in Latvian too?

VIDVUDS: Someone who doesn't want to believe his eyes.... And you are this grown man's mother? You! Tell me that I am mistaken!

RASMA (*climbing down*): You are not mistaken. Excuse me, I'll put away the bag.

(*Goes inside.*)

VIDVUDS: Yes. Of course. (*Hums.*) Come back, come back....
(*Turns his attention to the sea.*)
JURIS (*leafs through a "Dainas" volume.*)
(*RASMA suddenly screams loudly in the house.*)
VIDVUDS (*spins around. Silence.*): What was that?
(*JURIS shrugs his shoulders. VIDVUDS starts decisively for the door, but RASMA herself comes out first in her black dress, her coat pulled off.*)
RASMA: I am so sorry. I got startled.
VIDVUDS: It happens to the best of us.
RASMA: I wasn't expecting that in my room... but it's nothing. In other words, I apologize. I'm ashamed now that I couldn't control myself.
VIDVUDS: Everything's okay then and the matter is ended. I am Vidvuds. And if you don't mind, let's dispense with last names.
RASMA: Rasma.
VIDVUDS: Delighted. Your son, the scholar of folklore, and I have already introduced ourselves.
RASMA: How nice.
VIDVUDS: I think it necessary to offer some explanations, even though you are not asking for any. First of all, my unduly familiar behavior may seem to you...
RASMA: Not at all, I just thought that...
VIDVUDS: You just thought that I had a few too many, I understand, but the real fault lies in the breathtaking beauty of the South and summertime in December, so those few glasses of vermouth can hardly be an issue here.... In the second place, I am here as an escort to your son's former classmate, who found out this address yesterday quite by accident.
RASMA: That's really nice of you, thank you very much.
VIDVUDS: I was afraid, that the local hot blooded young men, wishing the girl their very best, might do her an injustice.
RASMA: You are the first visitors since we moved in here.
VIDVUDS: Are we to believe that?
RASMA: Well, our neighbors, the Rozanov's drop in now and then.
VIDVUDS: Neighbors, of course, are not visitors.
RASMA: Of course, although, they are wonderful people, so open and sincere...
VIDVUDS: And still they are only neighbors. You are used to them, naturally... like a picture on the wall, which nobody sees anymore, even if they look....
RASMA: But just try and take it down!
VIDVUDS: This concept of yours as a measure of value, I must reject

categorically...

RASMA: Categorically?

VIDVUDS: Everything around us evolves and changes, around us and inside us, thus we constantly crave for new paintings, new songs, new faces.... Why is style being changed so often, you tell me that? Just because people are afraid they'll become like that old picture on the wall: noticed only when it's gone.... People know that they must change and change for the better, as Rainis* once said, but in themselves they knew they cannot change that much, thus they at least change their outer appearances.... As long as we live, we crave for novelty.

RASMA: I still think we crave for something lasting in this changing world.

VIDVUDS: Like what?

RASMA: We don't tend to change friends all that often.... Also, are you, for example, against having a family?

VIDVUDS: I hope to God not! Me? Families, I have had more than one!
(*RASMA spreads her hands and sends forth peals of laughter and we realize that she is actually full of joy and humor. Her normal vitality has been subdued and blunted by the family tragedy and her son's illness. LINDA appears in the doorway. RASMA stops short in her laughter.*)

LINDA (*not looking at anyone*): The terrible headache I had seems to be going away.... If you could escort me, Vidvuds, I would like to go home now.

VIDVUDS: As you wish! I just can't help wondering what happened to you? A half an hour ago you were quite chipper.

LINDA: You don't think a person can get a headache? All of a sudden?

VIDVUDS: And how!

LINDA: It comes and it goes and there's nothing more to be said, I believe.
(*Goes towards the steps.*)

VIDVUDS: Thank you, Rasma, for the wonderful interlude up here. If there was a little more time, and fortunately there isn't, we would most certainly have a quarrel...

RASMA: Are you sure?

VIDVUDS: Absolutely, and we would part as two enemies...

JURIS: Linda, I found it!
(*LINDA stops at the top of the stairs and looks back. Even VIDVUDS and RASMA turn towards JURIS. Silence. "Bolero" is being heard on*

---

* A well known Latvian poet and dramatist.

the neighbors' radio.)
RASMA (*after a pause*): What did you find?
JURIS: About cattle, in the index of the fourth volume. On page 124. "Cattle breeding, raising, feeding," and so on.
(*JURIS leafs through the volume, finds the right page, reads. The sound of "Bolero" keeps increasing in intensity.*)
VIDVUDS (*after a pause, since no one says anything*): The youth of today is caught up in sports, cybernetics, cinema, and who knows what else.... Being caught up in folklore, I must admit is a new one for me....
RASMA: For me to...
LINDA: Vidvuds!
VIDVUDS: Okay, okay. We're going.
LINDA (*all the time feeling terribly uncomfortable, aside*): See you.
RASMA (*cooly*): 'By.
(*LINDA goes up the steps and disappears.*)
VIDVUDS: Good luck in your work, Juris! And get well soon, do you hear!
(*JURIS, absorbed in his reading, does not react.*)
RASMA: Juris...
JURIS (*looks up*): Yes, I... Thank you.
(*Continues his reading.*)
RASMA: Please, excuse us.
VIDVUDS: That's all right, Rasma, I understand.... I know that it's hard on you.... Yes, well. Happy New Year! It won't be long now, only a couple of days to go...
RASMA: And many happy returns. Stop by again if the long climb doesn't scare you. Maybe on New Year's eve?
VIDVUDS: Thank you. I don't want to bother you but I must confess that I really love it here...
RASMA: Wonderful! We can make a fire in one corner of the garden and roast some shashlik, and there is also a small fir tree down there, do you see? All we need to get are some candle holders and candles, which is a problem here.... Do come. The only others will be the Rozanovs.
VIDVUDS: How many are there, those Rozanovs?
RASMA: About seven or eight.
VIDVUDS: Oh?
RASMA: And imagine, they don't think of changing their clothing every day or dying their hair or something like that, in order to see, respect and love another!
VIDVUDS: An exception, as always, reaffirms the rule.... Thank you

235

again, and perhaps we'll be seeing you soon!
RASMA: See you soon. (*VIDVUDS follows LINDA to the top of the stairs. Disappears. RASMA shifts her attention to JURIS. JURIS has found what he has been looking for. It makes him happy and upsets him at the same time, and he gets to his feet.*) Juris.... Well, what's going on? (*"Bolero" finishes playing and stops abruptly. JURIS looks at his mother and sits down.*) Juris, don't scare me....
JURIS: I found it. Exactly what I was looking for. I knew it had to be here, but when I found it, it made me feel funny....
RASMA: But what is it?
JURIS: Listen... (*Reads.*)
    Blue is my little cow, blue
    Like little wagtail bird.
    Did not eat the marsh hay,
    Didn't drink the marshwater.
(*Raises his head and looks at his mother.*)
RASMA: I don't understand it. This little song, well, it's... it's pretty, but... but it's hardly worth the...
JURIS: It's very important to me.... Here, it looks like there's another one. I'll read that one, too.
RASMA: Go 'head, but I would still like an explanation.
JURIS: Later, okay? Here it is. Listen. (*Reads.*)
    Blue is my little cow, blue
    Like little wagtail bird.
    Brookwater slaked her thirst
    Riverwater washed her feet.
(*Looks at his mother.*)
RASMA: The first two lines sounded alike.
JURIS: They are exactly the same. Mamma, have you ever heard of a breed of cattle called "Latvian blue?"
RASMA: I don't know if they were considered a special breed, but there used to be these blue cows, yes. In one seaside village, I even caught a glimpse of a whole herd. They were called sea cows.
JURIS: Tell me about it!
RASMA: What is there to tell? Son, aren't you... you're not feeling well, are you?
JURIS: No, no.... Tell me everything you remember. About cows.
RASMA: About cows...
JURIS: Yes.
RASMA: At that time, during my childhood, in Livland there were mainly the Latvian browns, but in Courland, where we lived, were all kinds of mixed herds roaming the woods. There were black cows and

all sorts of the so called "raibalas" or spotted cows—red, yellow, black spots.... Big and little, some with huge horns and some without, the polled ones were called "toles".... The blue ones or the sea cows, some also called them mooncows, as I now recall....

JURIS: Moon?

RASMA: Yes, and their color was bluish-gray, but the horns seemed uncommonly white, they even glowed slightly in the dark...

JURIS: Yes! Spaced wide apart, curved to the front and upwards?

RASMA: How do you know?

JURIS: Mamma, you're looking at me and thinking that something psychic is going on, I know, but I'll tell you everything, and you'll see it's not that at all... I'm going to tell you everything, about the last moments before... well, before the accident, I have never told anyone, not you, not... I'll tell it to you and you'll see....

RASMA: Don't you want anything to eat today?

JURIS: Mamma, the cows had names, too, didn't they?

RASMA: Of course.

JURIS: What kind?

RASMA: Well, in this one place where I used to drive the cows to pasture and look after them, there was one called Betsy—long legs, leader of the herd, had to be constantly watched.... There was Valentine, Star—red with a white mark on her forehead.... Gypsy, black all over.... Dove...

JURIS: Blue?

RASMA: No, that was probably a descriptive name of her disposition. She was dark brown, and when she got wet in the rain, she looked like a second Gypsy.... I'm going to boil up some potatoes.
(Goes towards the door.)

JURIS: Tell me one more thing. Why did you scream?

RASMA (stops): Because I was startled, I already explained that.

JURIS: You are not the type to scream and holler.

RASMA: Among other things, Linda is at least five years older than you.

JURIS: What is that supposed to mean?

RASMA: How could she have been your classmate?

JURIS: She wasn't.

RASMA: Vidvuds said so.

JURIS: No.

RASMA: I don't think Linda will be coming here anymore.

JURIS: Did you tell her not to?

RASMA: She understood herself.

JURIS: Then why did you invite that character?

RASMA: Vidvuds?

JURIS: Yes.

RASMA: You mean you overheard our conversation?

JURIS: Yes.

RASMA: You were lost in your book.

JURIS: Yes, but I heard.

RASMA: Look son, how can I make you understand.... In Riga, when I had to constantly think about how to set you on your feet, I did not feel it as much, but here, I sometimes don't know what to do. I'd gladly work at something. I hate to lie around, but what can I do in Gagra? Lately, I have been wishing for people, I want to talk, sing... Strange, isn't it? At my age. After all that has happened.

JURIS: Looks like your dear Rozanovs are making an appearance down there.

RASMA: Why mine?

WOMAN'S VOICE (*from the neighboring garden, which is located much lower*): Mozshno k vam, Rasma Arvidovna.

RASMA: Mozshno.

MAN'S VOICE: Predstavtye, spichek nyet doma!

RASMA: Odnu minutu. (*She goes inside. JURIS goes back to his "Dainas" volumes. RASMA returns.*) Dyerzshitve!
(*Throws match box at the neighbors.*)

MR. ROZANOV: Spasiba vam, Rasmochka!

MRS. ROZANOV: Gosti Pozshalovali!

RASMA: Da, iz Rigi.

MRS. ROZANOV: Vesma sympatychniye, dolzshna vam skazat!

RASMA: Vi nahoditye?

MRS. ROZANOV: Vesma!

MR. ROZANOV: A Urik sevodnya kak?

RASMA: Spasiba, nichevo. (*Starts to go back in the house.*)

JURIS: Mamma, wait...

RASMA (*stops*): Yes?

JURIS: Just came across this, by chance... I'll read it to you Listen
(*Reads.*)

> The wagon is empty
> The pine box gone
> The passing is marked
> By a mound of sand.

Nice isn't it? Short and somehow... well, to the point.... I hadn't imagined that folk songs can also be so.... Why do you look at me like that? You know, I am going to read all of them now, from the first volume through the seventh. There must certainly be something more about the blue cows.

RASMA: Only don't over exert yourself. (*Off.*)
(*JURIS reads. A happy tune is heard in the loudspeaker.*)

ACT TWO

(*The same, a day later. A sunset is illuminating the sky in yellow, green, and blue, while the sea is silvery gray. JURIS has on a white woolen sweater and is sitting behind his desk. In front of him there are three volumes of "Dainas." RASMA appears in the doorway. She is dressed in a light colored costume and has made herself up to go out.*)

RASMA: What a cool, blue-green yellow evening sky. Yesterday it was flaming red.

JURIS: Yes, it seemed like Turkey was on fire.... It's not burning tonight. Tonight they have placed a glass dome over Turkey.

RASMA: I guess Turkey is more to the left, though.

JURIS: Are you going?

RASMA: No, it's early. The Rozanovs said something around nine.... Nothing special is going to happen, we'll just sit around. The same tomorrow night at our place.

JURIS: Here, for the first time...

RASMA: Are you by any chance afraid?

JURIS: No.

RASMA: You know we agreed to spend New Year's Eve at our place. There's more room here, a fireplace, a living fir tree and...

JURIS: And I, who otherwise should be left alone. Mamma, Rozanov's garden is right beside us and in full view...

RASMA: You mean that?

JURIS: I'd be near by... almost there.

RASMA: We can do it that way, if you wish. The Rozanovs will understand and won't get offended.

JURIS (*gets up*): Even the snow on the mountaintop looks blue.

RASMA: The afterglow of your Turkey.

JURIS (*takes a few steps up to the veranda post, leans against it and gazes in the sunset over the ocean; the reflection colors his face and sweater blue*): Mamma, listen.... The cow was standing in a meadow near the highway. That must have been the blue cow of Latvia. Gro called out that I ought to stop.... I stopped. They got out: gro, Madame Schwan, and papa, and went back to take a look. I also got out. For no reason, since I had absolutely no interest in the cow, but I did have a splitting headache. Oh yes, first I backed the car up and only then did I get out.... Yes, that's how it was.... Well, one way or another, we all four stood at the edge of the highway and looked at the cow, and the cow looked at us...

RASMA: Was she blue?

JURIS: Well, sort of... yes, bluish. Gun metal blue. With these strange eyes, like that of a human. She was tied down not with a chain but with a knotted rope.... I remember if all very clearly. Gro's last words I also remember.... After that we got back in the car and no more than ten minutes had gone by when...

RASMA (*interrupting*): What did she tell you?

JURIS: Gro? She... It was about cows. There were no houses around, only some alder and willow trees in the morning mist, and the cow stood in the meadow, she wasn't very big, with white horns and a white udder which appeared to be so white as if made out of white paper.... I said that in a zoo, such a roadside attraction could outdraw a monkey, but gro reprimanded me, it wasn't nice to talk like that... In the old days, there had been plenty such cows. They had even been classified as a species, the Latvian Blue.... To her, gro, it seemed only that the blue ones had long since disappeared from this world, because all one could see now were the brown ones.... This one we had seen, was probably some kind of a throwback, coming from a stubborn stock, like a weed....

RASMA (*after a pause*): Did you stay there long?

JURIS: No, not too long, but do you want to know what happened?

RASMA: Yes.

JURIS: The blue cow... sea cow, as you called it, mooncow... stood by the highway among some willows and looked at us and at our black Volga, and I also sort of looked—from the cow's viewpoint.... At us, you understand, the way we were there.... The way gro was with her dyed hair and powdered nose, short skirt, high-heeled shoes.... Madame Schwan, older than gro, but decked out in necklaces and earrings.... Did she really work for landowners as a maid when she was young?

RASMA: She did. Long years.

JURIS: She had to milk the cows then?

RASMA: Most certainly.

JURIS: Papa was suffering from a terrible hangover, his handsome face appeared ashen and puffy, hair matted... I myself felt also like... and glanced in the mirror... Well, I'll tell you, it was some picture... In short, that's how we stood there in front of the cow, four... four... I don't know what... four somethings, who at high speed were rushing through Courland from Mindau to Riga, and there was nothing really waiting for them in Riga, not... Mamma, it could all be read in the blue cow's eyes, there in the willows!

RASMA: You made this all up, later, during the long months when you were confined to your bed.

JURIS: No, that's the way it was, and I was not the only one who understood it, gro and papa understood it too, I saw it.... Afterwards we got in the car and drove on. Madame Schwan said that Latvian browns, as she had heard it, were suffering from undulent fever, and therefore, it couldn't hurt to think about a new breed, if only those blue ones were still somewhere to be found, those were her last words.... Gro's last words were that the blue cows came from the distant past, the same way as folk tales and myths, and that the cows had already been mentioned in the folk songs.... Those actually were the last words, because suddenly we...

RASMA (interrupting): Did papa say anything?

JURIS: Papa.... The women were talking behind us in loud voices like those who have trouble being heard. It made papa mad, because he had an awful hangover, that's why he growled something about old babblers and turned on the music, and we passed a truck and met the other one head-on, at full speed, with music.... The other one was blue and had some sort of... stripes which looked like horns, and there was also something resembling eyes.... Eyes that were looking... And that was all. Nothing more to it, everything happened so fast.

VOICE OF VIDVUDS: Good-evening! (RASMA and JURIS look up.) I'd gladly knock, if there were a place.... May I?

RASMA: But, of course! (VIDVUDS climbs down and shakes hands with RASMA. Hands her a package.) What is it?

VIDVUDS: Here you are. I brought you some candle holders and candles and threw in a bottle of black balsam.

RASMA: I'm speechless.

VIDVUDS: Which is quite alright. Just don't ask who or what, but it looks like I'll be in Riga for New Year's, at least flying in that direction, so I brought this over tonight.

RASMA: Thank you, but...

VIDVUDS: And no "buts", please.

RASMA: Yes, but... where did you get them? I searched high and low, in vain.

VIDVUDS: Did you go to the commission house?

RASMA: No I didn't...

> (*JURIS turns around and starts to go inside. He does not limp, neither is it the walk of a paralyzed man, he only moves slowly. RASMA and VIDVUDS stare. JURIS disappears behind a door.*)

VIDVUDS: I will take with me to Latvia two sunsets from the Black Sea. The one last evening raged like a holocaust of flaming tongues, but this one glitters cool, aloof and elegant in its refinement of blue tones... How's the patient?

RASMA: Pretty good, thank you. You saw how he walked with such confidence needing no assistance.... Oh, I'll get him back in shape. I am also stubborn like a weed... just now he told me something which probably six months ago would have... I don't know what I would have done, but now I am glad that he is able to talk and think about it all without fainting and screaming that there was darkness creeping up to him. And I am even more pleased that there seems to be nothing mixed-up in his strange passion for...

> (*Looks at "Dainas."*)

VIDVUDS: For studying folklore?

RASMA: Forgive me for speaking so openly, we are really strangers.... I'll leave you for a moment.

VIDVUDS: Of course.

RASMA: I must see if he...

VIDVUDS: Rasma, I beg of you.... Don't explain anything to me. I understand. Do not inconvenience yourself. (*RASMA goes inside. VIDVUDS directs his attention to the sky which has by now visibly darkened. The change from night to day and vice-versa is rapid in the south. Some stars already are beginning to twinkle. And the lamps are turned on along the coastal road. Someone is strumming a guitar in the neighboring garden. RASMA comes back into the courtyard, with a shawl thrown across her shoulders.*) You said that we are strangers, but there are not that many people in the world, just think about it, who understands the language that you and I are talking in....

RASMA: You are right there....

> (*She collects the volumes of "Dainas" and sheets of paper which JURIS has spread out on the table. A few fall down. VIDVUDS picks them up.*)

VIDVUDS: I am curious, which ones is your son copying down.... Would he mind my peeking?

RASMA (*smiling*): I don't think it would cause an earthquake.

VIDVUDS: Just one little page.... I'll apologize to Juris later. Let's say, this one... (*Reads.*)

Can't, shan't, won't forgive
My brandy bottle anything!
I'll drink it all, smash it up
In a hundred little pieces.

Did you hear how they confronted the problem in those days, and quite cleverly.

(*Gives the page back to RASMA.*)

RASMA: And, I am afraid, just as unsuccessfully.

VIDVUDS: At least on a recognizable aesthetic level and without obvious didacticism.

RASMA: My grandmother, she was near ninety then, during one of our village festivals started to sing ancient drinking songs at the top of her voice. Someone asked her why was she doing it and she explained: "To sound the alarm, dear, to sound the alarm for a dire need to sober up!"

VIDVUDS: Did she teach any to you, by chance?

RASMA: Oh boy, did she.

VIDVUDS: For example.

RASMA: For example... (*Sings.*)

"I am a liquor-loving lass
And never have denied it.

One dizzy day I drank away
My brother's chestnut stallion.

If you keep on chattering
I'll drink away his pony.

He who wants me for a wife
Must build a courtyard still.

Then mornings I'll be able
To step over and get my fill.

(*When RASMA finishes the song, applause and shouts of bravo are heard from the neighbor's garden. RASMA takes it in good stride, she knew she had an audience and is at her ease, radiant and smiling.... An unseen accordian player below tries to repeat the melody just heard.*)

VOICES: Rasma Arvidovna, k nam! Zshdem vas!

RASMA: O myenya gost!

VOICES: No e chto? Vozmite s soboy! Priglasite! Gost dorogoy, milostu prosim! Igite oba! Rasma!

RASMA: Spasiba!
> (*The accordion player cuts loose now with a loud and fairly accurate rendition of the song, drowning out the voices.*)

RASMA: I was just about to go over there, when you came. They are entertaining some Abkhazian friends from the mountains, who must be back in their village tomorrow night for the New Year's Eve. What do you say?

VIDVUDS: Go empty handed to a strange house for the first time?

RASMA: Why empty, you have your black balsam bottle, I have a box of chocolates from Riga... I'll just tell my son.
> (*RASMA goes inside, taking along three volumes of "Dainas" and the notes JURIS had left on the table. The accordion player is playing Rasma's song, the neighbors are singing along without words. RASMA returns wearing a coat and carrying the chocolate box, and she and VIDVUDS both go up the stairs and disappear in the darkness. Almost immediately a woman comes down. She is wrapped in a coat with the collar turned up and her head is bundled up with a scarf. She goes to the door, knocks. JURIS turns on the veranda light from the inside and the courtyard becomes bright. The rest of the world, now in contrast to the pool of light from the bulb, has sunk into a deep darkness. JURIS appears in the doorway. The woman takes off her scarf, shaking loose her long blond hair and we see that it is LINDA.*)

LINDA: *Ciau!*

JURIS: "Budele"

LINDA: Is that a new cuss word?

JURIS: No, it's from the "Dainas." It's the same as a mummer.

LINDA: Oh.... It was necessary to disguise myself, otherwise I couldn't take a step out of the house.

JURIS: Aren't you exaggerating?

LINDA: Me? It's the other way around, to say the least! Juris, it's going to be the way you wanted it. Vidvuds is flying back tomorrow and I am going to be here alone. The way you wanted it.

JURIS: Congratulations.

LINDA: You're making fun of me, but I'm speaking to you seriously. I made a call this morning to Riga—from the telephone exchange, naturally, and asked Marusja to fix it up.

JURIS: Fix what?

LINDA: So you could have what you wanted.

JURIS: I don't understand.

LINDA: Look, Vidvuds soon got a long distance call, sort of garbled, you know, like about his wife's health, like something being up with his daughter at the University, like drastic changes in his job right after

New Year's.... The old boy didn't understand a thing, got all upset and wasted no time getting over to the ticket office to book a flight....

JURIS: Who is he?

LINDA: He is the head of our applied arts department and also does a bit of woodcarving himself. On the whole, he is supposed to be quite popular.

JURIS: And you?

LINDA: Me?

JURIS: What do you do there?

LINDA: Everyone is afraid of me because I know a lot, therefore, they try to please me, but actually, I am just a messenger. (*From the neighbor's garden come voices and laughter. Someone is again strumming guitar strings. JURIS listens attentively.*) You know I'm through with him. We had a violent quarrel.

JURIS: What about?

LINDA: Since I saw you again and saw how you've changed, I realized that I didn't and never will have anything in common with him. (*Silence. Sound of guitar.*) Juris! You're not going to say anything? When you wrote me and asked me to come, I specifically arranged for his accomodations at a holiday spot in Picunda, and I had the idea.... Most people can't do like you and your mother. They don't have cars and houses which to sell, so that they can rent cottages in Gagra where it's possible to get a tan even in winter.

JURIS: You mean our house is sold?

LINDA: Didn't you know that? Ask me, I'll tell you all the details.... But you, when I go through all that trouble to finally get here, you treat me as cool as you please, to say the least, and your stuck-up mother...

JURIS: Linda, I hadn't told her yet about the accident. It was hard to bring it up, and I was afraid of how she would take it, because... but right after that she was out in the courtyard laughing and singing.

LINDA: Singing!

JURIS: Never heard anything like that coming from her either.... That kind of song, I mean.

LINDA: Now you're beginning to see what she is, your mother.... Last night, on the other hand, she swore at me in the worst way and made me leave.

JURIS: What did she say to you?

LINDA: Her? It's not the words that are important, it's the tone of voice in which they are said. To another person, those same words would probably mean something totally different, but coming from her mouth, though she never said anything specific, they sounded so insulting and horrible that later I had a good cry.... And why, why, may I ask you, was I subjected to such remarks? Because of my good heart? When I decided to join you, did anyone tell me that you had changed completely? No, I came to see the same Mumbler; I came, because I felt I was needed here!

(*A man's voice in the neighbor's garden starts a song accompanied by a guitar, and all the visitors there join in the chorus. LINDA falls silent, studiously wiping her tears with a handkerchief. Both she and JURIS listen to the song.*)

>Tsiganka molodaya
>Kak noch ti provyela?
>Tsiganka otvechala:
>—Ya ve kabare bila!
>
>O, daete yei gitaru,
>Naleite yei vina,
>Prishlite yei malchishku,
>V kogo ta vlublena!
>
>I dali yei gitaru,
>Nalili yei vina,
>No—ne prishel malchishka,
>V kogo ta vlublena....

(*The solo part is now taken over by a high woman's voice.*)

>Malchishki, vi malchishkii,
>Holoniye serdtsa,
>Vi lubite slovami
>No serdtsem nikogda.

(*The song ends with applause, laughter, and tinkling of glasses.*)

LINDA: What a song, really hits home.... You all are just the same.... Always taking advantage....

JURIS: You said that our house is sold?

LINDA: Furniture and all. But the money the repaired Volga was worth, your mother gave to the family of the other driver, although actually he was to blame also and was never hurt that much, since he is working again, only in a different job. (*VIDVUD's voice is heard in the neighbor's garden. LINDA falls silent and listens.*)

VIDVUDS (*sings unseen*):

>And so tonight
>I sing
>my dark
>blue song...
>And so, tonight

246

> I sing
> my dark
> blue song!

Rasma, is that you? Why did you run off?

LINDA: No, it's me! (*VIDVUDS falls silent.*) He stopped.... We had quite a run-in, you know... Well, Juris? What's it going to be? Are you honestly going to stand by and let me be out in the streets of a strange city and without a cent in my pocket?

(*RASMA comes hastily down the steps. LINDA, startled, looks back at her.*)

RASMA: Linda, what did I tell you last night?

LINDA: Your son is a grown man and can make his own...

RASMA (*interrupts*): Go away, please, and don't come back to see us again.

LINDA: I am not coming to see you, if you'll forgive me, but...

RASMA: Linda! (*JURIS, who has been leaning against the doorframe up to now, sits down in a chair by the door.*)

LINDA: Juris, don't let her do this. You called me, and I am here, but your dear mother is probably afraid that in the future she's not going to be the only one handling the money which she, without your knowing it, got for the house...

RASMA: Juris, the night is chilly. Don't you think it would be better for you inside?

LINDA: If you allow her to drive me away, I'll go down and jump in the ocean, I mean that....

JURIS (*quietly*): Mother...

RASMA: Yes?

JURIS: What do you have against her?

RASMA: I had resolved never to tell it to you, never.

JURIS: Why?

RASMA: It concerns your father.

JURIS: Please, tell me. I have to know.

RASMA: Perhaps you, Linda, will leave without causing a scene?

LINDA: Not a chance! And that, which you are threatening me with, is hardly all that earth-shaking, if you want my opinion.

RASMA: Is that the way you see it?

LINDA: I can tell it to him myself, and why does it involve his father, it pertains only to me and no one else.

RASMA: What sort of person are you, I don't understand. When I look at you, I get frightened.

JURIS: Mother...

RASMA: I still must tell it to you, so you may understand that she...

JURIS: Say it.

RASMA: You asked me yesterday, son, why did I scream when I saw Linda in my bed.... Because, it wasn't the first time.

JURIS: Not the first?

(*LINDA turns away.*)

RASMA: Didn't your father tell you, while driving to Mindau, that I had left him?

JURIS: No. You mean you...

RASMA: Not a word?

JURIS: Not a word. Pop was very depressed and drank a lot, but...

RASMA: And didn't gro tell you anything?

JURIS: Gro?

RASMA: I have an awful suspicion that she, gro, went along with you to Riga just because of that.... Let's cut the conversation, you're not feeling well...

JURIS: No, I only... Keep going. You said, it wasn't the first time. When was the first?

RASMA: Father knew that I was on a business trip to Moscow for a week, but I flew back earlier, unlocked our house door, went into the bedroom and...

(*Looks at LINDA.*)

LINDA   You're lying if you're trying to say that.... Juris, your mother is lying.

RASMA (*looks carefully at her son*): Juris...

(*JURIS is staring at a point in space, and the stage becomes almost completely dark, the way JURIS now perceives his surroundings, and RASMA and LINDA on each side of him are only silhouettes. A guitar is heard in Rozanov's garden. The third silhouette moving down the steps looks like VIDVUDS.*)

LINDA: How can you lie like that! The truth was that...

RASMA: Shut up!

LINDA: I love him, although he always treated me like dirt, to say the least, and I also don't mind that he is now considered the murderer of three people and that he'll stand trial after he gets well, I am even ready for that, just so that I can be with him!

VIDVUDS: Linda, what you are saying, these terrible things...

LINDA: What do you care, you old goat?

VIDVUDS: Linda, Linda...

LINDA: Juris, you were jealous of him, therefore I'll tell him in front of you that he can just go back to his wife and children, because I am letting him.

RASMA: This is too much. Don't you see what's happening to Juris?

248

VIDVUDS: Rasma, shall I get a doctor?

LINDA: Juris!

RASMA: Go away, or I'll... No Vidvuds, it's not necessary, I'll handle this.... I know what to do... just help me get him to his room.

VIDVUDS: Allow me...

(*Lifts JURIS up with the whole chair and with RASMA's help, carries it inside. The stage becomes light again. In the neighboring garden a number of male voices start up a song, and from all the ones that were heard tonight, this song comes the closest in capturing the sea, the mountains, and the southern night. VIDVUDS returns to the courtyard.*)

LINDA: (*half afraid*) Did he lose consciousness?

(*VIDVUDS does not answer. Sound of the song. After a while, RASMA comes out. She goes straight to LINDA and it appears that she is about to hit the girl, therefore, LINDA retreats and flattens herself against the side of the house... But RASMA gets hold of herself and with an outstretched hand, commandingly points to the steps. LINDA obeys the silent command. With her head pulled in her shoulders, still warding off the blow, she moves to the steps, rushes up, and disappears in the night.*)

RASMA: Vidvuds, how old are your children?

VIDVUDS: My daughter will be twenty, my son eighteen.

RASMA: My son will soon be twenty one. The years go so fast.... Seems like not too long ago when I brought him his first schoolboy's cap.... Vidvuds, I'm sure you know approximately how I feel now, but let's not talk about it, I beg you, let's talk about something else. I guess it's those three Abkhazians singing...

VIDVUDS: Yes, I've been listening.... It's a song that was born high up in the hills. Have you noticed that songs from the flatlands are structured quite differently? The songs of the steppe or the desert, let's say.

RASMA: I heard an Arab in Egypt once, he was singing while sitting on his camel.... You're right. It was totally different. It sounded like—"water."

VIDVUDS: Latvian songs, of course, do not echo a cry for water, since they sprang from forests and marshes, a land full of rivers.... In our songs, one feels more of a longing for sunlight, for summer....

RASMA: "Come hither, summertime".... Vidvuds, they are actually singing in various voices.

VIDVUDS: The polyphony of a nation.... And they can sing with amazing harmony and beauty.

(*Both listen.*)

RASMA (*after a moment*): Shall we rejoin them? (*VIDVUDS looks at her in surprise. RASMA laughs.*) You have two grown children, Vidvuds, but you yourself are still just like a child. You came down south for the first time in your life, got acquainted with a platinum blond from Riga, and you don't have the slightest idea who she is or how to act towards her.... I have to laugh, excuse me, each time I think of how you escorted her here yesterday, so as to protect her from the advances of the local hotblooded young men.... Her, Linda! Actually what you should have done was to go a little ways in front of her and loudly warn those poor boys to get off the road.... You're so naive. (*Pause.*) Forgive me, I don't know what I'm saying.... When I have to sit by my son the way I have done it through countless long nights.... Thank you, Vidvuds, for coming, and say hello to Riga for me.
(*RASMA leaves quickly. The door slams shut behind her. VIDVUDS listens to the song. The song rises loud and full, telling about the hill tribe's way of life, and it has nothing in common with the dead end in which the few visitors from Riga find themselves in. It is a good song.*)

ACT THREE

(*Morning of next day. The sun is already up but as of yet, unable to disperse the fog. The ocean is not visible. The immediate surroundings are gray. In the corner of the veranda, someone is sleeping in the cane reclining chair, legs tucked under and covered with heavy carpet-like tablecloth. Roosters crow. Once, twice, somewhere further away, a third time, and their sounds somehow get smothered in the fog. RASMA comes out in her coat and scarf. She is holding a shopping bag. The sleeper pushes away the blanket, revealing LINDA. RASMA stares at her.*)
LINDA: Good morning...
RASMA: Good heavens, You!
LINDA: I'm frozen stiff....
(*Gets up, and shivering from the morning chill, spreads the tablecloth back on the table.*)
RASMA: You sat here the whole night?
LINDA: At first I walked.... That is, from the very first when you drove me away, I, of course, started to walk to Picunda, but realized on the

way, that I could not leave, because I had to tell you how it all really happened.

RASMA: I don't want to know. Nothing, do you understand? I don't want to see you.

LINDA: But why?

RASMA: Oh boy, oh boy....

LINDA: At first it seemed to me that you were just lying through your teeth, but later, when I had calmed down somewhat, it all became clear to me.

RASMA: Please, go away.

LINDA: It was simply a case of misunderstanding. You thought that...

RASMA: Linda...

LINDA: Yes, I'll go, but do you have any hot tea? I'm shivering... After this excruciating night I'm sure I'll be sick, and where am I going to be laid up here in Georgia...

(*Starts to cry.*)

RASMA (*after a moment of indecision*): Come in the kitchen.

LINDA (*through her tears, trying to stop her shivers*): Is Juris better?

RASMA: You leave Juris alone.

LINDA: Yes, but is he...

RASMA: Don't even try to go near him, do you hear me?

LINDA: I hear you...

RASMA: Last night you nearly killed him.

LINDA: Wasn't it you who...

RASMA: Yes, I also lost my self control for a moment and forgot myself, you're right. That's how far you pushed me; you can be proud of that, and have quite a laugh.

LINDA: What's there to laugh about....

RASMA: Come inside, you really don't look well. Even your teeth are chattering.

(*LINDA follows RASMA into the house. VIDVUDS comes down the steps. He is wearing a coat, hat and carries a suitcase. He puts the suitcase down in the courtyard, looks at the house... Then walks over to the low stone fence which borders off Rozanov's courtyard, and looks down at the ocean. Nothing much is to be seen there, the world has shrunk quite small all of a sudden. RASMA comes back to shut the door that has been left open and spots VIDVUDS.*)

RASMA: Good morning. Up so early?

VIDVUDS: Good morning. On my way to Adler...

RASMA: That's right, you're flying away.... At what time?

VIDVUDS: There's plenty of time, the flight to Riga leaves only in the evening, it's just that I felt restless.

RASMA: I understand.

VIDVUDS: Linda didn't get back in last night.

RASMA: Linda is here.

VIDVUDS: Here?

RASMA: She's drinking tea in the kitchen. Do you have any cognac?

VIDVUDS: Yes.

RASMA: Let me have some, if you don't mind. (*VIDVUDS opens his suitcase, searches.*) She caught a chill sitting outside all night long and has a slight fever.

VIDVUDS: Here you are. (*Hands RASMA a cognac bottle three quarters full.*) Do you think that's enough?

RASMA: More than enough. I'll make some grog and then she can go.

VIDVUDS: Aren't you supposed to lie down after drinking grog?

RASMA: I guess so... I just didn't think of that. Linda in our house, oh no! Take this back, thank you. Tea will do just fine.

VIDVUDS: You don't have to make grog, just pour a couple of fingers in a glass to drink with the tea.

RASMA: You think that's alright...

VIDVUDS: Sure.

(*Closes the suitcase and picks it up.*)

RASMA: Don't leave just yet, you don't have to hurry. Let's have some breakfast.

VIDVUDS: I don't want to trouble you, other than that I...

RASMA: Can't object, of course. Won't it be too cold outside? The living room is a mess, and in the kitchen...

VIDVUDS: Too cold? Now? C'mon. Look at the roses, in bloom, nothing wrong with them, nor the palm trees down on the boulevard, although it had to be near freezing in the early hours... Are we northerners going to appear weaker than these roses and palm trees?

RASMA (*smiling*): Tea or coffee?

VIDVUDS: What are you having?

RASMA: Coffee.

VIDVUDS: The same for me, please.

(*RASMA goes inside. VIDVUDS arranges the table, places the chairs. The Rozanovs turn on the loudspeaker and the morning news is heard in Russian, after that, music. RASMA returns with all the necessary breakfast items. Also on the platter are two small glasses and the cognac bottle which stands now half empty. VIDVUDS tries to help RASMA.*)

RASMA: Sit down, you are the guest... I'll manage.

(*VIDVUDS sits down dutifully. RASMA places everything on the table and pours the coffee, then sits herself. Neither RASMA nor*

VIDVUDS are actually hungry, therefore during their conversation, if they pick up something, it is for the sake of doing so. They drink their coffee, though.)

VIDVUDS: Your coffee is out of this world....

RASMA: Vidvuds, you said that everything around us must constantly change and transform, including people.... Were you serious?

VIDVUDS: I must have said that a long time ago.

RASMA: As far back as yesterday!

VIDVUDS: The punishment that I received for such thinking and talking, was at any rate serious....

RASMA: I don't know how it happened, but my husband and I, through all our twenty years of marriage, lived only for each other. Those were beautiful years, and if they were shadowed in any way, then only towards the end in the obvious failure of raising a son, which finally caught up with us and destroyed us....

VIDVUDS: Rasma...

(Points to the small open window pane, used for ventilation.)

RASMA: Juris is asleep behind two doors, and after his attacks, he is dead to the world for a long time.

VIDVUDS: You were probably quite young when you married.

RASMA: Yes, but my husband was already an engineer and after the wedding, his mother gave us a house, which we eventually fixed up in style; I put in a garden.... After that I started to work again since we wanted to live well, but could not make it on his salary—we wanted a car, we wanted to travel—every year we went somewhere, every year, and always together, the northern islands, Central Asia, around Europe in a ship, we also were in Italy, we were in Egypt....

VIDVUDS: Where was your son during all this time?

RASMA: Up until he was ten years old, my mother-in-law looked after him. By then he could take care of himself and my mother-in-law moved to Mindau to live with her relatives.

VIDVUDS: Because he was getting on her nerves....

RASMA: That wasn't too hard to guess. Of course. He was like quicksilver in those days.

VIDVUDS: The boy never lacked anything, am I right?

RASMA: Not a thing.

VIDVUDS: Obviously. The third generation...

RASMA: So what?

VIDVUDS: The first one has it really tough, it gets tempered through struggle, becomes strong, overcomes its obstacles and wins. The second generation, which by now has a base to step off from, and moreoever, during its childhood and youth had fought alongside the first, goes further on and climbs higher, but the third is handed everything on a silver platter...

RASMA: And starts to waste and squander?

VIDVUDS: Doesn't it?

RASMA: You can just keep your generalizations. Maybe it's true in... Turkey, where other circumstances and social conditions prevail. In our country, it should be different.

VIDVUDS: Should be, that's right.... Should be!

RASMA: Besides, you cannot make generalizations from one extreme example.

VIDVUDS: It is an extreme example, if we judge it by its consequences, but in truth, you'll be able to find something strongly resembling it even in my house, no need to look too far...

RASMA: Don't tell me.

VIDVUDS: A friend once gave me Pestalozzi to read, and according to Pestalozzi, all that so called good upbringing is love plus a personal example, do you follow me? Love plus personal example, we can even say—ideal.... But what kind of an example or an ideal can I be for my children who hardly even see me? And when they do see me... (*Throws up his hands.*) Maybe it's better that they don't....

RASMA (*stands up*): Yesterday, Vidvuds, you heard me raising my voice, and I wouldn't want you to leave taking with you the image of some hysterical woman...

VIDVUDS: Don't be silly.

RASMA: You must understand why I cannot look upon Linda and keep calm.... Listen. My husband and I knew everything about each other, we shared the joys, sorrows, everything; and when coming home unexpectedly, I found Linda in my bed, it was the most horrible experience in my life. It's not good to say this, I know, but even... even the tragic accident on the highway did not shake me up as much.... My whole world got turned upside down. I wrote a short note not to expect me home, and went away empty handed, just like I was at that moment. I don't know if Linda also left or stayed there, that didn't interest me in the least.... I never saw my husband again. The next day he took my son, drove down to Mindau to his mother, and then a day later.... Well, you know about the rest. That's all. I'm sorry that I still get upset although I promised myself to talk calmly. Let me pour you some coffee. Oh, it's cold.... Well, of course, how else. Outside.

VIDVUDS (*pours cognac in glasses*): I'd like to drink this strong stuff to you, Rasma....

RASMA: Thank you.

(*Takes a glass. VIDVUDS rises, they toast. At this moment a noise of something falling is heard inside. VIDVUDS and RASMA exchange glances. RASMA puts her glass back on the table, but VIDVUDS drinks his. The door opens slowly. JURIS appears in it, wearing his white sweater. He leans on the doorframe with one hand, while clasping to himself a volume of "Dainas" with the other.)*

RASMA: Why aren't you... sleeping?

JURIS: I heard everything.

RASMA: I was sure that you were asleep.

JURIS: I already heard it yesterday, but I somehow managed to shut myself off, and only now I realize why papa drank so much in Mindau and why he asked Gro to come along to Riga, although she didn't want to, and why Gro, on the other hand, insisted that Madame Schwan, the old attorney held by you in such high esteem, must come along also.... Mamma, why didn't you tell me this sooner? Why did you have to wait until there is a complete stranger present, who even drags along a streetwalker.

RASMA: Juris, please.

JURIS: He dragged her along from Riga.

RASMA: You know very well that they met in Picunda.

JURIS: You just go ahead and believe him.... Are you really that naive? Mamma I want to know about Madame Schwan. What kind of an authority did you think she was, that old...

RASMA: Be quiet.

JURIS: Dressed in the latest fashion, she...

RASMA: Juris! Just like Gro, she tried to keep herself elegant, she wouldn't for any reason wrap a warm woolen scarf around her head and make like an old biddy.... You ought to consider that and respect it, the pride in older ladies. You shouldn't be sarcastic about it.

JURIS: What kind of influence did she have over you?

RASMA: Don't go Vidvuds, because I feel there is a connection here between our conversation.... In school, she was not afraid to tell us girls, that our primary duty will be to sacrifice ourselves for the next generation and grow with it together, instead of attempting to compete with all our might with men in the stone quarries, the steel mills, on the tractor.... Only the strongest and the most talented of us would be able to do that, she said, that and much more, to get on the stage, shoot movies, write books and make scientific discoveries, but even the boldest and bravest of us would have to ask ourselves: how will it affect my child.

JURIS: You, of course, feel that you have followed her advice....

RASMA: To the best of my ability.

(LINDA appears behind JURIS.)

255

LINDA: Let me by! (*JURIS moves aside.*) He did not drag me here, I dragged him.... Just so it is clear, because I like everything to be clear.
(*Comes outside. It is obvious that the home remedy has taken an effect.*)
RASMA: Is your fever gone?
LINDA: Yes. Vidvuds, let's go.
VIDVUDS: Let's go. I to Adler and you to where?
LINDA: Aha.... If I hadn't tossed down your cognac, my teeth would probably still be chattering and I'd be snivelling about my cruel fate, but now I'm going to speak. First, about you, Vidvuds.
VIDVUDS: Listen to me, Linda...
LINDA: Don't interrupt me! It is now the thirty first of December, and on the first of January I have always started a new life with a clear conscience, therefore, I confess here publicly, that your long distance call from Riga was on my special orders.
VIDVUDS: On your... what did you say?
LINDA: You can take it easy, go back to Picunda and unpack your suitcase. There's nothing wrong with your better half nor with your dear student daughter, and there are no switcheroos expected in your job. That was about you. Now about Juris. A streetwalker, imagine that.... And who do I hear it from? The Mumbler! From...
(*Catches herself.*)
JURIS: Go on, why did you stop?
LINDA: It doesn't matter.... Next I have to talk about myself and I feel really ashamed, because what I have to say will be... but there's no other way, I have to say it all, now or never.... (*To RASMA*) You had it all figured wrong. The truth was this: Juris took me to your home and then ran off somewhere, he was so soused, he probably later forgot about me.... On his way out he said that nobody was home and not to expect anyone the next day either, and so I stayed there, in your house.... What did I do? I listened to records, turned on the TV.... Ate very well, because the fridge, I must say, was stocked something royal.... Then I took a bath, that was an occasion, such a bathroom.... I used to idolize Brigitte Bardo, and in one film she splashed around a tub like that with mirrors on the walls.... Well, and then, then I... then I went to bed. What else could I have done, it was already late.... (*RASMA is staring at LINDA and has turned quite pale. JURIS collapses in a chair.*) Yesterday I had no idea that you were going to tell Juris all this, because I expected that you were going to reveal my being fired from your company after that ruckus with the foreign sailors, where I, among other things, wasn't all that guilty.... I

256

happened to be in your bed because I found the couch in Juris' room too hard, and I decided that since I had bathed in a Brigitte Bardot bathtub, I'll just go ahead and sleep in a real bed.... When you turned on the light, I awoke and was nearly frightened out of my wits, because you were staring at me as at a corpse or at a...

RASMA: Enough... I have no more strength....

LINDA: Don't exaggerate, please. If it had happened like you said yesterday, it would have been very shocking, I agree with you there wholeheartedly, but nothing like that happened, phui! I've never even seen your husband!

JURIS: So thus it's me. Thus there, on the highway, I just ended it. Put in the period.

LINDA: Stop your babbling!

VIDVUDS: Rasma, do you want me to take her away? (*RAMSA nods silently.*) I guess there's nothing else I could do for you....

RASMA: Are you going to stay in Picunda?

VIDVUDS: No, I'm flying to Riga.

LINDA: And me?

VIDVUDS: Let's go, Linda.

LINDA: Okay. (*VIDVUDS picks up his suitcase and both go to the steps. On the steps LINDA stops and looks back.*) Happy New Year!

VIDVUDS: C'mon. Move.

(*Both disappear. JURIS opens the "Dainas" volume. Children are heard singing over the neighbors' loudspeaker.*)

JURIS (*reads*): Mara* locate me a cow,
               Locate me a white-backed one;
               Blue and...

Mamma, do you hear?
               Blue and motley for the others
               Let me have a white-backed one.

(*RASMA is silent. The fog has for the most part disappeared, and the sun is beginning to dominate once more. Down below, the ocean shimmers a bright blue.*) Mamma, what do you think it means here "locate"? "Locate, Mara"... From the word "locate" "to find"? It doesn't sound right... Aha, it must be from the word "allocate," shortened to "locate"... It's the same as "to give".... What do you think? It could be, couldn't it? (*RASMA is silent. The children sing. VIDVUDS' face appears behind the stone wall. He puts his elbows on the fence, looks at RASMA as if to speak to her. VIDVUDS is spotted*

---

* One of the many benevolent deities who accompanies and protects a person from his cradle to grave.

by JURIS.) Mamma, over there.

(*RASMA looks over.*)

VIDVUDS: Rasma, I'd like a word with you please. (*RASMA moves nearer him.*) It's I... Linda ran off and I stopped in at the Rozanovs. If you ever need something, just call. No need to go around on the street, there is a garden ladder here now. Cal Rozanov brought it over and put it up, but Salome asked if you wanted something from the store. You're not to leave little Juris alone even for a moment, that's what Salome said.

RASMA: Did you tell them anything?

VIDVUDS: Now what do you think! I, tell them!

RASMA: Sorry.

VIDVUDS: They were standing here yesterday in the dark not understanding what's going on, and were ready to come help... Cal even ran and got the ladder from another neighbor.

RASMA: Tell them thank you, and I'll ask Salome... later Vidvuds, right now I'm still unable to think, right now I feel like I've been run over and cut in half, and the two pieces...

VIDVUDS: Still I have to ask you... Rasma, I understand, but let's look at my situation together for a moment, shall we? I'll return the airline ticket and stay here, that I've decided. Before showing myself home with an egg on my face, I have to work out a certain philosophical platform. It's too much to hope for forgiveness, I'm not going to pretend about that, but somehow, I'll have to continue going on in the world, somehow and somewhere...

RASMA: At home say exactly what you told me here, about the egg...

VIDVUDS: You think so? It won't work.... While talking to you I was sort of musing on a solution, but to say something like that out loud, oh no! I'm not going to lose all of my self-respect.

RASMA: I believe that everything can be forgiven.

VIDVUDS: Everything?

RASMA (*looks back and sees that JURIS is leafing through the "Dainas" volume; she goes down on her knees so as to be nearer VIDVUDS and to be able to talk quietly*): Everything except that what I have done.... Vidvuds, even if I saw in that... that bed not only Linda alone, even then I should have made sure first if my eyes were not fooling me and to ask... later... if that wasn't some kind of a hallucination because of drinking or... oh God, what am I saying, that sounds almost insane, but you understand don't you...

VIDVUDS: I understand....

RASMA: If my husband would answer me and say, yes, and say, from now on I... Then, only then I could write my bitter note and run away from the house in the middle of the night, and no one could blame me for that.... Nothing like that happened, not even remotely, and by forsaking him, I destroyed him. He couldn't understand it at all, the way he was.... First of all he looked for me everywhere, in vain, and then he dashed off to his mother in Mindau for advice.... Vidvuds, I'm trying with all my might to hold myself back from screaming my head off, that wouldn't be proper, would it?

VIDVUDS: No, no... No! I'm going down to the airline booking office to return my ticket, but after that, I'll be here all day with the Rozanovs. They have a strange cypress root lying in their courtyard, actually it's a whole stump; and I'm going to carve them a New Year's present for decorating their wall outside. It will be a memento of my visit to Georgia.

RASMA: What will it be?

VIDVUDS: A billy goat's head... (*Looks at JURIS. RASMA looks back and sees that JURIS is getting up. RASMA stands up also.*) Rasma, I almost forgot... Take it. (*Hands her a copper bell.*) The Rozanovs sent it and said for you to just ring it, they'll be over like a flash.

RASMA: Thank you.

VIDVUDS: It's a cow bell, for hundreds of years it's been handed down from generation to generation in Salome's family. If it ever fell off a cow and got lost, the whole family would go up in the high pastures and look for it until they found it.... Now it hangs inside in the place of honor, over the color TV!
(*Off.*)

JURIS: Let me have it, please. (*RASMA crosses the courtyard to JURIS and hands him the bell. JURIS examines it carefully.*) Did we have these in Latvia also?

RASMA: Of course, only smaller. Looking after cows in a wooded area would have been impossible without a bell.

JURIS: Every cow had her own sound...

RASMA: Not everyone, the leader.

JURIS: Bessy?

RASMA: Also Bessy.
(*Down the steps comes LINDA with a shopping net, and around her head she again has tied a scarf. JURIS sits down in his place behind the desk and places the volume of "Dainas" and the bell in front of him. RASMA looks at LINDA. Her pronounced hate for the girl seems to have disappeared, at least she is able to look at her calmly.*)

LINDA: Because of me you didn't get to the store for bread, so I brought some. Also a couple of little things. (*She hangs up the shopping net on a nail and takes off her scarf. Instead of the long, platinum blond hair falling freely over the shoulders, we see a short, close cropped hairdo.*) The hair got left behind with the beautician, where I realized... No sense to hang around here with hair like that, especially at work, because I'm going to get myself a job, I got to make enough to get back to Riga. (*RASMA returns to the fence and looks at the ocean. LINDA comes over and stands beside her.*) Among other things, I know what it means to fight for one's son, becaue I too am a mother...

RASMA (*looks at her*): You?

LINDA: My son is three years old, and how I have fought, both with a smile on my lips and with tooth and nail, just to get him a father, but it looks like it's probably not worth it...

RASMA: Where is he being brought up?

LINDA: In the country, with my mother.... It's interesting, how you accomplished it, changing Juris so. You probably don't even know how he was earlier, because, at home, I'm sure he tried to behave.... Our friends then, let's speak openly, were from a lower level crowd, that's to say, they did a lot of boozing, but even they couldn't stand him, because actually being nothing, he pretended like he really was something, and nobody likes that anywhere.... He was only tolerated because he always had money, and he also drove us around willingly in his car whenever somebody had to go somewhere; he himself never had to go anywhere, one place was to him like another, a smirk and a snigger. Speed, that was the only thing that meant something to him.... The girls that stuck with him were from the bottom of the barrel, I may as well tell you, and that was why he probably, here in the south, remembered and specifically called me, because thinking of my son's future, I at least kept a cool head...

RASMA: I understood that you came here by yourself.

LINDA: I have his letter, but it has no more meaning, he is a completely different person—God, sitting there and learning little verses by heart, he is probably going to recite them tonight when you light the candles.... I am looking at him and still can't believe it.... How long do you intend to stay here?

RASMA: The house is rented until the first of April. We'll still have enough money then for one return trip and for the initial period while I get settled in Riga and get some kind of a job.

LINDA: Oh... But I had calculated, that...

RASMA: You miscalculated. Those who informed you obviously did not know anything about Silvia Schwan's foster-children nor about... nor about a lot of things.

LINDA: Oh... Well, then, I'm off.

RASMA: All right.

LINDA: No, you mistook my meaning, I only... May I come up for a visit some evening? (*RASMA shrugs her shoulders.*) Fine, I'll come up. So long, now. (*RASMA does not answer. LINDA goes up to JURIS and embarces him spontaneously.*) Don't be angry with me, chum... Ciau, for now, but don't worry, I'm not going to abandon you in your misery.

(*LINDA kisses JURIS, rushes up the steps and disappears JURIS rises. RASMA looks at him.*)

JURIS: Mamma, how am I going to live; how and why?

RASMA: I'm going to start working again either as a patternmaker or somewhere else, work doesn't scare me, and we'll...

JURIS: When I asked you how will I live, I wasn't thinking of what will I eat...

RASMA: You have never thought of that, never.... You were always well fed, clothed and sheltered, you never had to tend cows when you were seven like I did, you were able to go to school and even could have gone on to a university like most of your classmates did. Papa and I had provided you every opportunity, but nothing interested you, absolutely nothing, not even that what papa was doing in his factory, and what I was doing was also boring to you, so papa stopped talking of things at home and you therefore got an impression that he was just taking it easy, and that he could be looked down upon by others, even by an old, dumb cow near the main road.... For your information, the whole technical aspect of the factory was resting squarely on papa's shoulders, and during the first months without him, it was hard, a lot of people told me...

JURIS: But... why did I have to be interested in anything, maybe the blue cow should have come and talked to me?

RASMA: Juris... And you're saying *that* to me? Didn't I tell you hundreds of times, for you...

JURIS: Okay, okay, yes you did. I remember.... (*He absentmindedly rings the bell.*) If the Rozanovs knew what kind of a person I am, would they still want to wait for the New Year together with us?

RASMA: I'm afraid it would depress them, because seeing you, they would constantly be thinking about...

(*Catches herself.*)

JURIS: Just like you, right? (*RASMA is silent.*) Just like you... Very well. When Linda comes back I'm going to go away with her.

RASMA (*with unexpected, though unintentional vehemence*): Why don't you learn first to cross the courtyard and come back?

JURIS: Yes, I haven't been successful yet, but I'll try.

(He climbs down, leaving behind for the first time the elevation of the veranda, and slowly starts across the courtyard towards the ocean. Each step demands from him a great effort.)

RASMA *(startled and realizes that she has done something irreversible)*: That's far enough, come back... Juris! Do you hear me?

(JURIS, gathering all his physical and mental strength, crosses the courtyard. Not far from the stone wall, he stops, stretches his hand holding the bell towards the ocean. RASMA looks on, pressing the back of her hand to her mouth. The stage slowly grows dim. The bell tinkles shyly. Then the stage sinks into darkness. The bell falls down, rolls tinkling forward, slams against a stone, and grows silent.)

CURTAIN

CINDERELLAGAME

In six scenes
by
Paul-Eerik Rummo

Translated from the Estonian by
Andres Männik
and
Mardi Valgemäe

Introduction to ₍
Cinderellagame

One of the leading young poets of Soviet Estonia, Paul-Eerik Rummo was born on January 19, 1942, in the capital city of Tallinn. He is a graduate of Tartu University, where he majored in literature. In addition to authoring several highly acclaimed volumes of verse, Rummo has translated Russian, Finnish, and English poetry, including Dylan Thomas's *Under Milk Wood*, and has written children's plays as well as libretti for musicals. His dramatic works include "Of an Eagle and Prometheus," "Pseudopus," and "Strange People." *Cinderellagame* (*Tuhkatriinumäng*) opened at Tartu's Theatre "Vanemuine" on February 19, 1969.

The widely-known fairy tale of Cinderella ends with a rebirth as its heroine moves literally from ashes to diamonds. *Cinderellagame* begins where the fairy tale ends. The Prince, having married Cinderella nine years ago, leaves his entourage and journeys alone to the former home of his wife. There he encounters a new Cinderella, whose foot seems to fit the slipper, but the shoe turns out to be a fake. While trying to discuss matters with the Second Daughter, he is lured into the warm bed of the First Daughter. Both remind him of the girl in the kitchen. His problem is indeed complicated: with his wife, the Court Cinderella, hard at his heels, which of the four is the real Cinderella? Though he has two probing talks with the Master of the House, the Prince fails to unravel life's motives for giving him the wrong girl—if, indeed, he did get the wrong girl—until he encounters the Stepmother, here called the Mistress of the House, whereupon the annual visit draws quickly to a close.

The cyclical structure of Rummo's play, incorporating the journey metaphor, suggests some kind of archetypal seasonal pattern. According to the *Encyclopaedia Britannica*, the almost universal fairy tale of the little cinder girl originated in a nature myth, in which Cinderella was the dawn, oppressed by night clouds (cruel relatives), until rescued by the sun (the prince). Thus we begin our examination of *Cinderellagame* with overtones that conjure up the ancient ritual of seasonal change, of fertility, of death and resurrection, which lead to Euripides' *The Bacchae* and eventually to the Off-Off Broadway production of *Dionysus in 69*. The best drama of all ages reveals man's gradual—and painful—awareness of his human condition. Such movement toward tragic perception may be the legacy of ancient myths and rituals. As Claude Lévi-Strauss has argued in *The Savage Mind*, "Myths and rites are far from being, as has often been held, the product of man's 'myth-making faculty,' turning its back on reality." On the contrary, they constitute "the remains of methods of observation and reflection" and therefore "still remain at the basis of our own civilization." The major area in which these ancient forms flourish today is of course art, for art, according to Levi-Strauss, has retained the element of "savage thought."

How then does Rummo extract the "savage thought" from a shopworn fairy tale? Among the many devices at his disposal are the use of a ritualized *poesie de théâtre* and the injection of absurdist images. Rummo does indeed depict a universe that is devoid of the familiar and the comprehensible. Instead of a storybook Cinderella and her Prince Charming, there are several pretenders to these titles. Furthermore, the Prince not only has a double but is reputedly simply one of many princes who inhabit a multitude of·castles that abound in the hostile countryside. Though he is the legitimate heir to the country's throne, the Prince is powerless, for the ruthless and cunning dictator in the play is the crippled Mistress of the House who sits in a wheelchair. Is Rummo suggesting that usurped power not only corrupts but actually induces illness, that tyranny is a disease? Perhaps. But Rummo is clearly writing more than political allegory, for he creates another plane of meaning by equating the Mistress, who "choose(s) by chance," with capricious life. When she produces some sheets of paper that are supposed to reveal the "rules" of the game, no one is able to read the strange markings on the few pages that are not completely blank. Thus we are quickly transported from the realm of totalitarian politics into that of metaphysics and, like Tertullian of old, cry out: *credo quia absurdum est.*

Like Oedipus, Lear or even Willy Loman, Rummo's Cinderella asks, "Who am I?" The answer seems to be that she is simply a puppet playing interchangeable roles in a meaningless game of charades. Rummo concretizes the idea of the absurdity of man's condition in a visually brilliant scene in which the Prince chases after the crazily wheeling Mistress, while obstacles drop from the flies to impede his movement. It is at this point in the play that the Prince realized the meaninglessness of his quest to unmask the real Cinderella, who has come to represent truth and happiness. This tragic perception is dramatized by a shift from prose to blank verse and the literal opening up of the stage both in height and depth, for until that moment most of the action has taken place in a single, as it were, almost exclusively linear dimension. The Estonian production, directed by Evald Hemakülla, underscored the element of ritual and absurdity in the text by introducing techniques of Antonin Artaud's theatre of cruelty. (Both sexuality and violence, the secondary characteristics of the Dionysiac, are of course present in the text of the play.) In Scene Three, during the Prince's seduction by the First Daughter, members of the "Vanemuine" audience are on record as having yelled in derision, "Shame on the Estonian theatre." In the scene in which the Prince beats Cinderella, the agonizing depiction of violence brought gasps of "Oh my God" and "Enough" from the audience. In *The Theatre and Its Double*, Artaud speaks of "being like victims burnt at the stake, signaling through the flames." We all burn at the stake of life. The fire may stifle our cries, but our gestures reveal the pain. This is the "savage thought" that lies at the core of the theatre of cruelty. The cosmic agony of the Prince in search of his elusive Cinderella ranges from casual sex to calculated sadism, but he cannot free himself from the flames. In the recognition scene, Hermaküla bared the stage to the extent of exposing the lighting system as well as all the visible stage machinery, but even this did not bring forth the real Cinderella or reveal any carefully guarded secrets. For the ultimate truth may be that there is no ultimate truth.

Rummo's absurdist universe is indeed turbulent and savage. But the playwright's world view is not nihilistic. For it is the element of play in *Cinderellagame* that injects a significant note of meaning and order into an apparently meaningless and chaotic cosmos. As Johan Huizinga points out in *Homo Ludens*, "in acknowledging play you acknowledge mind, for whatever else play is, it is not matter... From the point of view of a world wholly determined by the operation of blind forces, play would be altogether superfluous. Play only becomes possible, thinkable and understandable when an influx of *mind* breaks down the absolute determinism of the cosmos." Thus one of the ways in which man could survive the absurdity of the universe or the terrors of tyranny would be to transform reality into play. This, of course, is precisely what happens in such key plays of the absurd as Jean Genet's *The Maids* and Samuel Beckett's *Endgame*. The Cinderella *game* involves a ritualized quest for truth (and happiness), represented by the title figure. The rules of the game are made by the Mistress, and each of the puppet-characters, except of course the Prince, receives orders from her. Cinderella plays unawakened innocence. The First Daughter flaunts her sensual charms. The Second Daughter poses as a bluestocking. Court Cinderella pretends to sophistication. The Master becomes the existential "foolosopher." The Mistress herself assumes the role of Mother Earth and points to the power of the play: "I am not old, as long as I can play. My strength is in the game." As the Prince says, "It seems that everyone is playing the part he was once given and puts up with that part." The Prince's own role is that of the seeker. Disillusioned with the life of the senses (First Daughter) as well as with the intellect (Second Daughter), not to mention phony sophistication (Court Cinderella), he eschews existentialism (the Master) and finds momentary release in the quest itself, for play has made it possible for his mind to conquer "the absolute determinism of the cosmos."

Hand in hand with the concept of play in the contemporary theatre of the absurd goes the awareness of multiple levels of time. The chief categories of performance time may be termed real time, play time and symbolic time. The passage of real time during the production of *Cinderellagame* takes roughly two and a half hours. Play time, however, lasts an entire day. Symbolic time involves the better part of a lifetime, with the action of the play representing the journey of life, the archetypal quest, and man's final perception that he is doomed to failure. In the last scene the Prince and Cinderella, like Didi and Gogo in Beckett's *Waiting for Godot*, talk about the passing of time:

PRINCE: What did you do here all this time?

CINDERELLA: Waited.

PRINCE: Is waiting doing something?

CINDERELLA: Waiting is very much doing something. There's a lot to do while you're waiting.

PRINCE: And what else did you do while you waited?

CINDERELLA: Waited some more.

PRINCE: And then?

CINDERELLA: Some more. And I baked beans. Scorched them.

PRINCE: They'll do.

(*The PRINCE sits... and pitches beans into his mouth...*)

CINDERELLA: But you?

PRINCE: What, me?

CINDERELLA: Prince.

PRINCE: Yes?

CINDERELLA: Yes. Prince. But what did you do all that time, Prince?

PRINCE: I? (*Chokes on a bean. CINDERELLA slaps his back.*) I didn't do a thing. Didn't bake, didn't wait.

A few moments later the fire dies in the hearth, lighted ceremonial candles create a funereal atmosphere, and the Prince steps out of the warm room into a snowstorm. The Cinderellagame is over. Real time, play time and symbolic time have all come to an end. But have they? The Prince is dead. Long live the Prince! As the final curtain falls, the

Mistress, who has been equated with life, winds up the alarm clock and tells Cinderella about the ball to which she will go tomorrow. Having once more failed in his quest, man may die but life goes on, forever holding up the glittering promise of tomorrow. Even though the performance has ended for tonight, tomorrow night the actors will play again.

The beans Cinderella has been baking in the play are used by her to decorate a cake with the number nine. According to James George Frazer's *The Golden Bough*, the European festival of Twelfth Night (in January) featured a King of the Bean and the baking of a great cake with a bean in it. Beans are clearly a variant of wheat, corn, or rice as fertility images, just as the eating of the vegetation gods frequently took place in the form of cakes. Frazer notes, furthermore, that certain Finno-Ugric tribes offered cakes in the shape of sacrificial animals to their gods and hints that the number nine may have been sacred to these people. A more suggestive political implication of the repeated references to the number nine in *Cinderellagame* involves the realization that ancient kings (like contemporary American presidents) held a maximum tenure of eight years, of which seven- and nine-year periods are common corruptions.

As in the ancient myths of seasonal change, the winter of Rummo's discontent must sooner or later yield to the eternally recurring thaw of spring, and, as we recall an earlier speech by the Prince, the fear of tyrannical wolves will eventually be replaced by a feeling of Dionysian ecstasy and release:

> February, February! Wolves scent you;... you, hungry, scent the thaw... The wolves stalk after you, and you stalk after hope... The thaw, the thaw! Where can it be? It has to come... soon all this will crack apart,... and the wolves' starved cadavers will crack on the roads and on the roadbanks. The thaw! The thaw! You run around as if drunk. How everything drips with joy!

By endowing the action of *Cinderellagame* with what at first appears to be an absurd cosmic happening which then developes into an artful—and meaningful—game, Rummo seems to be suggesting that though Dionysus may have been caught in the web of totalitarian *Realpolitik*, he can be released within each of us, if only for the space of two and a half hours, by means of ritualized play.

Mardi Valgemäe

CINDERELLAGAME

CHARACTERS

PRINCE
CINDERELLA
MASTER
FIRST DAUGHTER
SECOND DAUGHTER
COURT CINDERELLA
PRINCE'S DOUBLE
MISTRESS

Note: The above list of characters has been included for the sake of uniformity with the other plays in this volume. Rummo's text does not have such a list, for the Prince and his Double (as well as Cinderella and Court Cinderella) are to be played by the same actor.

(As the audience assembles, both the outer and inner curtain are open. The stage, however, is completely dark, and the outlines of the set cannot be seen.)

SCENE ONE

(As the houselights go out, a loud tinny noise is heard on the stage, the sound of an alarm clock set in a washbasin. When the house is dark, a match is struck stage right, a candle is lit, and someone jumps down from a Russian oven that becomes hazily visible in the candlelight. A gray shape, sleepy, barefoot, and carrying a candle, stumbles across the stage. Downstage left, on a bench, there is the alarm clock in the basin. The gray shape stops the ringing, takes a piece of paper from under the clock, and tries to read it in the candlelight, but without success. She retreats a couple of steps, a door becomes visible stage left, and next to

the door, a high candelabra. She lights the candles while still trying to spell out what is written on the paper. By the time all three candles are burning in the candelabra, she has finished spelling and says the word out loud: "Cake." *Now she is quite visible, wearing a long light-gray jumper, a gray spotted scarf on her head. This is* CINDERELLA. *Carefully and reverently she replaces the paper under the alarm clock and puts a dark gray smock, which hangs on the candelabra, on top of her jumper. While doing all this, she pronounces the word* "cake" *with varying loudness and timbre, sometimes also singing it. She returns to stage right and blows on the coals in the hearth, bringing them to a glow. From the glow of the hearth, the candles in the candelabra, and the candle that* CINDERELLA *puts on a bench near the stove, the stage is now sufficiently lit to see that there are no more parts to the set, no other actors. The oven is low, covered with tiles, which have pictures on them that cannot yet be clearly seen. One can sense from the depth of the stage that there is no cyclorama. Immediately after the shutting off of the alarm clock, a new sound is heard: knocking on the door. The sound changes randomly from timid, polite scratching to official, dry knocking to desperate or bold banging.* CINDERELLA *does not react to this before she has sifted, by means of a ladle, a cupful of baked beans from the ashes. She sets the cup on the bench where she had earlier put the candle and where there is a cake. Now she crosses the stage again and opens the door. Storm sounds. Enter the* PRINCE. *Sheepskin coat, soft boots, knapsack or bag. Snowy.)*

PRINCE: Hello.

CINDERELLA: God save you.

PRINCE: May I?

CINDERELLA: What?

PRINCE: May I come in?

CINDERELLA: Why not?

PRINCE: And warm myself by the fireplace?

CINDERELLA: That's what it's there for.

PRINCE: Great!

(He pulls the door shut; storm sounds stop. Both cross the stage toward the hearth. While walking, the PRINCE *eyes* CIN-DERELLA.*)*

PRINCE *(spryly)*: I was afraid that no one would let me into the house, that hospitality had vanished from the earth. Did I make a racket outside that door!

CINDERELLA: I was sleeping.

PRINCE *(with sincere concern)*: I didn't wake you up, did I?

CINDERELLA: No.

PRINCE *(immediately with a complete feeling of relief)*: Good. I was afraid I had.

(*When the PRINCE gets to the hearth, he takes the vacant bench, throws his coat on the oven to dry, pokes the coals until a small flame appears, and sits by the fire. He warms himself, from time to time pausing in his speech, at which time he eyes CINDERELLA. The latter squats by the other bench and, using the beans, begins to make a pattern on the cake. Toward the end of the conversation the PRINCE's erstwhile spryness wanes, his inquiring glances become more lifeless. CINDERELLA, on her part, gets more and more deeply involved in what she is doing and soon, without particularly developing a melody, begins to sing, while paying no attention to the PRINCE.*)

PRINCE: A good thing you woke up. I'd still be fighting the storm. (*Takes a watch from his pocket.*) You certainly are early; it's only five o'clock. If it shows the right time. If the works have not gotten fouled with water. As for me, there is not a dry spot left on my body. (*Listens.*) It's ticking. So it runs. So it must be right. So far, everything has gone as planned. It's five o'clock; you woke up early indeed. Anyway, I have been up for several hours already. A wonder I didn't get lost. (*Observation pause.*) What a storm! February, February! Can't see the tip of your nose, but you must keep moving. Hungry wolves watch and wait beside the road... Exactly nine years ago it was February, too.

CINDERELLA (*singing to herself*): Exactly nine years from now it will be February, too.

PRINCE (*continues by himself; his observation pauses are not determined by CINDERELLA's singing, which he does not even seem to notice*): Push on! Downwind? That's too much to ask for. Then at least let it be into the wind! Oh, no! First it whips from here, then from there. It lashes against one cheek, then under the other side of your coat, then it coils your body like a vine. February, February! Wolves scent you; (*Observation pause.*) you, hungry, scent the thaw; you can scent the thaw through this cacophonic fury. The wolves stalk after you, and you stalk after hope, hoping that the storm will cover the old tracks. Exactly nine years ago it was February, too.

CINDERELLA (*as before*): Exactly nine years from now it will be February, too.

PRINCE (*as before*): The thaw, the thaw. Where can it be? It has to come. Let the year be what it will, February is always the same. You can taste its rage. It tastes of hope. Just walk and breathe; you can taste that soon all this will crack apart, that soon all these roads now cloaked with snow (*Observation pause.*)—stalking and cracking roadbanks—and the wolves' starved cadavers will crack on the roads and on the roadbanks. The thaw! The thaw! You run around as if drunk. How everything drips with joy!... (*Quite tired by now.*) How everything oozes and drips and splashes and sloshes... how wet the world is then; there isn't a dry spot on your body... you go to the fire, wanting heat... some go home, some to the pub, some to the royal castle... (*Nodding off to sleep*)... home castle, or royal pub... works wet... (*Talking in his sleep.*)... rusty... workhouses... royal works... (*The PRINCE sleeps. Continuing to hum, CINDERELLA looks up from her activity for the first time and throws a fleeting glance at the PRINCE, then at her work. She leans back in order to see better, falls on her backside. The PRINCE awakens, jumps up.*)

PRINCE: Excuse me! How did I... it's so warm here.

(*CINDERELLA has managed to rise before the PRINCE gets there to help her. The PRINCE gives her his bench.*)

PRINCE: Sit here. No, no, I'll stand. I must not pass out. (*Vehemently rushing about the stage and making exercise-like movements.*) I have much to do. It's no joke, waking up so early.

(*The PRINCE, now on the other side of the stage, checks his watch against the alarm clock. Stays on that side, trying to place the candelabra so that it would throw light also on CINDERELLA. When this fails, he starts across the stage, carrying the candelabra, putting it down from time to time and eyeing CINDERELLA in the changed light.*)

PRINCE: There is much to do; a long and tense day is ahead, and when it is over you wouldn't know where it went. Time runs in only one direction, always in one direction. Time is the only thing that is not like the storm, be it even February. It runs in one direction and there is much to do... How come you let me in here at all?

CINDERELLA: You were the one who knocked.

PRINCE: You don't know who might come in like this and do a lot of harm.

CINDERELLA: Who to?

PRINCE: To... you.

CINDERELLA: Who wants to harm me?

PRINCE: Doesn't anyone?

CINDERELLA: Who would?

PRINCE: Nothing but good?

CINDERELLA: Why should they?

PRINCE: But you to them?

CINDERELLA: Who?

PRINCE: They... the others.

CINDERELLA: Not me.

PRINCE: Neither good nor bad?

CINDERELLA: How?

(The PRINCE finds a suitable place for the candelabra, center stage, (leaves it there and hurries to CINDERELLA, adjusting her in the light like a photographer.)

PRINCE: There now, sit like this, please; oh, yes, your work; we can move it closer; sit nice; watch the birdie; that's right; what are you really doing here? What are you up to, if you are doing neither good nor bad?

CINDERELLA: Cake.

PRINCE *(looks at the cake, which seems to remind him of something)*: With beans baked in ashes?

CINDERELLA: That's how it's done.

PRINCE: But the number nine? Why did you make the nine out of beans?

CINDERELLA: Orders. She drew it for me. I don't know what number that is.

PRINCE: And last year you made number eight? Like that? *(He draws "8" in the air with his finger.)*

CINDERELLA: When?

PRINCE: Last year. Exactly a year ago, in February.

CINDERELLA: Don't remember.

PRINCE: How come you don't remember? But do you remember one like that? And like that, like that, like that?...

(The PRINCE draws all the numbers down to one in the air; the further he gets the more uncomprehending and apathetic CIN-DERELLA becomes, until, at the end, she is again fingering the cake.)

PRINCE: All right, who drew that number for you? Who told you to decorate the cake with beans?

CINDERELLA: Mistress, who else?

PRINCE: Stepmother or...?

CINDERELLA: Whatever she may be.

PRINCE: To you, what is she to you?

CINDERELLA: Mistress.

PRINCE: Does she have any children?

CINDERELLA: She does.

PRINCE: How many?

CINDERELLA: Two.

PRINCE: Where are they?

CINDERELLA *(motions toward the back)*: There.

PRINCE: What do they look like?

CINDERELLA: Like always.
PRINCE: Beautiful, proud?
CINDERELLA: Go see for yourself.
PRINCE: But who is your mistress to them?
CINDERELLA: Y'know, their mother.
PRINCE: Real mother or stepmother?
CINDERELLA: Ask them.
PRINCE: Maybe they don't know.
CINDERELLA: And I?
PRINCE: Maybe you are wiser.
CINDERELLA: And how!
PRINCE: But does she have a husband, too?
CINDERELLA: Who?
PRINCE: The mistress, of course.
CINDERELLA: Yes, the husband; he's there, too.
PRINCE: Would you know whether that's her first or second husband?
CINDERELLA: No idea.
PRINCE: Who would? Is there someone who would know?
CINDERELLA: Well, he himself ought to know.
PRINCE: Who?
CINDERELLA: The master.
PRINCE: Which master?
CINDERELLA: Well, the master. My goodness, who are we talking about? Mistress's husband. He ought to know whether he is mistress's first or second husband.
PRINCE (*haltingly*): Don't know...
CINDERELLA: Well, if he doesn't know, at least mistress herself ought to know.
PRINCE: Yes, the mistress ought to know, after all. The mistress must certainly know. She knows... So it was she who ordered you to decorate the cake and drew the number for you?
CINDERELLA: She did.
PRINCE: When?
CINDERELLA: Just now.
PRINCE: When just now? Yesterday?
CINDERELLA: Yes, yesterday.
PRINCE: Or last year?
CINDERELLA: Yesterday, yesterday. Just now. The cake is for today.
PRINCE: What's the occasion? Did the mistress tell you what it was for?
CINDERELLA: Company is supposed to be coming.
PRINCE: Who?
CINDERELLA: Company.

PRINCE: Have you seen them with your own eyes?

CINDERELLA: How could I, if they haven't gotten here yet?

PRINCE: But the years before, the years before! Have you made the cake with beans every year? Haven't you even once peeked through the door, to see who eats the cake?... But then, I've never had the sense to peek into the kitchen any of those years. But for that, this year I will start here. And I intend to ask a lot of questions. A lot! (*Pause. It is as if the PRINCE had lost the thread of his thought. Concentrates again.*) Next. Yes. Excuse me if my next question is... a little personal. How old are you?

CINDERELLA (*naturally*): I don't know.

PRINCE: But even approximately? Approximately? Were you already grown up nine years ago? Have you sometimes looked at yourself in the mirror?

CINDERELLA: Once I saw myself in a tub.

PRINCE: Yes! Yes! And what did you see?

CINDERELLA: Myself.

PRINCE: What were you like?

CINDERELLA: Like I am.

PRINCE: Like what, like what?

CINDERELLA: Like you see me.

PRINCE: I see you the way you are now. Was that long ago? What were you like then? Your eyes, for instance? Your hair?

CINDERELLA: Hair... hair was gray.

PRINCE: Gray?... That's from the ashes. That comes off. Come over here.

(*The PRINCE leads CINDERELLA by the hand to the candelabra. With his free hand he pushes the scarf off her head and slides his hand over her long ash-gray hair that tumbles out from under the scarf. Looks at his hand in candlelight. Repeats the same with the other hand. Now it looks more like a caress. Then with both hands. He stares at his hands. CINDERELLA, who has up to now stood without moving, frozen into a somewhat uncomfortable pose, ducks under his arm, picks the scarf off the floor and goes over to the oven. Her hair is as gray as it was before. The emotional pause continues. Both stand without moving. Then the PRINCE, with increasing impatience, begins to lift first one hand, then the other, closer to the candles. In order to see better, his nose almost touches the flame. Finally, he lets both hands drop abruptly, as in resignation.*)

PRINCE (*quietly, reprovingly*): Do you sometimes wash your hair?

CINDERELLA (*without moving, naturally*): No.

PRINCE (*as before*): That's what I see. Ashes stick to it so that not a

279

single flake came off on my hand. Why don't you wash? Why didn't
you wash it in the tub right there?

CINDERELLA (*as before*): You don't do that.

PRINCE (*as before*): You don't do what?

CINDERELLA: That. The one who is Cinderella does not wash.

PRINCE: You are Cinderella?

CINDERELLA: Of course.

PRINCE: So that, yet... How do you know that?

CINDERELLA: Mistress said so.

PRINCE: Where, when?

CINDERELLA: Right here.

PRINCE: In the kitchen?

CINDERELLA: Yes, in the kitchen, just now.

PRINCE: Yesterday?

CINDERELLA: When she told me to top the cake. The one who tops the
cake with beans baked in ashes is Cinderella.

PRINCE: What else, what else? What else did she tell you about Cinderella?

CINDERELLA: Oh, a lot.... A lot, a lot, a lot.... Come over here, it is all
painted on here. These are the pictures she talked about, and that is
how I remember it.

`(*The PRINCE goes over to the oven with the candelabra. The flame
and the coals have gone out. All the light concentrates on the pictures.*)

CINDERELLA: See, here I am baking beans in the ashes. When I bake
these beans real nice and sift them out of the ashes, and do everything
that's called for, then I'll get on this picture. (*She points to the next
picture.*)

PRINCE: Do you know what this is here?

CINDERELLA: That's the ball. That's me.

PRINCE: Have you ever been there?

CINDERELLA: No, dummy, that's a picture. (*Points to the next one.*)
Here I lose my slipper.

PRINCE: But who is that?

CINDERELLA: That one? That's the Prince. Here, on the next picture,
he puts the slipper on *my* foot. And here we are riding in a sleigh to
the royal castle. In the storm. (*Laughs.*) Just like now! That's all.
There are no more pictures. I'll start to top the cake again.

(*CINDERELLA sits on the bench and starts to work. The PRINCE
sorts around in his bag, takes out a package wrapped in several
layers of paper and cloth, unwinds a lot of string from around it,
opens it—out comes a glittering slipper. The stage is filled with*

iridescent light. CINDERELLA raises her head, her mouth and eyes are wide open. The PRINCE festively blows out the candles.)

PRINCE: Now, here is the slipper. The one who has the slipper is the Prince. The one on whose foot it fits is Cinderella. The true Cinderella. (Dropping the festive tone.) We'll try right away. Give... (Sinks to one knee.), please, give me your foot.

CINDERELLA (more confused by the light than by the PRINCE's talk): Wwwwwwwhich?

PRINCE: Right. No. Left.

(CINDERELLA extends her right foot to him.)

PRINCE: Left, left. The other.

(CINDERELLA extends her left foot to the PRINCE. The PRINCE puts the slipper on her foot. CINDERELLA jumps up from her seat, screaming with delight.)

CINDERELLA: It fits! It fits! I'm wearing the real Cinderella slipper! I'm wearing the real Cinderella slipper! I am the real Cinderella! You are the real Prince! I am the real Cinderella! You are the real Prince!

(She whirls about the stage, singing and dancing. This does not lack an element of comedy, for the dancer has one foot bare, while on the other is a high-heeled slipper. The light revolves with her. The PRINCE has not found time to rise from his knee.)

PRINCE: Hold it! Hold it! I haven't had a chance to take a good look yet.

CINDERELLA: Look at me dance! Look at me dance! Look how I dance with the Cinderella slipper.

PRINCE: Hold it, you crazy nut! You'll break the slipper.

CINDERELLA: This slipper is not gonna break! The slipper is not gonna break! The real Cinderella slipper is not gonna break on the real Cinderella's foot.

PRINCE: Listen to me, listen. If you spill this cake, you'll never get on that picture!!

CINDERELLA: Oh, cake!

(She stops abruptly, very close to the bench the cake is on. The slipper flies off her foot. CINDERELLA sinks on to the bench, gasps, laughs. The PRINCE, enraptured, looks at her, then becomes business-like and worried again.)

PRINCE: Show me your foot, Cinderella.

CINDERELLA (playfully): Which?

PRINCE: The one the slipper was on.

CINDERELLA (laughing, stretches out the wrong foot): This one?

PRINCE (quickly kisses her foot, then again quite business-like): No, the other.

CINDERELLA: No, I won't.

PRINCE: Let me seė. Come on, show it. (*Manages to catch the foot by playing along with her.*) Ah, here is a fresh blister.

CINDERELLA: So what, it does not hurt at all.

PRINCE: Why·is that blister here? Didn't the slipper fit?

(*The PRINCE retrieves the slipper that had been flung away and places it once more on CINDERELLA's foot. Clearly, the slipper is too big.*)

CINDERELLA (*naively*): Don't you see, it fits.

PRINCE: Yes... and there is some left over. Why is your foot so small?

CINDERELLA: Well, does Cinderella's foot have to be big?

PRINCE: No, Cinderella's foot must be small.

CINDERELLA: Like mine is.

PRINCE: No, no, something is wrong here. This slipper should fit Cinderella exactly.

CINDERELLA: Don't be angry, Prince. Maybe my foot will grow yet.

PRINCE: Something is wrong. The matter has not become any clearer than it was when I was outside, standing in the storm, knocking on the door. It is even more muddled than it was out in the storm. Something is still wrong.

CINDERELLA: Prince.

PRINCE: What is it?

CINDERELLA: Nothing.

PRINCE: Listen.

(*Throughout the following dialogue, the PRINCE strokes CIN-DERELLA's hair. At the end of the dialogue, he casts an automatic glance at his hands.*)

PRINCE: I'll get this matter cleared up. Right? Naturally. That's what I came for. So. And then I'll come and tell you, too. But don't you tell anybody that you saw me.

CINDERELLA: Nobody?

PRINCE: Nobody?

CINDERELLA: I won't tell anybody. Don't stay away for long, Prince.

PRINCE: Especially not the mistress.

CINDERELLA: Others don't even come to the kitchen.

PRINCE: So that...

CINDERELLA: ... don't stay away for long, Prince.

VOICE OF MISTRESS (*from the depth of the stage*): Cinderella! Cinderella!

CINDERELLA: There's mistress. She is coming for the cake.

VOICE OF THE MISTRESS (*coming closer*): Is the cake ready, Cinderella? Cinderella, yoo-hoo!

282

(*The PRINCE is feverishly packing the slipper. Through each successive layer of cloth or paper its reflections gradually diminishes until, at the end of the following speech by CINDERELLA, the stage is completely dark.*)

CINDERELLA: She is calling Cinderella. Who has to answer her, me? Am I Cinderella? Who am I? Can I answer her?

VOICE OF MISTRESS: Yoo-hoo, Cinderella! Cin-de-rel-la!

(*The stage is dark. The inner curtain closes.*)

SCENE TWO

(*Again the tinny ringing of the alarm clock. Mingled with it will be heard cursing and grumbling. A hurricane lamp is lighted behind the inner curtain, stage left. The inner curtain opens. The hurricane lamp illuminates downstage left; the same bench with the washbasin and alarm clock as in scene one; also the same door. Near there, the end of it almost out of the door, is a linenless field cot. On it lies a stocky man with a Hemingway beard and balding head, wearing wet and wrinkled hunting clothes. This is the MASTER OF THE HOUSE. In front of the cot are scattered his boots, rifle, and several empty bottles. Without getting up from the cot, the MASTER tries to reach the alarm clock, with the result that the cot collapses. The MASTER rises, cursing. Shuts off the alarm. Takes a piece of paper from under the clock and reads it in the light of the hurricane lamp. Repeats mockingly. "Speech! Speech!" Spits into the washbasin. Puts the paper back very carefully. Walks around and lights several different lights. Pieces of furniture, of various styles, are lined up on the stage in a straight line, parallel with the front edge of the stage. This line, which extends, unbroken, across the entire stage, not much further back than the jamb of the side door, is arranged either so that all like objects are grouped together: chairs, tables, armoires, showcases, chests, display boards (with firearms and blades, hunting trophies, pipes, etc.), lamps, etc. or so that they alternate in strict pattern: chair, table, chest; chair, table... etc. All items face the audience, except the board with targets, which ends the line at the right, opposite the left door. Scattered on the tables are boxes and albums, all scrupulously in order. One of the chairs is a rocker, tightly squeezed between the others. The hunting boots, empty bottles, and the collapsed field cot, like at first the*)

MASTER himself, form an obvious contrast to the general order and neatness. The MASTER, having turned on the lights, huffs and puffs while pulling on his wet boots, pushes the bottles aside with his foot, and tries, not very successfully, for his hands are shaking, to fold the cot. While doing this, he repeats mockingly: "Speech! Speech!"; manages to fold the cot somehow, and throws it backhanded, behind the line of furniture toward the area where one guesses, as in scene one, the empty stage extends its depth. Then picks up the rifle and aims for a long time at the targets on the right, waiting for the trembling of his hands to cease. Moves closer to the targets, rifle leveled, then backs up to the left side of the stage. Finally the trembling of his hands ceases. The MASTER hangs the rifle with the others on the proper display stand. Coughs with anticipation and says: "Ahem. Speech!" Climbs hesitatingly and somewhat doubtfully over the furniture and comes back with the cot that he had earlier discarded so carelessly, places it sideways somewhere into the slot designated for it in the monolithic line of furniture. Arranges the empty bottles under one of the tables where there are others, all lined up according to size, labels facing the audience. Coughs once again and says: "Let's see now. Speech!" It appears from his facial expression as if he would begin the speech. Then his expression changes to sullen irritation, no longer that of a hangover but troubled now, as befits a master of the house. Instead of clearing his throat for the third time, the MASTER succumbs to a fit of neurasthenic coughing. He pounds himself on the back.)

MASTER: Listen... to a speech... everybody's always ready to listen to a speech... but when you've lost the text... where the hell are you then... nothing... nothing better to do than to throw pearls... (*Severe fit of coughing. He continues as it passes.*)... to swine.

(*He conquers the cough, straightens himself up, looks around. Then begins to look for the text of the speech in drawers, cupboards, and folders. The PRINCE steals into the room. At that moment the MASTER, now stage right, has his back almost to the door. A bundle drops from inside the PRINCE's coat. The MASTER whirls around with a revolver in his hand.*)

MASTER: Halt!

PRINCE (*raises his hands, whispers*): Good morning.

MASTER: What the hell! Is it you or...?

PRINCE (*chuckles to himself*): ... or my ghost, eh? Quiet, for God's sake.

MASTER (*without lowering his voice*): I don't care about ghosts. I leave it to your kind to play around with spooks and ghosts. No, I don't take you for a ghost, but for—bitch, what was it now?—a regent.

PRINCE: My regent is a doddering old man. The old king's double. You couldn't get us mixed up. Hang up the gun.

MASTER: But you had some creep in the castle who was your double. Come, let me see your birthmarks.

PRINCE: My double is the old king's regent. If you are that mixed up about the administration, birthmarks won't help you. Even my fingerprints are the same as my double's.

MASTER: Then who the devil are you? All this governing business doesn't mean a thing to me. No cooperation with the government. (*Brandishes the revolver.*)

PRINCE: Ssh. I am I.

(*Without a struggle, the PRINCE takes the revolver from the MASTER and hangs it with the others on the display board.*)

PRINCE: Good morning.

MASTER: If that's what you want, good morning. Where did *you* come from? I am still looking for the speech to welcome you and your wife with.

PRINCE: For the time being, I am here on a secret mission. The others are staying overnight at the last post station. It is now six o'clock. At this very moment they'll be starting out and they'll get here by eight. While they were all sleeping, I made a deal with the station master for a coat, and here I am.

MASTER (*examining the newly found text of his speech*): You're all right. All right. I went out hunting. To tell the truth, I didn't get a thing, but what the hell? This is not the season, anyway, as you know. The main thing is that I got to slog around in the fresh air. Must have caught a bit of a cold, too. Haven't been able to sleep right either. I've got a splitting headache; what'll become of my speech? You see, I'm no longer a spring chicken. Damn nice of you to come. Look at you! All night in a snowstorm, but you're none the worse for it, are you? There are still tough and strong men around, even some young ones. That's what I like. But you'd better pick up the bundle you threw on the floor. I don't like a mess.

PRINCE (*picks up the bundle and hides it under his coat*): It's still too early to talk about all that. I have to wait until I get to be your age.

MASTER: I'm not good for shit anymore. Be so good and rub my neck and shoulders. Maybe it'll help clear my head. After all, I must welcome you with a speech, you know.

(*The MASTER sits on a chair. The PRINCE looks hesitatingly at the line of furniture, then jumps over it in order to get behind the MASTER, and begins the massage.*)

MASTER: C'mon, come on, don't pussyfoot around. What do you think your fingers are made of, putty? Let me feel it, said the lady to the rake. I'm afraid I praised you too soon. Well, that's better. Now I am beginning to see the writing: "Your excellency, my royal children, my darlings...." Harder! Harder! Don't have to do it for long, you know; only until I memorize the speech again. (*Laughs.*) Listen, remember how the year before last I made a face at the most solemn moment? You saw that, didn't you? Well, perhaps it's better you didn't. It wasn't meant for you anyway. Harder! Harder! You are more or less OK, but all these others at court.... Tell me, is there anyone there one could make a deal with? Man to man?

PRINCE: I have yet to get a clear picture of the government.

MASTER: That's too bad. That's really too bad, I gotta say. I look at you guys and I think that all you want is not to get your hands dirty, stay honest, and pussyfoot around the political cesspool. Nothing else matters to you. The world can go to hell, but I am not getting myself mixed up in this dirty game, eh? But listen to an old friend. A friend, mind you, goddamn it, and not some old shriveled-up shark that wants to eat you. There is always something to be saved; there is always something to be done better than it could be done if you didn't get mixed up in it. And even if there's not, do it anyway, without hoping for anything. A goal is a goal, and if there is no goal, then your goal should be to set up a goal. A house is built brick by brick. The mills of God grind slow. You think that the world and you are two different things? That if you stand aside, the shit will miss you? Don't kid yourself! If you do not fight back, you'll turn to nothing yourself, and the turd that used to be your mouth, will talk.... Go to it, don't just stand there! The mills of God grind slow, but just. Every morning when I wake up I say to myself: You gotta hold on, man. Hold on!

PRINCE: I didn't sleep at all.

MASTER: Great. Who are you in cahoots with, anyway? Or do you want to take all the power yourself? By the way, who's on top now?

PRINCE: That's not too clear.

(*He stops massaging and walks back and forth behind the barrier of furniture, without wandering off upstage. From time to time, whenever he happens to be near the MASTER's chair, he massages him a little.*)

PRINCE: It's beginning to dawn on me that no one there is particularly interested in getting anything done.

MASTER: Come, now. Everybody is not like you.

PRINCE: But I *am* interested.

MASTER: For instance.

PRINCE: They all simply let things go and rely on whoever happens to be in power.

MASTER: That's what I meant. Who is *it* right now?

PRINCE: The old king, of course. As always. No one else has ever had any power.

MASTER: And everybody depends on the old man?

PRINCE: No one depends on him any more. At times it seems that no one ever has.

MASTER: But on who then, if they let things go like that?

PRINCE: They are not always just letting things go! There are times when they all wake up and say to themselves, like you or I have today, that now's the... (*Begins to massage.*)

MASTER: And then one takes arms against the insane chaos of things so as to win out and put things right.

PRINCE: Not a chance. They take arms against each other... whoever comes out on top.

MASTER: But the old man is still the toughest of them all?

PRINCE: No one touches him. No one touches the old king. At times, they praise him to no end. They fight each other. And when someone has won...

MASTER (*rubbing his hands*): Then you beat the swords into plow-shares, grasp the plow of reason by the handles and begin to till the barren plains.

PRINCE: ... then everyone is so tired that not a man can be found even to set the plow. Whoever wins, lets things slide. The others hope that he will do something and lick their wounds for the next fight.

MASTER (*disappointed*): Same old story. (*Joyfully.*) It's the same old story. The king is sovereign in name only. Actually, it's someone else who gets things done, who aims the pale blue light of law into the darkest corners. (*Calms down, sits.*) So this regent is the old king's chief deputy? Your double, eh?

PRINCE (*likewise calms down and begins to massage again*): Regents do not take part in the fighting. The king's regent, my double—in school we played hooky for each other—is being kept for the time when the king will be so old and feeble that even the name of power would be too heavy for him to bear. Then he'll pass it on to a new generation, to the regent.... I, too, have a regent. Now he is the old king's double. When they were young, each went to the queen, and she never knew the difference. It could be... could be that I am not even the king's son, but the regent's.

(*This thought strikes the PRINCE for the first time. Again he stops massaging for a moment and stares into space.*)

MASTER: Dig in, my son.

PRINCE (*continues the massage*): Well, my regent was kept in reserve in case it might have come into my head as a boy to try to run things myself. The king would never have let me—a fledgling prince—and control would have gone to my experienced regent. But the thought never occurred to me, and now that I myself have come of age and this danger has passed, my regent has been put out to pasture.... I look at him now and then and think that he's the spitting image of my father, the old king, only much, much more feeble...

MASTER (*understandingly*): Yes, yes. Age... age...

PRINCE: The same will happen to my double as well. And to me, if I don't start to fight the presidents and prime ministers, secretaries and chancellors, the queen, my mother, and Cinderella, my wife. (*Now the PRINCE massages the MASTER slowly, effectively, vigorously, speaking in the same rhythm.*) Cinderella, my wife, whom I got from this house exactly nine years ago. Cinderella, my wife, your daughter. Cinderella.

MASTER (*laughs*): Ouch! You rascal! You have strength enough when you want to. (*Jumps up and moves away from the chair; speaks slowly in a casual tone.*) Nine years ago, as you said. Yes, yes. That was the time I was getting along with my new wife. At first, when she came to this house, I thought I'd just go on with my own way of life: read books, mow the lawn, and practice the arts and sciences. If I remember it right, I was in the midst of tracing my family tree. One of the branches that I had just come upon, or perhaps it was the trunk, can you imagine... but let's drop that now. The new mistress was energetic and simply swept everyone along into what she was doing. At times this made her laugh, at times angry, but you couldn't get away from her. "I am life itself," she used to say. Or did I say that about her? Can't remember. But it isn't important. In any case, that expression has lasted in our house to this day. Some of my books she gave away so everyone could read them; some she threw away so no one could read them. I went along. And how we fought for this house! That was a beautiful time, though hard and pitiless. My brass balls and radicleism* are really from that time—and this arms collection, the jewel of all my collections. Here, for instance... oh well, who would want to listen to me talk my way through this whole rack, gun by gun. And here are the pipes. Oh, how we smoked while solving vital problems. And how we blew smoke into each other's eyes. And

---

* The Estonian original denotes a nerve disease that derives from the word "radicle" but contains the suggestion of "radical" as well. (Translators' note.)

together we practiced science to scare the sparrows, the thieves, and the spies from our garden.

(*The MASTER opens the lid of a chest; life-size devils on springs are flung out. The MASTER taps wistfully on their skulls. The PRINCE pets a couple of them hesitantly, as if petting a strange dog.*)

PRINCE: Yes, indeed. Magnificent collection.

MASTER (*theatrically slamming the lid*): Why talk about all this shit. Let bygones by bygones. My head is aching.

PRINCE: Come, sit here. I'll rub you some more. I've got the feel of it now.

MASTER (*sits*): And tell me more stories about court.

PRINCE (*massaging*): Why does everyone want to hear stories about court, as if they were really interested in power. You know what else I've noticed? However confusing the question of who is on top at court may be, having power over the palace does not mean having power over the country.

MASTER (*yawns pleasurably*): But who *does* rule the country?

PRINCE: By the way, I am not the first one at court to notice this. There's always some ruler who tries to proclaim himself so loudly you can't hear yourself think. But some who are in his field of vision are too far away to hear, and those who hear cannot see who is doing all the shouting. Others close their ears or keep their mouths open. Who can keep track of them all? Besides, I have lately begun to suspect that our palace is not the only one there is. It seems that there are other palaces elsewhere, and which one would then be the most important one? Even in the palace, the order of importance could begin from practically any point.... No one could recognize the real voice of power, everyone avoids hearing it. Yet there are many listeners whenever it's talked about. And until they find out what it really is, they keep trying to get into the palace to be closer to power. To see power. To touch power. To manipulate power, not knowing what it is. Nine years ago, they gave me someone from this house to take to court. Her name is Cinderella. *Is* she Cinderella? *Is* she your daughter? *Is* she your daughter?

(*The MASTER sits, head bowed, eyes closed, silent. The PRINCE ends the massage with a volley of sharp taps delivered with the sides of his hands.*)

PRINCE: Are you sleeping or sleeping or sleeping or sleeping or?

MASTER (*without shifting his position or opening his eyes*): To tell you the truth, I'm not sleeping.

PRINCE: Then please answer me.

MASTER (*as before*): Nine years ago. What was nine years

ago?... That's when I began to shift from collaborating with my wife to resisting her openly. My enthusiasm did not fade and everything seemed to remain the same.... The things you discovered here—all those palaces and the orders of importance—are news only to you. All this! All this and a thousand other things that you'll never get to see, if you rely only on your *own* eyes, have already been noted. In those books, for example, that I was lucky enough to get together again. Into these boxes over there. My library is the jewel of all my collections.

PRINCE: Why don't you answer when I ask about Cinderella?

MASTER (*after a pause*): A matter of breeding. It is not fitting to talk of things you know nothing about. (*Tries to get up.*)

PRINCE (*pushes him back into the chair*): You don't want to talk. Or don't remember. I could rub you some more, you know. To refresh your memory. Just speak.

MASTER (*rises*): Refresh my memory? That's no news.

(*The MASTER walks around, touching his collections and his furniture in the manner of Antaeus. By and by he begins to dislodge them a bit to free the rocking chair and allow it to rock.*)

MASTER: Who would know better than you who it was you took along at that time? Number one: you had seen her at the ball three times.

PRINCE: Cosmetics! Make-up! Spells, witchcraft!

MASTER: Number two: consider that I was not there at the time, but later I heard that you had rushed like a madman from the hall where the daughters were into the kitchen, and there found the right one. The shoe fit her, didn't it?

PRINCE: Plastic surgery, perhaps. Or the girls were switched on the way to the sleigh. It was snowing hard. Was it Cinderella?

MASTER: For nine years everyone has known it was Cinderella.

PRINCE: The official version.

MASTER: Go to hell with your childishly straightforward distrust. Why should the official version be false? That's real diplomacy when the official version could be the true one.

PRINCE: True... or false. That's what I'm trying to clear up.

MASTER: You want to find out that it's false. Then you could say, I was deceived. Otherwise it would be embarassing for you to end our collaboration.

PRINCE: No, no. That's not so. Makes no difference whether it's true or false. I only want to know...

MASTER: Stop. I know you. I am just like you. I am willing to help you.

(*The MASTER has sufficiently freed the rocker and begins to rock. The PRINCE cannot believe his ears.*)

PRINCE (*cautiously*): You are willing to help me?

MASTER: If you wish.

PRINCE: But... you don't really understand my motives.

MASTER: I don't want anything for my help. And let it be a lesson to you in how to temporarily collaborate with an individual whose interests partly coincide with your own. Someone with whom you go part way, but only part way. Or so you may think. Sit down and listen to me.

(*The PRINCE jumps in front of the furniture and sits on a chair next to the rocker. The MASTER rocks and speaks in the same rhythm.*)

MASTER: Nine years ago. What was nine years ago?... That was exactly the time I began to have some private jokes along with serious resistance. I began to boycott certain events that took place in this house so as to sabotage them. Unfortunately, I didn't always find out whether these events were really canceled because of my passive resistance or whether they were held without me. I couldn't just send out pickets. I worked alone and was divided. I was divided among all the actions I did not take part in. Let this be a lesson to you. One of these was the little operation which ended with one of the maidens of this house finding her way into the palace. Who she was, or who she was not, I really don't know. I heard it rumored in the house that the Prince was expected to end his matrimonial quest here. I guessed, guessed that the reason could be Cinderella, because I didn't think my stepdaughters could captivate anyone at the ball though I had seen them catch many a man. I asked Cinderella in a roundabout way, but there was no way to tell through the layer of ashes whether she blushed or blanched. And that's why I was so sure. Still water runs deep. But then vital intelligence reached my ears: the women with their wiles planned to palm off one of the stepdaughters on the Prince. I was angry. I must confess from the bottom of my heart I was very angry. I was all set to intervene, because I didn't like my child to be pushed aside so vilely, nor did I like it that the mistress would send one of her agents to the palace, nor did I like it that I was unable to send mine. But then I began to suspect that this rumor was leaked out for the purpose of confusing me. I was investigating this in the far end of the house when everything broke and I did not even get to say goodbye to my daughter... if she *was* my daughter. Too bad you can't be everywhere at once, especially where you are not expected!... Soon I changed my mind about what had happened. Was it not perhaps for the best that Cinderella did not get to the palace? Ever since she was a child she has reminded me of her mother. The same elusive character, the same misty conceptions. Had she come into power, could she have been able to realize herself or represent my interests?

PRINCE: What was her mother like?

MASTER: Just like her.

PRINCE: I don't really know her yet.

MASTER: You have been married for nine years.

PRINCE: What do you mean? This is not she. You see my wife every year when we come for our traditional visit. Does she remind you of your first wife, your Cinderella's mother?

MASTER: I never saw my first wife as the consort of a prince.

PRINCE: But Cinderella, Cinderella is in this house now. I came through the kitchen. I talked with her. I even...

MASTER: This house has always had a Cinderella. Already when my daughter was a child, there was a Cinderella here. And before that, when the house still belonged to my father and I was small. We never could manage without a Cinderella here.

PRINCE: But now? Who is the current Cinderella?

MASTER: Don't know. Haven't seen her. I have not set foot in the kitchen since that diplomatic failure nine years ago.

PRINCE: Stop the rocking. You're already asleep, you man of action. Wake up! Hold on! You were going to help me. (*The PRINCE wrestles with the rocking chair; pushes furniture together in order to stop the rocking. The MASTER seems to be napping.*) Right now there are three girls in the house, just as before. If the present Cinderella is the real Cinderella, then my wife is one of the daughters and a new stepdaughter has been taken into the house. If my wife is the real Cinderella, then they've taken in a new Cinderella or one of the daughters has become Cinderella and a new stepdaughter has come into the house. And, furthermore, it could... it could be like this: nine years ago the real Cinderella was brought into the hall and was decked out like a daughter so as to prevent me from recognizing her. One of the daughters was dressed as Cinderella and was sent to the kitchen, from where I took her with me, and the real Cinderella kept her place as a daughter and later a new Cinderella was taken into the house. (*The PRINCE manages to stop the rocking. The MASTER wakes up.*) Listen, I must know if one of the daughters is the real Cinderella.

MASTER (*incredulously*): What the hell?! (*Laughs.*) Don't know; which one!

PRINCE (*seiously*): Don't know; which one.

MASTER (*laughing*): One is... comme çi, the other... comme ça...

PRINCE: But which?

MASTER: Haven't you seen enough of them?

PRINCE: Haven't bothered to look.

MASTER (*makes a gesture of resignation with his hand*): Cinderella couldn't have become either of them.

PRINCE (*with great certainty*): In any case, I'll go see them now.

MASTER (*rises with the seriousness of an older colleague*): Go. That's the boy. If it should become clear that one of them is my daughter— my unfortunate child—and even if it does not (*He is struggling to keep from laughing.*), at least we'll have some fun. You, my son, are levelheaded, tough, and strong. Young and hot-blooded.

PRINCE (*sincerely*): What is my one thrust compared to your per- severance. To assemble and preserve all these collections—through thick and thin.

(*They shake hands. The voice of the MISTRESS is heard from the depth of the stage.*)

VOICE OF MISTRESS: Dear! Yoo-hoo! Dear! Do you have your speech, darling?

(*Upon hearing the voice, both the MASTER and the PRINCE quickly begin to extinguish the lights, until the PRINCE disappears into the darkness. The MASTER hurriedly reads the text of his speech by the light of the hurricane lamp.*)

VOICE OF MISTRESS: Dear! Have you memorized your speech? Darling!

(*The MASTER extinguishes the hurricane lamp. The inner curtain closes.*)

SCENE THREE

(*Ringing of the alarm clock as in the beginning of previous scenes. Somewhat to the left of stage center, a pink lamp is lit. The inner curtain opens. Stage left are a door, bench, washbasin, and clock, as before. Left of stage center, in line with the far jamb of the side door, is a comfortable, inviting bed, with its foot toward the door, head toward stage center, side to the audience. In front of the bed are a low cocktail table with something on it, covered with a napkin, and a hassock. At the foot of the bed is a pink screen. All this is lit by the pink lamp, which is held by a large statue of Aphrodite at the head of the bed (In profile to the audience, face to the bed.) The lamp was lit by the FIRST DAUGHTER who, in arresting pink pajamas, now rises from the bed with a consciously beautiful and deliberately energetic movement, puts on pink slippers, and goes to shut off the alarm. Takes a sheet of paper from under the clock and reads:* "Looks." *Ponders seriously for a moment, eyes down, the tip of a finger almost in her mouth, then smiles:* "Oh, looks!" *Goes and lights a blue lamp held by a large statue of Athena. The latter stands slightly right of center stage, at the head of an iron bed, back to back with Aphrodite. In front of the iron bed are a couple of stools, covered with books and ashtrays. At the foot of the bed is a blue screen. Stage right, facing the door on stage left, is the door leading to the bathroom. In the iron bed, curled in a ball, sleeps the SECOND DAUGHTER.)*

FIRST DAUGHTER: Good morning, sis. How did you sleep? Time to rise. We have to look decent for the reception. (*Hurries behind the pink screen. The SECOND DAUGHTER tosses and turns lazily in her bed.*)

SECOND DAUGHTER (*annoyed*): Mother has gone nuts. Nothing but a three-ring circus.

FIRST (*from behind the screen*): I don't understand either what mama had in mind, waking us at seven o'clock. Who could get ready in an hour!

SECOND (*without rising from bed*): Only seven o'clock? Madhouse. Why don't you let me sleep?

FIRST (*emerges from behind the screen in tank suit, with a hula hoop*): Who told you to stay up all night again? I feel completely rested. I think a bit of exercise would do you good.

SECOND: Exercise yourself; you need it.

FIRST: I am exercising.

SECOND: You've got to look beautiful. I'll see to it that I look intriguing.

FIRST (*turning the hoop*): Oh dear! Inner and outer beauty, outer and inner.

SECOND: Go to the bathroom; or you won't be ready in time. And be a dear, leave me some toothpaste.
(*The SECOND DAUGHTER pushes herself into a sitting position— she is wearing rumpled blue pajamas—stretches with gusto, picks a butt out of the ashtray, can't find matches, lights her cigarette from the Athena lamp without getting out of bed.*)

FIRST (*on her way to the bathroom*): Every night you finish with a cigarette, every morning you start with one. Soon you'll look like Cinderella. You didn't forget to pick out those books you promised me, did you? I ought to look at them before the guests get here.

SECOND: I put them under your pillow. Didn't you feel the lump?

FIRST: You don't say! (*Goes into bathroom; immediately shrieks.*) OOOOOOOOOH! You frightened me, sir! Oh, it's you, isn't it? I can't believe it. How dare you? (*To her sister.*) Surprise! Look who I found waiting for me in the bathroom!

SECOND: What are you jabbering now?

(*The FIRST DAUGHTER comes out of the bathroom, letting the PRINCE go first.*)

SECOND: Oh-ho! Good morning, Prince. Welcome.

PRINCE: Good morning. Please excuse me, but...

FIRST: I think I can proceed back to the bathroom, or is someone else waiting to pounce on me?

PRINCE: Pounce! Was I there to pounce on you?

FIRST (*quickly casts an inspecting look at herself*): Why not?

(*She traipses past the PRINCE into the bathroom. He follows her with an extremely attentive look. From the bathroom door, the FIRST DAUGHTER casts a superior glance over her shoulder, then stops for a measured moment and throws a coquettish smile over the other shoulder. Disappears into the bathroom.*)

SECOND: Listen, how come you're here? I don't even know if I'm properly made up to receive you. Sit down. I read as long as I could last night.... Listen, do you have a smoke?

PRINCE (*sits down, searches for a cigarette*); Last one.

SECOND: Let's have it together. What was I talking about? Oh yes, still the same old thing. Some progress can be noted, but generally no one wants to understand that the formation of inner grace and the formation of outer grace are equally important, but the methods are somewhat different in each case. Don't argue with me. I understand that we both, my sister as well as I, must be ready to receive you at eight o'clock. But, Jesus Christ, that doesn't mean that we have to do it the same way! I spent the whole night getting ready. Why must I wake up now, at the same time as my sister? Because *she* starts to prepare herself *now*. Well, if she were told to prepare herself at night—for instance: do her hair, paint her face, loosen up with exercise—and then go to sleep, what would she say? But if *I* raise my voice, it's cynicism, estheticism, intellectual snobbism, nihilism...

PRINCE: Where did you get all these books?

SECOND: Here and there.

PRINCE: From your father or...?

SECOND: Which father? Oh, you're thinking of the Master.

PRINCE: Well, father... or stepfather... or...

SECOND: What's he good for? Only for stepping on. His are all out of date. And anyway, what's the use of talking.... You want another drag?

PRINCE: No, thank you, you finish it.

(*The SECOND DAUGHTER takes a last deep puff and then goes to the bathroom door. Throughout the preceding dialogue, the PRINCE has been eyeing her attentively, sometimes secretly trying to compare the slippers in front of her bed with his package, but without success, for his slipper is inside the closed package.*)

SECOND (*speaking through the bathroom door*): Come on, get out. I wanna ablute myself, too. The Prince is pining for you. (*Conspiratorially winking at the PRINCE.*) I told the Prince you'd know how to take care of him.

FIRST (*from the bathroom*): Don't be snide. You can't imagine how hard it is to do all this.

SECOND: Hard, but beautiful.

FIRST (*comes out of the bathroom wearing a bathrobe*): All yours, my dear. You'll find the cold cream in the jar, the toothpaste in the tube, the shampoo in the bottle, and the shower in perfect order. And you better be quick about it, time is flying.

SECOND (*while disappearing into the bathroom*): What do you mean it's flying? It's flown already. The Prince is here.

FIRST: Heavens! (*Remains standing in a thoughtful pose; then.*) Yes, yes. Oh dear, how could I forget? Do excuse me, please. I hope you weren't bored.

PRINCE: We talked.

FIRST: Yes. My sister.... I must admit she has something. She knows so much. But to say what I really feel—which is the proper thing to do in our relationship—I must say that I prefer more agreeable people. Did she manage to bore you?

PRINCE: Oh no.

FIRST: Not yet? By the way, would you sit on my side, too? (*Leads the PRINCE to her side of the room, seats him on the hassock.*) I hardly have anything as interesting to offer as sister does. She really poses a riddle in our family: elusive character, misty conceptions.

PRINCE: What did you say?

FIRST: Elusive character, misty conceptions. That's how our father always puts it. And he can't be wrong.

PRINCE: Pardon me, whose father?

FIRST: Our father, the father of us all. You know him! Every year he greets you with a speech. Oh, I forgot again. This time you arrived so early. You couldn't have had a meal. But of course you must be hungry, and all we do is talk instead of offering you something... warm.

PRINCE: Don't bother.

FIRST: When a man comes in from the cold...

PRINCE: A man?

FIRST: You are a man. And it is cold outside. It's the same kind of February it was nine years ago, which we all remember.

PRINCE: Really, you do remember?

FIRST: Who could forget? (*Lifts napkin from the cocktail table, baring a tastefully arranged breakfast on a curious tray.*) Bon appetit, mon Prince. Enjoy your meal. Don't let me keep you from eating. If it tastes good, I must admit it was all my own modest effort. Don't worry, even though it was made last night, it's still warm in the morning, thanks to our mother's foresight. She invented this thermos tray. It was our mother who coined the phrase: "When a man comes in from the cold...".

PRINCE: Whose mother are you speaking of, may I ask?

FIRST: Our mother, the mother of us all, who can't be wrong. But now, let me serve you, and I won't bother you again.

(*The FIRST DAUGHTER squats by the cocktail table in the same position as did CINDERELLA in the first scene by her bench. The PRINCE's looks remain fixed on her. The FIRST DAUGHTER loses her balance and falls on her backside. The PRINCE hurries to help her up and wants to give her his hassock.*)

PRINCE: Please sit.

FIRST: No, no. You sit and enjoy your meal.

PRINCE: I'll sit over here, on the edge of the bed.

FIRST: Later, later. Which cereal would you like to begin with?

PRINCE: Thank you.

(*The PRINCE eats. The FIRST DAUGHTER watches him, handing him the right utensils or food when needed. The PRINCE eats with an increasing appetite, but does not forget to glance at the FIRST DAUGHTER from time to time, who, squatting on the other side of the table, indeed reminds one of CINDERELLA busy with the cake in scene one—if CINDERELLA's uncramped angularity were replaced with cramped fluidity. When their glances meet, the FIRST DAUGHTER lowers her eyes and fiddles with the opening of her dressing gown. The SECOND DAUGHTER emerges from the bathroom, wearing a correct but somehow military-looking dress. Barefoot as before, she walks familiarly over to the table and picks some food from right under the PRINCE's nose.*)

SECOND: Let's see what the Prince is getting.

FIRST: Aren't you ashamed of yourself! If I had your intelligence...

SECOND: Hmmm. That's not bad at all.

FIRST: By the way, the recipe comes from one of your books.

SECOND: Then I can have some more.

FIRST: Leave it alone. It's for the Prince. I prepared it just to make him happy. Look how hungry he is.

SECOND: Listen, sister. How would you like it if I went to the reception barefoot? It would be cold, too. Give me a pair of shoes, will you?

PRINCE: Are your feet the same size?

FIRST: That's why she can live off me all the time.

PRINCE: You know, I have a slipper with me. Would you care to try it?

FIRST: And you haven't even tried my preserves.

PRINCE: Really, a very tasty meal. If I didn't know that my wife was due within half an hour.... What did I say, within half an hour? (*Looks at his watch.*) Yes; right. (*To the SECOND DAUGHTER.*) If you are interested in that slipper... it's in that package. (*To the FIRST DAUGHTER.*)... I'd think, judging from the way you take care of me, that I'm your husband. Yes, you take even better care of me. As if you'd been meant for me, but something went wrong—nine years ago.

FIRST: Thank you, my Prince. No one has ever paid me such kind compliments; no one has ever appreciated my care so much. But nine years ago, my Prince, you got the wife who was meant for you—our beloved Cinderella, so dear to us all! May I clear the table?

PRINCE: Yes. Thank you.

(*The FIRST DAUGHTER covers the dishes with a napkin and wheels the table away. The SECOND DAUGHTER is having trouble opening the package with the slipper.*)

FIRST: And now I'd really like to sit for a while. These chores are so tiring. What do you men know about it? Present parties excepted, of course. Parties present and the dead. Parties present and the dead do not need to know anything. Their duty is to be happy. (*The PRINCE frees his hassock for her. The FIRST DAUGHTER sits on it.*) But you may sit on the edge of the bed as you wished. (*The PRINCE sits.*) Myself, I never sit on the bed. (*The PRINCE rises. The FIRST DAUGHTER gently pushes him back on the bed.*) When a man comes in from the cold, tired of battle.... Who can be pedantic here?

PRINCE (*to the SECOND DAUGHTER*): How are you doing?

SECOND (*hides the fact that she can't get the package open and makes a face as if she wanted to examine it from the outside*): Judging by the size and shape it doesn't seem to me there could be more than one shoe in there.

PRINCE: But what a shoe!

FIRST: Let me arrange the bed a little.

(*The PRINCE rises and finds himself standing directly opposite the*

FIRST DAUGHTER: the same position as in scene one, when the PRINCE wanted to clean CINDERELLA's hair. Momentary fixation. The FIRST DAUGHTER ducks under the PRINCE's arm and begins to smooth the blanket. The SECOND DAUGHTER wrestles with the package.)

SECOND (*noticing that the PRINCE is watching her*): A single shoe is not going to help me at all. Either all or nothing.

PRINCE: This shoe is more than everything and less than nothing. This, my dear ladies, is the real Cinderella slipper.

(The SECOND DAUGHTER is stunned by what she has heard. The FIRST DAUGHTER, having finished arranging the bed, gently pushes the PRINCE into a sitting position.)

FIRST: There you are. Comfy now?

PRINCE (*to the FIRST DAUGHTER*): Aren't you interested in that shoe?

FIRST: Why? What good is somebody else's fairy tale? Everyone has to make his own fairy tale.

(The FIRST DAUGHTER caresses the PRINCE, while he observes the SECOND DAUGHTER. The latter is running around barefoot, reminiscent of the dancing CINDERELLA in scene one. She has the package in her hand, waving it excitedly.)

SECOND: I've got the real Cinderella slipper! I've got the real Cinderella slipper! What a moment! I am holding this historic relic in my own hands.

FRIST (*to the PRINCE*): Why don't you hold me?

SECOND: It really exists! It really exists! The legend is rooted in reality. In my hand! In my hand! In my hand is the object that serves as the focal point of dozens of divergent variations. Dozens of opposing interpretations. Contending truths cross swords, flashing in my palm!

FIRST (*to the PRINCE*): Naturally, there should be conversation, but once she gets her mouth onto the bit...

PRINCE (*while responding to the caresses of the FIRST DAUGHTER, speaks to the SECOND DAUGHTER*): You know these variations? Speak, speak!

FIRST (*loudly to the SECOND DAUGHTER*): Be quiet! (*Silently to the PRINCE.*) Quiet...quiet...

(The PRINCE calms the FIRST DAUGHTER, responding to her caresses and at the same time fending her off, which the latter takes as qualified encouragement. During all this, the PRINCE is observing the SECOND DAUGHTER.)

SECOND (*excitedly*): I'm not going to bother repeating the generally known vulgar legend that has petrified into dogma. No scientific approach will come close...

FIRST (*to the PRINCE*): Closer... closer...

SECOND: ...to even considering this. All, even the most opposing theories, unite in one postulate...

FIRST (*to the PRINCE*): Unite... unite...

SECOND: ... that there must have taken place an intrigue to exploit the absent-minded ecstasy of a Prince blinded by passion, or, better yet, the historically ripened social inevitablilty that the Prince had to marry. An intrigue, in short, with the object of planting a person suitable to us into palace circles.

PRINCE: Who is us?

SECOND: Well, they.

PRINCE: Who?

FIRST: Nobody.

SECOND: The instigators of the intrigue. With that object in mind, the Prince was given one of the so-called daughters, that is, my sister or I. From here on, opinions differ. Some schools of thought hold the main question to be: Which one of the daughters was sent to the palace as the False Cinderella? Others deal mainly with the question: What happened to the real Cinderella? First, let us take a look at number one. There...

FIRST (*to the PRINCE*): Don't listen to her. Don't listen. She is crazy. All she knows is rumors. She herself wasn't there when it happened. She was taken into this house later, much later. (*Carefully assuming seductive poses.*) Do you like it like this? Or like this, my Prince?

PRINCE: Later? (*To the SECOND DAUGHTER.*) You were taken in later?

SECOND (*to the FIRST DAUGHTER*): Even once a year you don't let me talk to an intelligent person. (*To the PRINCE.*) If this matter interests you, listen and don't let yourself be distracted. She can only slavishly repeat the canonic version she was taught by rote when she was taken into this house. And the other you can get later from me, too.

PRINCE: What? How? (*To the FIRST DAUGHTER.*) When were you taught this?

FIRST: Lies... she lies, my Prince.

SECOND: And if this is a lie, then it is by way of lies that we may arrive at truth! Therefore: which of the daughters was sent to the palace? It couldn't have been me, because I am here. Nevertheless, it is logical that I was the one, because power demands intellect, knowledge, brilliance. Other authors hold that the main characteristic of power is a striving toward unity, harmony, and external representation. According to them, my sister must have been sent to the palace—a theory that is also easily carried ad absurdum, because my sister is here, which is, I must admit, argumentum ad hominem.

FIRST (*to the PRINCE who has in the meantime distanced himself from her*): You hear... I am here...

SECOND: The other schools of thought deal with the problem: What happened to the real Cinderella? One widely accepted version is that the cheated Cinderella was given a place as a daughter of the house for compensation.

PRINCE: Bravo! Bravo! (*Enthusiastically embracing the FIRST DAUGHTER: to her.*) You know, I arrived at the same thought all by myself.

SECOND (*with rising involvement*): And here again, we have a number of debatable issues! It would be an oversimplification to think that if we know which one of the daughters went to the palace, we would automatically know which daughter's place was given to Cinderella. According to one bold hypotheses, there was first a shifting of places, whereby the daughter who was left behind took the place of the False Cinderella who had gone to the palace, and Cinderella got the place of the daughter who was left behind. Ergo, she would have been left twice, the False Cinderella would have departed twice, and the other daughter been left behind once! (*Reaching a climax.*) This hypothesis has found no confirmation!

(*The PRINCE, who has tensely followed her, while mechanically continuing to embrace the FIRST DAUGHTER, is disappointed. Lets go of the FIRST DAUGHTER, but she rises with him.*)

FIRST: Don't go... don't go, my Prince... where are you going?... Come...

PRINCE: Are you... are you the real Cinderella?

FIRST (*also at her climax*): Oh, I don't know. I don't know, my Prince... what all this means... Your Cinderella's the one who takes good care of you.

(*Embracing the PRINCE, she pulls him into the bed, puts out the lamps. The SECOND DAUGHTER is standing up in her bed, the package with the slipper triumphantly held above her head.*)

SECOND: On top of all interpretations, my Prince, there remains a good possibility that I am the real Cinderella!

PRINCE (*speaking to the SECOND DAUGHTER from the embrace of the FIRST DAUGHTER*): Once you try this slipper on your foot, it should be clear right away.

SECOND: What importance does it all have, my Prince? All truths are relative! We must understand them all and not be prejudiced by any one of them!

VOICE OF MISTRESS (*from the depth of the stage*): Girls! Girls! Are you ready? Yoo-hoo, girls! The Prince and Cinderella will be here in a moment. Are you all made up? Girls!

(*Panic. The PRINCE jumps out of the bed, grabs the package from the SECOND DAUGHTER, and disappears into the bathroom. The FIRST DAUGHTER relights her lamp, rises and disappears behind the screen. The SECOND DAUGHTER runs behind the screen on her side.*)

FIRST: Oh heavens, the Prince will be here in a moment and I am still naked.

SECOND: Shoes. Listen, you were going to give me a pair of your shoes.

(*Both the stage and the house are slowly becoming fully lit. As the lights rise, a hunting horn is heard; a festive voice increases in volume along with the lighting.*)

VOICE OF MISTRESS (*festively*): Welcome, Prince and Cinderella. Again I am pleased to greet you on your anniversary.

(*The curtain closes.*)

INTERMISSION

SCENE FOUR

(*The setting as in scene two. Only the bench with the washbasin and alarm clock is missing. Sober daylight, which does not reach farther or higher than the playing area in front of the line of furniture. On stage are the MASTER, COURT CINDERELLA, and the PRINCE'S DOUBLE, the King's Regent. The latter is identical with the PRINCE: both are played by the same actor. Nevertheless. he is differentiated from the PRINCE by his flabbier, more vacuous bearing and facial expression. Thus he resembles the PRINCE when the latter has lost his train of thought and his self-control. The COURT CINDERELLA resembles both daughters, but her training has been stricter, more rooted in essences. Her bearing is more supple, her mien more intelligent. She sits on a chair, near the table, looking at collections that the MASTER lays out, sheet by sheet, in front of her. From time to time, she gazes about with a restless, searching look, but on the whole she controls herself admirably. On a chest and within an arm's length from her sits the PRINCE'S DOUBLE, staring into space and dangling his legs, which he bangs from time to time against the chest, whereupon COURT CINDERELLA gives him an admonishing look. Upon receiving the sheets, the PRINCE'S DOUBLE fingers them with no apparent interest and places them, willy-nilly, on the chest or on the floor, whence the MASTER gathers them up. There is a bottle on the table and each person has a full glass.)*

MASTER: As you may well imagine, this stamp collection is the jewel of all my collections. It dates from the time you went to court. Ever since that time we have had diplomatic relations and official correspondence.

COURT CINDERELLA: I haven't had a chance to thank you for the cordial words of welcome, father.

MASTER: Father? My God, you called me "father."

COURT CINDERELLA: Well, this isn't the first time you have heard me call you "father," is it?

MASTER (*chuckling*): You did not hear the speech for the first time, either.

COURT CINDERELLA: But each time, each time it grips my heart as if it were new. (*To the PRINCE'S DOUBLE, who makes a racket with his feet.*) Quiet, Prince.

MASTER: And likewise it grips my heart each time I hear you call me "father."

COURT CINDERELLA: I believe you, I do. Who could compete with you in sincerity? How you cared for us, all three of us. There was no discrimination. It was as if you were the real father of us all.

MASTER (*to himself*): See... (*Continuing to introduce his collections.*) This stamp here, please take note of this one here. Do you remember the first letter you sent from the palace?

COURT CINDERELLA: You do keep everything!

MASTER: I keep everything. Everything. (*Begins to forget his role; rapidly and confidentially.*) The mistress does not understand, or does not want to understand, that I devote so much energy to keeping these resources in order. But at times, when she happens into this room, I can see it in her face that she is jealous of my system, my organization. Then, goddamn it, I know that my work has paid off.

COURT CINDERELLA (*with gentle, dignified reproach*): Why do you talk like that?

MASTER (*somewhat confused*): I... oh, well... there's really nothing to it... it doesn't really concern you, does it? Excuse me, I wasn't thinking... After all, she's not your real mother, you know.

COURT CINDERELLA: How she cared for us all. There was no discrimination. I have always felt as though she were my real mother.

MASTER: You are right. Yes, she too can get wistful when she looks back at what she has accomplished. Especially now that her memory is beginning to slip, if I may say so. Sometimes she comes here with a guest or two; without a doubt these are my happiest days. As I was saying, this stamp here. Where did...? (*The PRINCE'S DOUBLE has the sheet with the stamps, which he is at this moment sliding under his posterior.*) Oh... permit me, please... dear son-in-law... yes, yes... this one, this one here... thank you... As I was saying, this stamp here comes from your letter, the letter that did so much for us because you had not forgotten us, because there was still a warm place in your heart for your old home, because when you got to court you did not give up the name of Cinderella.

COURT CINDERELLA: What would be more detestable than to deny your past? If the Prince didn't mind—(*To the PRINCE'S DOUBLE.*) Sssh!—why should I be ashamed of having been a scullery maid?

MASTER: Golden words, my daughter, golden words. Who would have thought.... Just between the two of us, how are things at court? Are you happy? Do you have a good piece of the action? And how is the, ha-ha-ha, the Prince?

COURT CINDERELLA: You certainly don't beat around the bush, do you? You wouldn't expect me to tell a stranger...

MASTER: But I am your father... as you said yourself.

COURT CINDERELLA: True, but not when he is present. (*Points in the direction of the PRINCE'S DOUBLE.*)

MASTER (*conspiratorially, taking a chance*): Well, no, but that's not him, is it?

COURT CINDERELLA: Yes, you certainly have good reason to be proud of your collections. Seeing these stamps really touched me. (*To the PRINCE'S DOUBLE.*) Let's go, Prince. We have a lot to do. Farewell, daddy.

(*Exit the PRINCE'S DOUBLE and COURT CINDERELLA. From the door the latter casts a probing look around the room, sighs as if moved, smiles at the MASTER, and closes the door. The MASTER reassembles his stamp collection with care, then drinks up the three glasses that remained untouched, places one of them in a cabinet, which houses a glass collection, and refills the other two. He slinks to the door, listens, peers out. Satisfied with what he sees, takes a key from among the many on a display board and opens the chest the PRINCE'S DOUBLE had sat on. The PRINCE emerges from the chest, stretches, straightens his back, touches his shoulder and neck muscles, massages his temples. He seems thoughtful and worried. The MASTER hands him a glass, which the PRINCE mechanically empties.)*

MASTER: The danger has passed. The coast is clear. Don't worry, things are moving. It's too bad you didn't see the formal reception we gave you. That stupid regent of yours, I mean your double, didn't doubt for a moment that everyone thought he was you. Your wife, of course, suspected that you'd gotten here first and were up to something, but she kept a perfectly straight face. Such opponents must be respected.

PRINCE: Then what did I accomplish?

MASTER: I was in such goddamn good spirits that I just couldn't resist. I had to do something. Well, I managed to turn the cake around—in my wife's lap—so that when the time came for her to say a few words, she would look at the cake and say six instead of nine. But the bitch remembered. Just as well! The bloodier the battle, the greater the glory!

PRINCE: Pour me one more. I have a headache. *(Both drink.)* No sleep. And then all this exhaustive questioning here. Exhaustive, but no results. Didn't get a thing done before they tracked me down. Stuff yourself into a box! *(Gives the chest an angry kick.)* And that alter ego of mine has to dangle his legs right there! *(Sinks down to sit on the chest and again falls into a revery.)*

MASTER: Had he but known what a precious thing he was kicking! How many great men have found a hiding place in this chest! Great spirit, thou who used to rule this land, art now but building castles in the sand.... Of course, you must be careful moving about the house, but you have touched all the bases, haven't you? Man! You should have seen your wife's eyes darting around the room. Never before, you know, had she gotten further than the hall and your room. I was itching to let you out just to see her explain why there were two princes all of a sudden. *(Even though the PRINCE does not react to any of this.)* Don't worry, my boy. Don't worry. I know when to stop joking. It's coming along. Thank you, my boy, for stirring me to action once more. At last I took a chance. I wanted to lead her into a state of mutual confidence so that she would blab out what we need to know. This time I failed, but one has to take chances. One must always take chances. That's what I want to tell you. That's what I mean.

PRINCE: It seems... it seems that... *(Gathering his thoughts.)* It seems that no one remembers how it all began... it seems that no one

305

cares.... It seems that everyone is playing the part he was once given and puts up with that part.... What's the meaning of it all?

MASTER: One must take chances, again and again.

PRINCE (*to himself*): Everyone is a prince in his own world.... Everyone is more than a prince, because I, the Prince, do not have a part to play. The Prince's role is to hunt and shoot animals that have been clubbed senseless.... The Prince has no power, because... the Prince has not sought power? No, that's not it.... Right now when I must arrive at tentative conclusions, I have such a splitting headache. (*Sits on the chair on which the MASTER sat in scene two.*) Rub my neck a bit, good and hard.

(*The MASTER jumps resolutely over the line of furniture to get behind the PRINCE and begins to massage. Frowning, the MASTER stares straight ahead with an intense, radiant look. The PRINCE sinks once more into thought; here his facial expression must differ noticeably from that of his double.*)

MASTER (*massaging systematically*): Taking chances is what keeps us on our toes. We gotta have guts, guts! Life, the lady of the house we are in, is a cruel and compassionless mistress. She takes upon herself to do everything, and she does it all badly for us. She holds on to power with her teeth and blows it up like an infinite balloon. Singly, in groups of tens, hundreds, thousands, she stuffs us down the maw of time, in order to last forever herself. We shall not give her an inch. We must be ready to stand up for ourself at any moment, as if it were our last.

(*The PRINCE stands up as if in a trance, walks around thoughtfully with his head held high, eyes half-closed, then sinks into the rocking chair, which, however, rocks rather reluctantly. Slowly gaining in momentum, the PRINCE begins to rock himself, hard, with his whole body. The MASTER does not notice the PRINCE's departure, for he is carried away by his own words. He continues to massage the back of the chair.*)

MASTER: There is no avoiding the issues. There is nowhere to hide. Compromises are temporary ruses. There is no alternative. This is the only world. It is a hostile world. There's no purpose in basking in luxury or in suffering, searching for the meaning of life. Only to persist. Only to resist. That's the only choice. The only alternative. The only role. The only power we have.

PRINCE (*giving himself a push*): Haven't I wished for power over the way things are? Haven't I cared about life?... Somewhere there must be what I need.... A Cinderella is waiting for me in the kitchen; is she the one?... My part does not have to be just a part. It must be everything all at once. All at once I must be able to see everything for once, so that I may tell them all: Go and live your life your way. All power, all power must for once be in the hands of the one who wants no more power. All at once I must have everything for once in my grasp so that I may release it like a bird. Like the bird that flies out of the camera. All these pictures can be left untaken; all these moments can be left unrecorded.

MASTER (*massaging the back of the chair*): Not to lose firmness of mind. Not to sink back into hope. Emptiness contains us; we must fill it again and again. Fear lurks in us; we must conquer it again and again. So that at the hour of death, when we are no longer able, and when we look back, fear won't be too frightening nor the void too empty. Tranquillity cannot be hoped for. Getting into deep shit.... that's what we can do and must do. Unequal, unequal contest.

PRINCE: What did you give me, girls? What was it I wanted from you? I wanted to know whether one of you was Cinderella. No, I didn't want that, I didn't want that at all. Then the one who is waiting for me in the kitchen would not be Cinderella. What are you waiting for? That I would return and tell you that.... What did I want to tell you? Yes, I wanted to take you to the palace so that everything could begin again from the beginning. No. I didn't come here for that, through the storm, nine years ago—no, today.... I came to fight for power. Power must be taken away from the usurper. My wife is the False Cinderella. She is a usurper. Do you hear me, you are a usurper! When I have proved that, I will take your power away from you. No. What's the point, what's the point of fighting you over power that you do not have? You have nothing but your role, which you yourself don't see or understand. If indeed you had power, then you might as well hold on to it, and I will stay with you, no matter who you really are.

MASTER (*massaging*): Unequal, unequal contests. Unselfishly, not burdening your comrades. One must be like a craftsman who is forever training apprentices and forever losing them. We will not stop you, Mistress? What else can we do?

PRINCE: Then what is left? What was it I really wanted? Ah, yes! I wanted to know, only to know, only to know, to know how it all was and is.... Still, there's a Mistress left in this house. She must be the one who knows everything. Even I might bow to her power.

MASTER (*finishes the massage with a volley of sharp blows delivered with the sides of his open palms against the frame of the chair*): What do we have left? We can't hold you back? Very well! But we must keep irking you constantly. We can't keep track of your tricks! Very well! But we must constantly demand an accounting. Yes. Yes. Yes.

PRINCE (*calmly, rhythmically rocking in an immobile chair*): You are the only one who can give answers. I'll go to you for explanations. You will tell me what I need to know. You will tell me everything I need to know.
(*The inner curtain closes.*)

SCENE FIVE

(*From stage left in front of the inner curtain enter the MISTRESS in a wheelchair that she herself wheels; a monumental matron of uncertain but doubtlessly honorable age (as are all who take part in this play, for what age would not be honorable?). The edge of the shawl that covers her shoulders catches from time to time in the wheels; she pulls it loose with quiet, powerful rage. That does not occur often. From stage right enter COURT CINDERELLA and the PRINCE'S DOUBLE. The former's good-natured machine-like gait shows simpleminded, half-awake indecision, same as CINDERELLA'S at the end of scene one. The PRINCE'S DOUBLE shuffles in behind her. Catching sight of the MISTRESS, they hurry to her aid on COUR CINDERELLA'S initiative and push her to center stage, while the MISTRESS keeps protesting energetically.*)

MISTRESS: No need. No need, I tell you. I don't need any help. Enough now, enough. I don't need to go any further. (*Wipes off the perspiration, fans herself, pants—not from wheeling around but from protesting.*) Do I really look so weak? I'm strong enough to help others! Well, what did you hear?

COURT CINDERELLA: I am just as wise as before.

MISTRESS: Just as dumb, you were about to say.

COURT CINDERELLA: Yes, mother dear.

MISTRESS: Once a Cinderella, always a Cinderella. Well, sit down.
(*She takes two folding stools from beside her in the wheelchair and hands them to the others. The PRINCE'S DOUBLE sits, away from the others, and begins to file his nails. COURT CINDERELLA sits at the MISTRESS'S feet.*)

MISTRESS: Tell me everything you found out.

COURT CINDERELLA: When we left the post station early this morning, I did not have time to find out anything, or we would have been late. I don't think anyone in the party noticed that I had replaced the Prince with his Double. The Double had come along secretly; no one in the party knew about him.

MISTRESS: If someone needed to, he would have known. With all this searching for the Prince you have not managed to let me know how things are in the palace. Do you have everything under control? Is anybody trying to push you aside?

COURT CINDERELLA: I'm satisfied with my position. But being pushed aside... so far there didn't seem to be anything, but now.... If all of a sudden the Prince...?

MISTRESS (*contemptuously*): Come now! (*Indicating the DOUBLE.*) That there!

COURT CINDERELLA: Mother, dear, that's not he.

MISTRESS: Right, right. Yes. But the other one is no better. Go on.

COURT CINDERELLA: We've checked everywhere here.

MISTRESS: The girls?

COURT CINDERELLA (*dismisses them with a wave of her hand*): One started right away to offer him (*Pointing to the DOUBLE.*) food and tried to get him into bed; the other one tried to involve him in a book.

MISTRESS: And you?

COURT CINDERELLA: We looked around and left.

MISTRESS: Stupid. You should have let him take everything they offered. Was the book half-read? Was the food still warm? Was the bed in order or rumpled?

COURT CINDERELLA: But mother dear, I couldn't...

MISTRESS (*indicating the DOUBLE*): Well, this is not he!

COURT CINDERELLA: Right... but they are really so much alike. Do you think the Prince has already been there today?

MISTRESS: *You* think that he is in the house and that he got there ahead of you. I am interested in it only because you are. I had hoped that you would be in power. Nine years have passed, and still it pains me to see that you're dependent on him. I cannot be satisfied with you. This time I must say it right out.

COURT CINDERELLA (*sobbing*): But after all, he is my Prince and I... I'm his Cinderella.

MISTRESS (*impatiently*): Stop that. Calm yourself, calm down. Go on.

COURT CINDERELLA: Daddy... daddy seemed to know something. He kept hinting at something.

MISTRESS (*not at all worried*): That old fool! Just a trifle he amuses himself with in the attic. What else?

COURT CINDERELLA: Finally, I grilled the master of ceremonies on duty in the post station. I tortured him with my own hands.

MISTRESS: You should have started with him. What did he tell you?

COURT CINDERELLA (*unhappily*): With my own hands, I tortured him.

MISTRESS: You already bragged about that. I ask, did he tell you anything?

COURT CINDERELLA: Only that I was right. The Prince is here. But what's the use of being right if he's not here? The Prince had said to the master of ceremonies that he was going to arrange a little ceremony for the anniversary. A hike along the same route he took before. Nine years ago, he came from the last post station on foot, leaving his whole retinue in ignorance and confusion. He came, anxious to find me, his Cinderella....

MISTRESS: Is that all?

COURT CINDERELLA (*hesitates*): No, not quite. One more weird thing that the master of ceremonies confessed. But is that little master of ceremonies going to get it from me!

MISTRESS: Well?

COURT CINDERELLA: After the Prince had left... the master of ceremonies said that he hadn't noticed it before, but he's lying; he saw it right away, but he was afraid to speak, the bastard; maybe he himself gave the slipper to the Prince!

MISTRESS: The slipper? (*Becomes very attentive.*)

COURT CINDERELLA: After the Prince had left, the master of ceremonies discovered that the historic slipper used by the Prince to find his Cinderella was missing from the traveling exhibit. Who else but the Prince would have taken it?

MISTRESS (*very downcast*): What carelessness! First, to keep it at all! You over there in the palace don't have any more sense than our Master here. And secondly, to drag it around all over creation! What all could not happen on the road! Purely out of absentmindedness couldn't it be left somewhere? Purely out of royal distain couldn't it be lost? Don't I know what all can happen by chance.

COURT CINDERELLA (*meekly*): Mama, don't. This was not the same slipper. This was a mass produced item for traveling exhibits... slightly altered...

MISTRESS (*relieved*): So?! (*Very inconsiderately.*) Then there is no need to worry about it.

COURT CINDERELLA: But still... why did he need it?

MISTRESS (*looks at her for a while, then decisively*): Well and good! Now, go to your room and leave me alone. You'll get new instructions before you leave. Go.

(*COURT CINDERELLA and the PRINCE'S DOUBLE fold their stools, return them to the MISTRESS, and leave. The MISTRESS rides back and forth on the stage apron. Seems more tired and weaker than at the beginning of the scene.*)

VOICE OF PRINCE (*from behind the inner curtain*): Hello-o-o!

MISTRESS: Yooo! Who's calling?

VOICE OF PRINCE: It's me, the Prince. I'd like to talk to you, Mistress.

MISTRESS: Let's hear it.

PRINCE(*caught in the inner curtain, thrashing about*): Where are you? I can't see you.

MISTRESS: If you do have to see me...

(The MISTRESS waves her hand. The curtain rises. The stage is empty. Worklights—even, neutral—over the whole stage, also in the corners where so far no action has taken place. The PRINCE stands center stage, his hands the way they were from thrashing about in the curtain. The package with the slipper inside his coat. Pause.)

MISTRESS: The sight of me has struck you blind and dumb.

PRINCE: No... I'm dumb with amazement that, having seen you, I am not blind.

MISTRESS: A nice compliment. (*Laughs.*) You aren't seeing me for the first time. We met this morning.

PRINCE: Didn't you really notice that it wasn't me? Is it true that even you...

MISTRESS: Right, right. Nevertheless, we see each other once a year. Or has it always been your double?

PRINCE: No, no.

MISTRESS: Perhaps that time it was the Prince's Double, too? That time, nine years ago. Perhaps it was the senile king's senile regent looking for a wife, hoping power would soon drop into his lap? That time... nine years ago.

PRINCE: It was me.

MISTRESS: Perhaps it was the Prince's Double who was given... Cinderella's double. (*Laughs to herself, but openly.*)

PRINCE: I...

MISTRESS: Who knows?

PRINCE (*very firmly*): It was me. And about Cinderella, that is why I came to you. You are the one who knows the truth. Isn't that so?

MISTRESS: What is the sense in asking me anything if you have to ask that? (*Begins to wheel away.*)

PRINCE: No, don't go away. I must find out... I must at least hear what you have to say.

MISTRESS: I am not going anywhere. I am just moving around a bit.

(The MISTRESS rides in an illogical, unfounded pattern with unexpected turns and stops about the stage, which acquires for the

first time during the play its third dimension, except for CIN-
DERELLA's dance in scene one. So far, all props have been placed in
one line, fairly far downstage, and there the action has also been
carried out lineally. Exaggerating slightly, one could say that up to
this point the stage has been one-dimensional, because also the height
of the stage has been unlit and unused and all scenery and props
have been, at most, no higher than the actors. Now, during the
MISTRESS's moving about, the pipes begin to move up and down at
random. Both the PRINCE and the MISTRESS tire as the result of
moving about. From time to time some pipe will drop between them
unexpectedly like a barrier. Then the PRINCE jumps over it or
crawls under it; sometimes he swings from a pipe and propels
himself after the MISTRESS. After a while he learns to react more
quickly to her sudden turns. In the interest of more natural play, the
movement of the pipes could be different at each performance,
unexpected for the actors.)

PRINCE: I want to hear what lies behind your plans,
What is the goal of all your cold intrigues.
MISTRESS: Intrigues?
PRINCE: Yes, things that you arrange,
Arrangements that you've made inside this house
And elsewhere, too.
MISTRESS: And elsewhere?
PRINCE: Yes, in the palace.
MISTRESS: I've never felt the need to see your palace,
But you once came from there to visit us.
And since that time, once each and every year,
Come here, have you come here.
PRINCE: I come to you
Because my wife is from this house. And you,
You were the one who gave her to me then.
And now I want, I want, I want to hear
What was your goal, what lies behind your plans.
MISTRESS: A goal, again a goal....
PRINCE: Don't evade!
MISTRESS: Ah, come evade with me.
PRINCE: You're panting now.
Come on, give up this game, you are too old.
MISTRESS: I am not old, as long as I can play.
My strength is in the game.
(She makes a virtuosic turn and rolls directly under a pipe, quickly
distancing herself from the PRINCE. The PRINCE remains in place

312

and speaks louder or softer, according to how the MISTRESS circles
around, while listening to him.)
PRINCE: You didn't know,
In your omniscience were so ignorant,
That all the land is full of palaces,
Each palace full of those who think that they
Have power, wield power, are in power.
Did you really think that cheating one
Demented prince—one heir to just one throne—
By palming off an agent as his wife
You'd gain your end, arrive at something real?
But since you did not give me Cinderella,
Not seeing fit to let us have a happy
Life, then best you gave no one at all.
You and your agent did not gain by this,
Because the palace where you planted her
Is not the heart of power. Power is not
Centered there. And nowhere else.
MISTRESS (*Stops*):
                                                                  It's here.
Here. In this house. Here.
PRINCE (*Swings to her*):
                                                                     Here?
MISTRESS (*Changing position*):
No, here.
PRINCE: Here?
MISTRESS: No, here.
PRINCE: Then here.
MISTRESS: Yes, here
And here and here and here and here and here
And wherever I might be.
(*The MISTRESS throws the PRINCE a folding stool.*)
MISTRESS: Sit, rest.
(*The PRINCE automatically catches the stool.*)
PRINCE (*Contrarily*):
Thank you, I'm not tired.
(*The MISTRESS continues riding, breathing hard.*)
MISTRESS: Oh yes, you are,
My dear Prince.
(*She rides up to the PRINCE, fleetingly puts her hand on his*
shoulder. The PRINCE sits with unexpected obedience.)
MISTRESS: How well, how well I know

313

How everything that lives wears down and tires.
(*Both catch their breath. The MISTRESS breathes hard, asthmatically, fans herself.*)
PRINCE (*Strained*):
And life itself, it seems, must rest a space.
MISTRESS (*Quite lightly with amusement*):
Now, then, where did we leave off, my Prince?
PRINCE: My god, how many houses now hold crones
Like you, who gloat: I am all power!
MISTRESS (*In a conversational tone, without pathos*):
The storm has ended, we'll have a clear night,
We'll see a batch of stars above our house.
Among those stars and far beyond them yet
A lot of those that our eyes can't see,
All kinds of galaxies, where there are lives
We could not dream about. How many, Prince?
Who on earth would know? I don't care.
I've always had enough to mess with here....
PRINCE: So, then, you are not all, all of life?
MISTRESS: I've got enough for you and some to spare.
Yes, true, you're not the only suitor
Who's left the only palace in the land
To court a country girl. You're not the only Prince.
You're not the only royal heir who has
Been married to a girl from our house.
You're not the only one who every year
Duly comes to visit, nor your palace
The only place where I have sent an envoy.
Does that console you now?
PRINCE: Oh no, oh no!
You are a wholesale pimp!
MISTRESS: If you will.
PRINCE: But all those princes.... Not a single prince
Did ever get his real Cinderella?
MISTRESS: I wouldn't know. Not everyone is so
Aggressive... and comes to me demanding truth...
PRINCE: Thank you for that at least.
MISTRESS: ... or quite so stupid.
Now, what else can I console you with?
PRINCE: Wait. Let me collect myself.... So that
If you have placed your agents everywhere...
Then *you* pull the strings and lead us—where?

Again, what is your goal?
MISTRESS: I choose by chance.
   A bullet strikes; its hole decides the target.
   (*She begins to wheel again. The PRINCE remains in place.*)
PRINCE: So that's your goal, that's the end for which
   You turn to any means?
MISTRESS: My means, dear Prince,
   I said, is chance. My moves a game, my acts
   Experimental. And how they end is all
   The same to me.
PRINCE: But not to me! No!
MISTRESS: Yes, yes. Maybe. But you have memories,
   Your head is full of neat and useless trash,
   Collections and accounts that lull your brain to sleep.
   I'll see to it that nothing too essential
   Would suddenly disturb your peace of mind.
   You could not stand to face the truth.
   Myself, I keep a double set of books.
   (*The PRINCE jumps up and hurries after her. He chases her as before.*)
PRINCE: You keep a double... double set of books?
   Then you must have it written down somewhere
   Whose foot the slipper really fit and how.
   And a report on how your scheme paid off.
   And for a game, there must be written rules.
   For instance, if an agent fails your hopes
   What happens to her? Do you call her back?
   As compensation for the wrong you've done me,
   I demand the truth! Then I'll try
   To live without my real Cinderella.
MISTRESS: Maybe you did get her.... I can't remember.
   Well, since you are so persistent...
PRINCE: Thanks.
MISTRESS: ... a sorry sight and so insistent, too:
   Could be some things were once recorded here—
   But I don't know where I have laid my glasses—
   Read for yourself what interests you. Catch.
   (*While riding around, the MISTRESS throws up sheets of paper of different colors and sizes, some bound together, some loose, some rolled. The PRINCE gathers them.*)
MISTRESS: But unsuccessful Cinderellas—no,
   I don't call them back. They simply fade from sight.

(From this point on, the MISTRESS begins to age again, her voice subsides, she moves upstage. The PRINCE sits on the stool and examines the sheets.)

PRINCE: I cannot understand! What's this? Most
Pages are blank, others full of signs
I cannot read... strange alphabets,
Weird symbols, scribbles, scratches... Again an empty page...
MISTRESS: I am illiterate, as you might say.
PRINCE: And how do you read them yourself?
MISTRESS: I don't. And now
I should go. I've taken all your time.
PRINCE: But I insisted, I....
MISTRESS: Maybe you did.
Maybe you now regret it. No, don't help.
I don't need help. You're leaving soon, prepare.
You can keep those papers if you want them, and
In exchange give me the slipper, if you wish.
Some day, to amuse myself, I'll try it on
my withered foot.
PRINCE: I will not give it up.
MISTRESS: Well, so let it be. You yourself know best. *(The MISTRESS rides upstage, signals with her hand, whereupon the inner curtain drops.*

(The PRINCE remains sitting in front of the inner curtain, papers on his knees and spread around him on the floor. He leafs them quite thoughtlessly and arranges them according to color and size. Sings to himself quietly, improvising, without tragic pathos.)

PRINCE: Mother earth, from whom all things once came, is the mean old woman who would keep me as a slave? And life recedes just like an aging dame, sitting in the wheelchair that's headed for the grave? The prince did not have any great illusions; he has become a sad, unhappy, little fella? And all his hopes turned out to be delusions, because he has not found his sooty Cinderella?

(During the third sentence, there can be heard from behind the curtain, as if it were accompaniment—the tunes need not harmonize—CINDERELLA's syllabic song, which the PRINCE does not notice at first. When he finishes his song, CINDERELLA's continues—a distant humming. Through the inner curtain the glow of the fireplace can be seen. The PRINCE listens. The inner curtain rises slowly.)

SCENE SIX

(*The setting as in scene one. CINDERELLA, wearing the prince's coat and with her gray hair undone, sits by the hearth, from whence comes the only illumination. The PRINCE carries his stool to her side. Both sit facing the hearth, with their backs to the audience. Immediately, without looking at the PRINCE, CINDERELLA leans against him and rests her head on his shoulder while continuing her song. The PRINCE throws sheets of paper into the fire, at first slowly and singly, then more impatiently and in groups. Each time the flame becomes brighter and leaps higher.*)

PRINCE: Now we'll really have a fire. Watch them burn. Next page. Can't hear the storm. Next page. It must have stopped. Next page. I wonder what time it is. (*Takes out his watch.*) It's stopped. (*Looks around, sees the alarm clock in its usual place.*) Aah... (*Tries to get up.*)

(*CINDERELLA puts her arm around the PRINCE without saying anything or looking at him or interrupting or changing her song. The PRINCE remains seated.*)

PRINCE: Must be dark by now. Next page. (*Excitedly.*) I guess. It's always dark here. Can never tell what time of day it is. (*Throws a large handful of papers into the hearth so that, for a moment, the flame rises quite high.*) That's better. (*Opens the casing of his watch.*) Of course, wet as could be. The snow has melted.

(*Throws more papers into the fire and swings the watch by its chain over the hearth, while reaching over the head of CINDERELLA. With his other hand he begins again, now more calmly, to toss papers into the fire. CINDERELLA continues to sing.*)

PRINCE: I want to see if I can get this watch going again—page—or not. Page. I want to see if I can accomplish anything—page—here today—page—or if I can't get anything done at all—page—here today. Will that watch start working—page—and show the time I must leave—page—or (*Rapidly, with excitement.*) will it show the time I must leave before I can get it going?

(*Pause. The PRINCE tries to look at the face of CINDERELLA who has not changed her position or song. He does not succeed very well. Then the PRINCE puts his watch to his ear and listens. It does not work. The PRINCE continues what he was doing.*)

PRINCE: Yes, Cinderella. Page. Cinderella?... Page.... No matter what, I must leave. Page. To the court. Page. I promised you (*Rapidly.*)

317

that I will solve this riddle, but now I am not sure that the riddle isn't my own invention.

(*Throws the remaining papers into the fire all at the same time. A huge flame. CINDERELLA exclaims softly: "Oh!" Her song stops. The PRINCE tries to jump up, but her arm is around him. The flame subsides.*)

CINDERELLA: Want beans?

PRINCE: Yes. Beans.

(*While CINDERELLA is fishing the beans from the hearth, the PRINCE rises, listens to his watch, shrugs his shoulders in a gesture of hopelessness, and pockets the watch. He lifts up the sheepskin coat that has fallen off CINDERELLA's shoulders and hangs it on the candelabra by the door. Looks at the alarm clock, makes an uncomprehending face, puts the alarm clock to his ear, listens, shakes his head, and places the clock back in the washbasin. Again moves across the stage toward the hearth.*)

PRINCE: What did you do here all this time?

CINDERELLA: Waited.

PRINCE: Is waiting doing something?

CINDERELLA: Waiting is very much doing something. There's a lot to do while you're waiting.

PRINCE: And what else did you do while you waited?

CINDERELLA: Waited some more.

PRINCE: And then?

CINDERELLA: Some more. And I baked beans. Scorched them.

PRINCE: They'll do.

(*The PRINCE sits with his back to the hearth, facing the audience. He holds a cup of beans in his hand and pitches beans into his mouth. CINDERELLA remains facing the hearth.*)

CINDERELLA: But you?

PRINCE: What, me?

CINDERELLA: Prince.

PRINCE: Yes?

CINDERELLA: Yes. Prince. But what did you do all that time, Prince.

PRINCE: I? (*Chokes on a bean. CINDERELLA slaps his back.*) I didn't do a thing. Didn't bake, didn't wait.

(*The PRINCE jumps to his feet. The beans scatter. He begins to pick them up. CINDERELLA joins him. At first the PRINCE gathers them rapidly and sloppily, but then a thought comes to him. He stops to consider it, throwing occasional scowling looks at CINDERELLA, quickly turning away when she returns his gaze. The PRINCE arrives at some decision. He continues to pick up the beans, now*

318

calmly and rhythmically. Thus all the beans are picked up. The PRINCE *sets the cup on the bench and remains standing, facing the pictures on the stove, his back to the audience.*

CINDERELLA: They're dirty now. You want more?

PRINCE: They'll do.

CINDERELLA: Prince.

PRINCE: What is it?

CINDERELLA: I would like to see that slipper again. I won't put it on, if you don't want me to. I just wanna see it. Why not, Prince...?

PRINCE: Prince. Prince. Prince. (*Icily, monotonously.*) You get nothing for nothing from the Prince. That's the Prince's role. There's a picture missing here. How do you suppose Cinderella gets to go to the ball? Where does she get all her clothes, her hairdo? Where will she get her regal bearing? And where will she get her shining slippers?

CINDERELLA: For beans.

PRINCE: You get nothing for beans.

CINDERELLA: Cinderella has nothing but the beans she bakes in the ashes. If she does that well...

PRINCE: You'll get nothing for beans. Unless someone wants to give you everything anyway. That's it. That's the way Cinderella gets to the ball. That's the way she gets her shining slippers. There must be a Fairy Godmother!

CINDERELLA: F-a-i-r-y G-o-d-m-o-t-h-e-r? F-a-i-r-y G-o-d-m-o-t-h-e-r?

PRINCE: You haven't heard about that?

CINDERELLA: No.

PRINCE: Try to remember. Try hard to remember.

CINDERELLA: I've never heard of a Fairy Godmother.

PRINCE (*monotonously*): Cinderella must have a mother in the fairy kingdom. Cinderella is being mistreated. Cinderella's whole life is miserable. Others are rich and happy, she has to cower in the kitchen. Cinderella has to cower in the kitchen. She has to root in the ashes. She has to root in the ashes. Tedium seeps from the cracks in the chimney like fumes, or like water trickling from a leaky tap. But Cinderella knows how to call her fairy godmother for help. And then you'll get compassion. Then you'll get justice and redemption. Then you'll get revenge! (*Small pause.*) Everyone has gone to the ball. Cinderella is alone. Cinderella knows how to call her Fairy Godmother. Cinderella will call her Fairy Godmother. How does Cinderella call her Fairy Godmother?

CINDERELLA: Me?

PRINCE: You.

CINDERELLA: I don't get it.

PRINCE: Or are you not Cinderella?

CINDERELLA: I don't understand. I don't know. I don't know how.

PRINCE: Cinderella must understand, must know, must know how. Otherwise what'll happen to justice and revenge? Otherwise how does she get to the ball? Otherwise how does she rise to power?

CINDERELLA: What is this justice? What is this revenge? I don't really need the ball. All I want is this shiny slipper.

PRINCE: That would be revenge on the others. Call your Fairy Godmother. Call your Fairy Godmother.

CINDERELLA: What Fairy Godmother?

PRINCE (*turning*): Very well. The Fairy Godmother should come when her Cinderella is being mistreated. Oh, you poor Cinderella, you haven't even heard of your Fairy Godmother. How could it possibly be worse?

(*The PRINCE steps up to CINDERELLA and strikes her. CINDERELLA just stands there, wide-eyed.*)

PRINCE: Well? (*Strikes her again.*)

CINDERELLA: Prince.

PRINCE: Nothing but Prince, and Prince, and Prince.

(*He beats CINDERELLA. She retreats. He follows her, accompanying each sentence with blows. Thus they move across the stage to the door.*)

PRINCE: I'm not leaving this house until I know everything. If you are Cinderella, I'll take you with me to the palace. Then there will be justice and revenge and you will get your shiny slippers. Why don't you call your Fairy Godmother? Why not, if I'm beating you?

(*They have reached the door. Suddenly CINDERELLA turns around and runs across the stage, back toward the hearth.*)

PRINCE (*by the door*): Only your Fairy Godmother is left. Only your Fairy Godmother knows everything and wishes no evil. Call your Fairy Godmother. (*Runs after her, reaching out.*) What horrible gray hair you have. (*He pulls her hair.*) What an ugly, sooty face you have. (*Crushes her face with his fingers.*) What dull and idiotic eyes. (*Reaches his spread fingers towards her eyes.*) Disgusting, stupid Cinderella, fit only to be beaten and tortured. Why don't you come, Fairy Godmother? Can't you hear? Fairy Godmother!

(*The PRINCE kicks CINDERELLA with all his strength, but she ducks unexpectedly, grasps a handful of ashes from the hearth and throws it in the PRINCE's eyes. She flees to the top of the stove, where she remains, crouching. At that moment, as if in response to the PRINCE's last shout, the MISTRESS appears from the depth of the stage in her wheelchair. She is accompanied by COURT CIN-*)

DERELLA, dressed for a journey, and the members of the house-hold: MASTER, FIRST DAUGHTER, and SECOND DAUGHTER. The PRINCE, having backed up across the stage, stands by the door and is busy clearing his eyes. Ceremoniously, the MASTER lights the candles by the door. All newcomers except COURT CINDERELLA and the MISTRESS have candles in both hands.)

MISTRESS: Here he is.

COURT CINDERELLA: Where on earth did you disappear to? We looked all over for you. I was beginning to get worried. What's this package under your coat? (*She takes it.*) We have come to the sad moment of parting. Everything is set. The sleds are here. Our party awaits. Here is your coat. (*She tries to put the greatcoat on the PRINCE, but his hands are busy with his eyes.*) Goodness gracious, what's the matter with your eyes?

PRINCE: The storm.

COURT CINDERELLA: It has stopped snowing, thank heavens. I'm having the roads cleared. Let us say farewell.

PRINCE: Us?

COURT CINDERELLA (*to all*): Once more the sad moment has arrived when we must take leave of this kind and loving household for the time being. We thank you for an incomparable reception. Good-bye, daddy. Good-bye, my dear sisters. Good-bye, mamma.

(She kisses everyone goodbye. All stand, arms spread, candles in their hands. Upon being kissed, the MASTER sputters. While the PRINCE is taking his leave of everyone, the MISTRESS keeps talking quietly to COURT CINDERELLA, who bends over her.)

FIRST DAUGHTER (*to the PRINCE*): Farewell, my Prince. Have a good journey. We shall meet again? (*Prolonged kiss.*)

SECOND DAUGHTER (*to the PRINCE*): Well, take it easy and come see us again, won't you? (*Gives him one of the candles and heartily shakes his hand.*)

MASTER (*to the PRINCE*): That's it, my boy. (*Shakes his hand for a long time without saying anything, also giving him one of his candles.*)

(The PRINCE, seeing that the MISTRESS is still talking with COURT CINDERELLA, does not go near her wheelchair. He places his candles in the candelabra, takes the sheepskin coat, and laboriously puts it on top of his greatcoat. Looks across the stage, but it is all dark there; the fire in the hearth has gone out.)

MISTRESS (*ends her conversation with COURT CINDERELLA; to the PRINCE*): Well, my noble Prince, good-bye.

PRINCE (*staring into the darkness*): Good-bye. Good-bye.

ALL (*to one another*): Good-bye. Good-bye.
  (*COURT CINDERELLA and the PRINCE go out the door. The others wave after them.*)
FIRST DAUGHTER: It certainly is quiet outside.
SECOND DAUGHTER: Inside too.
MASTER (*with deep inner suffering, with complete sincerity*): Ah, endless storm.
MISTRESS: Let us carry on.
  (*At a signal from her the door is closed, and all gather around the wheelchair.*)
MISTRESS: Now everyone will go to his or her room and will do whatever he'll do. It would be best to go to sleep. There's a ball tomorrow to which we have all been invited.
FIRST DAUGHTER: Oh, a ball. Strange our guests didn't mention it.
SECOND DAUGHTER: Evidently, my dear, it's taking place in some other palace.
FIRST DAUGHTER: You didn't scuff my shoes up again, did you?
MISTRESS: Be ready to get ready in the morning. (*Waves her hand. They all begin to leave. To the MASTER.*) Oh yes. Here's something for you. You can put it with your other collections. (*Gives him the package containing the slipper that she had confiscated from COURT CINDERELLA.*) Good night.
ALL: Good night.
  (*Exit all, except the MISTRESS. She wheels herself to the alarm clock, picks it up, and begins to wind it with a clatter, while driving across the stage toward the stove. At the same time the lights come gradually on until the stage is evenly flooded with the same neutral light as in scene five.*)
MISTRESS: Cinderella! Cinderella! Yoo-hoo! Still sleeping? Sleep well. Sleep well. Sleep well. Tomorrow's the ball. Tomorrow you must get up early and dress your sisters. Tomorrow, when they have all left and you are alone, you will go to the room I'll tell you about, and you'll become beautiful. I'll show you how. Then you must put on the shining slippers and hurry to the ball, because tomorrow is your turn. Tomorrow is your turn. Sleep well. Sleep well. Sleep well. Tomorrow is your turn to go to the ball in shining slippers. Cinderella. Cinderella. Sleep. Cinderella, yoo!
  (*She has wound up the clock and has reached the stove. She touches CINDERELLA's shoulder. The curtain closes.*)

THE END

ILLUMINATIONS

For A Globe of Lightning and Nine Actors
(with a bang at the end)

by

Enn Vetemaa

Translated from the Estonian by
George Kurman

Introduction to
Illuminations

One of the better known younger writers of Soviet Estonia, Enn Vetemaa is the author of opera libretti, two collections of verse, several volumes of widely translated prose, and four plays. Born in Tallinn on June 20, 1936, he graduated from the Polytechnic Institute as a chemical engineer and later studied composition at the Tallinn Conservatory. Vetemaa has worked as the chief literary and art editor of Estonian television and as poetry consultant for the League of Estonian Writers. Among his stage works are "St. Susan, or the School for Masters" and "Supper for Five," which played a successful engagement in Finland in 1974. *Illuminations*, scripted as a teleplay, was produced by the Tallinn TV Studio on May 11, 1969.

Set in an isolated research station on Mt. Parnassus, *Illuminations* concerns a group of people who are menaced by a growing sphere of ball lightning. As the threat from lightning increases, the characters reveal their true selves, but, at a climactic moment, it becomes apparent that there is no real danger, for the building is protected by lightning rods, and the electrical display itself is being monitored by a safety engineer. In other words, the battle against lightning is meaningless. Having come to a similar realization, one of the characters tears the lightning rods from the building, thus triumphing over inevitability by once more making man the master of his own fate, whereupon a gigantic ball of electricity invades the room, concluding the play with a bang.

The character who precipitates the violent ending of *Illuminations* declares that his actions provide "an escape from the absurd." Throughout the work, he has been busy, in the manner of a latter-day Sisyphus, rolling the globe of lightning away from the building. Another character, not unlike Samuel Beckett's Krapp, conducts a dialogue with his tape recorder. Vetemaa is here parodying certain key images of the absurd that are familiar even to Estonian audiences, for both Camus and Beckett have appeared in translation, and Beckett's *Krapp's Last Tape* was shown on Soviet Estonian television in 1967, less than a year and a half before the staging of *Illuminations*. The very title of Vetemaa's play, which in full is *Illuminations for Ball Lightning and Nine Actors (with a Bang at the End)* (*Illuminatsioonid keravälgule ja uheksale näitlejale (pauguga lõpus)* pokes fun at such Western examples of verbosity in the titles of absurdist plays as Arthur Kopit's *Oh Dad, Poor Dad, Mamma's Hung You in the Closet and I'm Feelin' So Sad* and, perhaps more specifically, Peter Weiss's *The Persecution and Assassination of Jean-Paul Marat as Performed by the Inmates of the Asylum of Charenton Under the Direction of the Marquis de Sade*, which was translated into Estonian as early as 1966.

The mock absurdity of Vetemaa's *Illuminations* is tempered, however, by the ominous words of yet another character who has spoken moments before the fiery end. "Yes," he says, "a microcosm of the world stands before you. There is lightning at our windows; perhaps it will soon be at yours." Vetemaa's burlesque assumes even more serious dimensions when we recall a still earlier speech that has by now acquired a tragically ironic meaning. "Dear fellow humans," it begins. "We are all living in the twentieth century. Can't you really understand that this tiny ball of fire does not amount to anything important? If it were really dangerous, then... then all of contemporary humanity would join us. All men of good will would unite with us to roll it into the trash bin of history." Yet instead of doing anything of the sort, the firemen of our political world, as the absurdists—and Vetemaa—so well know, are all arsonists.

Though there is a reference to "all kinds of bombs" in *Illuminations*, Vetemaa's metaphoric ball lightning represents more than a nuclear holocaust. The color of the menacing globe is blood red, and it could easily be emblematic of any kind of political tyranny that leads to massive destruction. Thus one of the basic philosophical issues of the play deals with the following question: "Are we, as bystanders, forced to interfere in the atrocities for which we are not to blame?" The effects of anticipating the arrival of a tyranny of such proportions are reflected in the actions involving the allegorical characters of the play. These include a Classic, a Sufferer, an Orator, a Profligate, One in Search of His Identity, and the inevitable camp follower, here called a Muse. In a teleplay within a teleplay, each of the characters delivers his last words to the viewing audience back home as the red death, now "huge" and "radiant," rolls in through the door, veering "first to the left" and bringing utter panic to the inhabitants of Vetemaa's microcosm.

Illuminations is significant, finally, because an oft-recurring image in Vetemaa's Aesopian allegory is that of a dead sea gull, which immediately brings to mind a seminal work of the Russian theatre. Chekhov's sea gull, once the proud emblem of the Moscow Art Theatre, and hence symbolic not only of the wide-ranging influence of

Stanislavsky's realism but of Russian imperialism as well, now lies dead and rotting, polluting the very atmosphere.

Mardi Valgemäe

ILLUMINATIONS

CHARACTERS

BERNHARD—*an amateur painter.*

THE CLASSIC—*formerly a poet, now a butterfly collector.*

A SUFFERER—*makes his living being unhappy; has attempted suicide seventeen times as a result of agreements made with various communications media.*

IN SEARCH OF HIS IDENTITY—*a self-employed introspectionist.*

A PROFLIGATE—*a professional brawler and drunkard; has worked for bar owners by entertaining customers in the two aforementioned capacities.*

THE SPEECHMAKER—*who is simply a boring person.*

A MUSE—*before the start of* Illuminations *she was employed as a typist by Portobonia's television station.*

A MASTER OF CEREMONIES—*whose name is not revealed.*

THE ELECTRICIAN ON DUTY—*the electrician on duty.*

A GLOBE OF LIGHTNING—*ball lightning.*

All of the characters (with the exception of the Globe of Lightning) are citizens of the republic of Portobonia.

The scene of the broadcast: the summit of Mount Liakoura in central Greece—the Mount Parnassus of mythology. Elevation 8,068 feet above sea level.

The time: exactly one month ago.

I would like to express my gratitude to the International Research and Exchanges Board of the American Council of Learned Societies for financial support during the preparation of this translation.   G. *Kurman.*

In order to arrive at the correct perception of three-dimensional figures... it is useful to view models of such figures along with drawings of them. For our models we use flat pieces of plywood or cardboard to represent planes, and wire or dowels to represent lines. In employing such models, however, it should not be forgotten that both plywood and dowel represent but a limited portion of the figure under consideration. We must remember that:

> *a straight line continues without limit in both directions, and a plane extends without limit in every direction within that plane.*

E. Etverk, Stereometry

SCENE ONE

A television studio: the rear wall of the studio is heavily covered with advertisements, the majority of which portray modern electrical fuses and lightning rods of recent design. The MASTER OF CEREMONIES enters. He is an imposing man of about thirty-five, and is at ease in his white tie and tails.

MASTER OF CEREMONIES: Ladies and gentlemen of the television audience! Taking into account your considerable sophistication, good taste, and great experience in drawing correct and dynamic conclusions from televised material, today we would like to present to you the tragic final program of our recently concluded mammoth series—a program which, for numerous reasons, has not been seen on the air until now.

Perhaps you're a bit surprised that for the viewing of our video tape we have chosen this evening, Monday, at which time we usually present a television drama. Although it is true that, strictly speaking, the piece you are about to see is not a television play, it fails to be one for the sole reason that no one author has written it. My dear friends out there in the television audience, life itself has edited the final chapter of our popular series *The World and I,* and fashioned it into a tragedy.

We are presenting *Illuminations* to you not only because it is considerably more forceful than the works of our professional television playwrights, but also because, by presenting it, we are observing the emphatic joint request of the Portobonian Weather Bureau and the PFDVL (Portobonian Fire Department's Volunteer League). These two respected organizations have repeatedly asked us to call your attention to the danger of ball-lightning, which is especially great in this year of sunspot activity.

My dear viewers! There are many technical flaws in tonight's program. However, these are not technical difficulties in the usual sense. Life itself, the ball-lightning itself, has created these flaws by imposing extremely difficult atmospheric conditions for our program. Of course, we could have simply edited out a number of the defects but we feel that the flaws we are dealing with in the present case represent reality elevated to artistic truth, and for this reason we haven't tampered with the video tape.

Finally, we would like to call your attention to the fact that the tragedy in the shepherd's hut occurred as a direct result of the negligence of those present, and for this reason we are not dealing with an industrial accident. The Prosecutor's Office has ascertained that Portobonia's television station is not responsible for the regrettable tragedy which follows.

In closing, we would like to express our sincere gratitude to Delphic Television, which aided us in every respect during the preparation of our program, and kindly furnished us with mobile relay stations and relay lines.

Pleasant viewing!

A spacious, poorly-lit room, which at first glance reminds one of a barracks. This impression is created by military-style double bunks and footlockers, but is dispelled by the general disorder. There are two double bunks (for a total of four beds), and two single bunks set next to each other and partially separated from the others by an old-fashioned screen. In addition we notice a large, empty wine barrel lying on its side and a black, three-sided wardrobe. In the left-hand corner there is a television camera by means of which our esteemed TV viewers can see into the room in the first place. As the camera's red eye is not lit, those in the room ignore it. Nearby there is also a television set (more exactly a TV monitor). The room has two doors. One of them resembles a door leading to the bathroom, because that's exactly what it is. The second door leads outside. Another essential is a broad, low window, because through it the splendid scenery of Parnassus opens to view. Through the same window we also see numberous lovely but hazardous flashes of light, thanks to the ball-lightning. People are sleeping in the beds. We hear snoring. Only one of the residents of this odd room—namely BERNHARD—is already up. He is seated on a chair in front of the footlocker and is gluing rubber patches, in the light of a table lamp, onto something resembling a snow shovel. The glue-laden patches are spread out on the footlocker. BERNHARD is wearing very shabby overalls which are full of stains and burns; he has a puny physique and a sickly appearance. A bald spot makes him about fifty-five years of age.
 Silence.

THE CLASSIC (*from above, softly*): What time is it?

BERNHARD: Six.

THE CLASSIC: Are you putting on patches?

BERNHARD: What else can I do?

THE CLASSIC—*about seventy years of age, but still a rather stately, tall man in striped pajamas—climbs down and carefully sits on the lower bunk.*

BERNHARD (*without raising his eyes*): That big triangular one... if you'd... (*THE CLASSIC passes him the patch requested.*)

BERNHARD (*respectfully*): I have a big favor to ask you...

THE CLASSIC: Yes?

BERNHARD: If anything should happen to me today, then please send my things to Matilda. And write her that I saw her in my dreams every night—just like I promised. Each and every night. I didn't miss a single one. I kept my word. (*Still doesn't raise his eyes.*)

THE CLASSIC: Now why put it that way, Bernhard... Things will go all right today, too.

BERNHARD: I don't know. It's already so huge, that globe of lightning. Like a pumpkin. I can't even lift it on the shovel any more, I can only roll it. I'm afraid that it'll soon explode. And then...

THE CLASSIC: I'm not so sure. If it hasn't exploded up to now, will it ever explode?

BERNHARD: But at first it was as little as a tennis ball.

THE CLASSIC: Bernhard...

BERNHARD: Yes?

THE CLASSIC: Suppose it turns out not to be a globe of lightning after all? Ball-lightning that acts, so to speak, in such a way is unheard of. Is there any point in taking risks and endangering your health?

BERNHARD: You're right, that stench of burnt rubber really is terrible! It makes me sick. Every fifteen minutes I have to vomit.

THE CLASSIC: Perhaps the globe of lightning will turn out to be no more than a bad practical joke.

BERNHARD: But perhaps it won't.

THE CLASSIC: You're right, who can tell...

Silence. THE CLASSIC passes a new patch to BERNHARD, who glues it on.

BERNHARD: I've thought of just forgetting about the globe of lightning, but I simply can't. After all, it keeps rolling around the house and heading, dammit, right for the window. If I'd stop rolling it, it would suddenly plop right inside. No, I don't have the heart to give up. I have very little education; I'm just a country boy and can't understand those high ideas that the others here talk about.

THE CLASSIC (*passes him a new patch*): Now why bother mentioning the matter of education...

BERNHARD: Education's just the point. (*Raises his eyes for the first time.*) I'm not worthy of a man like you.

THE CLASSIC: I... I'll try to convince some of the others. And if no one is willing to help you, then... Then I will myself!

BERNHARD (*shocked*): You? Not under any conditions! You're very kind to me but... but I couldn't allow you to desert your principles for my sake.

THE CLASSIC: Now those principles, really...

BERNHARD (*in search of the proper words*): That's what I mean. The whole of your noteworthy, century-spanning, titanic... (*Gets tangled.*)

THE CLASSIC (*tormentedly*): Oh, enough of that! My creative work is really very modest.

BERNHARD: ... in your titanic works you've demonstrated the senselessness of life and praised death as the ultimate of harmony and equilibrium. It would be horrible if for my sake you'd renounce your ideals by resisting the danger. I can't allow it under any circumstances! What would my Willie say in that case?! Oh, yes... if something really should happen to me today, then please tell Matilda to let my dear son Willie study to be a ventriloquist after all. If his heart is set on that profession, there's no sense in forbidding it. I believe, my dear Mr. Classic, that a good ventriloquist will never go hungry, whatever kind of laws or government there might be. What's your opinion?

THE CLASSIC: Maybe; that may well be true. Certainly... of course, but what does my joining you to roll the globe of lightning have to do with your son Willie?

BERNHARD: It would be a great disappointment to him! After all, he knows your famous "Gunpowder Poem" by heart from start to finish, including the first and third stanzas that aren't printed in the school readers. Oh, how nicely he reads it!

(*Recites.*)

> ...into the fire I'd roll you,
> putrescent pumpkin,
> I'd blow you all to bits,
> you reeking head of cheese....

No, I can't do it nearly as well as he can. I can't get the right tone. I can't figure out where the kid got his talent for ventriloquism.

THE CLASSIC: Do you mean he ventriloquizes when reciting?

BERNHARD: Exactly. He's recited your poem several times at school parties. He's learned the whole poem by heart, even by ventricle. Yes, if my boy were ever to find out that I had allowed you to act in contradiction to your life's work, it would be a great blow to him.

THE CLASSIC (*with melancholy irony*): It would probably knock the wind out of him.

BERNHARD: Precisely. (*Continues gluing patches.*)
Silence. Then a low and distant roll of thunder. A glow outside the window.
BERNHARD: There, you can hear it! The lightning's gotten up too. It's a good thing that at least it doesn't attack at night... I've got to go soon. (*The blanket on the adjacent upper bunk is turned aside and a husky man—A SUFFERER—sits up and stretches contentedly. He then takes a revolver from under his pillow, points it to his temple, and clears his throat.*)
SUFFERER: I am replete with anguish! (*Yawns and then repeats with an even deadlier seriousness.*) Oh, I am replete with anguish! (*Looks at his wristwatch.*) It's only a quarter after six. (*Lies down once more and covers himself with the blanket.*)
THE CLASSIC (*speaking upward*): If perhaps you might be able to help Bernhard today...
SUFFERER: You idi-ots!
THE CLASSIC: He really can't go on alone.
SUFFERER: And he doesn't have to.
THE CLASSIC (*softly*): Aren't you at all... sorry for Bernhard then?
SUFFERER: There's no way to help a fool. And who's ever felt sorry for me?
BERNHARD (*softly to THE CLASSIC*): You'd better not bother. They might start thinking badly of you. (*Takes his shovel and exits.*)
SUFFERER (*who nevertheless has heard*): And for good reason. (*Smirking*): "Into the fire I'd roll you, reeking head of cheese..."
THE CLASSIC: Young man, you should be ashamed of yourself!... No, I still think that someone should help Bernhard, or at least notify the studio that we're having trouble with the lightning.
SUFFERER (*gently*): Why that's just what they're waiting for—that we either notify them or roll the globe down a cliff by ourselves. We're guinea pigs! They want to see how we'll react, to observe how this nonsense affects our frame of mind, especially your frame of mind, Mr. Death-Glorifier. I'd bet my life that this is one more of those sociological experiments. And the television program for which we've been assigned to come here will be put on the air as soon as we do something with the lightning—something that they would expect.
THE CLASSIC: But what if you're wrong?
SUFFERER: Oh, my God, how tiresome! (*Didactically.*) My dear man, we both are living in the twentieth century. Can you really fail to understand that this little ball of fire doesn't amount to anything important. If it were really dangerous, then... then all of contemporary humanity would join us; all men of good will would unite

337

together to roll it into the trash-bin of history. Yes sir! (*Yawns, looks at his watch.*) Oh, I am replete with anguish! (*Lies down again.*)

THE CLASSIC: All men of good will... would roll it away—all three of them. (*Sighs.*)

IN SEARCH OF HIS IDENTITY (*awakens and raises the blanket from his face*): Phew! The shovel's been inside all night again. Is there any real reason why Bernhard can't leave it outside? What a disgusting stench! I can't concentrate at all in this atmosphere.

THE CLASSIC (*to IN SEARCH OF HIS IDENTITY*): Maybe you might go to help Bernhard?

IN SEARCH OF HIS IDENTITY (*with regret*): I can't. I can't allow myself to be distracted. (*His round, simple-minded face slowly assumes an expression of happiness.*) I think that very soon I'll have it!

THE CLASSIC: Do you mean your identity?

IN SEARCH OF HIS IDENTITY: Exactly. (*Confidingly.*) You know, I think it's all a question of a dead seagull. The carcass of a seagull.

THE CLASSIC (*without interest*): Oh really?

IN SEARCH OF HIS IDENTITY: When I was five, one Sunday I saw the carcass of a seagull on the beach. It left a deep impression on me. It was during my formative years, after all... And when a little later—when I was six, I think—I was sitting on the roof of a shed, looking at the beautiful white clouds, you know, those soft, fleecy clouds; then suddenly I realized with a shock that I didn't like those clouds one bit. Why? What do you think?

THE CLASSIC: I don't know what to think.

IN SEARCH OF HIS IDENTITY (*triumphantly*): My unconscious projected that stinking seagull's carcass into the clouds. Can you imagine? Entire clouds full of dead seagulls. That's how the clouds were ruined for me. (*Sadly.*) That's how I spoiled that symbol of purity and lightness for myself. And its been decisive for my entire life.

THE CLASSIC (*forcing himself to be patient*): I see; entirely plausible. So now you've almost caught up with the deeper you.

IN SEARCH OF HIS IDENTITY: Yes, I think so.

THE CLASSIC: But its full discovery will require a little more time, eh?

IN SEARCH OF HIS IDENTITY: Of course.

THE CLASSIC: But tell me: what will happen if we're all blown up in the meantime? That ball-lightning doesn't necessarily have to be a stage prop. In any case, we can't be absolutely certain that is.

IN SEARCH OF HIS IDENTITY: You're right. For some reason I personally believe that it's real lightning. (*THE CLASSIC flinches.*)

Those ball-lightnings are really a strange and unexplained fee-nomenon. They're supposed to be different each time.

THE CLASSIC: All right, all right! But then it's possible that we might perish before you finally catch up with the secret of the deeper you. Wouldn't that be a terrible tragedy!

IN SEARCH OF HIS IDENTITY: Maybe it would.

THE CLASSIC: Why "maybe?"

IN SEARCH OF HIS IDENTITY: "Maybe" because I can't be sure about anything. I don't know how my inner self feels about the lightning. What if it has an overdeveloped death-wish? Maybe it would be enthusiastic about a death through lightning. (*Embarrassedly.*) I'm really very sorry but right now I can't help you. I simply don't know my attitude toward the lightning yet. (*Pulls the blanket over his head once more.*)

Silence. Rolling thunder. A glow outside the window. The SPEECH-MAKER climbs out of the barrel lying on its side. He is wearing a white tie and tails, and also has on spats and a monocle.

SPEECHMAKER: O golden sun, I greet you! (*Wipes the dust from his spats.*) I'm so stiff that...

THE CLASSIC: It's an occupational disease.

SPEECHMAKER: Yes sir, I simply have to admire Diogenes, who lived in a barrel all of the time. (*Yawns.*) I hear that the ball-lightning is worrying you. (*Softly to THE CLASSIC.*) Don't get nervous about such a trifle. It's only a provocative stage prop. Actually we should feel grateful to it... a special assignment, a daily allowance—we've got it made living here. Instead of worrying, we should get ready for the television program. (*More loudly.*) May I commence with my lecture?

THE CLASSIC: It's early yet. They're sleeping.

SPEECHMAKER: Don't worry about that. I can speak softly. It's just to keep in practice. But if you really think... All right. I'll get into the wardrobe for ten more minutes. I might even get some sleep.

THE CLASSIC: Why not get into Bernhard's bed?

SPEECHMAKER: Under no conditions. The bed of an opponent.... (*Walks to the wardrobe, opens it, and begins to empty it of women's clothes and underwear.*)

MUSE: Be careful! Those are my last good stockings. Look out that they don't run. (*The MUSE is sleeping with the PROFLIGATE. At first only her head is visible behind the screen.*)

SPEECHMAKER: All right, Miss Muse. I won't put them on the chair. I'll put them here on the footlocker. (*Stacks the underclothes on IN SEARCH OF HIS IDENTITY's footlocker.*)

339

PROFLIGATE: What is this jawing in the middle of the night! Let me sleep, you bastards!

The PROFLIGATE's bed and its environs are extremely filthy. The broken screen separating the MUSE and PROFLIGATE from the others is covered on the inside with photos of nudes from the borderline between art and pornography. Under the bed there is a pile of empty bottles and a transistor radio; curiously enough there is also a seventy-pound weight with a handle attached. Contrary to expectations, the PROFLIGATE himself is a thin little man of sickly appearance. There is something comically helpless about him. Nevertheless, he tries to appear supremely vital—the PROFLIGATE even speaks in a voice slightly deeper than the one granted him by nature.

MUSE: The night is ended, dearest.

PROFLIGATE: There never was a night.... Somebody here was blathering something about some seagull carcasses. What a group! (*Takes a half-empty bottle from under his bed and drinks the last few mouthfuls. Then he turns back to bed.*)

IN SEARCH OF HIS IDENTITY (*nervously to the SPEECHMAKER*): This underwear annoys me; the rags won't let me concentrate.

MUSE: Rags!... Watch your language, you miserable faggot.

IN SEARCH OF HIS IDENTITY: Put the bra at the very bottom, please.

SPEECHMATER: To the very bottom it goes.... I'll just be five minutes.... (*Steps into the wardrobe.*) It's far more private here than in the barrel.

THE CLASSIC: What are you doing with your monocle in the wardrobe?

SPEECHMAKER (*significantly*): Even darkness can be seen more clearly through a corrective lens. (*Closes the door. Silence.*)

SUFFERER (*from above*):

These nights, beneath the raven lid of sky,
from suffering I swoon upon the white-bloomed clover,
My heart is trampled by the hoof of agony,
my grief is without end, is never over.

(*Politely to THE CLASSIC.*) Is that version any better?

THE CLASSIC(*amiably*): I think it is a little better, yes. But in general... you'd really better not trouble yourself with writing poetry. Yours doesn't turn out too well.

SUFFERER: It has to turn out well! However much effort it takes, it finally has to. And it will!

THE CLASSIC: Believe me, young man, writing verses is the most thankless way to make a living. Why in the world would you want to learn such a crazy trade?

SUFFERER: I don't have any other choice. I've already attempted suicide seventeen times; for the newspapers' gossip columns, for television, even for makers of documentary films. I've hanged, drowned, taken poison, leapt from a cliff. I'm one of Portobonia's best suicides, but the public is getting bored. I think they sense that there's a contract in it somewhere. The public is so ungrateful. I simply *must* find a new profession. I'm going to begin writing elegies on unrequited love, and so forth. If a person has attempted suicide seventeen times, that should serve as a good recommendation for writing elegies. I'm going to make my debut on the TV program that's coming up. They should believe me.

THE CLASSIC: If they do believe you, then all is lost. But go right ahead and practice, although...

SUFFERER: I would consider failure insufferable.

THE CLASSIC: Taking your profession into account, I suppose you would.

The SUFFERER takes paper and pencil and starts to work. Silence.

IN SEARCH OF HIS IDENTITY (*motions THE CLASSIC to come nearer*): It looks like a bicycle pump is also very important. You know, when I was sitting on the roof of that shed looking at the clouds—those clouds full of dead seagulls—then one more thing was bothering me. One of the boys in our building had a beautiful, silvered bicycle pump. I wanted it for myself very much. It became a kind of fetish for me. If I had had the courage to steal that pump and even take it with me to the roof, then maybe I'd have gotten the best of those spooky seagulls. Who knows—maybe in that case I might have become somebody entirely different; someone more powerful—a bank robber for example. (*Sighs.*) But I didn't have the courage, and the only thing that came of it was complexes. A bundle of intricate complexes—so intricate that it can't be unraveled. And soon it'll be time for the live telecast, for which I'd like to present an exhaustive self-analysis.

PROFLIGATE: What are you raving about! Keep it down. Goddam seagull carcasses... (*Crosses his hands beneath his head.*) Be damned if I don't already smell them. (*To the MUSE.*) You too... get the hell into the bathroom and brush your teeth.

MUSE: I...

PROFLIGATE: Don't give me any "I, I." And by the way, I think I'm starting to get tired of you. You know, when we finished up our little caper and went to sleep I saw women in my dreams. *Other* women: plumper, Rubenesque; like lady wrestlers. You know, you really are a scrawny bitch.

341

MUSE: But we're actually starving. You order vodka with our subsistence allowance, and how long are even my savings supposed to hold out like that? (*Sleepily.*) Look under the bed—that's where our salary is!

IN SEARCH OF HIS IDENTITY: Going hungry sharpens the inner eye. There's nothing more disgusting than a person who's gorged himself to the limit.

PROFLIGATE: Right! So we can take you off the chow line right now. (*Jumps out of his bed and grabs a bag of cookies from the floor by the side of IN SEARCH OF HIS IDENTITY's bed.*)

IN SEARCH OF HIS IDENTITY (*monotonously*): That's rotten.

The PROFLIGATE starts munching the cookies. The MUSE goes into the bathroom and sounds of running water and gargling are heard.

IN SEARCH OF HIS IDENTITY (*monotonously*): Vulgar drunkard.

PROFLIGATE: Crunch, crunch. (*Mimics.*) When I was six months old I saw a dead camel.

A growing rumbling outside. A bright flash.

MUSE (*at the bathroom door*): Come wash my back, lover.

PROFLIGATE: Get lost!

SUFFERER (*rises and goes to the PROFLIGATE's bed*): Are you really very hungry?

PROFLIGATE: What's that to you?

SUFFERER (*quietly*): I'd offer you a tin of ham if... if you'd still continue... I mean, with the Muse...

PROFLIGATE (*amazed*): Really?

SUFFERER: I'd like it very much if your ardor wouldn't cool...

PROFLIGATE: Have you gone crazy?

SUFFERER: You know, last night when you... then I experienced first-rate suffering; top-notch heartache. I wept until a quarter of five and wrote three poems. I'm a professional sufferer and I have to keep in condition... By the way, it's a very good ham.

PROFLIGATE: Ah, so that's it.... Let's see the ham!

SUFFERER: Right away. And you'll still continue?...

PROFLIGATE: We'll see about that. (*The SUFFERER, after a brief hesitation, brings a tin of ham.*) Open it up.

SUFFERER: All right. (*Opens the tin. The PROFLIGATE helps himself to a good-sized slab of ham.*)

PROFLIGATE: Not bad.

The SUFFERER takes the seventy-pound weight from under the PROFLIGATE's bed and exercises masterfully with it.

THE MUSE'S VOICE: That lightning has really gotten big. I can see it from the window here. Poor Bernhard can just barely roll it. He's crowbarring it like he would a treestump. And it's so fiery red... How's it all going to end?

The MUSE returns into the room. She stops in admiration to see the SUFFERER exercising. The PROFLIGATE attracts her attention.

PROFLIGATE (*annoyedly*): Leave the weight alone! (*The SUFFERER complies.*)

THE CLASSIC (*goes into the bathroom*): The ball-lightning is enormous...

PROFLIGATE: Now you've really found something to be nervous about. What a bore—wasting their whole lives complaining! And if that little bugger of a ball-lightning really would blast us sky high, then so what! A few cockroaches less and that's that. You've got to croak sooner or later anyhow. (*Scratches himself contentedly.*) No, there's no sense in complaining. You only live once and you might as well take advantage of it so that... (*A shot showing the bottles underneath his bed. The MUSE returns.*) Did'ya brush your teeth good? D'ya know what—go brush them again! There's never too much of a good thing. (*Continues eating the ham.*)

MUSE: You're mean. (*Goes unhappily to THE CLASSIC's bed and sits down. The PROFLIGATE turns on his transistor radio.*)

TRANSISTOR RADIO: So let us begin with our morning exercises. Stretch your arms forward!

The PROFLIGATE tunes in some jazz.

MUSE (*to THE CLASSIC*): He doesn't care for me at all any more. Oh, what's going to happen to me?

THE CLASSIC: Don't worry daughter. You still have your entire life ahead of you.

MUSE: Daughter? Daughter? I may well have a daughter of my own soon... What was it that made me climb up here! I risked my life. *You* were brought here in a helicopter but I climbed up by myself. Several times I came near to tumbling down off the glaciers, but I kept going, thinking that death was preferable to my dull workaday life. And I had it good as a typist for the television series. (*Wipes her eyes.*)

THE CLASSIC: Well, soon they'll be showing a program about us. You'll become famous.

MUSE: Yes, but he doesn't want me any more. If he doesn't let me sit next to him and doesn't tickle me during the program, then what else can I do? I don't know how to be anything else but a woman. (*Wipes her eyes once more.*) That one there (*points to IN SEARCH OF HIS IDENTITY*) stares at his navel and groans about his seagulls. The Sufferer is really cute, but he's only interested in suffering. You're old enough to be my grandfather and the Speechmaker won't take me into his barrel. Bernhard dreams of Matilda, and on top of that he's got a terrible smell of burnt rubber about him. No, all of my hopes are pinned to him (*Points to the PROFLIGATE*). Only he can make me famous.

THE CLASSIC: Well, I'm not so sure... why not become Little Red Riding Hood. I'll write you a couple of children's poems. Pick some flowers. On the television program you can be a good little girl.

MUSE: It's too late for that. That parasite took me for a roll in the hay. People found out about it and our pictures were published in *Foto & Frase*. I was so proud of it then....

A growing roll of thunder. A glow outside. All listen.

THE CLASSIC (*takes his butterfly collection from under his bed and views it anxiously*): It's a terrible thing. The atmospheric electricity is ruining all of my butterflies—the work of a lifetime. The *papilii* are tarnished and the *Oxyptilus didactylus* has been twisted up. At night I could even see St. Elmo's fire playing on the antennae of the swallowtails... (*Sighs.*) I think I really will have to help Bernhard after all.

SPEECHMAKER (*opens the door of the wardrobe*): I must have snored myself awake, or was that the lightning? It doesn't matter... (*Climbs out of the wardrobe.*) My lady, and gentlemen! I feel that I lack the right to remain silent any longer. I shall begin. Quiet there! (*To THE CLASSIC in a whisper.*) Excuse me, did I speak in favor of the lightning yesterday or against it?

THE CLASSIC: In favor, I believe. You called it a tonic for the spirit, the golden apple of the Hesperides.

SPEECHMAKER: I thank you. Today I will indict it then. (*Prepares to make a speech.*) My lady, and gentlemen! We are living in a strenuous age. I have it on good evidence that there is an abominable globe of lightning prowling around our dwelling. Hannibal is at the gates, my dear comrades-in-arms! And we must reach a decision as to how to arrive at a decision about whether or not to decide anything. *Nobody is listening to him. Everyone finds an agreeable pastime. THE CLASSIC opens his butterfly collection and begins to examine the butterflies with a magnifying glass; the SUFFERER cleans his revolver; IN SEARCH OF HIS IDENTITY is thinking intensely— presumably about a bicycle pump; the MUSE is mending runs in her stockings; the PROFLIGATE mixes the liquor remaining on the bottom of several bottles together. From time to time the SUF- FERER repeats: "I am replete with anguish."*

MASTER OF CEREMONIES (*from the TV studio*): My dear television viewers: As the SPEECHMAKER's lecture probably doesn't interest you very much either, it might be a good idea to eat during his monologue, or to knit, or to spend the time in running some other urgent errand. You might also turn down the volume of your TV sets.

SPEECHMAKER: It seems to me that we should view this matter of the ball-lightning in two differing ways: the ethical-theoretical, and the practical-utilitarian. The former, I dare say, is appreciably simpler. Let us begin with it.

Are we the ones who are to blame for the creation of that globe of lightning? No, we are not the ones. We are not responsible for the differing levels of electrical tension in the atmosphere which give rise to lightning. My lady, and gentlemen! In this matter our hands are clean. *Eo ipso*, we have every right to present a resolute protest about the matter of the ball-lightning. We condemn the lightning. Do you agree? (*No one responds.*) I interpret your behavior as indicating agreement. My lady, and gentlemen! Thus we have taken the same position *vis-a-vis* the aforementioned ball-lightning as Voltaire took against the Lisbon earthquake in a fine, effectively-worded tract. I, too, am prepared to write such a tract. What is more, I feel that it's my obligation to do so. I propose that from this day forth we refer, among ourselves, to the ball-lightning as a "vile fire-wheel," a "foul stink-ball," a "depraved little lightning bugger..." (*A loud crackling. Flashes.*) Let it rumble. We will not retreat from our decision.

Now we should move to the consideration of a second question: What should we do about the depraved little lightning bugger? What is to be done? The problem is even more complicated than that. Nothing would change if we were to regard our little house as the entire world. I can report to you with pride that the question is a global one. The biological instinct for self-preservation, which is concealed in all of us, compels us all to take up shovels, galoshes, and other available rubber objects in order unanimously to repel the lightning. I do not doubt that we could easily roll it down a cliff. But along with the lightning we would also be rolling down a supremely important philosophical question, namely, "Are we, as bystanders, forced to interfere in atrocities for which we are not to blame?" We would also be rolling *responsibility* down the cliff—the responsibility of providing the problem with a philosophically correct solution. I feel that we cannot simply roll our responsibility away. Once we have destroyed one globe of lightning, then we must do the same with the next one, and with the next one after that. But do the lightnings have the right to turn people into lightning-rollers? In such a case, it seems to me, the lightning would have achieved its objective.

An exhausted BERNHARD enters. The handle of his shovel is broken.

PROFLIGATE: Shut up for a second! (*Takes his shoe and threatens to throw it at the SPEECHMAKER.*)

SPEECHMAKER: You can't talk like that. I have the right to practice for the telecast!

PROFLIGATE: Go ahead, then, but in a whisper... and very softly.

The SPEECHMAKER continues mutely, moving his lips and gesticulating violently, but we hear nothing.

BERNHARD (*sits on the barrel*): I've had enough... I can't go on...

SUFFERER: There you are! He's had enough. Simple, isn't it! Of course the lightning is nonsense, but it's disgusting to see people who so readily turn back from the road they have chosen.

PROFLIGATE (*quite amiably*): Don't give up, old man! You... you're the only man of action in this bunch of twaddlers and, well, these so-called heroics suit you damn well.

BERNHARD: I'm out of gas.

IN SEARCH OF HIS IDENTITY: How can you be so sure about that? I don't believe that anyone knows himself *so* completely as to be able to make such categorical decisions.

SUFFERER: Turncoat!

SPEECHMAKER: May I have the floor?

THE CLASSIC: Do you really have something to say?

SPEECHMAKER: Yes, I do.

THE CLASSIC: Make it short then.

SPEECHMAKER: I want to accuse Bernhard of ingratitude.

BERNHARD: Me? Of ingratitude?

SPEECHMAKER: Yes, you; and yes, of ingratitude! (*To the others.*) Have any of us interfered with Bernhard's hobby—rolling the globe of lightning? No, we have not interfered. Why? Because if we all had joined him, then the lightning would now be resting at the bottom of the cliff, and Bernhard could no longer carry out his favorite activity; he could not longer play the role which he chose voluntarily, prompted by his conscience—a role which obviously is very dear to him. It's sufficient to cast a glance at his clothes and at his person in order to see how earnestly he has pursued this hobby. He's wanted to play the hero, at least within the limits of his imagination, and has been able to do so freely and without interference. He should be content. That's right. And what has our role been? We have chosen the role of bystanders—a difficult role demanding great mental control in the continual struggle against the fear aroused, for biological reasons, in every living organism by the menace of lightning. We have chosen the overcoming of this fear as our means of self-realization. We demand that Bernhard should create the conditions to make this possible for us, even as we have created the conditions for his self-realization. And we shall persist in our demand as long as the notion of human gratitude continues to exist. (*The SPEECHMAKER takes a conservative bow.*)

SUFFERER: Not at all bad; he's right. That man really does want to deprive us of the conditions needed for creativity. And on top of that, if we were to take after him, we'd be mere imitators.

PROFLIGATE: And it's not only him. The whole world's full of whiners who tell us that people should get together to wipe out dangers. Everyplace is full of them. We simply can't join them in echoing that tiresome bilge. (*Amiably.*) Come on, Bernie, keep trying. Don't give up. Maybe we'll really think of something by tomorrow.

IN SEARCH OF HIS IDENTITY: Oh, my Lord! How can I concentrate here. At least stop shouting back and forth! Elect a commission or...

THE CLASSIC: There's not much good to expect from a commission which, after all, would be based on the existence of the lightning; if there were no ball-lightning, the commission would have no importance; the lightning would thus be necessary for the continued existence of the commission and the commission would hardly undertake anything to undermine its own foundation. That's how it is with most commissions in this world.

MUSE: Don't give up, Bernhard!

THE CLASSIC quietly takes BERNHARD's shovel and replaces the broken handle with the handle of a broom.

BERNHARD: I'd go back, but, darn it, I'm just worn out. The globe of lightning's already so big and heavy. (*Softly.*) And so beautiful! (*Fumbles among his painter's supplies.*)

A loud roll of thunder.

BERNHARD (*shyly, struggling with himself*): You know... I... I'd like to paint the ball-lightning. (*A long pause.*) I'm slowly starting to develop... really, I heard the SPEECHMAKER's learned speech through the window and I feel that I'm really beginning to understand some things... Before we're all blown up, I'd like very much to paint that ball-lightning. What colors! (*The CLASSIC gets up and goes toward the door with the shovel. He is certain that he will be stopped.*)

BERNHARD: No, no! Anyone but him! My Willie... (*Runs and snatches the shovel from THE CLASSIC, casts a sad glance at his box of paints—which he has placed on the window sill—and exits again. Everybody breathes a sigh of relief. A pleasant calm pervades the room once more. Everybody resumes their former activity. THE*

CLASSIC *takes a rubber raincoat from his footlocker and wraps it around his butterfly collection. The MUSE helps him.*)

THE CLASSIC: It may help a little. It's an insulator.

SUFFERER (*to the PROFLIGATE in a whisper*): Our agreement, Matthew...

PROFLIGATE (*swallows a chunk of ham, then nods to the MUSE*): Listen... come on back. It's kind of cold here alone. Come on, daddy'll give you some ham.

MUSE (*slinks back to where the PROFLIGATE is sitting*): You aren't angry any more, are you? Oh, I know, you aren't really angry at all.

PROFLIGATE: Now, now. Here! (*They draw the blanket up under their chins and munch on the ham and cookies. The SUFFERER takes a small tape recorder from his footlocker and places it next to him on the bed. He checks to see that it's working properly.*)

TAPE RECORDER: Oh, I am replete with anguish!

The MUSE's giggling is heard from behind the screen. Then once more there is silence.

SUFFERER (*takes his head in his hands, starts the tape recorder and extemporizes*): That silence. That silence there behind the screen... Her tiny, golden-tressed head resting on his manly chest. What could be more painful for me than to hear that musical silence. They do not need words. (*Stops, rewinds the tape recorder and checks the quality of the recording. The tape recorder repeats the above sentences.*) That silence which is happiness and harmony, peace and plentitude. No ardent lovers' whispers, no vows of faithfulness, trembling with tenderness, can compare to that silence. And I have to endure it all! Ooh! If I could only crumble into dust. Destruction lurks outside and by tomorrow we may no longer be among the living; it's terrible to pass into non-being all alone. (*Starts getting carried away.*) I am replete, replete, replete...

MUSE (*tiptoes out from behind the screen*): Please be a little more quiet if you can. He fell asleep again. (*The MUSE is holding a piece of paper which she is going to read by the light from the window.*)

THE CLASSIC: What paper have you got there?

MUSE: I think that Matthew writes poetry too. (*Begins to read, softly but audibly.*) "To the Directorate of Portobonia's Television Station: I would like to remind you once more of the demands presented in my last letter concerning the...the removal of your typist from our base. She is vulgar in her person, deeply unintelligent, repulsive in appearance and an utterly unfeminine girl. Her presence on the hilltop is interfering with the creative work of all of us, as well as with our preparations for the television program. I would also like to remind you that I wish to leave Mount Liakoura together with the aforementioned girl, as I have reached retirement age and am suffering from chronic gastritis..."

The MUSE drops the letter, rushes to the PROFLIGATE's bedside, knocks over the screen, and wakes the PROFLIGATE up with a box on the ear.

MUSE: You... you... you...

PROFLIGATE: What's going on?

MUSE (*through tears of anger*): That letter there... you disgusting crook, you cretin, I... I'll...

PROFLIGATE: Well, I mean... it's all a joke. I swear.

SUFFERER (*startled*): What's going on? Why are you hitting him?

THE CLASSIC and the SPEECHMAKER pick up the letter from the ground and read it.

MUSE (*shrieking*): Vulgar, am I! Repulsive in appearance, am I! (*The PROFLIGATE leaps out of bed and stands helplessly. He is utterly grotesque; a sneaker on one foot, the other foot bare; his partly open robe reveals athletic shorts which are too long, drooping nearly to his knees.*) So I'm repulsive, eh? Look at what he's like himself! Miserable rag! And this thing took me to bed... I put up with it all, even though...

PROFLIGATE: Dearest, I can explain it to you. It was all because...

MUSE: Oh "dearest," am I! You wanted to ruin my life. Now I'll be taken back down, away from here. It's all over... So I'm unfeminine, am I? You're a miserable lush yourself and not a real man at all!

PROFLIGATE: Won't you wait a minute. (*Takes the MUSE's hand; she tears it away.*)

SUFFERER But if he took you to bed, after all... then he had to...

MUSE: I just don't know. Oh, I don't know anything any more. Maybe I took him instead...(*Weeps.*)

SUFFERER (*to the MUSE, frightened*): Don't you love him anymore?

MUSE: That thing there? No way. I've never loved him a bit.

The PROFLIGATE appears as though he had received a slap in the face; he lies face down on his bed.

SUFFERER: So that it's all over?

MUSE: All, all of it's over.

SUFFERER (*genuinely*): I am replete with anguish.

SPEECHMAKER: Then everything is all right.

SUFFERER (*furiously*): God dammit! I won't permit myself to be made fun of! Shut up! (*To the MUSE.*) It's not all over for you, but for me, you bloodsucker! Where are the necessary conditions for suffering? They want to destroy me. (*Spits.*) I won't let things stand like this. March! Back to Matthew! (*Picks the MUSE up in order to carry her*

to the PROFLIGATE's bed. She resists, thrashing, but is then silent.)
MUSE (*admiringly*): How strong you are!
SUFFERER: Shut up! I'm a weak, betrayed pessimist. (*In fact, the SUFFERER leaves rather an imposing impression.*)
MUSE: My sweet!
PROFLIGATE: She called him "my sweet"...But I love you, why can't you understand that! (*He has been transported from his usual role and is almost moving in his sincerity.*) I wanted to save you...
MUSE (*to the SUFFERER*): I've always admired you. Before, when you were lifting that weight...
SUFFERER: Be quiet!
MUSE: Behind the house there are violets as well as hay. Take me for a roll in the violets.
SUFFERER: I'm a weak, unhappy person.
MUSE: If you reject me, I'll be replete with anguish.
    The SUFFERER throws the MUSE onto a bed, clutches his head and rushes out of the room.
PROFLIGATE: Please, listen to me!
    The MUSE rushes out after the SUFFERER.
THE CLASSIC (*goes to the PROFLIGATE's bed*): Calm down now, I beg of you! Now, what about that letter?
PROFLIGATE (*dully, after a silence*): I wanted to take her away from here.
THE CLASSIC: Did you really love her? An unbelievable story.
PROFLIGATE: I have a little house and garden in the country. I wanted to take her there.
THE CLASSIC: You, the profligate and brawler? On several occasions you've said that your only wish is the free life of a bachelor and a death from liquor. Why were you pretending, then?
PROFLIGATE: Who isn't pretending then? Which one of us is honest? Are you? You (*He tries to laugh.*) would like to go out and roll the lightning, but you don't dare. Because of your life's work. (*Presses his face into the pillow.*)
THE CLASSIC (*tormentedly*): It's true. But take some sugar-water. (*Pours a glass of water and adds some sugar. The PROFLIGATE obediently drinks.*)
PROFLIGATE: I... I have to go out after them. The Sufferer can't be trusted.
THE CLASSIC: That young man has nerves of steel. He won't allow himself to be tempted out of his role.
PROFLIGATE: Do you think so? Ahh, it doesn't matter now. Nothing matters.

THE CLASSIC: Matthew, the notorious barroom brawler, Portobonia's biggest drunkard and profligate, is crying.

PROFLIGATE: I'm no real profligate!

THE CLASSIC: What do you mean? Explain!

PROFLIGATE (*through his tears*): What is there to explain? I started out as a waiter. A horrible job! The smell of the tavern, drunken people—all of it disgusted me. Once I lost my head and started throwing bottles; I broke the mirrors and windows. Ahh!

THE CLASSIC: Why, you're completely pale. And your pulse is weak.

PROFLIGATE: Of course my pulse is weak. Profligacy is a difficult profession. Profligacy is a perilous profession... so I broke the mirrors. The next day I was offered a job as a paid brawler. I was poor and didn't have any other trade. And of course I was good at my job; I threw only cracked bottles specially filled with colored water; and I never missed. The number of customers grew—after all, people love spectacles. On Mondays a row in the Red Heart Tavern, Tuesdays in the Silver Heart, Wednesdays in the Heart of Gold... Oh, I'm such an unhappy person. I fell in love with that girl. I'm miserable, miserable, miserable...

SUFFERER (*enters*): You, miserable? If anyone here is allowed to be miserable then it's me. That's my profession.

THE CLASSIC: What happened to the girl?

SUFFERER: I tied her to a tree.

THE CLASSIC: Tied her to a tree?

SUFFERER: What else could I have done? You don't know how difficult it was. She bit and scratched me. (*Sadly.*) Ah! And she really is some girl. I like her, yes sir! (*To the PROFLIGATE.*) Look, cut the blubbering. We all have it tough, I understand, but... God dammit, cut it out. I'll report you to the copyright board. I have ten years experience in suffering; for ten years I've had to cry by the bucketful—beneath the windows of older ladies whose husbands paid me for it. Do you think that it was easy for a healthy young man? You can't imagine how my insides have boiled in anger. I'd have liked to have heaved bottles at mirrors, screamed, brawled... Cut it out! I'll knock you right on your ass!

PROFLIGATE (*staggered*): "I'll knock you right on your ass?"—why that's my line. You're the one who's plagiarizing.

A disheveled-looking MUSE rushes in.

MUSE (*to the SUFFERER*): Punch him out!

THE CLASSIC (*shocked*): My God, what kind of world are we living in!

MUSE: What are you waiting for?

THE CLASSIC (*leaps between the SUFFERER and the PROFLIGATE in order to separate them. He is reeling from the excitement.*): Oh, my God!

SUFFERER: Control yourself! A man of your age...

THE CLASSIC sits down on a bed.

PROFLIGATE: Take some sugar-water. Your pulse...

THE CLASSIC drinks from the glass of water given to him.

SPEECHMAKER (*calmly*): Into the fire I'd roll you, reeking head of cheese.

The roll of thunder has grown louder once more. There is a bright glow outside. The television monitor in the room comes to life.

MASTER OF CEREMONIES (*from the monitor's screen*): Base 13. Group "Art, Science, Love." Do you read me?

THE CLASSIC rises and staggers to the microphone on the table.

THE CLASSIC: Group "Art, Science, Love" here. We read you.

MASTER OF CEREMONIES: Because of worsening atmospheric conditions and the threat of thunderstorms, we must begin at once with the video taping of your program. (*Looks at his watch.*) Well, let's say in fifteen minutes. I hope that you'll be ready.

THE CLASSIC (*as though in a dream*): We'll be ready.

IN SEARCH OF HIS IDENTITY: I'm not prepared yet! I feel a bit nervous, somehow.

THE CLASSIC (*automatically*): Some of us are not quite prepared yet. Some of us feel a bit nervous, somehow.

MASTER OF CEREMONIES: Unfortunately, delay is no longer possible. I hope that you can pull yourselves together.

THE SPEECHMAKER steps beside THE CLASSIC.

SPEECHMAKER: Don't worry. We can do it. Although... but we have no idea of what you really expect from us.

MASTER OF CEREMONIES: Very good. Your assignment is as easy as can be. You'll tell our audience about your impressions. We had you sent to Parnassus, the home of lofty spirits. Surely the locale and its renowned traditions—along with a worry-free life and financial security—has inspired some interesting ideas among you. It's exactly these ideas that we'd like to hear about. Be relaxed and speak plainly—we wouldn't know how to recommend any more than that. In about ten minutes we'll be on the air. (*The image on the monitor fades.*)

MUSE: Oh my Lord, what's going to happen to us! In the present situation...

SPEECHMAKER: I think... well, I'll tell you what we can do: Mr. Profligate and Mr. Sufferer can simply exchange roles. (*Eyes them for a moment.*) Incidentally, I think I'm a bit late with my advice—

your roles have already been exchanged.

SUFFERER: I'll agree to that. (*Enthusiastically.*) Yes sir! I'll agree. God dammit, at least once I can play a part that I really like.

MUSE: Great. I'll agree too—with you, my sweet. (*Leans on the SUFFERER's breast as though weak.*)

PROFLIGATE (*softly*): I won't go along with it. I won't agree to anything any more. For me nothing has any meaning any longer.

MUSE: Listen! He's doing pretty well.

SUFFERER: Not bad at all.

PROFLIGATE (*decisively*): I won't go along with it!

SUFFERER: Don't be so decisive. Speak in a trembling voice. Those tears... no, those tears of yours do seem pretty real.

There is a knock at the door and the ELECTRICIAN ON DUTY enters. He is wearing overalls, and several electrical gauges are visible in his breast pocket; he wears rubber gloves on his hands. He remains shyly standing by the door.

SUFFERER: And who might you be?

ELECTRICIAN ON DUTY: I beg your pardon.

MUSE: How did you get here? Has the helicopter come?

ELECTRICIAN ON DUTY: I beg your pardon. I've been here the whole time. I'm the Electrician on Duty.

THE CLASSIC: Where? Here?

ELECTRICIAN ON DUTY: In the cave. In the power station.

SUFFERER: What, a power station up here on Parnassus? Don't give me that. (*Assumes a boxer's stance.*) Tell me the truth now or I'll knock you right on your ass.

ELECTRICIAN ON DUTY: I beg your pardon. My job is this lightning business.

IN SEARCH OF HIS IDENTITY, THE CLASSIC, MUSE: What lightning business?

ELECTRICIAN ON DUTY: Oh, you gentlemen surely know... Would you please let me get in touch with the studio from here? The lightning should be disconnected for half an hour. It's gotten overheated. The poles might burn out. The ball-lightning needs continual maintenance.

VOICES: What? You mean the lightning...

SPEECHMAKER (*steps forward and quiets the others with a wave of his hand*): Ahem... I thought so, that is... (*Pulls himself together.*) Of course we know that it isn't real lightning, but... what right do you have to disconnect it just now?

ELECTRICIAN ON DUTY: It might be burnt out... it could be wrecked completely. Those ball-lightnings are very tough to repair and the guarantee's run out too... We've got to report this to the studio.

SPEECHMAKER (*angrily*): Under no conditions can you disconnect the lightning now. That would be sabotage! Now, right before the television program. And... what right at all do they have to send us such defective globes of lightning? Really—that *is* going too far.

ELECTRICIAN ON DUTY: It's really not defective. It just can't be heated for such a long time without being disconnected. A different type of lightning should've been chosen, only... only who would've known that you gents would want to stick it out for so long. The globes of lightning have been removed from some of the other stations long ago, and those other gentlemen have long since rolled theirs down the cliff.

SPEECHMAKER: Which other gentlemen?

ELECTRICIAN ON DUTY: All of the others. From all of the nearby mountain peaks.

SPEECHMAKER (*with new found pride*): So that we're the last ones?

ELECTRICIAN ON DUTY: Well, you gents know that well enough yourselves. The last ones by far. And now could I... Do you have a phone here?

SPEECHMAKER (*pacing back and forth*): Right now you can't disconnect the lightning under any circumstances. Our program begins in five minutes. (*To himself.*) So that we... we're the last ones. (*To the ELECTRICIAN ON DUTY.*) How much longer can the lightning be connected to the circuit?

ELECTRICIAN ON DUTY: It's not in any circuit. It works on condensers.

SPEECHMAKER: Of course, of course, on condensers. But answer my question.

ELECTRICIAN ON DUTY: It's... well, she might go another fifteen minutes.

THE CLASSIC (*frightened*): And then what? Will it explode? In that case it must by all means be...

ELECTRICIAN ON DUTY: No, it won't just explode. But by then it'll be so hot that... now wait a minute... if you gents aren't afraid of a little bang, then... then we might just...

SPEECHMAKER: We're not afraid, not afraid of any bang.

ELECTRICIAN ON DUTY: In that case we could ground her after the program with your lightning-rod. That would be the only way.

THE CLASSIC (*quietly*): Ah, so we even have lightning rods?

SPEECHMAKER: Would it be dangerous?

ELECTRICIAN ON DUTY: Naw, it won't be too dangerous. It's all been checked. Before this house was approved, we checked the rods five times. I've grounded this very same globe of lightning with your lightning-rods five times. All according to the book. It's only that the blast is fierce. If that lady...

SPEECHMAKER: Don't worry. She'll plug her ears.

ELECTRICIAN ON DUTY: In that case we could do it; but you should still let the studio know.

SPEECHMAKER: We'll see to it. (*Looks at his watch.*) Move on along now. We'll soon be on the air. When we're finished we'll let you know.

ELECTRICIAN ON DUTY: Are you sure about that?

SPEECHMAKER: Why ask any more questions? Get on with your work!

ELECTRICIAN: I mean, that... well, all right. (*Exits at a half-run.*)

THE CLASSIC: The Profligate Matthew and I refuse. We'll have no part of this farce.

MUSE: That's not a bit comradely of you. At such a decisive moment... (*Takes a mirror from the table.*) Oh my heavens! What a fright I am! (*Begins combing herself quickly. Goes behind the screen to change her clothes.*)

SUFFERER (*looks in the mirror*): And me too. (*Goes to the PROFLIGATE's bed and begins to dress himself in Matthew's clothes. He is taller than the PROFLIGATE and this doesn't make his task any easier.*)

SPEECHMAKER: D'you know what: we're the last ones on the mountain. The most fearless ones. A moment has arrived, a great moment the like of which comes only once in a lifetime. We can become famous. And we will. Gentlemen, and my lady! We will address humanity about lightning and the threat of death, and about the place of man in an absurd universe. Tremendous!

SUFFERER: But I don't know how.

The TV monitor begins to flicker.

SPEECHMAKER: What is there to know! You're a profligate. Everything is all the same to you. Ignore the lightning. Eat something. Do everything the way that Matthew did.

SUFFERER: Eat during the telecast? And what?

SPEECHMAKER: Anything at all. Ham for example.

SUFFERER: I sure could eat some ham. (*Laughs.*) And why not.

MUSE: Could I have some too?

SPEECHMAKER: No. You're to do what you know best. That is to say, don't do anything. (*In a friendly tone.*) Be just what you are—an insignificant, simple-minded, giggling little girl.

MUSE: Watch your language.

SPEECHMAKER: I beg your pardon, but is everything clear now?

MUSE: Yes, it's clear.

SPEECHMAKER (*to the SUFFERER*): Get ready. You'll begin.
The very same room appears on the television monitor's screen.

MONOLOGUES

THE SUFFERER

(*rises, takes a fork on which there is a large piece of ham, and begins, simultaneously eating and walking around*): Dearly beloved! A king-sized globe of lightning is rolling around our hut. It looks like it'll soon blow up and we'll be blasted to smithereens, yes sir. I dare to humbly hope (*Grins.*) that it'll be a whopping blast big enough to smash your TV sets to bits too. Of course, you're interested in how we feel right about now? Personally, I'd gladly get the hell out of here, but it won't work—the mountain is iced up and I'd break my neck anyhow. It makes me feel better, though, dearly beloved, that one day all of you'll have to croak just like us, 'cause ya can't live forever, ya know.... And by the way, those scientists are inventing all kinds of bombs so that who knows how our little globe will soon be doing. (*Grins.*) Those who are about to die salute you! To each of you I recommend that, as long as you're still alive and kicking, you enjoy your food and don't turn your nose up at the bottle. (*Goes to the MUSE and grabs her by the arm.*) No, there's no sense in our wasting any time. What say we go behind that screen there and present a little pantomime, eh? (*The MUSE giggles.*) Au revoir [aw, rewire], dearly beloved! My name is Humpfree. I never lose my nerve. And she's my little Muse, yes sir! Well, let's take a bow for all the nice people.
(*They bow and disappear behind the screen.*)

THE SPEECHMAKER

(*has in the meantime pulled a pajama over his white tie and tails; in the striped pajamas he looks like a convict*): Humanity! We are going to our deaths! Soon the ball-lightning will kill us all.
The window is open and we see BERNHARD's face as he takes his box of paints from the windowsill and then stops to listen to the SPEECHMAKER. He listens attentively. During the speech BERN-HARD's face reveals an idea taking shape.

My predecessor has given you an account of the situation in

boisterous tonalities. He, a man of the common people, has already answered the question, What shall we do?, simply and with good old-fashioned horse-sense which nevertheless grasped the global significance of our situation. Yes, a microcosm of the world stands before you. There is lightning at our window and it soon might be at your window as well. Perhaps it might also soon be time for your last thoughts on this earth. Think on it, ladies and gentlemen! Think and soon we shall see how hopeless, how absurd, and how final our situation is. Why? Simply because we want to preserve our personal freedom, to which we after all are entitled. We do not wish to soil our hands in the battle against evil, for such a battle would destroy our Parnassian aloofness, to which we are entitled just as we are entitled to having clean hands. From up here on Parnassus we look down upon the world with heartache and concern, yet we still have the strength not to be untrue to ourselves. And this strength makes us happy, happy in spite of everything. Let the world crumble and let us perish—there is nothing more beautiful than the innocent perishing. O world, you bear the responsibility for man not being able to live as he would like; for his not being able to die as he would like, but only as the forces of evil beyond him might dictate. I have lived like a philosopher and I will die like a philosopher; and I will be free in spite of my convict's clothes. Adieu!

THE PROFLIGATE:

Go to Hell, all of you! To Hell with you all! I'm the unhappy profligate, Matthew; all my life I've existed in order to entertain you. But I won't do it any longer... (*Starts crying.*) Now I'm crying, I have a right to cry, and all of you can go to Hell; all, all, all of you. (*His voice is drowned in tears. Matthew presses his face into the pillow.*)

SPEECHMAKER

(*whispering*): Bravo! You were brilliant.

IN SEARCH OF HIS IDENTITY

(*from his bed*): I have nothing to say to you. What could I tell others if I don't know anything decisive about myself yet. In my childhood I once saw the carcass of a seagull and since then for me every cloud is filled with dead seagulls. (*Changing his tone.*) These people here are playing some kind of game which is so sick that everything inside me is growing more and more confused. Yes, I saw the carcass of a seagull, and my powers of imagination are so damaged that the only possible explanation is that all of this here is nothing more than the product of my diseased brain. If this actually is the case, then please forgive me. Good evening! I have no more time for you because I have to attend to myself. My name is Benjamin. I'll search for my identity until I find it.

THE CLASSIC

(*examines his butterflies with a magnifying glass: speaks resignedly*): I have nothing to say. This is all a bad comedy. It's a wanton flirtation with death, and although we're protected by the lightning-rods, it might all end unhappily. I have begun to love every one of you, my dear foolish humans. I'm afraid for you. I'm an old man now and all I have left is this fear and my butterfly collection. I am the classic Erasmus. Don't put too much faith in what I have written. Don't toy with death. I am the classic Erasmus who loves all of you as much as he does these butterflies.

MASTER OF CEREMONIES: Dear viewers. I would like to ask you to turn your sets down. It would also be advisable to plug your ears with cotton. There will soon be an explosion.

The door opens and BERNHARD backs into the room. He is painting with passionate care. There is crackling, flashes of light, and static which causes the television transmission to appear defective.

BERNHARD:

I am thankful to you. Accept me, slow-witted as I am, among you. (*Still painting.*) Splendid lightning! Exciting lightning!... I heard the learned words of our Speechmaker and all of a sudden everything became clear to me. Everything, everything became clear! I began to understand that I was a poor fool, fighting a senseless battle in a world of inevitabilities. But I thought even further beyond that. I know that man can still be the master of his fate. Yes he can! There is an escape from the absurd. And I, the poor painter Bernhard, have found this escape. We are still the masters of our fate. I have done the deed. The deed is done!

A huge, radiant globe of lightning, one meter in diameter, rolls in through the door. It moves by fits and starts, veering first to the left and then to the right. Panic. Static which causes the television transmission to appear defective.

SPEECHMAKER: Help! *What* did you do? Which deed? Where's the Electrician?

BERNHARD (*proudly, shouting through the crackling*): I ripped the lightning-rods from the house; trampled them to bits. We are the masters of our fate. We have overcome inevitability! (*Static which causes the television transmission to appear defective.*) Fare-thee-well, my Matilda! I saw you in my dreams every night just like I promised. Matilda and Willie! You can be proud of me now... (*Expressionless faces. Rumbling to the extent permitted by technical facilities. Darkening. Flashes of lightning.*)

BERNHARD (*through the rumbling*): Brothers! Let's sing something.
Let us sing.
A blinding explosion.

THE END

CONTRIBUTORS

GEORGE KURMAN is an Associate Professor of English at Western Illinois University. He received his Ph.D. degree from Indiana University and was Fulbright-Hays Graduate Fellow and Honorary Fellow of the Scandinavian-American Society in Helsinki, Finland. Mr. Kurman is the author of two books, *The Development of Written Estonian*, and *Literatures in Contact: Finland and Estonia*. His articles and reviews have appeared in journals such as *Canadian Slavic Studies, Comparative Literature, Books Abroad*, and *Journal of Baltic Studies*, among others.

ALGIRDAS LANDSBERGIS is an Assistant Professor of history at Fairleigh Dickinson University and has lectured on history, literature, and theatre at universities all across the United States. He received his M.A. degree from Colombia University. Mr. Landsbergis is the author of more than ten plays, a novel, *The Journey*, and many short stories, radio scripts, and film reviews. He has co-edited two anthologies of Lithuanian poetry and folksongs, *The Green Oak* and *The Green Linden*. His plays and critical articles have appeared in books and journals, *Baltic Literature and Linguistics* and *Lituanus*, among others.

ANDRES MÄNNIK has spent his adult life in New York theatres where his experiences range from video engineer to mixed media artist and from dancer to producer.

ANDRE SEDRIKS is a Ph.D. candidate in Theatre at Southern Illinois University. He received his M.A. degree from University of Kansas. Mr. Sedriks has acted and directed in off-Broadway, resident, and university theatres and T.V., as well as has taught acting at HB Studio and SIU Theatre Department.

RIMVYDAS ŠILBAJORIS is a Professor of .Slavic languages and literature in The Ohio State University. He received his Ph.D. degree from Columbia University. Mr. Šilbajoris is the author of two books, *Russian Versification: the Theories of Trediakovsky, Lomonosov, and Kantemir*, and *Perfection of Exile: Fourteen Contemporary Lithuanian Writers*, and co-editor of two books on Baltic studies. More than fifty articles by Mr. Šilbajoris have appeared in books and journals, such as *Baltic Literature and Linguistics, World Literature Since 1945, Slavic and East European Journal, Moderne Weltliteratur, Russian Literature, Books Abroad, Slavic Review, Acta Baltica,* and *Lituanus,* among others.

JURIS SILENIEKS is a Professor and Head of Modern Languages and Literatures at Carnegie-Mellon University. He received his Ph.D. degree from University of Nebraska. Mr. Silenieks is the author of a book, *Themes and Dramatic Forms in the Theatre of Armand Salacrou,* and his articles have appeared in books and journals, such as *Problems of Mininations: Baltic Perspectives, Encyclopedia of World Literature in the Twentieth Century, Modern Drama, Lituanus, Journal of Baltic Studies,* and *Books Abroad,* among others.

KRISTINA ŠKEMA-SNYDER, after receiving her B.A. degree in English, considers raising a family her main duty. She specializes in translating her late father's works; recently she finished *Ataraxia* for a production at Southern Illinois University, and presently is working on the translation of *The White Shroud,* last of her father's novels.

ALFREDS STRAUMANIS is an Assistant Professor of Theatre at Southern Illinois University where he also is Director of the Baltic Theatre project. He received his Ph.D. degree from Carnegie Institute of Technology while being an Andrew Mellon Fellow. Mr. Straumanis has travelled all over the world as actor, singer, director, lecturer, and drama critic. His plays—original and translated—have been produced in the U.S.A., Australia, New Zealand, and Canada. He is the author of a novel, short stories, and the co-author of a book, *In the World of Martins Zīverts.* His essays have appeared in journals, such as *Southern Theatre,* and *Journal of Baltic Studies,* among others.

MARDI VALGEMÄE is a Professor of English at Herbert H. Lehman College of the City University of New York. He received his Ph.D. degree from the University of California, Los Angeles. Mr. Valgemäe is the author of *Accelerated Grimace*, a book on expressionism in the American drama, and a co-editor of three books on Baltic studies. He has written more than thirty articles for journals, such as *Modern Drama*, *Comparative Drama*, *Educational Theatre Journal*, *Books Abroad*, and *Journal of Baltic Studies*, among others.